Lecture Notes in Computer Science   16363

Founding Editors

Gerhard Goos
Juris Hartmanis

The series Lecture Notes in Computer Science (LNCS), including its subseries Lecture Notes in Artificial Intelligence (LNAI) and Lecture Notes in Bioinformatics (LNBI), has established itself as a medium for the publication of new developments in computer science and information technology research, teaching, and education.

LNCS enjoys close cooperation with the computer science R & D community, the series counts many renowned academics among its volume editors and paper authors, and collaborates with prestigious societies. Its mission is to serve this international community by providing an invaluable service, mainly focused on the publication of conference and workshop proceedings and postproceedings. LNCS commenced publication in 1973.

Maurice H. ter Beek · Leopoldo Teixeira
Editors

Formal Methods: Foundations and Applications

28th Brazilian Symposium, SBMF 2025
Recife, Brazil, December 3–5, 2025
Proceedings

 Springer

Editors
Maurice H. ter Beek
CNR-ISTI
Pisa, Italy

Leopoldo Teixeira
Federal University of Pernambuco
Recife, Pernambuco, Brazil

ISSN 0302-9743   ISSN 1611-3349 (electronic)
Lecture Notes in Computer Science
ISBN 978-3-032-12085-4   ISBN 978-3-032-12086-1 (eBook)
https://doi.org/10.1007/978-3-032-12086-1

This Springer imprint is published by the registered company Springer Nature Switzerland AG
The registered company address is: Gewerbestrasse 11, 6330 Cham, Switzerland

If disposing of this product, please recycle the paper.

Preface

This volume contains the papers presented at the 28th Brazilian Symposium on Formal Methods (SBMF 2025), held in Recife, Brazil, from December 3–5, 2025. The SBMF conference series is devoted to the development, dissemination, and use of formal methods for the construction of high-quality computational systems.

The main topics discussed at SBMF include the following. Formal aspects of specification languages and theoretical foundations, such as the development of new domain-specific languages, the formalization of existing languages, and the study of the foundations of software engineering. Formal aspects of systems development, such as the application of formal methods to the development of cyber-physical systems, embedded systems, and software-intensive systems. Verification and validation, such as the formal verification of the correctness of software systems, the model checking of the requirements of software systems, and the fuzz testing of software systems. Formal verification of neural networks, such as the application of formal methods to the verification of the correctness of deep learning models. Self-formalization and formal aspects in practice, such as the automation of formal methods, the use of formal methods in industrial settings, and the teaching of formal methods.

SBMF 2025 solicited high-quality papers with a strong emphasis on formal methods, whether practical or theoretical, in the form of regular or short papers. The Program Committee (PC), with members from 14 different countries spread over 5 continents, originally received a total of 25 submissions from 8 different countries spread over 4 continents: 24 regular papers and 1 short paper. Of these, 24 papers went through a rigorous single-blind review process according to which all papers were reviewed by three PC members, with the help of a few external reviewers. The decision to accept or reject a submission was based not only on the review reports and scores, but also and in particular on the in-depth and sometimes intense discussions. In the end, the PC of SBMF 2025 decided to accept 1 short and 12 regular papers, resulting in an acceptance rate of 54%.

The conference also featured three inspiring keynotes by our invited speakers:

- *Formal Reasoning for Assuring Product Lines of Complex Systems* by Marsha Chechik (University of Toronto, Canada)
- *Safe Evolution of Smart Contracts Supported by LLMs and Bounded Model Checking* by Augusto Sampaio (Federal University of Pernambuco, Brazil)
- *Exploring Modelling Language Engineering* by Hans Vangheluwe (University of Antwerp, Belgium)

We are very grateful for the contributions of our invited speakers.

Thanks are due to all involved in SBMF 2025. Specifically, all PC members and external reviewers for their accurate and timely reviewing, all authors for their submissions, and all attendees for their participation. We also thank in particular the conference General Chair, Lucas Lima from the Federal Rural University of Pernambuco (UFRPE,

Brazil), as well as the Web and Social Media Chair and of course the Steering Committee, all itemised on the following pages.

We are very grateful for the support of the Brazilian Computer Society (SBC), promoting this event, with local support from UFRPE, Centre for Strategic Technologies of the Northeast (CETENE), and the Informatics Center at Federal University of Pernambuco (CIn-UFPE). We also acknowledge our sponsors: AWS, Cadence, CAPES, CNPq, FACEPE, and Formal Methods Europe (FME).

Finally, we would like to thank Springer for publishing these proceedings and we gratefully acknowledge the support from EasyChair in assisting us in managing the entire process from submissions through these proceedings to the programme.

We hope you enjoyed the conference!

December 2025

Leopoldo Teixeira
Maurice H. ter Beek

Organization

General Chair

Lucas Lima — Federal Rural University of Pernambuco, Brazil

PC Chairs

Leopoldo Teixeira — Federal University of Pernambuco, Brazil
Maurice H. ter Beek — CNR–ISTI, Pisa, Italy

Web and Social Media Chair

Diego Ferreira — Federal Rural University of Pernambuco, Brazil

Steering Committee

Vince Molnár — Budapest University of Technology and Economics, Hungary
Lucas Lima — Federal Rural University of Pernambuco, Brazil
Yoni Zohar — Bar-Ilan University, Israel
Haniel Barbosa — Federal University of Minas Gerais, Brazil
Ciprian Teodorov — ENSTA Bretagne, France
Sidney C. Nogueira — Federal Rural University of Pernambuco, Brazil

Program Committee

Jefferson O. Andrade — Federal Institute of Espírito Santo, Brazil
Luís Soares Barbosa — University of Minho and INESC TEC, Portugal, and UNU-EGOV, Brazil
Haniel Barbosa — Federal University of Minas Gerais, Brazil
Davide Basile — CNR–ISTI, Pisa, Italy
Armin Biere — University of Freiburg, Germany
Laura Bussi — University of Amsterdam, The Netherlands
Sérgio Campos — Federal University of Minas Gerais, Brazil

Gustavo Carvalho	Federal University of Pernambuco, Brazil
Valentina Castiglioni	Eindhoven University of Technology, The Netherlands
Márcio Cornélio	Federal University of Pernambuco, Brazil
Katalin Fazekas	TU Wien, Austria
Mathias Fleury	University of Freiburg, Germany
Rohit Gheyi	Federal University of Campina Grande, Brazil
Ahmed Irfan	SRI International, USA
Juliano Iyoda	Federal Rural University of Pernambuco, Brazil
Thierry Lecomte	CLEARSY, France
Michael Leuschel	University of Düsseldorf, Germany
Lucas Lima	Federal Rural University of Pernambuco, Brazil
Alberto Lluch Lafuente	Technical University of Denmark, Denmark
Alvaro Miyazawa	University of York, UK
Vince Molnár	Budapest University of Technology and Economics, Hungary
Alexandre Mota	Federal University of Pernambuco, Brazil
Sidney Nogueira	Federal Rural University of Pernambuco, Brazil
Marcel Oliveira	Federal University of Rio Grande do Norte, Brazil
José Proença	CISTER and University of Porto, Portugal
Pedro Ribeiro	University of York, UK
Philipp Rümmer	University of Regensburg, Germany, and Uppsala University, Sweden
Augusto Sampaio	Federal University of Pernambuco, Brazil
Hans-Jörg Schurr	University of Iowa, USA
Volker Stolz	Western Norway University of Applied Sciences, Norway
Ciprian Teodorov	ENSTA Bretagne, France
Nils Timm	University of Pretoria, South Africa
Jim Woodcock	University of York, UK
Yoni Zohar	Bar-Ilan University, Israel

Additional Reviewers

Bertalan Zoltán Péter	Budapest University of Technology and Economics, Hungary
Caio Ribeiro	Federal University of Minas Gerais, Brazil
Kangfeng Ye	University of York, UK

Invited Talks

Formal Reasoning for Assuring Product Lines of Complex Systems

Marsha Chechik

University of Toronto, Canada
`chechik@cs.toronto.edu`

Abstract. Assuring the reliability of complex systems is a difficult and expensive undertaking. These costs are further exacerbated when a family of similar products with varying features need to be assured, or when products evolve due to changing requirements or to introduce new functionalities. In this talk I will discuss methods for assuring reliability of such systems, from their representation as product lines to their efficient analysis to methods for building and maintaining assurance cases for such systems using templates. The focus would be on formal techniques underlying these methods.

Keywords: Assurance cases · reliability · product lines · theorem-proving · consistency

Acknowledgments. The author would like to thank her group members and collaborators: Logan Murphy, Torin Viger, Aren Babikian, Alessio Di Sandro, Claudio Menghi, Jeff Joyce, Simon Diemert, Ramesh S., Sahar Kokaly. This research was funded by NSERC, General Motors and Critical Systems Lab.

Safe Evolution of Smart Contracts Supported by LLMs and Bounded Model Checking

Augusto Sampaio

Universidade Federal de Pernambuco, Brazil
`acas@cin.ufpe.br`

Abstract. The talk presents a trusted deployer framework for safely deploying and upgrading smart contracts within the design-by-contract (DbC) paradigm. The inputs are (i) a reference interface specification, which defines invariants and pre- and postconditions for each function, and (ii) an implementation to be verified. The framework ensures that any deployed implementation must conform to the given specification. Both specification and implementation evolution are supported. Specifications might evolve by changing data representations or extending the interface with new functions, provided that the evolved specification is a (data) refinement of the current reference one. A new implementation must conform to the current reference specification. A distinguishing feature of the overall approach is the automation of the verification process in a hidden formal methods style. Since developers tend to be reluctant to provide formal specifications for software components, we are investigating state-of-the-art natural language processing technologies—particularly Large Language Models (LLMs) from the GPT family—to automatically infer formal (DbC) interface specifications from textual requirements. Furthermore, when a specification upgrade involves a change in data representation, we use a strategy built with the Alloy Analyzer to automatically infer the relation between the two data representations. The applicability of the framework is evaluated in the context of Solidity smart contracts implementing Ethereum standards.

Keywords: Solidity smart contracts · Ethereum standards · Formal verification · GPTAlloy

Acknowledgments. This project is being developed by a consortium including the Universidade Federal de Pernambuco (Brazil), the University College Oxford Blockchain Research Centre (UK), and the Blockhouse Technology Limited (UK). This is a collaboration with Pedro Antonino, Filipe Arruda, Juliandson Ferreira, Gabriel Leite and Bill Roscoe.

Exploring Modelling Language Engineering

Hans Vangheluwe

University of Antwerp, Belgium
`hans.vangheluwe@uantwerpen.be`

Abstract. Models described in a plethora of modelling languages are ubiquitous. They allow us to encode knowledge for various purposes at an appropriate level of abstraction, using appropriate notations. A floor-plan model for example allows an architect to specify the structure of a building so that a contractor can use it as a specification for building. A differential equation model, based on laws of physics allows an engineer to describe the behaviour of a physical system, either to explain observed system behaviour, or as a means to find, through simulation-based experimentation, an optimal design of the system. Programming languages are also modelling languages, which allow programmers to specify, at a computing-platform independent level, what a computer should do. Such programs are commonly either interpreted or compiled (or just-in-time compiled, as a hybrid). In addition to general-purposes modelling languages, so-called domain-specific languages (DSLs) have limited expressiveness, restricting their use to a specific application domain. This often makes them easier to learn by non-programmers and more amenable to the application of advanced analysis techniques such as model checking. Recently, Low Code, closely related to DSLs, have gained in popularity. Designing these modelling languages, with their associated modelling editors, simulators, debuggers, code-generators, … is hard. That is why modelling language engineering requires rigorous techniques. After some definitions of modelling language engineering concepts, the question arises what the most appropriate modelling formalisms are to precisely model/specify all aspects a modelling language. Models of modelling languages should encompass all aspects: concrete syntax, abstract syntax, semantics, the interaction behaviour of a model editor, of a simulator, and a debugger. Furthermore, from the onset, evolution of all these aspects should be taken into consideration.

An overview will be given of some techniques to model modelling languages, with a focus on graph-based approaches. This leads to some interesting insights into the co-design of requirements-, design-, trace- and property-languages. Furthermore, if the semantics of a modelling language is expressed in the form of graph transformation rules, this specification is not only easy to understand, even to non-computer scientists, but it is also amenable to certain kinds of analysis.

Contents

Formal Methods and AI

Teaching and Foundations

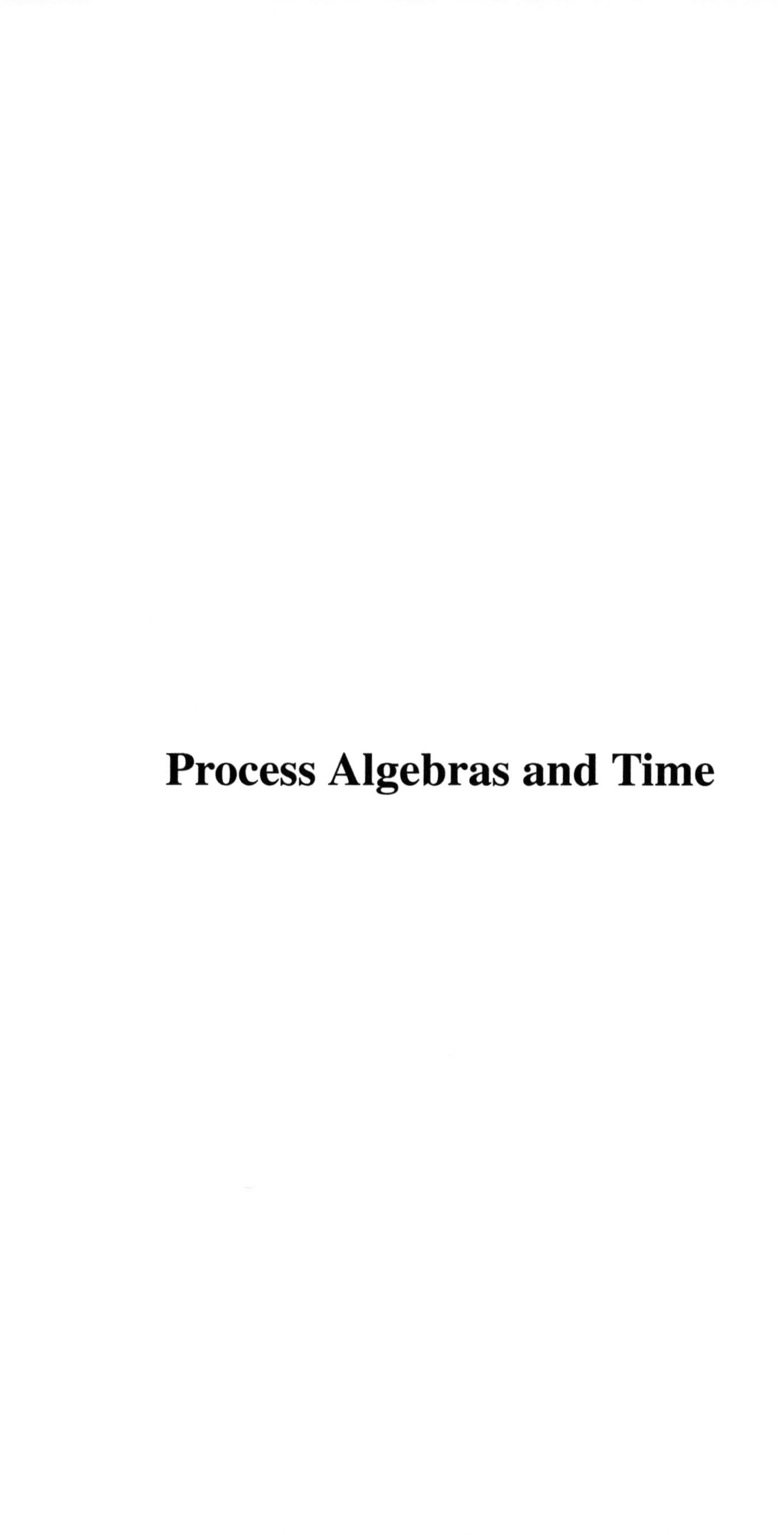

Process Algebras and Time

State-Based Security and Time-Inserting Supervisors

Damas P. Gruska$^{(\boxtimes)}$ [iD]

Department of Applied Informatics, Comenius University, Mlynska dolina, 842 48 Bratislava, Slovakia
`gruska@fmph.uniba.sk`

Abstract. This paper investigates the enforcement of state-based security properties in process systems through supervisory control. We introduce a supervisor that operates under the assumption of incomplete system knowledge, mirroring the challenges faced in real-world deployments where both the supervisor and potential adversaries possess limited information. The proposed supervisor rectifies insecure process behaviors by strategically restricting actions or injecting timed events. Our study focuses on analyzing the necessary and sufficient conditions for the existence of such a supervisor capable of guaranteeing process security despite the knowledge limitations.

1   Introduction

A key focus of current research involves the application of formal models and methods to analyze and mitigate system vulnerabilities, especially concerning security threats. In this work, we concentrate on the information flow approach, where a system is considered secure if an intruder, by observing its public behavior, cannot infer any private properties. System security in our framework is expressed through a state-based property known as process opacity. This property is capable of representing a wide range of security concerns. Furthermore, because our formal model can also account for the time-dependent aspects of system behavior, process opacity can also be used to express vulnerabilities to timing attacks. These attacks use timing information leakage, which is the ability of an attacker to deduce internal (private) information depending on timing information. They, as side-channel attacks, represent a serious threat to many systems. They allow intruders "break" "unbreakable" systems, algorithms, protocols, etc. For example, by carefully measuring the amount of time required to perform private key operations, attackers may be able to find fixed Diffie-Hellman exponents, factor RSA keys, and break other cryptosystems (see [18]). This idea was developed in [5] where a timing attack against smart card implementation of RSA was conducted. In [15], a timing attack on the RC5 block

Work funded by the EU NextGenerationEU through the Recovery and Resilience Plan for Slovakia under the project No. 09I03-03-V04-00095.

encryption algorithm is described. The analysis is motivated by the possibility that some implementations of RC5 could result in data-dependent rotations taking a time that is a function of the data. In [17], the vulnerability of two implementations of the Data Encryption Standard (DES) cryptosystem under a timing attack is studied. It is shown that a timing attack yields the Hamming weight of the key used by both DES implementations. Moreover, the attack is computationally inexpensive. A timing attack against an implementation of AES candidate Rijndael is described in [19], and the one against the popular SSH protocol in [23]. In [2] several novel timing attacks against the common table-driven software implementation of the AES cipher are described. Also possible attacks on most of the currently used processors (Meltdown and Spectre) belong to timing attacks. Timing attacks on web privacy and some corresponding formal models can be found in [7].

Now, consider a system that has been proven insecure for process opacity. We then focus on the problem of system insecurity. To address this, we can either redesign the system or employ supervisory control. Redesign can be challenging and expensive, particularly for embedded or proprietary systems. Supervisory control, (see [8, 21, 22, 27, 28]) or other means ([16]), which restricts system behavior by enabling or disabling actions, provides a more flexible solution, albeit at the cost of reduced functionality (see also [14]). For an unsafe process P, we propose a way how protect it by means of a supervisor. The supervisor (Sup) is modeled as an entity with partial observability over the system's behavior. This lack of complete information is explicitly defined by the observational function $\mathcal{O}_S$.

A supervisor, having partial information on the behavior of a process, tries to prohibit unwanted behavior by restricting certain actions or by inserting time delays. Hence, it is stronger than traditional supervisors, which can only prohibit actions and typically assume complete information about the process behavior. The process, the observation function, and the supervisor cooperating together will be modeled using the same formalism as a new, single process. This new process can only perform traces that could also be performed by the original process alone (see Fig. 1).

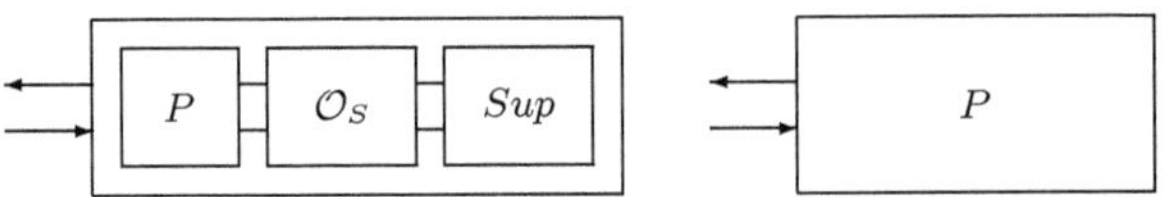

Fig. 1. Supervisory Control.

We utilize timed process algebra and state-based opacity to formalize security properties and analyze the effectiveness of our proposed supervisor. This approach allows us to model complex systems and timing-related vulnerabilities. We examine the conditions under which time-inserting supervisors can be effectively employed, and we explore the decidability and undecidability of supervisor existence in this context. Our work extends beyond traditional supervisory control, which typically focuses on finite automata, by considering a formalism equivalent to a Turing machine (see [20]). In [12,13] we studied conditions under which a timed insertion function exists for a given process and state-based security property and presented some decidability and undecidability results. Here we study this concept for a state-based security property and combine insertion functions with supervisors.

Furthermore, this work proposes a novel approach to system observation, departing from the conventional binary classification of actions into observed and unobserved categories. Instead, we introduce the concept of an observation function, which maps system states and actions to observation values, thereby enabling the modeling of complex, context-dependent observability. We also propose methods for the formal verification of some of the properties introduced. *Key Contributions:* 1. Development of supervisors with partial observability. 2. Extension of supervisory control to include time delay insertion. 3. Modeling supervisors as interacting processes within a timed process algebra framework. 4. Several properties related to the existence or non-existence of a supervisor are presented. 5. Formal verification of selected properties. The paper is structured as follows: Sect. 2 introduces the timed process algebra (TPA). In Sect. 3 state-based security property process opacity is defined. Section 4 presents and analyzes the time-inserting supervisors.

2 Working Formalism

In this section, we briefly recall our working formalism, which will be based on Timed Process Algebra, TPA for short (see [10]). TPA itself is based on Milner's Calculus of Communicating Systems (for short, CCS, see [20]), so we will start with this. To define the CCS language, we first presuppose a set of symbols of atomic actions A that do not contain symbols τ, and that for every $a \in A$ there exist an $\bar{a} \in A$ and $\bar{\bar{a}} = a$ i.e. actions that represent receiving and sending from a channel a, respectively. We define $Act = A \cup \{\tau\}$ where τ represents an internal action, for example, a result of internal communication. We let $a, b, \ldots$ range over A; $x, y, \ldots$ range over Act. The set of CSS terms is defined by the following BNF expression where $x \in Act, X \in Var$, Var is a set of process variables, S is ranging over relabeling functions, $f : Act \rightarrow Act$ is such that $\overline{f(a)} = S(\bar{a})$ for $a \in A, f(\tau) = \tau$ and finally, $L \subseteq A$:

$$P ::= Nil \mid X \mid x.P \mid P + P \mid P \mid P \mid \mu X.P \mid P \setminus L \mid P[f]$$

We use the usual definitions for free and bound variables, open and closed terms and guarded recursion. The set **CCS** of *processes* consists of closed and guarded CCS terms.

Nil represents process doing nothing, X is a process variable. Process $x.P$ can perform action x and then behaves as process P (prefix operator), $+, \mid$ represents nondeterministic choice and parallel operator, respectively. A recursion operator is denoted by $\mu X.P$ i.e. recursive definition of the process given by equation $X = P$. The unary operators $P \setminus L$ and $P[S]$ represent restriction and relabeling, respectively. The formal definition of structural operational semantics for **CCS** is defined in terms of Labeled transition systems.

Definition 1. *A Labeled Transition System is a triple* $(S, T, \{\xrightarrow{x}, x \in T\})$ *where* S *is a set of states,* T *is a set of labels and* $\{\xrightarrow{x}, x \in T\}$ *is the transition relation such that each* $\xrightarrow{x}$ *is a binary transition relation on* S. *We write* $P \xrightarrow{x} P'$ *instead of* $(P, P') \in \xrightarrow{x}$ *and* $P \xrightarrow{x}\!\!\!\!\!/\,$ *if there is no* P' *such that* $P \xrightarrow{x} P'$.

As a set of states, we use the set of CCS terms, the set of labels is equal to *Act*, and the transition relations are defined as follows.

Definition 2. *The transition relations* $T = \{\xrightarrow{x}_{CCS}, x \in Act\}$ *are defined as the least relations satisfying the following inference rules:*

$$\frac{}{x.P \xrightarrow{x} P} \qquad\qquad \frac{P \xrightarrow{x} P'}{P + Q \xrightarrow{x} P', \, Q + P \xrightarrow{x} P'}$$

$$\frac{P \xrightarrow{x} P'}{P \setminus L \xrightarrow{x} P' \setminus L}, (x, \bar{x} \notin L) \qquad \frac{P[\mu X.P/X] \xrightarrow{x} P'}{\mu X.P \xrightarrow{x} P'}$$

$$\frac{P \xrightarrow{x} P'}{P[f] \xrightarrow{f(x)} P'[f]} \qquad \frac{P \xrightarrow{a} P', Q \xrightarrow{\bar{a}} Q'}{P \mid Q \xrightarrow{\tau} P' \mid Q'}$$

$$\frac{P \xrightarrow{x} P'}{P \mid Q \xrightarrow{x} P' \mid Q, \, Q \mid P \xrightarrow{x} Q \mid P'}$$

We are now ready to define the working formalism, which is the time extension of CCS. In TPA we use the special time action t, which expresses the elapsing of (discrete) time is added and hence the set of actions is extended from *Act* to *Actt*. The presented language is a slight simplification of Timed Security Process Algebra (tSPA) introduced in [6]. We omit an explicit idling operator ι used in tSPA, and instead of this we allow implicit idling of processes. Hence processes can perform either "enforced idling" by performing t actions which are explicitly expressed in their descriptions or "voluntary idling", i.e., for example, the process $a.Nil$ can perform t action despite the fact that this action is not formally expressed in the process specification. In other words, the process $t.a.Nil$ must idle for one time unit before it can perform action a. In contrast, the process $a.Nil$ can perform immediately, but it also has the option to idle until a becomes available. The elapsing of time in this context does not lead to a deadlock. In both cases, internal communication takes priority over the time action t in the parallel composition, a consequence of the principle that a system should not idle unnecessarily if an internal action is ready. Furthermore, we do not categorize actions as private and public (in contrast to approaches like tSPA); our methodology for modeling information flow will be established through alternative mechanisms later in this work. TPA differs also from the tCryptoSPA (see [9]). TPA does not use value passing and strictly preserves *time determinancy* in the case of the choice operator $+$ which is not the case for tCryptoSPA (see [10]). To define $At = A \cup \{t\}$, $Actt = Act \cup \{t\}$, we also suppose that $f(t) = t$ for every relabeling function f. We give a structural operational semantics of terms again using labeled transition systems. The set of terms represents a set of states, and the labels are actions of $Actt$. The transition relation $\rightarrow$ is a subset of TPA $\times$ Actt $\times$ TPA. We define the transition relation as the least relation satisfying the inference rules for CCS plus the following inference rules for the action t (for more details see [10]). Here, we provide labels for each rule to facilitate its explanation. Rule $A1$ allows time to elapse for the Nil process, and Rule $A2$ allows idle for processes prefixed by a visible action. The rule Pa establishes the priority of the internal transition τ with respect to the temporal action t. Rule S specifies that the passage of time does not necessitate the resolution of non-determinism.

$$\frac{}{Nil \xrightarrow{t} Nil} \; A1 \qquad \frac{}{u.P \xrightarrow{t} u.P} \; A2$$

$$\frac{P \xrightarrow{t} P', Q \xrightarrow{t} Q', P \mid Q \xrightarrow{\tau}\!\!\!\!\!\!/}{P \mid Q \xrightarrow{t} P' \mid Q'} \; Pa \qquad \frac{P \xrightarrow{t} P', Q \xrightarrow{t} Q'}{P + Q \xrightarrow{t} P' + Q'} \; S$$

For $s = x_1.x_2.\ldots.x_n, x_i \in Actt$ we write $P \xrightarrow{s}$ instead of $P \xrightarrow{x_1}\xrightarrow{x_2} \cdots \xrightarrow{x_n}$ and we say that s is a trace of P. The set of all traces of P will be denoted by $Tr(P)$. By ϵ we denote the empty sequence, and by M^* we denote the set of finite sequences of elements from M. We use $\xRightarrow{x}$ as an abbreviation for transitions that include τ actions , that $(\xrightarrow{\tau})^* \xrightarrow{x} (\xrightarrow{\tau})^*$ (see [20]) By $Tr_w(P) = \{s \in (A \cup \{t\})^* \mid P \xRightarrow{s}\}$ we denote the set of all visible traces of P, i.e., traces that do not contain τ. By $s|_B$ we denote the sequence obtained from s by removing all actions not belonging to B. By $L(P)$ we denote a set of actions that can be performed by P, i.e. $L(P) = \{x \mid P \xrightarrow{s.x}, s \in Actt^*\}$. We define $\hat{x} = x$ if $x \neq \tau$ and $\hat{x} = \epsilon$ otherwise. We define $\lambda(P) = \{P' \mid$ such that there exists $s \in Actt^*, P \xrightarrow{s} P'\}$, i.e., $\lambda(P)$ is the set of all successors of P. If $\lambda(P)$ is a finite set, we say that the process P is a finite state process.

We now formally define two behavioral equivalences utilized in later analysis: weak trace equivalence and bisimulation, respectively (see [20]).

Definition 3. *Two processes P and Q are weak trace equivalent (denoted as $P \approx_w Q$) iff $Tr_w(P) = Tr_w(Q)$.*

Definition 4. *Let $(TPA, Actt, \rightarrow)$ be a labeled transition system (LTS). A relation $\Re \subseteq TPA \times TPA$ is called a bisimulation if it is symmetric and satisfies the following condition: if $(P, Q) \in \Re$ and $P \xrightarrow{x} P', x \in Actt$ then there exists a process Q' such that $Q \xrightarrow{x} Q'$ and $(P', Q') \in \Re$. Two processes P, Q are bisimilar, abbreviated $P \sim Q$, if there exists a bisimulation relating P and Q.*

3   Opacity

To formalize an information flow, we do not divide actions into public and private ones at the system description level, as it is done for example in [9], but we use a more general concept of observation and opacity. This concept was exploited in [4] and [3] in a framework of Petri Nets and transition systems, respectively. Opacity is a general notion for defining an absence of information flow, and many other security properties can be viewed as its special cases. For example, noninterference (see [9] for process algebras or [24] for timed automata) is a special case of trace-based opacity. In this work, however, we focus on state-based opacity, which considers system states rather than execution traces as the confidential information.

Firstly, we define the observation function on sequences from $Actt^\star$. Various variants of observation functions differ according to the contexts that they take into account. For example, an observation of action can depend on the previous actions. We assume a set Θ of elements called observables. These could be actions from $Actt \cup \{\epsilon\}$, but not necessarily. In this paper, we use $\Theta \subseteq Actt \cup \{\epsilon\}$.

Definition 5. (Observation) *Let Θ be a set of elements called observables. Any function $\mathcal{O} : Actt^\star \to \Theta^\star$ is an observation function. It is called static/dynamic/orwellian/m-orwellian $(m \geq 1)$ if the following conditions hold respectively (below we assume $w = x_1 \ldots x_n$):*

- *static if there is a mapping $\mathcal{O}' : Actt \to \Theta \cup \{\epsilon\}$ such that for every $w \in Actt^\star$ it holds $\mathcal{O}(w) = \mathcal{O}'(x_1) \ldots \mathcal{O}'(x_n)$,*
- *dynamic if there is a mapping $\mathcal{O}' : Actt^\star \to \Theta \cup \{\epsilon\}$ such that for every $w \in Actt^\star$ it holds $\mathcal{O}(w) = \mathcal{O}'(x_1).\mathcal{O}'(x_1.x_2) \ldots \mathcal{O}'(x_1 \ldots x_n)$,*
- *orwellian if there is a mapping $\mathcal{O}' : Actt \times Actt^\star \to \Theta \cup \{\epsilon\}$ such that for every $w \in Actt^\star$ it holds $\mathcal{O}(w) = \mathcal{O}'(x_1, w).\mathcal{O}'(x_2, w) \ldots \mathcal{O}'(x_n, w)$,*
- *m-orwellian if there is a mapping $\mathcal{O}' : Actt \times Actt^\star \to \Theta \cup \{\epsilon\}$ such that for every $w \in Actt^\star$ it holds $\mathcal{O}(w) = \mathcal{O}'(x_1, w_1).\mathcal{O}'(x_2, w_2) \ldots \mathcal{O}'(x_n, w_n)$ where*

$$w_i = x_{max\{1, i-m+1\}}.x_{max\{2, i-m+1\}+1} \cdots x_{min\{n, i+m-1\}}.$$

In the case of the static observation function, each action is observed independently from its context. In the case of the dynamic observation function, an observation of an action depends on the previous ones, in the case of the orwellian and m-orwellian observation function an observation of an action depends on the all and on m previous actions in the sequence, respectively. The static observation function is the special case of m-orwellian one for $m = 1$. Note that from the practical point of view the m-orwellian observation functions are the most interesting ones. An observation expresses what an observer - eavesdropper can see from a system behavior and we will alternatively use both the terms (observation - observer) with the same meaning. Note that the same action can be seen differently during an observation (except static observation function) and this expresses a possibility of accumulating some knowledge by an intruder. For example, an action not visible at the beginning could become somehow observable. An observation function can be naturally extended to a set of sequences. From now on we will assume that $\Theta \subseteq Actt^*$ or $\Theta \subseteq Actt'^*$ where $Actt' = A' \cup \{t, \tau\}$ with $A' = \{a' | a \in A\}$.

Now let us assume that an intruder is interested in whether a given process has reached a state with some given property which is expressed by a (total) predicate. This property might be process deadlock, capability to execute only traces with some given actions, capability to perform the same actions from a given set, incapacity to idle (to perform τ action), etc. We do not put any restrictions on such predicates but we only assume that they are consistent with some suitable behavioral equivalence. The formal definition follows.

Definition 6. *We say that the predicate ϕ over processes is consistent with respect to relation $\cong$ if whenever $P \cong P'$ then $\phi(P) \Leftrightarrow \phi(P')$.*

As the consistency relation $\cong$ we could take bisimulation, weak bisimulation, weak trace equivalence or any other suitable equivalence.

An intruder cannot learn the validity of predicate ϕ observing process's behaviour, iff there are two traces, undistinguished for him (by observation function $\mathcal{O}$), where one leads to a state which satisfy ϕ and another one leads to a state for which $\neg\phi$ holds. The formal definition follows.

Definition 7. (Process Opacity) *Given process P, a predicate ϕ over processes is process opaque w.r.t. the observation function $\mathcal{O}$ whenever $P \xrightarrow{w} P'$ for $w \in Actt^*$ and $\phi(P')$ holds then there exists P'' such that $P \xrightarrow{w'} P''$ for some $w' \in Actt^*$ and $\neg\phi(P'')$ holds and moreover $\mathcal{O}(w) = \mathcal{O}(w')$. The set of processes for which the predicate ϕ is process opaque w.r.t. the $\mathcal{O}$ will be denoted by $POp_{\mathcal{O}}^{\phi}$.*

Process opacity offers plenty of interpretations and applications. We illustrate one of them by the following example.

Example 1. Let us consider a very simple system modelling a controller which tries to fill a tank with fuel. The system can receive command to start filling *open*, then it reports that it is *filling* and after three time units it can receive command *close* and reports it is *full* or if something goes wrong, for example pipeline for fuel does not work, it can receive command *close* without tank beeing full and reports *nonfull*. For an intruder, it is important to know whether the tank is full or not but does not see actions $\overline{filling}, \overline{full}, \overline{nonfull}$. The system can be expressed by process $P = open.(\overline{filling}.t.t.t.close.\overline{full}.Nil + close.\overline{nonfull}.Nil)$. Let us consider a static observation function ($\mathcal{O}$ such that $\mathcal{O}(\overline{filling}) = \mathcal{O}(\overline{full}) = \mathcal{O}(\overline{nonfull}) = \epsilon$ and $\mathcal{O}(x) = x$ for $x \notin \{\overline{filling}, \overline{full}, \overline{nonfull}\}$ and ϕ such that $\phi(R)$ iff $R \xrightarrow{\overline{nonfull}}$. Then we have $P \notin POp_{\mathcal{O}}^{\phi}$ since by observation sequence *open.close* we know that for the resulting process ϕ holds, and there is no other sequence with the same observation such that after it ϕ does not hold. Hence, the intruder can learn whether the process reaches a state for which ϕ holds. To make process P opaque, it is enough to insert three actions t before action $\overline{nonfull}$.

4   Time Inserting Supervisor

In this section, we will deal with the problem of what to do if a process is not secure in the sense of process opacity. Changing its design is often not a solution because of the high price, already existing hardware implementation, etc.

We introduce a supervisory mechanism designed to safeguard sensitive information during process execution. This supervisor operates by continuously monitoring the process and upon detecting a potential data leakage threat, it intervenes in one of two ways: either by abruptly terminating the process to prevent any further compromise or by dynamically modifying its behavior to eliminate the leakage risk while allowing the process to continue. A key aspect of this modification involves the insertion of timed actions. By strategically introducing delays or precisely timed operations, the supervisor proactively mitigates time-based attacks, which exploit temporal information to infer sensitive data. Our formal framework, as illustrated by rules A1, A2, Pa, and S in Sect. 2, supports the insertion of these timed actions while ensuring the resulting action sequence remains feasible and inconspicuous, thus avoiding suspicion. Recognizing the inherent limitations of real-world systems, we acknowledge that the supervisor, like a potential attacker, operates with incomplete information. To model this partial observability, we introduce a supervisor-specific observational function, $\mathcal{O}_S$, which defines the supervisor's perception of the system's state. This function, analogous to an attacker's observational function, allows us to analyze the supervisor's effectiveness in scenarios where it lacks full knowledge of the system's activity. By considering both the supervisor's control capabilities and its information constraints, we aim to develop a robust security framework that can effectively protect sensitive information in complex and dynamic environments.

We employ Timed Process Algebra as our modeling framework to represent not only the target system, whose security we aim to enforce, but also the crucial elements of our security model: the observation functions of both attackers and supervisors, the security predicate ϕ that defines sensitive information, and the supervisors themselves. By encapsulating all these components within a unified TPA model, we gain the capability to formally investigate the fundamental question of supervisor existence for a given process. This allows us to precisely determine the conditions under which a supervisor can be constructed to effectively enforce security. We then define a set of "safe processes," which are characterized by processes that, under a given observation, do not reveal the validity of the security predicate ϕ. In essence, these safe processes represent the desired behavior where sensitive information remains protected. The core objective of the supervisor is to dynamically manipulate the execution of process P, ensuring that all its successors invariably fall within this set of safe processes. By achieving this, the supervisor effectively prevents any potential leakage of sensitive information, thereby guaranteeing the system's security.

Definition 8. (Safe Processes) *Assume process P, a predicate ϕ over TPA processes and the observation function $\mathcal{O}$. We define $K^{P,\phi,\mathcal{O}} \subseteq \lambda(P)$ as $Q \in$*

$K^{P,\phi,\mathcal{O}}$ *iff* $\neg\phi(Q)$ *holds or* $\phi(Q)$ *holds but if* $P \xrightarrow{w} Q$ *then there exists a sequence* $w', w' \in Tr(P)$ *such that* $P \xrightarrow{w'} Q'$ *and* $\neg\phi(Q')$ *holds and* $\mathcal{O}(w) = \mathcal{O}(w')$.

Clearly, we have $K^{P,\phi,\mathcal{O}} = \lambda(P)$ iff $P \in POp_{\mathcal{O}}^{\phi}$, hence if $P \notin POp_{\mathcal{O}}^{\phi}$ we have $K^{P,\phi,\mathcal{O}} \subset \lambda(P)$. Now we define a set traces such that if P performs any of them then resulting process belongs to $K^{P,\phi,\mathcal{O}}$. Hence, safe process traces are such traces that they lead either to a process for which ϕ does not hold, or if ϕ holds for it, then there shoudd be another indistinguishable trace (by $\mathcal{O}$) which leads to a process for which ϕ does not hold.

Definition 9. (Safe Processes Traces) *Assume the process* P, *a predicate* ϕ *on the TPA processes, and the observation function* $\mathcal{O}$. *We define* $T^{P,\phi,\mathcal{O}} \subseteq Tr(P)$ *as* $w \in T^{P,\phi,\mathcal{O}}$ *iff* $P \xrightarrow{w} P'$ *then* $P' \in K^{P,\phi,\mathcal{O}}$.

So to keep process P to be secure with respect to process opacity, we need to prohibit it from performing any trace from $Tr(P) \setminus T^{P,\phi,\mathcal{O}}$. To do so we exploit a special concept of supervisor Sup, which can prohibit some actions and it can also insert a sequence of actions t so that the resulting trace performed by the supervised process always belongs to $T^{P,\phi,\mathcal{O}}$.

Example 2. Referring back to Example 1, adding a three-time-unit delay before the *close* action in the second branch suffices to prevent an intruder from determining the tank's fill level.

We assume that, similarly to an attacker also the supervisor cannot see all process actions, which can be expressed by its own, possibly different, observation function $\mathcal{O}_S$(see Definition 5).

Example 3. Let $\phi(Q)$ hold iff Q can perform the action h. $\mathcal{O} = \mathcal{O}_s$ are static observation function such that $\mathcal{O}(h) = \mathcal{O}(h') = \epsilon$ and $\mathcal{O}(x) = x$ otherwise. Then for $P_1 = l_1.h'.l_2.h.Nil$ we have $P_1 \notin POp_{\mathcal{O}}^{\phi}$ and a supervisor has to prohibit action l_2 to keep process P_1 secure. For $P_2 = l_1.h'.l_2.h.Nil + l_1.h'.l_2.Nil$ we have $P_2 \in POp_{\mathcal{O}}^{\phi}$ and a supervisor need to do nothing. For $P_3 = l_1.t.l_2.h.Nil + l_1.l_2.Nil$ the supervisor has to insert action t after performing l_1 in the second branch to keep process P_1 secure.

To refine the supervisor's control, we impose a constraint: the supervisor, denoted as Sup_C (or simply Sup when the set C is clear), is restricted to disabling only actions belonging to a predefined set of controllable actions, C, where C is a subset of the process's visible action set A (i.e., $C \subseteq A$).

Conceptually, the supervisor Sup operates as a mapping function. It receives as input the trace w of the process P, as perceived through the observation function $\mathcal{O}_S$. Based on this observed trace, the supervisor makes decisions regarding the permissibility of subsequent actions. However, its control is limited: it can only intervene to disable actions that are within the controllable set C.

Furthermore, we extend the supervisor's capabilities beyond simple action disabling. Specifically, Sup can insert a sequence of "time" actions, denoted as

t. These time actions represent deliberate delays introduced to manipulate the timing of the process. The purpose of these insertions, along with the action enabling/disabling, is to ensure that the resulting modified trace always belong to $T^{P,\phi,\mathcal{O}}$.

In essence, the supervisor aims to reconcile the observed behavior of the process with the desired security constraints. It does this by selectively preventing controllable actions and strategically inserting time delays, thereby shaping the system's execution to conform to the security specification. This combination of action control and time manipulation allows for a more nuanced and effective approach to securing systems against timing-related and other vulnerabilities. Formally, $Sup_C \circ \mathcal{O}_S : Tr(P) \to T^{P,\phi,\mathcal{O}}$ such that $Sup(\mathcal{O}_S(w.x)) = Sup_C(\mathcal{O}_S(w)).x.t^i$ iff $x \in Actt \setminus C$, $Sup(\mathcal{O}_S(w.x)) = Sup_C(\mathcal{O}_S(w)).y.t^i$ iff $x \in C$ where $y \in \{x, \epsilon\}$ and $i \in N$.

We will model both the supervisor and its observational function as separate processes that communicate with process P (see Fig. 1). A trace w of process P is first translated to a sequence seen by the supervisor by process $\mathcal{O}_S$ and then the supervisor decides whether to forbid the next action or insert t action.

We model the supervisor and its observational capabilities as distinct processes that engage in communication with process P, as depicted in Fig. 1. This approach effectively illustrates the flow of information: the trace w of P is first filtered and transformed by the observation process $\mathcal{O}_S$, resulting in the sequence available to the supervisor, which subsequently decides on action control or time insertion.

We use contexts to model communications between a process, observation function and supervisor. By context $\mathcal{C}$ we mean a process term with placeholders $\mathcal{H}$. Formally, the set of TPA contexts is defined by the following BNF notation:

$$\mathcal{C} ::= \mathcal{H}_i \mid op(\mathcal{C}_1, \mathcal{C}_2, \ldots \mathcal{C}_n)$$

where $\mathcal{C}, \mathcal{C}_1, \ldots \mathcal{C}_n$ are TPA contexts, $op \in \{[S], \setminus, |\}$ (i.e. operations relabelling, restriction and parallel composition) and $\mathcal{H}$ is the place holder.

By $\mathcal{C}(P, \mathcal{O}, Sup)$ we denote the process obtained from process context $\mathcal{C}(\mathcal{H}_1, \mathcal{H}_2, \mathcal{H}_3)$ by substituting holder $\mathcal{H}_1$ by P, $\mathcal{H}_2$ by $\mathcal{O}$, $\mathcal{H}_3$ by Sup, i.e. $\mathcal{C}(P, O, Sup) = \mathcal{C}[P/\mathcal{H}_1, O/\mathcal{H}_2, Sup/\mathcal{H}_3]$. We require that

$$Tr(\mathcal{C}(P, \mathcal{O}_S, Sup)) \subseteq T^{P,\phi,\mathcal{O}}.$$

Our formalism allows us to express vulnerability to timing attacks. Let $\mathcal{O}, \mathcal{O}'$ be observation functions such that $\mathcal{O}(w|_{Act}) = \mathcal{O}'(w)$ where $w|_{Act}$ represents the sequence w without t actions. Then P is vulnerable to timing attacks iff $P \notin POp_{\mathcal{O}}^{\phi}$ but $P \in POp_{\mathcal{O}'}^{\phi}$. In this case we can put $C = \emptyset$ for a supervisor to guarantee P security.

Now we define a set of all the supervisors that guarantee state-based security for a given process P and the corresponding observation functions and the predicate.

Definition 10. (Set of Supervisors) *Assume process P, a predicate ϕ over processes, $C \subset A$ and the observation functions $\mathcal{O}, \mathcal{O}_S$. We define $Sup(P, POp_{\mathcal{O}}^{\phi}, C, \mathcal{O}_S)$ as a set of all supervisors such that $Tr(\mathcal{C}(P, \mathcal{O}_S, Sup_C)) \subseteq T^{P,\phi,\mathcal{O}}$.*

Clearly, $Sup(P, POp_{\mathcal{O}}^{\phi}, C, \mathcal{O}_S) = Sup(P', POp_{\mathcal{O}}^{\phi}, C, \mathcal{O}_S)$ if P and P' are trace equivalent, i.e. $P \approx P'$. We assume that a supervisor has influence only over a subset of actions. Since the supervisor tries to prohibit a process from performing an unsafe execution (trace), it requires control over those actions that could lead to an unsafe trace.

Definition 11. (Controllability) *Assume process P, a predicate ϕ over processes, $C \subset A$ and the observation functions $\mathcal{O}, \mathcal{O}_S$. We say that set $T^{P,\phi,\mathcal{O}}$ is controllable iff for any $w \in T^{P,\phi,\mathcal{O}}$ and $x \in A \setminus C$ we have $w.x \in T^{P,\phi,\mathcal{O}}$.*

The following proposition formulates a controllability condition that determines when a supervisor can effectively prohibit unsafe behaviour of a supervised process, by precisely characterizing the relationship between the language of unsafe traces and the set of actions the supervisor can restrict.

Proposition 1. *Assume process P, a predicate ϕ over processes, $C \subset A$ and the observation functions $\mathcal{O}, \mathcal{O}_S$. Let set $T^{P,\phi,\mathcal{O}}$ be not controllable. Then $Sup(P, POp_{\mathcal{O}}^{\phi}, C, \mathcal{O}_S) = \emptyset$.*

Proof. Let set $T^{P,\phi,\mathcal{O}}$ be not controllable. Hence there exists $w \in T^{P,\phi,\mathcal{O}}$ and $x \in A \setminus C$ such that $w.x \notin T^{P,\phi,\mathcal{O}}$ i.e. no supervisor can prohibit process P to reach an unsafe state.

As a direct consequence of the previous proposition, we have the following corollary.

Corollary. Assume process P, a predicate ϕ over processes, $C = A$ and the observation functions $\mathcal{O}, \mathcal{O}_S$. Then $Sup(P, POp_{\mathcal{O}}^{\phi}, C, \mathcal{O}_S) \neq \emptyset$.

We can define partial ordering on the set of observation functions which reflects strength of observations.

Definition 12. (Ordering on Observation Functions) *Assume two observation functions $\mathcal{O}_1, \mathcal{O}_2$ we say that observation function $\mathcal{O}_2$ is stronger than $\mathcal{O}_1$, denoted as $\mathcal{O}_1 \preceq \mathcal{O}_2$ iff whenever $w, w' \in Actt^*$ such that $\mathcal{O}_2(w) = \mathcal{O}_2(w')$ then also $\mathcal{O}_1(w) = \mathcal{O}_1(w')$. If $\mathcal{O}_1 \preceq \mathcal{O}_2$ and $\mathcal{O}_2 \preceq \mathcal{O}_1$ we say that the observation functions are comparable (denoted as $\mathcal{O}_1 \simeq \mathcal{O}_2$)*

Now we can formally relate the observational capabilities of an intruder and a supervisor to the system's protection properties, allowing us to define precise conditions under which opacity can be guaranteed.

Proposition 2. *Assume process P, a predicate ϕ over processes and the observation functions $\mathcal{O}, \mathcal{O}_S$ such that $\mathcal{O} \preceq \mathcal{O}_S$ and $C = A$. Then $Sup(P, POp_{\mathcal{O}}^{\phi}, C, \mathcal{O}_S)$ contains at least one nontrivial supervisor, i.e. such that does not prohibit all actions.*

Proof. Main idea. Let $w \in Tr(P) \setminus T^{P,\phi,\mathcal{O}}$. If such w does not exist, then a supervisor that does not prohibit any action and does not insert actions t, guaranties the security of P. The supervisor's job is to prohibit P from performing w. Since $\mathcal{O} \preceq \mathcal{O}_S$ the supervisor does not see less than an attacker and can prohibit only actions that would help an intruder learn the validity of ϕ.

Due to the strength of bisimulation, two bisimilar supervisors represent the same protection of a process, as is stated by the following proposition.

Proposition 3. *Let Sup, Sup' be processes corresponding to supervisors and let $Sup \sim Sup'$. Then $Tr(\mathcal{C}(P, \mathcal{O}_S, Sup)) = Tr(\mathcal{C}(P, \mathcal{O}_S, Sup'))$.*

Proof. The proof follows from the fact that bisimulation $\sim$ is the congruence relation and it is stronger than the trace equivalence.

Corollary For any supervisor Sup, if $Sup \sim Q$ than also Q is a supervisor.

To guarantee a minimal restriction of process behavior, our aim is to find a maximal process supervisor in the sense that it minimally restricts the behavior of the original process. The formal definition is the following.

Definition 13. (Maximal Supervisor for Process Opacity) *Process $Sup \in Sup(P, POp_{\mathcal{O}}^{\phi}, C, \mathcal{O}_S)$ is called a maximal process supervisor for process opacity $POp_{\mathcal{O}}^{\phi}$ iff for every $Sup' \in Sup(P, POp_{\mathcal{O}}^{\phi}, C, \mathcal{O}_S)$ we have $Tr(\mathcal{C}(P, \mathcal{O}_S, Sup')) \subseteq Tr(\mathcal{C}(P, \mathcal{O}_S, Sup))$.*

Unfortunately, it is undecidable to verify whether the process Sup is a process supervisors for P and process opacity as it is stated by the following proposition.

Proposition 4. *The property that Sup is a process supervisor for process opacity is undecidable in general.*

Proof. The proof is based on the idea that the opacity of the process is already undecidable (see Proposition 2. in [11]). Suppose that the property is decidable. Let $Sup = \mu X. \sum_{x \in Actt} x'.x.X$ i.e. Sup does not restrict anything. We have that Sup is a supervisor for process opacity for process P iff $P \in POp_{\mathcal{O}}^{\phi}$). Hence, we would be able to decide the process opacity, which contradicts its undecidability.

Using a similar argument, we can prove the following statement, which claims that we cannot even decide whether there is at least one supervisor that guarantees the security of systems.

Proposition 5. *It is undecidable whether $Sup(P, POp_{\mathcal{O}}^{\phi}, C, \mathcal{O}_S) = \emptyset$ in general.*

To obtain a decidable variant of the previous propositions, we insert some restrictions on trace processes. First, we model predicates by special processes called tests. The tests communicate with the processes and produce $\sqrt{}$ action if the corresponding predicates hold for the process. In the following proposition, we show how to exploit this idea for process opacity.

Definition 14. *We say that the process T_ϕ is the test representing the predicate ϕ if $\phi(P)$ holds iff $(P|T_\phi) \setminus At \approx_t \sqrt{}.Nil$ where $\sqrt{}$ is a new action indicating a passing of the test. If T_ϕ is the finite state process, we say that ϕ is the finitely definable predicate.*

Due to the Turing-complete computational power of process algebras such as CCS, there is a fundamental limitation on their expressiveness. Specifically, not all behavioral properties (predicates) defined over processes can be captured or represented by another process. This infeasibility is a direct consequence of the undecidability of problems like the halting problem. Suppose that both ϕ and $\neg\phi$ are finitely definable predicates. Then we can reduce the check whether *Sup* is a process supervisor for process opacity to check bisimulation. Since we can reduce the problem of decidability to finite automata (see [26]) we obtain the following result.

Proposition 6. *Let ϕ and $\neg\phi$ be finitely definable predicates and $\mathcal{O}$, $\mathcal{O}_S$ are static. The property that Sup is a process supervisor for process opacity for a finite state process P and is decidable. Moreover, we can always find a maximal supervisor for state opacity.*

Moreover, for static observation functions $\mathcal{O}$, $\mathcal{O}_S$, and ϕ and $\neg\phi$ finitely definable predicates, there exists a finite state maximal process supervisor for process opacity for any finite state process P. This follows from the fact that such an observation function can be emulated by finite-state processes since only finite memory is required.

Proposition 7. *Let ϕ and $\neg\phi$ be finitely definable predicates and $\mathcal{O}$, $\mathcal{O}_S$ are static. Then for any finite-state process P there exists finite-state process Sup which is the maximal supervisor for corresponding process opacity.*

Note that the above-mentioned properties can be directly extended to m-orwellian observation functions. As regards dynamic and orwellian observation functions, it is more complex and we will leave it to future research.

For the formal verification of some properties introduced in this sections, we leverage the established capabilities of the CAAL system [1]. This system serves as the core verification engine, allowing us to exploit its robust model-checking algorithms and comprehensive state-space exploration methods, thereby ensuring the rigor and scalability of our analysis. Specifically, we consider a property ϕ (as defined in Definition 7) that can be represented as a formula in the μ-calculus [25]. To determine whether a process P can reach a state satisfying this property, we can utilize a model checker with an appropriate temporal logic formula. This approach provides a rigorous method for confirming the system's behavior against its specified properties, moving beyond informal reasoning to a provably correct analysis.

The μ-calculus formula $\mu Z.\phi \vee <-> Z$ expresses reachability to a state satisfying ϕ ($-$ means any action). The CAAL system can verify this by checking if $P \models min\ Z.\phi \vee <-> Z$ is valid, where "min" is CAAL's equivalent of the μ

operator for the minimal fixed point [25]. A key finding is that any consistent predicate ϕ with a finite state process test $T\phi$ (Definition 6) can be formulated in μ-calculus. Beyond reachability, CAAL can check for other properties like bisimilarity (Proposition 3), weak trace equivalence, and trace inclusion. This functionality is crucial for formally validating if a process Sup is a supervisor for process opacity, provided that ϕ and $\neg\phi$ are finitely definable predicates and $\mathcal{O}$, $\mathcal{O}_S$ are static. The verification technique is similar to that in Definition 14. A more detailed exploration of this and other verification methods is left for future work.

Our work employs a timed variant of the CCS. We note that this specific extension is representative, not unique; the field includes a variety of timed process algebras (extensions of CCS, CSP, ACP, etc.) and a corresponding range of verification tools. Our specific selection of TPA and the tool CAAL serves primarily as a concrete demonstration of the principles of protecting timed systems via time-inserting supervisors. The underlying methodology, however, is paradigm-independent: the supervisory control principles presented are transferable to other process algebraic formalisms and can be verified using other model checkers and verification environments. Consequently, the choice of our specific formal framework and verification tool is not a limitation on the applicability of our results.

5   Conclusions

Future research will focus on the optimization and extension of the proposed supervisory control framework, specifically targeting the minimization of inserted time delays while maintaining process security with respect to opacity. This involves quantifying the inherent trade-off between security guarantees and the introduction of artificial delays, seeking to identify optimal control strategies that minimize temporal perturbations.

The presented framework's inherent flexibility allows for the seamless integration of process algebras enriched with operators representing diverse system parameters. Future work will investigate the application of this approach to systems characterized by spatial constraints, probabilistic distributions, complex networking architectures, and power consumption limitations. For instance, we can extend the current framework to analyze the impact of temporal delays on network latency and bandwidth utilization in distributed control systems. Similarly, we can investigate the interplay between temporal delays and energy consumption in battery-powered embedded systems.

Our future plans include investigating additional relationships between the supervisor's observation function, as specified in Definition 11. Even when two such functions are incomparable with respect to the ordering $\preceq$, they may still exhibit differences in their discriminatory power. For example, one function might be sensitive to a narrower range of actions, or more acutely sensitive to timing variations.

References

1. Andersen, J.R., et al.: CAAL: concurrency workbench, aalborg edition. In: Leucker, M., Rueda, C., Valencia, F.D. (eds.) ICTAC 2015. LNCS, vol. 9399, pp. 573–582. Springer, Cham (2015). https://doi.org/10.1007/978-3-319-25150-9_33
2. Bonneau, J., Mironov, I.: Cache-collision timing attacks against AES. In: Goubin, L., Matsui, M. (eds.) CHES 2006. LNCS, vol. 4249, pp. 201–215. Springer, Heidelberg (2006). https://doi.org/10.1007/11894063_16
3. Bryans, J.W., Koutny, M., Mazaré, L., Ryan, P.Y.: Opacity generalised to transition systems. **7**, 421–435 (11 2008)
4. Bryans, J.W., Koutny, M., Ryan, P.Y.: Modelling opacity using Petri nets. Electronic Notes in Theoretical Computer Science, **121**, 101–115 (2005). In: Proceedings of the 2nd International Workshop on Security Issues with Petri Nets and other Computational Models (WISP 2004)
5. Dhem, J.-F., Koeune, F., Leroux, P.-A., Mestré, P., Quisquater, J.-J., Willems, J.-L.: A practical implementation of the timing attack. In: Quisquater, J.-J., Schneier, B. (eds.) CARDIS 1998. LNCS, vol. 1820, pp. 167–182. Springer, Heidelberg (2000). https://doi.org/10.1007/10721064_15
6. Focardi, R., Gorrieri, R., Martinelli, F.: Information flow analysis in a discrete-time process algebra. In: Proceedings 13th IEEE Computer Security Foundations Workshop. CSFW-13, pp. 170–184 (2000)
7. Focardi, R., et al.: Formal models of timing attacks on web privacy. Electron. Notes Theor. Comput. Sci. **62**, 229–243 (2001)
8. Fuchiwaki, K., Cai, K.: Marking data-informativity and data-driven supervisory control of discrete-event systems. Proc. Japan Joint Autom. Contr. Conf. **67**, 102–107 (2024)
9. Gorrieri, R., Martinelli, F.: A simple framework for real-time cryptographic protocol analysis with compositional proof rules. Sci. Comput. Programm. **50**,23–49 (03 2004)
10. Gruska, D.P.: Process opacity for timed process algebra. In: Voronkov, A., Virbitskaite, I. (eds.) PSI 2014. LNCS, vol. 8974, pp. 151–160. Springer, Heidelberg (2015). https://doi.org/10.1007/978-3-662-46823-4_13
11. Gruska, D.P.: Process opacity for timed process algebra. In: Voronkov, A., Virbitskaite, I. (eds.) PSI 2014. LNCS, vol. 8974, pp. 151–160. Springer, Heidelberg (2015). https://doi.org/10.1007/978-3-662-46823-4_13
12. Gruska, D.P.: Security and time insertion. In: Manolopoulos, Y., Papadopoulos, G.A., Stassopoulou, A., Dionysiou, I., Kyriakides, I., Tsapatsoulis, N.eds., In: Proceedings of the 23rd Pan-Hellenic Conference on Informatics, PCI 2019, Nicosia, Cyprus, November 28-30, 2019, pp. 154–157. ACM (2019)
13. Gruska, D.P.: Time insertion functions. In: Bellatreche, L., Chernishev, G., Corral, A., Ouchani, S., Vain, J. (eds.) MEDI 2021. CCIS, vol. 1481, pp. 181–188. Springer, Cham (2021). https://doi.org/10.1007/978-3-030-87657-9_14
14. Gruska, D.P., Ruiz, M.C.: Opacity-enforcing for process algebras. In: Schlingloff, B.H., Akili, S., eds., In: Proceedings of the 27th International Workshop on Concurrency, Specification and Programming, Berlin, Germany, September 24–26, 2018, volume 2240 of CEUR Workshop Proceedings. CEUR-WS.org (2018)
15. Handschuh, H., Heys, H.M.: A timing attack on RC5. In: Tavares, S., Meijer, H. (eds.) SAC 1998. LNCS, vol. 1556, pp. 306–318. Springer, Heidelberg (1999). https://doi.org/10.1007/3-540-48892-8_24

16. Hernández-Rueda, K., Meda-Campaña, M.E., Arámburo-Lizárraga, J.: Enforcing diagnosability in interpreted Petri nets. IFAC-PapersOnLine **48**(7), 58–63, 2015. 5th IFAC International Workshop on Dependable Control of Discrete Systems
17. Hevia, A., Kiwi, M.: Strength of two data encryption standard implementations under timing attacks. ACM Trans. Inf. Syst. Secur. **2**(4), 416–437 (1999)
18. Kocher, P.C.: Timing attacks on implementations of Diffie-Hellman, RSA, DSS, and other systems. In: Koblitz, N. (ed.) CRYPTO 1996. LNCS, vol. 1109, pp. 104–113. Springer, Heidelberg (1996). https://doi.org/10.1007/3-540-68697-5_9
19. cois Koeune, F., Quisquater, J.J.: A timing attack against rijndael. Technical report (1999)
20. Milner, R.: Communication and Concurrency. Prentice-Hall Inc, USA (1989)
21. Ramadge, P.J.G., Wonham, W.M.: The control of discrete event systems. Proc. IEEE **77**(1), 81–98 (1989)
22. Rashidinejad, A., Reniers, M., Fabian, M.: Supervisory control synthesis of timed automata using forcible events (2021)
23. Song, D.X., Wagner, D., Tian, X.: Timing analysis of keystrokes and timing attacks on SSH. In: Proceedings of the 10th Conference on USENIX Security Symposium - Volume 10, SSYM'01, USA, 2001. USENIX Association (2001)
24. Spriet, A., Lime, D., Roux, O.H.: Timed non-interference under partial observability and bounded memory. In: 21st International Conference on Formal Modeling and Analysis of Timed Systems (FORMATS 2023), vol. 14138 of LNCS, pp. 122–137, Antwerp, Belgium, September 2023. Springer Nature Switzerland
25. Stirling, C.: Modal and temporal logics for processes. In: Moller, F., Birtwistle, G. (eds.) Logics for Concurrency. LNCS, vol. 1043, pp. 149–237. Springer, Heidelberg (1996). https://doi.org/10.1007/3-540-60915-6_5
26. Tong, Y., Li, Z., Seatzu, C., Giua, A.: Current-state opacity enforcement in discrete event systems under incomparable observations. Discret. Event Dyn. Syst. **28**(2), 161–182 (2018)
27. Wonham, W.: On the control of discrete-event systems **135**, 542–562 (01 1970)
28. Xie, G., Tong, Y., Wang, X., Seatzu, C.: Resilient supervisor synthesis for labeled Petri nets against sensor attacks. IEEE Transactions on Automatic Control, pp. 1–8 (2025)

A Modular Orthogonal Integration of Operational and Prescriptive Timing Requirements Using TASTD

Alex Rodrigue Ndouna[1]([⊠]) [iD], Marc Frappier[1] [iD], and Frédéric Mallet[2] [iD]

[1] Université de Sherbrooke, Sherbrooke, QC J1K 2R1, Canada
{Alex.Rodrigue.Ndouna,Marc.Frappier}@USherbrooke.ca
[2] Université Côte d'Azur, CNRS, Inria, I3S, Nice, France
Frederic.Mallet@inria.fr

Abstract. Designing and verifying safety-critical systems requires giving equal importance to non-functional and functional requirements from the start, especially those related to time. Since no single method can address all system aspects, a combination of formal methods is needed for accurate modeling and analysis. This paper proposes an integration of the CCSL (Clock constraints Specification language) and TASTD specification languages for the modular modeling of timing requirements. CCSL allows for the modular expression of timing constraints, whereas TASTD allows for the combination of state machines using CSP process algebra operators, to foster the construction of a system specification using the composition of small components specification. We propose rules to translate a CCSL specification into a TASTD specification, which can use the CSP [14] operators of TASTD to compose the CCSL constraints with other specification elements, like operating modes of a system. The CCSL part of the specification can be verified using CCSL tools. The global specification can be simulated using TASTD tools. The approach is demonstrated on a temperature control system which has been previously modeled using UML MARTE and CCSL, but for which no formal combination was available.

Keywords: TASTD · CCSL · formal method

1 Introduction

The formal design and verification of safety-critical systems requires capturing non-functional requirements with the same importance as functional requirements, right from the beginning. Among all, time plays a special role as many non-functional requirements directly depend upon it (e.g., energy, security). Time requirements include real-time constraints imposed by hardware or

Supported by Public Safety Canada's Cyber Security Cooperation Program (CSCP) and NSERC (Natural Sciences and Engineering Research Council of Canada).

software components, but also timed or temporal functional requirements from the application itself. The literature provides plenty of rich models of time (e.g., Time(d) Automata [1], Petri nets [28], synchronous languages [6], timed process algebra [26], real-time scheduling [23]) that each come with ad-hoc efficient verification tools. To be efficient, each tool targets a decidable sub-class of problems but then demands to capture the requirements accordingly thus often altering the initial intents and very frequently omitting the functional part of the requirements as it falls outside the reach of the decidable sub-domain.

Real systems (whether industrial or not) have several characteristics, and most of the formal methods available today are either very general or focus on specific characteristics. No method can therefore simultaneously take into account all the different facets of a system to be developed or analyzed. Hence there is a need to use a combination of formal methods to model as faithfully as possible all aspects of a system before refinement and decomposition.

The Unified Modelling Language (UML) is one such method which intentionally attempts to provide a unified notation to capture all aspects of a system. So it has certain extensions, called profiles, which offer specialised notation for specific domains. The UML profile for MARTE is dedicated to modelling real-time and embedded systems. CCSL [2] has been designed as a formal companion language for MARTE to deal with time and causality in a very precise and concise way. The paper [27] shows two examples where a UML model is refined first with MARTE and second with CCSL to model two case studies. While CCSL comes with a formal semantics, the subset of UML/MARTE that was used does not give such guarantees. In this paper, we replace UML with TASTD [3], a strong, formal, state-based modeling language whose notation is syntactically close to UML State Machines, and which allows for the orthogonal combination of state machines using process algebra operators.

The contribution of this paper is as follows. We provide rules to translate CCSL operators into TASTD expressions and to combine them with other parts of a TASTD specification specifying other operational requirements like modes, to allow for a complete integration of CCSL within a TASTD specification. We prove the correctness of our translations to ensure that the translated expression have the same trace semantics as their corresponding CCSL expressions. The combination enables one to benefit from the advantages of each of the two languages, in particular the great expressiveness and modularity of the TASTD language and the verification tools offered by CCSL. The aspects modeled in CCSL can be verified using the tools offered by CCSL. We are currently developing several verification tools for TASTD, e.g., for proving local invariants in a TASTD specification [7] and a general meta-model framework for proving temporal properties [9], which will enable us to prove more properties on a CCSL-TASTD specification. This gives us a powerful heterogeneous formal modeling framework.

This paper is structured as follows. Section 2 presents an overview of the TASTD notation. Section 3 describes CCSL. Section 4 presents the translation rules from CCSL to TASTD and a proof of their correctness. Section 5 presents the CCSL and TASTD model of our case study, a temperature control system. Section 6 discusses the verification and validation of this model, while Sect. 7 concludes the paper.

2   TASTD

2.1   An Overview of TASTD

Timed Algebraic State-Transition Diagrams (TASTD) [3,4] is a time extension for ASTD [22]. TASTD allows for the composition of automata using CSP-like process algebra operators: sequence, choice, Kleene closure, guard, parameterized synchronization, flow (the AND states of Statecharts), and quantified versions of parameterized synchronization and choice. Each TASTD operator corresponds to a TASTD type. Elementary TASTDs are defined using automata. Automaton states can either be elementary or composite; a composite state can be of any TASTD type. Within a TASTD, a user can declare attributes (i.e., state variables). Actions written in C++ can be declared on automata transitions, states, and at the TASTD level; they are executed when a transition is triggered. These actions can modify TASTD attributes and execute arbitrary C++ code. Attributes can be of any C++ type.

TASTD introduces time-triggered transitions, i.e., transitions triggered when conditions referring to a global clock are satisfied. In ordinary ASTDs, only the reception of an event from the environment can trigger a transition. The special event Step labels the timed-triggered transitions. Step is treated as an event; its only particularity is that it is evaluated on a periodical basis. The specifier determines the value of the period according to the desired time granularity required to match system timing constraints. TASTD also introduces new timing operators that can perform Step transitions: delay, persistent delay, timeout, persistent timeout, and timed interrupt. TASTDs rely on the availability of a global clock called cst, which stands for *current system time*. If the guard of a Step transition is satisfied, the transition can be fired. TASTD is algebraic, in the sense that TASTD operators can be freely mixed as in a process algebra. The operational semantics of TASTD is formally defined in [4] using transition rules in the usual Plotkin style.

2.2   TASTD Support Tools

TASTD specifications can be edited with a graphical tool called eASTD [13] and translated into executable C++ programs using cASTD [13]. The generated C++ programs can be used as an actual implementation of the TASTD specification. cASTD can generate code for simulation, where a manual clock, which the specifier controls during the simulation, replaces the system clock. The specifier can decide to advance the clock to a specific time; the simulator generates the Step events necessary to reach the specified time. Environment events can be submitted at these specified times. We use a simulation to validate the provided scenarios discussed in Sect. 6. Invariants can also be declared in TASTD expressions and automaton states. Proof obligations for invariant preservation are currently being developed and available for 4 ASTD types (automaton, guard, sequence and Kleene closure). A Rodin plugin to generate and discharge these proof obligations is currently under development [7].

3   The Clock Constraint Specification Language (CCSL)

3.1   An Overview of CCSL

In CCSL, logical clocks are used to model occurrences of events [29]. Each event that may occur in the system is represented by a clock that ticks when the corresponding event occurs. Constraints over clocks are used to specify causal and temporal relations between system events. Global physical time does not exist for the clocks and their constraints. A logical clock c is defined by an infinite sequence s_c with each $s_c(i)$ being *tick* or *idle*. The value of $s_c(i)$ indicates whether the associated event of c occurs or not at step i. If $s_c(i)$ is *tick*, then the event occurs, otherwise not.

The semantics of CCSL of a CCSL operator is defined using traces called *schedules*. Given a set C of clocks, a schedule of C is a total function $\delta : \mathbb{N}^+ \to 2^C$ such that $\forall i \in \mathbb{N}^+, \delta(i) = \{c \in C \mid s_c(i) = tick\}$ and $\delta(i) \neq \emptyset$. A schedule defines a partial order between the ticks of the clocks. $\delta(i)$ is a subset of C such that $c \in \delta(i)$ iff c ticks at step i. For a given schedule δ, the *history function* $\chi : C \times \mathbb{N}^+ \to \mathbb{N}$ returns the number of *tick* of a clock c between steps 1 and $i - 1$ in a schedule δ. It is defined as follows:

$$\chi(c,i) = \begin{pmatrix} 0, \ if \ i = 1; \\ \chi(c, i - 1), \ if \ i > 1 \ \wedge \ c \notin \delta(i-1); \\ \chi(c, i-1) + 1, \ if \ i > 1 \ \wedge \ c \in \delta(i-1); \end{pmatrix}$$

CCSL operators are defined in Table 1, where $b \geq 0$, $d \geq 0$, $p > 0$, c_1, c_2, c_3 are logical clocks and w is a word over $\{0, 1\}$. An operational semantics of CCSL operators, by means of a clock-labeled transition system (LTS), has also been defined in [16]. The traces of a CCSL expression (constraint), defined in Table 1, are the same as the traces of its LTS.

The semantics of a set of CCSL constraints $S_1, \ldots, S_n$ is their "conjunction", which is given by the synchronized product of $A_1 \times \ldots \times A_n$, where each A_i is the LTS representing S_i. Let C_i be the clocks occurring in CCSL constraint S_i. A transition (s_i, B, s_i') in this LTS denotes that the set of clocks $B \subseteq C_i$ tick when transitioning from s_i to s_i'. The translation of S_i into A_i is given in [18] and omitted here for the sake of concision. The LTS of the synchronized product $A_1 \times A_2$ is defined on the Cartesian product of the states of each LTS as follows:

$$((s_1, s_2), B_1 \cup B_2, (s_1', s_2'))$$
$$\Leftrightarrow \tag{1}$$
$$(s_1, B_1, s_1') \wedge (s_2, B_2, s_2') \wedge B_1 \cap C_2 = B_2 \cap C_1$$

Table 1. Semantics of CCSL with respect to schedules

CCSL operator	Condition for a valid trace
Precedence ($c_1[b] \prec c_2$)	$\forall n \in \mathbb{N}^+ . \chi(c_2, n) - \chi(c_1, n) = b \Rightarrow c_2 \notin \delta(n)$
$c_1 \prec c_2$	$c_1[0] \prec c_2$
$c_1 \prec_b c_2$	$c_1 \prec c_2 \wedge c_2[b] \prec c_1$
Causality ($c_1 \preccurlyeq c_2$)	$\forall n \in \mathbb{N}^+ . \chi(c_1, n) \geq \chi(c_2, n)$
Subclock ($c_1 \subseteq c_2$)	$\forall n \in \mathbb{N}^+ . c_1 \in \delta(n) \Rightarrow c_2 \in \delta(n)$
Exclusion ($c_1 \mathbin{\#} c_2$)	$\forall n \in \mathbb{N}^+ . c_1 \notin \delta(n) \vee c_2 \notin \delta(n)$
Union ($c_1 \triangleq c_2 + c_3$)	$\forall n \in \mathbb{N}^+ . c_1 \in \delta(n) \Leftrightarrow c_2 \in \delta(n) \vee c_3 \in \delta(n)$
Intersection ($c_1 \triangleq c_2 * c_3$)	$\forall n \in \mathbb{N}^+ . c_1 \in \delta(n) \Leftrightarrow c_2 \in \delta(n) \wedge c_3 \in \delta(n)$
Infimum ($c_1 \triangleq c_2 \wedge c_3$)	$\forall n \in \mathbb{N}^+ . \chi(c_1, n) = max(\chi(c_2, n), \chi(c_3, n))$
Supremum ($c_1 \triangleq c_2 \vee c_3$)	$\forall n \in \mathbb{N}^+ . \chi(c_1, n) = min(\chi(c_2, n), \chi(c_3, n))$
Periodicity ($c_1 \triangleq c_2 \propto p$)	$\forall n \in \mathbb{N}^+ . c_1 \in \delta(n) \Leftrightarrow$ $(c_2 \in \delta(n) \wedge \exists m \in \mathbb{N}_+ . \chi(c_2, n) = m \times p - 1)$
Filtering ($c_1 \triangleq c_2 \blacktriangledown w$)	$\forall n \in \mathbb{N}^+ . c_1 \in \delta(n) \Leftrightarrow (c_2 \in \delta(n) \wedge w[\chi(c_2, n) mod |w|])$
DelayFor ($c_1 \triangleq c_2 \$ d\ on\ c_3$)	$\forall n \in \mathbb{N}^+ . c_1 \in \delta(n) \Leftrightarrow (c_3 \in \delta(n) \wedge \exists m \in \mathbb{N}_+$ $.(c_2 \in \delta(m) \wedge \chi(c_3, n) - \chi(c_3, m) = d))$
discretizedBy ($c_1 \triangleq c_2$ *discretizedBy d*)	$\forall n \in \mathbb{N}^+ . c_1 \in \delta(n) \Rightarrow c_2 \in \delta(n)$ where c_2 ticks every d units of time
alternatesWith ($c_1 \sim c_2$)	$c_1 \prec c_2 \wedge c_2[1] \prec c_1$

CCSL constraints can be structured into 3 groups: *synchronous constraints*, *asynchronous constraints* and *mixed constraints*.

Synchronous Constraints rely on the notion of coincidence of clock instants. For example, the subclock constraint $a \subseteq b$ specifies that each occurrence of a (called the *subclock*) must coincide with exactly one occurrence of b (called the *superclock*). Other examples of synchronous constraints are *discretizedBy* and *exclusion* (denoted $\#$). The latter prevents two clocks from ticking simultaneously. The former discretizes a dense clock to derive discrete chronometric clocks, mostly from *IdealClk* as the value for parameter c_2 of the operator, a perfect dense chronometric clock, predefined in the MARTE Time Library, and assumed to follow 'physical time' faithfully.

Asynchronous Constraints are based on instant *precedence*, which may appear in a strict ($\prec$) or a non-strict ($\preccurlyeq$) form. The clock constraint $a \preccurlyeq b$, also called *fasterThan,* specifies that clock a is (non-strictly) faster than clock b, i.e., clock b can produce its kth tick only if a has produced at least k ticks. The strict version ($\prec$) forbids the kth ticks of a and b to be synchronous, while the non-strict version ($\preccurlyeq$) allows it. The constraint $a \sim b$ or $a \prec_1 b$ states that $\forall k \in \mathbb{N}; a[k] \prec b[k] \wedge b[k] \prec a[k+1]$, i.e., an instant of a precedes the instant of b which in turn precedes the next instant of a. The conjunction $\wedge$ of two

CCSL constraint is represented by the synchronised product of the LTS of these constraints.

Mixed Constraints combine coincidence and precedence. The constraint $c = a$ *delayedFor* n *on* b enforces a delayed coincidence, i.e., imposes c to tick synchronously with the nth tick of b following a tick of a. It is considered as a mixed constraint since a and b are not assumed to be synchronous.

3.2   CCSL Support Tools

CCSL was introduced as part of UML MARTE by OMG in 2011. The main tool to handle CCSL and conduct verification is TimeSquare [12][12]. TimeSquare can produce simulations for a given CCSL specification but also decide whether no schedule is possible. It can build both explicit (when finite) and symbolic representations of the possible schedules. If no schedule is possible, there is a flaw in the specification. Usually there is an unbounded number of possible schedules, in which case the tool looks for schedules that can be implemented with finite memory (called *safe* schedules). When it is safe, the tool exports a representation that can be used to conduct LTL model-checking. Output formats available include NuXMV [8], UPPAAL [5], Z3 [20], Kieler [25], which are third-party tools that are largely used by the community. Specific experiments to exploit SMT tools like Z3 in an efficient way have been conducted on a separate tool called *MyCCSL* [10][3].

4   Translating CCSL Operators in TASTD

4.1   General Concepts Used in Translation

Before proposing our different translations of CCSL operators in TASTD, we first describe how the basic concepts of CCSL in TASTD are modeled.

Given a system with n logical clocks, we use an ASTD event called Schedule(?*clock*) that takes a vector $clock \in 0..(n-1) \rightarrow$ bool as an input parameter (decoration "?") to receive clock values. We have $clock[i-1] = 1$ when the ith clock has ticked in that step.

One might be tempted to trivially model CCSL's notion of history χ by an array of integers of size n, called *history*, which would keep track of the number of ticks of each clock. The *history* array would be unique and global for the entire specification. In accordance with CCSL's definition of history, each element of the *history* would be initialized to 0. Taking advantage of TASTD's ability to inject utility functions implemented in C++ into our specification, we would have an *updateHistory*(*history*, *clock*) function that will be called at each step to update *history* using *clock*. But using a *history* array to save history could lead to memory overflow. To avoid memory overflow, each CCSL constraint is translated into an ASTD, each ASTD contains local variables to store

---

[1] https://timesquare.inria.fr.

[2] https://github.com/frederic-mallet/ccsl-sts.

[3] http://re4cps.org/download.

the necessary information, implemented by counters, to represent the CCSL constraint. These ASTDs are then composed using synchronization to represent the conjunction of these constraints.

In [17,19] it is shown how to prove that a CCSL constraint can be implemented using bounded memory. This approach transforms a specification of a CCSL operator into A directed marked graph [11] where it is easier to demonstrate memory bounding. Based on this work, we optimize our translation by using local counters in the ASTD representing a CCSL constraint that refers to history in its semantics. The counters associated with the CCSL operators are updated at each transition execution in the system. To update the counters we will define three functions. Function $clockCounterDiff\,(counter, c_1, c_2, clock)$ which takes the counter, two clocks and the clock array as parameters and updates the counter by performing the action $counter := counter + clock[c_1] - clock[c_2]$. This function will be used to update the counters for the operators $Precedence$, $Causality$, $Infimum$ and $Supremum$. We have the function $clockCounterMod(counter, c_1, clock, p)$ which updates the counter by applying the action $counter := (counter + clock[c_1])\%p$. This function will be used to update the counters for the operators $Periodicity$ and $Filtering$ with $p = w.size()$.

4.2   Translation

The translation of a CCSL specification consisting of a set of constraints $A = \{S_1, \ldots, S_n\}$ is given by a synchronization TASTD $T(S) = T(S_1) \parallel \ldots \parallel T(S_n)$, where $T(S_i)$ is a TASTD automaton representing the CCSL constraint S_i. TASTD's synchronization operator "$\parallel$" is CSP's parallel operator $\parallel$. It represents the conjunction of the CCSL constraints. Figure 1 illustrates the structure of $T(S)$.

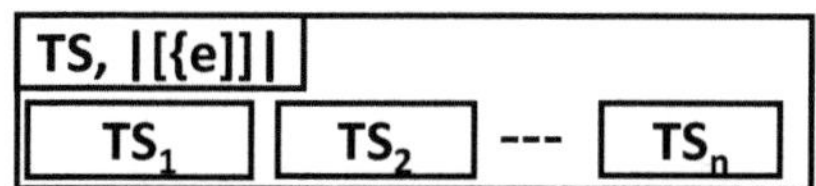

Fig. 1. The TASTD $T(S)$ represent a CCSL specification $S = \{S_1, \ldots, S_N\}$.

For the translation of a CCSL constraint into an automaton TASTD, we use the template automaton TASTD shown in Fig. 2, which simply consists of a state s_0 with a single reflexive transition Schedule($clock$). The guard and the action of the transition depend on the CCSL operator to translate. Table 2 shows, for each of the CCSL operators, the guard of the transition, written using the C++ syntax. One can see that the translation is directly derived from Table 1. For example, for precedence ($c_1\ [b] \prec c_2$), the difference $\chi(c_2, n) - \chi(c_1, n)$ will be implemented by using a counter variable which, for each tick, will keep track of the difference between the number of times c_2 and c_1 appear in the system. The semantics of CCSL for accepting a clock tick at step n only refers to $\chi(\ldots, n)$. Condition $c \in \delta(n)$ is represented by $clock[c] == 1$, i.e., the value of the clock c in parameter $clock$.

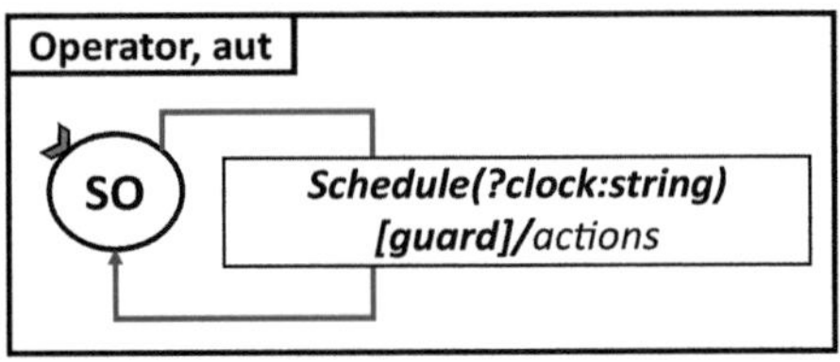

Fig. 2. TASTD representing a CCSL constraint.

For the translation of $DelayFor$ ($c_1 \triangleq c_2\$d$ on c_3) operator, we use an array of size d of Boolean initialised at 0 called $Buffer$. This array will allow us to keep track of the appearance of the clocks affected by the operator. $Buffer$ works like a right-shift register and to update it we use the function $updateBuffer(c2, c3, clock, Buffer, d)$ which, when clock c_2 ticks, sets a value of 1 in the first position of $Buffer$, and if c_3 ticks, all the values in $Buffer$ are shifted to the right by resetting the first position of $Buffer$ to 0. In this way, a tick from c_1 can only be obtained when c_3 also has a tick and $Buffer[d-1] == 1$, $Buffer$.

To translate the $discretizedBy$ operator, we need to implement the notion of $idealClock$ in ASTD, and to do this we use its ASTD equivalent, the $Timer$ object. A $Timer$ in ASTD is a C++ class with a timestamp attribute of type $std::time\_t$, which defaults to the current time when instantiated, and has functions such as $expired(double\ duration)$, which determines whether a duration (in nanoseconds) has elapsed between the timestamp value and the current time, and the object has a $reset\_clock()$ function, which resets the timestamp to the current time. The $discretizedBy$ operator is therefore translated by declaring a local variable $ideal\_clock$ of type $Timer$, which only accepts the transition when $ideal\_clock.expired(d)$ is true, and after the transition has been executed, the $ideal\_clock.reset\_clock()$ action is called to reset our clock for the next iteration of the periodicity.

Table 3 shows the logic for updating the counters associated with each operator. Depending on the operator, the transition will execute either $updateBuffer$, $clockCounterMod$ or $clockCounterDiff$.

Figure 3 shows an example of an ASTD automaton obtained at the end of the complete translation of a CCSL constraint, in this case the complete translation of the precedence constraint.

4.3   Correctness of the Translation

Since the translation of each CCSL operator into an automaton TASTD is straightforward, it remains to show that the synchronized product of CCSL constraints is equivalent to the synchronization operator of TASTD, which is defined

Table 2. Transition guard of event Schedule($clock$) for each CCSL operator, expressed in C++

Operators (Parameters)	guard
Precedence ($c_1[b] \prec c_2$)	$(counter \; != b) \; \| \; (clock[c_2] == 0)$
Causality ($c_1 \preccurlyeq c_2$)	$(counter + clock[c_1] - clock[c_2]) \; >= 0$
Subclock ($c_1 \subseteq c_2$)	$((clock[c_1] == 0) \; \| \; (clock[c_2] == 1))$
Exclusion ($c_1 \# c_2$)	$((clock[c_1] == 0) \; \| \; (clock[c_2] == 0))$
Union ($c_1 \triangleq c_2 + c_3$)	$(clock[c_1] == (clock[c_2] \; \| \; clock[c_3]))$
Intersection ($c_1 \triangleq c_2 * c_3$)	$(clock[c_1] == (clock[c_2] \; \&\& \; clock[c_3]))$
Infimum ($c_1 \triangleq c_2 \wedge c_3$)	$(counter == 0)?(clock[c_1] == (clock[c_2] \; \| \; clock[c_3]))$ $: (counter > 0)?$ $clock[c_1] == clock[c_2] : clock[c_1] == clock[c_3]$
Supremum ($c_1 \triangleq c_2 \vee c_3$)	$(counter == 0)?(clock[c_1] == (clock[c_2] \; \| \; clock[c_3]))$ $: (counter < 0)?$ $clock[c_1] == clock[c_2] : clock[c_1] == clock[c_3]$
Periodicity ($c_1 \triangleq c_2 \propto p$)	$(clock[c_1] == clock[c_2]) \; \&\& \; (counter == 0)$
Filtering ($c_1 \triangleq c_2 \blacktriangledown w$)	$clock[c_1] == (clock[c_2] \; \&\& \; (w[counter] == 1))$
DelayFor ($c_1 \triangleq c_2 \$ d \; on \; c_3$)	$(clock[c_1] == clock[c_3]) \; \&\& \; (Buffer[d-1] == 1)$
discretizedBy ($p = IdealClk$ $discretizedBy \; d$)	$!(clock[p] == 1) \; \| \; ideal\_clock.expired(d)$

Table 3. Counter update logic for each type of operator

Operators	Counter update action
Precedence ($c_1 \; [b] \prec c_2$)	$clockCounterDiff(counter, c_2, c_1, clock)$
Causality ($c_1 \preccurlyeq c_2$)	$clockCounterDiff(counter, c_1, c_2, clock)$
Infimum ($c_1 \triangleq c_2 \wedge c_3$)	$clockCounterDiff(counter, c_2, c_3, clock)$
Supremum ($c_1 \triangleq c_2 \vee c_3$)	$clockCounterDiff(counter, c_2, c_3, clock)$
Periodicity ($c_1 \triangleq c_2 \propto p$)	$clockCounterMod(counter, c_1, clock, p)$
Filtering ($c_1 \triangleq c_2 \blacktriangledown w$)	$clockCounterMod(counter, c_2, clock, w.size())$
DelayFor ($c_1 \triangleq c_2 \$ d \; on \; c_3$)	$updateBuffer(c_2, c_3, clock, Buffer, d)$

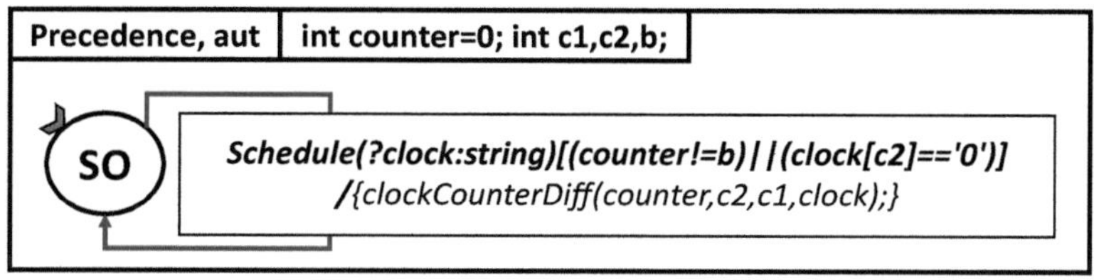

Fig. 3. Complete translation of a precedence constraint.

as CSP's parallel product. Given CCSL specifications $S_1, \ldots S_n$, and their corresponding LTS $A_1, \ldots, A_n$, we must prove that $A_1 \times \ldots \times A_n$ is trace-equivalent to $T(S_1) \parallel \ldots \parallel T(S_n)$.

In TASTD, $T(S_i)$ is represented by a TASTD automata with a single transition of the form $[G_i]e(?B)$, where the guard G_i refers only to clocks of C_i and B is the set of all clocks occuring in S (i.e., $B = \cup_i C_i$). Since the evaluation of the guard G_i depends only on the clock of C_i, we have that $G(B) \Leftrightarrow G(B \cap C_i)$. We have already argued that $T(S_i)$ and S_i are trace equivalent by construction. This means that for any trace accepted by both, each transition (s_i, B, s_i') in a run of A_i is matched by a transition $Q_i \xrightarrow{B} Q_i'$ in $T(A_i)$, and vice-versa. To prove the equivalence between the synchronized product of two CCSL constraints and parallel synchronization in TASTD, we establish Theorem 1 that we will demonstrate next.

Theorem 1. *Let A_1, A_2 be two LTS that represent two CCSL constraints. Then $A_1 \times A_2$ and $T(A_1) \parallel T(A_2)$ are trace equivalent.*

To demonstrate this, we are going to prove that a transition in a run of $A_1 \times A_2$ is matched by a transition in a run of $T(A_1) \parallel T(A_2)$ and vice-versa. For the sake of concision, we denote $(s_i, B, s_i') \in A_i$ by simply writing (s_i, B, s_i'), and we denote a transition in $T(S_i)$ by $Q_i \xrightarrow{B} Q_i'$. The equivalence to be demonstrated is as follows.

$$((s_1, s_2), B_1 \cup B_2, (s_1', s_2')) \Leftrightarrow (Q_1, Q_2) \xrightarrow{e(B)} (Q_1', Q_2')$$

with $B = B_1 \cup B_2$.

- Proof of direction $\Rightarrow$
$$((s_1, s2), B, (s_1', s2'))$$
$$\Leftrightarrow \qquad\qquad\qquad\qquad\qquad\qquad\qquad\qquad \langle \text{ definition of } \times \ (1) \ \rangle$$
$$(s_1, B_1, s_1') \wedge (s_2, B_2, s_2') \wedge B_1 \cap C_2 = B_2 \cap C_1$$
$$\Rightarrow \qquad\qquad\qquad\qquad\qquad\qquad \langle \text{ Trace equivalence of } A_i \text{ and } T(S_i) \ \rangle$$
$$Q_1 \xrightarrow{e(B_1)} Q_1' \wedge Q_2 \xrightarrow{e(B_2)} Q_2' \wedge B_1 \cap C_2 = B_2 \cap C_1$$
$$\Rightarrow \qquad\qquad\qquad\qquad\qquad\qquad\qquad\qquad \langle \text{ lemma 1 (see below) } \rangle$$
$$Q_1 \xrightarrow{e(B \cap C_1)} Q_1' \wedge Q_2 \xrightarrow{e(B \cap C_2)} Q_2'$$
$$\Leftrightarrow \qquad\qquad\qquad\qquad\qquad\qquad\qquad\qquad \langle \ G(B) \Leftrightarrow G(B \cap C_i) \ \rangle$$
$$Q_1 \xrightarrow{e(B)} Q_1' \wedge Q_2 \xrightarrow{e(B)} Q_2'$$
$$\Rightarrow \qquad\qquad\qquad\qquad\qquad\qquad\qquad\qquad \langle \text{ semantics of } \parallel \text{ in TASTD } \rangle$$
$$(Q_1, Q_2) \xrightarrow{e(B)} (Q_1', Q_2')$$

– Proof of direction $\Leftarrow$

$$(Q_1, Q_2) \xrightarrow{e(B)} (Q'_1, Q'_2)$$
$\Leftrightarrow$ $\qquad\qquad\qquad\qquad\qquad\qquad\qquad\qquad\qquad$ $\langle$ def. of $\parallel$ $\rangle$
$$Q_1 \xrightarrow{e(B)} Q'_1 \wedge Q_2 \xrightarrow{e(B)} Q'_2$$
$\Leftrightarrow$ $\qquad\qquad\qquad\qquad\qquad\qquad\qquad\qquad$ $\langle$ $G(B) \Leftrightarrow G(B \cap C_i)$ $\rangle$
$$Q_1 \xrightarrow{e(B \cap C_1)} Q'_1 \wedge Q_2 \xrightarrow{e(B \cap C_2)} Q'_2$$
$\Rightarrow$ $\qquad\qquad\qquad\qquad\qquad$ $\langle$ Trace equivalence of A_i and $T(S_i)$ $\rangle$
$$(S_1, B \cap C_1, S'_1) \wedge (S_2, B \cap C_2, S'_2)$$
$\Leftrightarrow$ $\qquad\qquad\qquad\qquad$ $\langle$ identity $B \cap C_1 \cap C_2 = B \cap C_2 \cap C_1$ $\rangle$
$$(S_1, B \cap C_1, S'_1) \wedge (S_2, B \cap C_2, S'_2) \wedge (B \cap C_1) \cap C_2 = (B \cap C_2) \cap C_1$$
$\Rightarrow$ $\qquad\qquad\qquad\qquad\qquad\qquad\qquad$ $\langle$ definition of $\times$ (1) $\rangle$
$$((S_1, S_2), (B \cap C_1) \cup (B \cap C_2), (s'_1, s'_2)) \in T$$
$\Leftrightarrow$ $\qquad\qquad\qquad\qquad\qquad\qquad\qquad\qquad$ $\langle$ set theory $\rangle$
$$((S_1, S_2), B \cap (C_1 \cup C_2), (s'_1, s'_2)) \in T$$
$\Leftrightarrow$ $\qquad\qquad\qquad\qquad\qquad\qquad\qquad$ $\langle$ $C = C_1 \cup C_2$ $\rangle$
$$((S_1, S_2), B \cap C, (s'_1, s'_2)) \in T$$
$\Leftrightarrow$ $\qquad\qquad\qquad\qquad\qquad\qquad\qquad\qquad$ $\langle$ $B \subseteq C$ $\rangle$
$$((S_1, S_2), B, (s'_1, s'_2)) \in T$$
$\Leftrightarrow$ $\qquad\qquad\qquad\qquad\qquad\qquad\qquad$ $\langle$ $B = B_1 \cup B_2$ $\rangle$
$$((S_1, S_2), B_1 \cup B_2, (s'_1, s'_2)) \in T$$

$\square$

Lemma 1. $(B_1 \cap C_2 = B_2 \cap C_1) \Rightarrow B \cap C_1 = B_1 \ \wedge \ B \cap C_2 = B_2$
We only show $B \cap C_1 = B_1$; the proof of $B \cap C_2 = B_2$ is similar.

5 Case Study: Temperature Control System (TCS)

We consider a simplified version of a temperature control system [27] that regulates the temperature inside a nuclear reactor core, by using thermal-controlling rods. The rods are inserted into the core of the reactor when the temperature reaches a given upper limit, denoted by constant MAX, causing the temperature to gradually reduce (as neutrons in the reactor are absorbed by the control rods). Similarly, the control rods are removed when the temperature in the reactor falls below MIN. TCS operates in two modes, *Diagnostic* and *Control*.

In *Diagnostic* mode, the following actions are triggered that execute the corresponding behaviors: *Diagnostics* examines the current status of the control rods, *Reconfig* replaces the ineffective control rods if any, and *StatusUpdate* updates the status of a rod configuration in the reactor. In *Control* mode, the system triggers three actions; *PeriodicSense* senses the temperature in the reactor, *InsertRod* inserts a control rod, and *RemoveRod* removes a rod from the reactor.

After 100 s in *Diagnostic* mode, the system changes to *Control* mode. However, the mode change from *Control* to *Diagnostic* is triggered by an event occurring when the sensed temperature in the reactor is within the specified limits. The following properties specify the functional and timing aspects for TCS:

$TCS1$: *Diagnostics* is always followed by *Reconfig.*
$TCS2$: The behavior of *Reconfig* is 'extended' by *StatusUpdate*, only when there is a change in the control rod configuration.
$TCS3$: *PeriodicSense* executes periodically with a period of $10s$.
$TCS4$: *PeriodicSense* is followed by *InsertRod* or *RemoveRod* but not both.
$TCS5$: At most two rods can be used in sequence, for cooling the reactor core.

The correspondence between the actions and the logical clocks in the CCSL constraints is as follows: *Diagnostics* : d, *Reconfig* : c, *StatusUpdate* : s, *PeriodicSense* : p, *InsertRod* : i, and *RemoveRod* : r. The functional and timing properties of the TCS, as CCSL constraints, are: $TCS1 : d \sim c, TCS2 : s \subseteq c, TCS3 : Clock\ p = IdealClk\ discretizedBy\ 10\,s, TCS4 : p \sim (i \cup r) \wedge i \# r, TCS5 : i \prec_2 r$.

We translate the CCSL constraints using the translation described in the previous section, and we combine the resulting TASTDs using the TASTD synchronization operator. The $TCS1$ constraint can be translated into a CCSL base constraint as follows: $d \prec c \wedge c\,[1] \prec d$. The basic CCSL constraints refer to the CCSL constraints listed in the Table 1. Following the same logic, we decompose the $TCS4$ constraint into the product of basic operators and we have: $p \prec z \wedge z\,[1] \prec p \wedge z = i \cup r \wedge i \# r$.

All the basic CCSL constraints to be translated into TASTD for our study, after decomposing all our initial constraints into products of basic CCSL operators are: $TCS1\_1 : d \prec c, TCS1\_2 : c\,[1] \prec d, TCS2 : s \subseteq c, TCS3 : Clock\ p = IdealClk\ discretizedBy\ 10\,s, TCS4\_1 : p \prec z, TCS4\_2 : z\,[1] \prec p, TCS4\_3 : z = i \cup r, TCS4\_4 : i \# r, TCS5 : i \prec_2 r$

(a) TCS TASTD

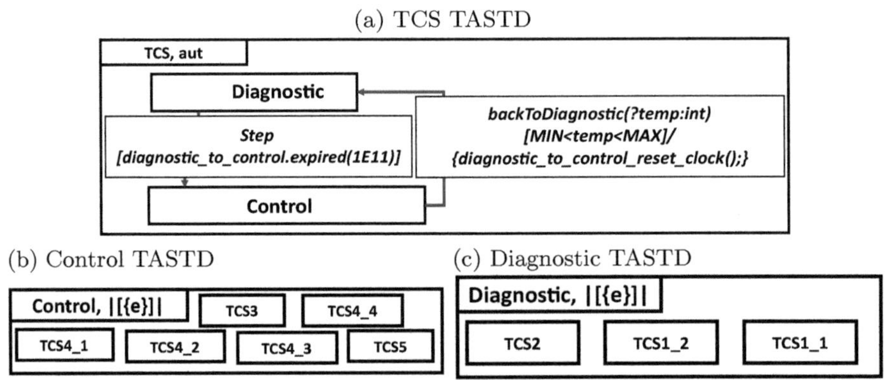

Fig. 4. The TASTD specification of the TCS case study.

Our case study has 2 operating modes: *Diagnostic*, which is responsible for implementing the constraints $TCS1\_1$, $TCS1\_2$, $TCS2$, and *Control*, which implements constraints $TCS3$, $TCS4\_1$, $TCS4\_2$, $TCS4\_3$, $TCS4\_4$, $TCS5$. Each constraint is implemented according to the generic TASTD model shown in

Fig. 2 and, depending on the type of operator to be translated, the guard and actions is defined as shown in Table 2.

Figure 4 (c) shows the TASTD for the behaviour of the *Diagnostic* mode. It is a synchronization of $TCS1\_1$, $TCS1\_2$ and $TCS2$. Mode *Control* is carried out using a synchronization of $TCS4\_1$, $TCS4\_2$, $TCS4\_3$, $TCS4\_4$, TCS_3 and $TCS5$. Figure 4 (b) shows the general structure TASTD control, synchronising the constraints relating to this mode. Switching from *Diagnostic* mode to *Control* mode is done automatically after running the *Diagnostic* mode for 100 *s*. To model it in TASTD we first initialise a timeout variable to 0, in this case the *diagnostic_to_control* variable. This variable counts the time spent in the mode. To switch from *Diagnostic* mode to *Control* mode we use a Step transition, which is a transition that is periodically automatically triggered in a TASTD, following the system clock. We associate a guard with the Step transition so that it is only executed when the variable accounting for the time spent in *Diagnostic* mode has a value greater than or equal to 100 *s*. So, after 100 *s* spent in *Diagnostic* mode, the Step transition is triggered and *Control* mode is launched. The basic unit of time being the nanosecond in TASTD, in the implementation we check instead that $1E + 11$ *nanoseconds* have elapsed, corresponding to 100 *s*, which explains the appearance of the value $1E11$ in Fig. 4 (a).

On the other hand, to switch from mode *Control* to mode *Diagnostic*, the reactor temperature must be between a minimum and a maximum temperature, called MIN and MAX respectively in our model. To model this transition from *Control* to *Diagnostic*, we use a backToDiagnostic transition between the two modes, which take an integer *temp* parameter as input, representing the current reactor temperature, and use its guard to check whether the temperature taken as input meets the $MIN < temp < MAX$ constraint. If the constraint is met, we go into *Diagnostic* mode, otherwise we continue in *Control* mode. Figure 4 (a) shows the TCS TASTD modelling our case study, focusing only on communication between the two modes.

The TCS TASTD takes 9 variables as parameters: MAX and MIN corresponding respectively to the maximum and minimum values of the reactor temperature, then we have d, c, s, p, i, r and z which correspond respectively to the indices of the *Diagnostics*, *Reconfig*, *StatusUpdate*, *PeriodicSense*, *InsertRod* and *RemoveRod* events in the binary sequence of clock ticks. The z parameter corresponds to a clock which ticks when one of the *InsertRod* or *RemoveRod* event occurs; it has been added to take into account of the $TCS4\_3$ basic constraint.

6   Validation and Verification

One of the advantages of TASTD is the ability to generate C++ code ready for compilation and execution to test the modelling of the problem to be solved. The ability to translate a CCSL specification into a TASTD therefore extends CCSL by providing an environment for testing specifications in simulation mode. Since CCSL is an extension of MARTE, which is itself a UML profile for specifying real-time systems, with this translation of CCSL into TASTD we can have a problem specification path going from UML to the generation of executable C++ code that can be tested in simulation mode to ensure the accuracy of our modelling.

To validate our model, we use an interactive animation of the specification with the executable code generated by the cASTD compiler for the simulation. Compilation is automatic and no human modification is required after code generation. We execute the compiled code and compare the results obtained with the requirements demanded by the case study to ensure that all the constraints are met each time an event is executed. However, execution of the compiled code and comparison with the trace provided is manual. We implemented four test cases to test our specification: one test case to simulate the execution of actions in *Diagnostic* mode, one test case to simulate the execution of *Diagnostic* mode then switch to *Control* mode after 100 *s*, one test case to test the execution of actions in *Diagnostic* mode followed by a switch to *Control* mode after 100 *s* and execution of actions in *Control* mode, one test case to test execution of *Diagnostic* mode followed by a switch to *Control* mode and a return to execution of *Diagnostic* mode after a change in system temperature. Our TASTD specification for the TCS study case is available here [21], with the executable source code for our specification and the various test cases presented for validating and verifying our specification.

Prior to this work, TASTD had no tools for verifying certain properties such as LTL and safety properties. One of the relevant aspects of this work is to enable this translation to fill this gap in TASTD by equipping it with certain tools enabling the verification of certain safety properties thanks to CCSL. CCSL would enable certain properties to be verified before translation, and which would then be kept true by the translation so that they would always remain verified on the TASTD specification resulting from the translation, whether in a complete modeling logic in TASTD or in a heterogeneous modeling system in both TASTD and CCSL. The first verifiable safety property is the bounding of the counters used to track the history. We perform a counter bounding check to ensure that there is no capacity or memory overflow for local counters. Here we ensure that, for translation purposes, the counters are finite, but this only depends on the use of these operators or the modeling of the specification, as we may come across cases where the counter cannot be bounded according to the modeling. We can translate all CCSL specifications into TASTD, whether they are partial or not, and then use CCSL to say whether it's safe or not, and saying it's safe means that all counters are bounded. If not all counters are bounded, this implies potential undesirable behavior during simulation due to a potential memory overflow of one of the unbounded counters.

Other properties that can be checked using CCSL include the consistency of the specification, because requirements are usually translated into CCSL from English, and English is often ambiguous, which means that problem specifications are not written in a consistent way. So CCSL allows us to know and check whether the problem posed has a potential solution before translation into

TASTD, which is possible but very complex to do directly with TASTDs. But the absence of a solution to a problem can also be caused by deadlocks, which can be partial or local, or even called a bad path in CCSL, referring to an often infinite execution of the program without reaching an acceptance state. With CCSL, we can also detect these deadlocks beforehand.

Figure 5 shows the CCSL specification for our case study. Using the tool LightCCSL [15], we can generate its LTS, which helps to visualise all possible states and transitions according to the specified constraints, thus ensuring that the behaviour of the system respects the defined temporal and logical requirements.

```
Specification tcs {
   Clock d c p s i r[
         Precedence d < (max:1) c
         SubClocking s <- c
         Let ir be i xor r
         Precedence p < (max:1) ir
         Precedence i < (max:2) r]}
```

Fig. 5. CCSL case specification.

Another important advantage of our translation is the possibility of using it to set up an observer system to validate the actions taken by an ASTD specification which was independently and manually derived. As TASTD is a more expressive language than CCSL, this means that in certain cases, it is more efficient to implement the system using a manually derived ASTD, rather than using the ASTD obtained from the CCSL to ASTD translation. But in this case, the ASTD obtained by translation remains important, as it will enable us to carry out the necessary checks on safety properties. The ASTD obtained by translation will be coupled with the manually derived ASTD. An event is submitted to both. It must accepted/rejected by both ASTDs to be valid. The ASTD obtained by translation is called an *Observer*. This ensures that the manually derived ASTD satisfies safety properties that have been checked on the CCSL specification of the observer.

7   Conclusion

We have presented the methodology for translating CCSL operators into TASTD. For each CCSL operator, we define rules to construct an equivalent TASTD, which generally consists of an automaton TASTD with a state that has a reflexive transition and whose guard and actions depend on the operator being translated. We then proved that the product of CCSL operators is equivalent to the synchronization of TASTD, which allows us to translate a CCSL system specification into an equivalent TASTD system specification.

We tested our approach for translating CCSL into TASTD by applying it to the TCS system case study. We then validated and verified the translation using several test cases. The work presented here is a solid the basis to integrate TASTD and CCSL together to specify critical systems and thus take advantage of the benefits of both languages. Certain parts of the system shall be specified in CCSL and others in TASTD, like transfer between operating modes, which cannot be done in CCSL. We shall then be able to check certain important properties of the system on the parts specified in CCSL by taking advantage of the model checkers associated with CCSL.

The next stage of our work is therefore to determine how global properties of a TASTD specification can be proved from local properties checked using TASTD or CCSL verification mechanisms. This allows for modular verification, which should hopefully streamline the proving of global properties on large systems, using its TASTD decomposition. Event-B theories will be used to construct and verify the derivation of global properties from local properties, following the approach described in [24]. A theory of a TASTD meta-model has been recently developed [9]; we also plan to develop one for CCSL.

References

1. Alur, R., Dill, D.L.: A theory of timed automata. Theor. Comput. Sci. **126**(2), 183–235 (1994). https://doi.org/10.1016/0304-3975(94)90010-8
2. André, C.: Syntax and Semantics of the Clock Constraint Specification Language (CCSL). Research Report RR-6925, INRIA (2009). https://inria.hal.science/inria-00384077
3. de Azevedo Oliveira, D., Frappier, M.: TASTD: A real-time extension for ASTD. In: Glässer, U., Campos, J.C., Méry, D., Palanque, P.A. (eds.) ABZ 2023. LNCS, vol. 14010, pp. 142–159. Springer (2023). https://doi.org/10.1007/978-3-031-33163-3_11
4. de Azevedo Oliveira, D., Frappier, M.: Technical Report 27 - Extending ASTD with real-time. https://github.com/DiegoOliveiraUDES/astd-tech-report-27 (2023)
5. Behrmann, G., David, A., Larsen, K.G., Pettersson, P., Yi, W.: Developing UPPAAL over 15 years. Softw. Pract. Exp. **41**(2), 133–142 (2011). https://doi.org/10.1002/SPE.1006
6. Benveniste, A., Caspi, P., Edwards, S.A., Halbwachs, N., Le Guernic, P., de Simone, R.: The synchronous languages 12 years later. Proc. IEEE **91**(1), 64–83 (2003)
7. Cartellier, Q., Frappier, M., Mammar, A.: Proving local invariants in ASTDs. In: Li, Y., Tahar, S. (eds.) ICFEM 2023. Lecture Notes in Computer Science, vol. 14308, pp. 228–246. Springer (2023). https://doi.org/10.1007/978-981-99-7584-6_14
8. Cavada, R., et al.: The nuxmv symbolic model checker. In: CAV 2014. LNCS, vol. 8559, pp. 334–342. Springer (2014). https://doi.org/10.1007/978-3-319-08867-9_22
9. Chen, C., Rivière, P., Singh, N.K., Dupont, G., Ait Ameur, Y., Frappier, M.: A proof-based ground algebraic meta-model for reasoning on astd in event-b. In:

O'Conner, L. (ed.) IEEE/ACM 13th International Conference on Formal Methods in Software Engineering (FormaliSE) (2025)

10. Chen, X., Mallet, F., Liu, X.: Formally verifying sequence diagrams for safety critical systems. In: Aoki, T., Li, Q. (eds.) TASE 2020, pp. 217–224. IEEE (Dec 2020). https://doi.org/10.1109/TASE49443.2020.00037

11. Commoner, F., Holt, A.W., Even, S., Pnueli, A.: Marked directed graphs. J. Comput. Syst. Sci. 5(5), 511–523 (1971)

12. DeAntoni, J., Mallet, F.: TimeSquare: treat your models with logical time. In: Furia, C.A., Nanz, S. (eds.) TOOLS 2012. LNCS, vol. 7304, pp. 34–41. Springer, Heidelberg (2012). https://doi.org/10.1007/978-3-642-30561-0_4

13. Frappier, M.: ASTD support tools repo. https://github.com/DiegoOliveiraUDES/ASTD-tools (2023)

14. Hoare, C.A.R.: Communicating Sequential Processes. Prentice-Hall (1985)

15. Mallet, F.: LightCCSL tools repo. https://github.com/frederic-mallet/ccsl-sts

16. Mallet, F.: Automatic generation of observers from MARTE/CCSL. In: RSP 2012, pp. 86–92. IEEE (2012).https://doi.org/10.1109/RSP.2012.6380695

17. Mallet, F., Millo, J.V.: Boundness issues in CCSL specifications. In: ICFEM 2013 . LNCS, vol. 8144, pp. 20–35. Springer (Oct 2013). https://doi.org/10.1007/978-3-642-41202-8_3

18. Mallet, F., de Simone, R.: Correctness issues on marte/ccsl constraints. Sci. Comput. Program. 106(C), 78–92 (Aug 2015). https://doi.org/10.1016/j.scico.2015.03.001

19. Mallet, F., Millo, J.V., de Simone, R.: Safe ccsl specifications and marked graphs. In: (MEMOCODE 2013), pp. 157–166 (2013)

20. de Moura, L.M., Bjørner, N.S.: Z3: an efficient SMT solver. In: Ramakrishnan, C.R., Rehof, J. (eds.) TACAS 2008. Lecture Notes in Computer Science, vol. 4963, pp. 337–340. Springer (2008). https://doi.org/10.1007/978-3-540-78800-3_24

21. Ndouna, A.R., Frappier, M.: Case Study TCS ASTD. https://github.com/ndounalex/CCSL-to-ASTD-translation (2024)

22. Nganyewou Tidjon, L., Frappier, M., Leuschel, M., Mammar, A.: Extended algebraic state-transition diagrams. In: 2018 23rd International Conference on Engineering of Complex Computer Systems (ICECCS), pp. 146–155. Melbourne, Australia (2018)

23. Peraldi-Frati, M., DeAntoni, J.: Scheduling multi clock real time systems: from requirements to implementation. In: 14th IEEE ISORC 2011, pp. 50–57. IEEE CS (2011). https://doi.org/10.1109/ISORC.2011.16

24. Rivière, P., Singh, N.K., Aït-Ameur, Y.: Reflexive event-b: Semantics and correctness the EB4EB framework. IEEE Trans. Reliab. 73(2), 835–850 (2024). https://doi.org/10.1109/TR.2022.3219649

25. Spönemann, M., Schulze, C.D., Motika, C., Schneider, C., von Hanxleden, R.: KIELER: building on automatic layout for pragmatics-aware modeling. In: Kelleher, C., Burnett, M.M., Sauer, S. (eds.) 2013 IEEE VL/HCC, pp. 195–196. IEEE Computer Society (2013). https://doi.org/10.1109/VLHCC.2013.6645265

26. Sun, J., Liu, Y., Dong, J.S., Liu, Y., Shi, L., André, É.: Modeling and verifying hierarchical real-time systems using stateful timed CSP. ACM Trans. Softw. Eng. Methodol. 22(1), 3:1–3:29 (2013). https://doi.org/10.1145/2430536.2430537

27. Suryadevara, J., Seceleanu, C., Mallet, F., Pettersson, P.: Verifying marte/ccsl mode behaviors using uppaal. In: Hierons, R.M., Merayo, M.G., Bravetti, M. (eds.) Software Engineering and Formal Methods, pp. 1–15. Springer, Berlin Heidelberg, Berlin, Heidelberg (2013)

28. Winskel, G.: Event structures. In: Petri Nets: Central Models and Their Properties, Advances in Petri Nets 1986, Part II, Proceedings of an Advanced Course. LNCS, vol. 255, pp. 325–392. Springer (1986). https://doi.org/10.1007/3-540-17906-2_31
29. Zhang, M., Song, F., Mallet, F., Chen, X.: SMT-based bounded schedulability analysis of the clock constraint specification language. In: Hähnle, R., van der Aalst, W. (eds.) FASE 2019. LNCS, vol. 11424, pp. 61–78. Springer, Cham (2019). https://doi.org/10.1007/978-3-030-16722-6_4

Formal Verification

Bridging the B-Method and ACSL:
Towards Verified C Code

Fagner M. Dias[1]([✉]), Marcel V. M. Oliveira[1], and Thierry Lecomte[2]

[1] Universidade Federal do Rio Grande do Norte, Natal, Brazil
`fagner.dias.082@ufrn.edu.br`
[2] CLEARSY, Aix-en-Provence, France

Abstract. The B-Method is a formal specification and development methodology that ensures system correctness with a design-by-contract approach. However, translating these high-level specifications into C code introduces challenges, particularly in verifying that the generated code respects the specified properties. To address this, we propose a systematic translation process from the B-Method to ACSL, which enables the formal verification of the C code using Frama-C, a static analysis tool. The proposed method provides a set of ACSL specifications that correspond to B-Method abstractions, allowing for deductive verification of the C code to ensure compliance with safety and correctness requirements. A case study demonstrates the practical application of this translation strategy, showing its effectiveness in verifying a simple runner-counting system.

Keywords: Formal Verification · C Code Verification · Software Safety

1   Introduction

Software systems are now ubiquitous and indispensable across numerous domains, from embedded systems in consumer electronics to mission-critical applications in finance, healthcare, and transportation. As their influence on modern society increases, so does the need to ensure their dependability. In particular, for safety-critical systems, any failure can have catastrophic consequences, which makes safety and security key concerns in software engineering [3,18].

While *security* focuses on protecting systems from external attacks and preserving data integrity, *safety* is concerned with ensuring that software behaves correctly and does not cause harm to users, environments, or physical assets. Failures in either domain can lead to disastrous results, as evidenced by incidents like the $440 million loss due to a software fault at Knight Capital Group [22] or recent cyberattacks on European financial institutions [11].

To mitigate such risks, formal methods offer a mathematically rigorous approach to software specification and verification. Techniques such as the B-Method [23] enable developers to formally specify system behaviour and verify correctness properties through proof obligations. However, although these methods support the development of correct models, flaws can still arise during code generation or implementation.

© The Author(s), under exclusive license to Springer Nature Switzerland AG 2026
M. H. ter Beek and L. Teixeira (Eds.): SBMF 2025, LNCS 16363, pp. 39–60, 2026.
https://doi.org/10.1007/978-3-032-12086-1_3

Usually for Safety Integrity Level (SIL) 3 or 4 applications [8], software and hardware redundancy is required to detect divergent behaviour due to systematic and random failures. In particular, a voting mechanism is used to compare the results obtained by isofunctional software compiled differently. The possibility of the same error occurring at the same time in two software applications developed with different tool chains and by two independent teams from a common specification is neglected by the standards. However, for SIL 1 and SIL 2 applications where this redundancy is not required, the correctness of the generated source code becomes central once again. To address this, complementary strategies are needed to ensure that the generated code, particularly in C, is also safe and reliable. The use of a proven compiler such as COMPCERT [21] is not an option, as it is not adapted to the specificities of embedded systems and the variability of the processors used.

In this context, formal static verification tools, such as Frama-C [19] have gained traction for the analysis of C programs. Frama-C uses the ACSL (ANSI/ISO C Specification Language) [5] as its annotation language, allowing developers to write contracts that specify the expected behaviour of functions, invariants, assertions, and pre/postconditions. These annotations are analysed through deductive verification techniques, enabling the formal proof that the implementation respects its specification. By leveraging plugins like WP (Weakest Precondition), Frama-C can automatically generate and attempt to discharge verification conditions using various automated theorem provers.

This paper presents a translation strategy from the B-Method [23] to ACSL, establishing a bridge between abstract formal models and the verification of low-level C code, and an ACSL library that represents data structures of the B-Method and their functions. Section 2 reviews the background on both the B-Method and ACSL. Section 3 introduces a library that encodes the types of the B-Method and their operations in ACSL. Section 4 describes the mapping process from B components to ACSL specifications, and Sect. 5 illustrates the approach with a case study. Finally, Sect. 6 presents related work and Sect. 7 concludes the paper.

2   Background

In this section, we present the background of this work. Section 2.1 presents the structure of the B-Method and the syntax used in this work. Section 2.2 presents ACSL, the contract language used with the tool that uses it, presenting the constructs on which we rely (predicates, logic functions, axioms, and `axiomatic` blocks) and the verification workflow.

2.1   The B-Method

The B-Method [1] is a formal specification language and development methodology that provides a mathematically rigorous approach to software construction. The B-Method employs a design-by-contract paradigm, where system behaviour is precisely specified through preconditions, postconditions, and invariants, ensuring that all operations maintain the mathematical properties defined for the system. A B-Method development starts with the writing of an abstract machine (abstract model) that specifies what the system should do. Then this abstract machine is refined to a more concrete machine through the refinement machine(s) and finally, the implementation machine, which can be translated to code. Each refinement level must demonstrate that it preserves all properties of the more abstract specification, creating a correct-by-construction development path that culminates in implementable code. Atelier-B [9] is a tool that fully supports the development process by automatically generating proof obligations, providing automatic and interactive theorem proving, and producing C or Ada code from the implementation machines to ensure that the software preserves all established correctness properties. Even if the B models and refinements are proved to be correct, the generated source code may still contain errors because the code generation tool has not been formally developed.

The strength of the B-Method comes from its solid mathematical foundation in set theory, allowing advanced operations on key data types like sets, relations, functions, and sequences. Set operations such as power set (POW), union (\/), intersection (/\), difference (-), cardinality (card), membership (:), and non-membership (/:) allow for precise specification of data collections and their properties, while relation operations enable the modelling of complex associations between data elements through constructs like domain restriction (<|), range restriction (|>), and relational composition (;). Function types in the B-Method support both partial (+->) and total (-->) functions with operations for function application (f(x)), domain (dom), and range (ran) extraction. Sequence operations include concatenation (^), element access (s(x)), head (->) and tail (<-) insertions, and head (/|\) and tail (\|/) restrictions, enabling the specification of ordered data structures and their manipulations.

Listing 2.1. Example of B-Method's abstract machine.

```
MACHINE findmax VARIABLES st INVARIANT st <: NAT & st : FIN(st)
INITIALISATION st := {} OPERATIONS
    reset = BEGIN st := {} END;
    enter(ee) = PRE ee : NAT THEN st := st \/ {ee} END;
    mx <-- maxi = PRE not(st = {}) THEN mx := max(st) END
END
```

Listing 2.1 presents an example of an abstract machine that has a state variable st. The INVARIANT establishes that st is a finite set of natural numbers, and the INITIALISATION defines a starting state with the empty set, which is consistent with the invariant. The operation reset empties the set st and has no preconditions; enter(ee) has a precondition ee : NAT, which ensures that only natural numbers are added, using set union; finally, maxi requires st to be non-empty and returns its maximum value (max(st)).

2.2 ACSL

ANSI/ISO C Specification Language (ACSL) is a behaviour interface specification language (BISL) [17] designed for formal verification of C programs. The design of ACSL is based on JML [20] while inheriting key features from the Caduceus specification language [13,14], a previous development of one of the partners in the Frama-C [19] project. As JML, ACSL utilizes the design-by-contract methodology to specify contracts in C code. As a formal language, ACSL enables a precise specification of function contracts. That makes the specification not only understandable by a human but also manipulable by an analyser.

ACSL provides comprehensive specification primitives that cover both low-level aspects of C programming, such as memory management and pointer operations, and high-level abstract reasoning through mathematical and logic types. The language supports the definition of concepts such as "valid linked lists" and allows partial contract specification, allowing developers to verify specific properties of interest without requiring complete formal specifications. Within the Frama-C verification framework, ACSL annotations are processed by specialised plug-ins, including WP (Weakest Precondition) [7], which employ Hoare-style weakest precondition computations to generate verification conditions. These verification conditions can be automatically discharged using external theorem provers such as Alt-Ergo [10], Z3 [12], and CVC4 [4], or are handled interactively through the built-in WP prover or the Coq proof assistant. Another Frama-C plug-in is the ACSL importer [2], which allows importing external ACSL specifications written in files, separated from the C source files. In ACSL, a contract specification is written directly in the code in the form of comments starting with `//@` (line) or between `/*@ e @*/` (block).

The specification of preconditions and postconditions can be written using the keywords **requires** and **ensures**, respectively. The preconditions will specify conditions that must be true before the function call, while the postconditions are conditions that must be true after its execution. The **assigns** clause specifies the memory locations that can be modified during the execution of the function. In ACSL, a **predicate** is a logical expression that evaluates to either true or false; a **logic function** is a mathematical function that can be used within specifications to express complex computations and relationships; a **type** is a statement that creates new logic types to be used within specifications. These new types can also be defined as polymorphic types such as in `//@ type list<A>`; a **axiom** is a logic statement that is assumed to be true without proof, serving as a building block for logical reasoning within specifications; finally, an **axiomatic**[1] is a structured container that groups related logical definitions, including types, logic functions, predicates, and axioms.

---

[1] Although "axiomatic" is grammatically an adjective, ACSL uses it as a keyword (noun) to define a structured container that groups related logical definitions. In this paper, we keep ACSL's use of this word, but use **verbatim** font in such cases.

Listing 2.2. Example of ACSL's <code>axiomatic</code>.

```
axiomatic sign {
   logic integer get_sign(real x);
   axiom sign_pos:  \forall real x; x > 0. ==> get_sign(x) == 1;
   axiom sign_neg:  \forall real x; x < 0. ==> get_sign(x) == -1;
   axiom sign_zero:  \forall real x; x = 0. ==> get_sign(x) == 0;
   predicate is_positive(real x) = get_sign(x) == 1;
   predicate is_negative(real x) = get_sign(x) == -1;
   predicate is_zero(real x) = get_sign(x) == 0;
}
```

Listing 2.2 presents an `axiomatic` that contains a logic function `get_sign`, which receives a real number and returns an integer. To define this function, we have three axioms: the first describes the positive numbers, the second describes the negative numbers, and the third describes zero. Furthermore, the `axiomatic` contains the predicate `is_positive` that verifies if the number is positive, the predicate `is_negative` that verifies if the number is negative, and the predicate `is_zero` that verifies if the number is zero.

3 An ACSL Library for the B-Method

In order to be able to translate B machines to ACSL, we built an ACSL library to represent the B-Method data structures and their functions. This library contains the definitions of sets, tuples, relations, functions, and sequences, as well as the B-Method operations on these data structures. This section presents the `axiomatic` used to translate each data structure and the axioms that define their operations. The types described in this article were defined using a total of 46 axioms. For conciseness, this section presents the most basic and interesting definitions; a full account can be found in the Appendix A.

3.1 Set

The ACSL `Set` type represents one of the fundamental data structures in the B-Method, and its translation to ACSL requires a comprehensive axiomatic definition. The presented definition of ACSL `axiomatic` establishes a generic type `Set<A>` that can represent sets of any type `A`, providing the flexibility needed to model the various operations of sets found in the B specifications.

Listing 3.1. Set type <code>axiomatic</code>.

```
axiomatic set {
   type Set<A>;
   logic Set<A> empty<A>(Set<A> witness);
   logic int card<A>(Set<A> ss);
   logic Set<integer> singleton<A>(A xx);
   logic Set<A> set_union<A>(Set<A> ss, Set<A> tt);
   logic Set<A> set_intersection<A>(Set<A> ss, Set<A> tt);
   logic Set<A> set_difference<A>(Set<A> s1, Set<A> s2);
```

```
predicate  is_finite<A>(Set<A> ss);
predicate  belongs<A>(A xx, Set<A> ss);
predicate  not_belongs <A>(A xx, Set<A> ss);
predicate  inclusion<A>(Set<A> ss, Set<A> tt) =
    (\forall A xx; belongs(xx, ss) ==> belongs(xx,tt));
predicate  equals<A>(Set<A> ss, Set<A> tt) =
    ( (\forall A xx; belongs(xx, ss) ==> belongs(xx, tt)) &&
      (\forall A yy; belongs(yy, tt) ==> belongs(yy, ss)) );
logic Set<integer> NAT;
logic Set<integer> NAT1; }
```

Listing 3.1 presented the `axiomatic` built to define the type `Set` in ACSL. The `axiomatic` begins with the declaration of the generic type `Set<A>` and the essential logical functions that correspond to the fundamental set operations in the B-Method. The `empty<A>` function represents the empty set, which requires a witness parameter of type `Set<A>` to ensure proper type instantiation in the ACSL type system. The `card<A>` function provides the cardinality computation, returning an integer value representing the number of elements in a given set. The `singleton<A>` function creates a set containing exactly one element, corresponding to the singleton set of the B-Method. The set operations `set_union<A>`, `set_intersection<A>`, and `set_difference<A>` directly translate the B-Method's sets union, sets intersection, and sets difference operations, respectively, maintaining the same mathematical semantics while adapting to ACSL's functional specification style. The `belongs<A>` predicate determines set membership of an element, directly corresponding to the B-Method's membership operator. Its complement, `not_belongs<A>`, provides explicit non-membership. The `inclusion<A>` predicate defines subset relationships using universal quantification, stating that the set `ss` is included in the set `tt` if every element belonging to `ss` also belongs to `tt`. The `equals<A>` predicate establishes set equality through mutual inclusion. Furthermore, the `axiomatic` defines a logical variable: `NAT`, and `NAT1`, that represent, respectively, the set of natural numbers with a practical upper bound of 2147483647 (the maximum value of a 32-bit signed integer) and a similar set that simply excludes zero.

To define each function presented in this `axiomatic` block, we define some axioms that define the behaviour of the function and the properties related to the set type (Listing 3.2). For instance, three axioms were defined for the logical function `empty<A>`: `def_empty_integer` establishes that for all sets of integers S and integers `xx`, `xx` does not belong to the empty set witnessed with S; `def_empty_card` establishes that the cardinality of an empty set is 0, and `def_inclusion_empty` establishes that the empty set of `NAT` is included in every set of integers.

Listing 3.2. Empty function axioms.

```
axiom def_empty_integer:
   \forall Set<integer> S; \forall integer xx;
      not_belongs(xx, empty(S));
axiom def_empty_card: \forall Set<integer> S; card(empty(S))==0;
axiom def_inclusion_empty:
   \forall Set<integer> ss; inclusion(empty(NAT), ss);
```

Three axioms define the function `singleton<A>` (Listing 3.3): `def_singleton_card` establishes that the cardinality of a singleton is 1; `singleton_membership` establishes that for any two integers, xx and yy, xx belongs to the singleton of yy if and only if these two integers are equal, and `def_singleton_not_belongs` establishes that for any two different integers, xx and yy, yy does not belong to the singleton of xx.

Listing 3.3. Singleton function axioms.

```
axiom def_singleton_card:
   \forall integer x; card(singleton(x)) == 1;
axiom singleton_membership:
   \forall integer xx, integer yy;
       belongs(xx, singleton(yy)) <==> xx == yy;
axiom def_singleton_not_belongs:
   \forall integer xx, integer yy;
      xx != yy ==> not_belongs(yy, singleton(xx));
```

The axiom **def_card** provides a recursive definition for calculating set cardinality (Listing 3.4). It states that the cardinality of the union of a set with a singleton is equal to one plus the cardinality of the set. The **union_membership** axiom determines, for all integers, that an integer belongs to the union of two sets of integers `ss` and `tt` if and only if this integer belongs to `ss` or `tt`. The axiom **intersection_membership** determines, for all integers, that an integer belongs to the intersection of two sets of integers `ss` and `tt`, if and only if this integer belongs to `ss` and `tt`. The axiom **difference_membership** determines, for all integers, that an integer belongs to the difference of two sets of integers `ss` and `tt`, if and only if this integer belongs to `ss` and does not belong to `tt`.

Listing 3.4. Card, Union, Intersection and Difference functions axioms.

```
axiom def_card:
   \forall integer xx, Set<integer> ss;
      card(set_union(ss, singleton(xx)))
      == 1 + card(set_difference(ss, singleton(xx)));
axiom union_membership:
   \forall integer xx, Set<integer> ss, Set<integer> tt;
      belongs(xx, set_union(ss, tt))
      <==> belongs(xx, ss) || belongs(xx, tt);
axiom intersection_membership:
   \forall integer xx, Set<integer> ss, Set<integer> tt;
      belongs(xx, set_intersection(ss, tt))
      <==> belongs(xx, ss) && belongs(xx, tt);
axiom difference_membership:
   \forall integer xx, Set<integer> ss, Set<integer> tt;
      belongs(xx, set_difference(ss, tt))
      <==> belongs(xx, ss) && not_belongs(xx, tt);
```

Furthermore, the axiom **belongs_not_belongs** defines the relation between the predicate **belongs** and **not_belongs** (Listing 3.5).

Listing 3.5. Axiom for `belongs` and `not_belongs` function.

```
axiom belongs_not_belongs: \forall integer xx, Set<integer> ss;
      not_belongs(xx,ss) <==> !belongs(xx, ss);
```

The `is_finite<A>` function is defined through axioms that define when a set can be considered finite. In Listing 3.6, the axiom `is_finite_empty` establishes that all empty sets are finite, providing a base case for finite set reasoning. The axiom `is_finite_add` provides an inductive step, stating that if a set is finite, then the union of that set with any singleton set is also finite.

Listing 3.6. `is_finite` function's axiom.

```
axiom is_finite_empty: \forall Set<integer> S; is_finite(empty(S));
axiom is_finite_add: \forall integer x, Set<integer> t;
      is_finite(t) ==> is_finite(set_union(singleton(x),t));
```

Finally, in Listing 3.7, we present the axiom that defines the logic variable `NAT`. The axiom `def_NAT_set` defines that all integers between 0 and 2147483647, corresponding to `INT_MAX`, belong to the set defined by the logic variable `NAT`. A similar axiom defines the logic variable `NAT`, simply excluding zero.

Listing 3.7. Axiom to define the sets NAT and NAT1.

```
    axiom def_NAT_set:
      \forall integer xx;
        xx>=0 && xx<=2147483647 ==> belongs(xx,NAT);
    axiom def_NAT1_set:
      \forall integer xx;
        xx>=1 && xx<=2147483647 ==> belongs(xx,NAT1);
}
```

This concludes the definition of the `Set` ACSL type.

3.2 Tuple

The tuple data structure allows for the ordered grouping of elements of different types. Its translation into ACSL establishes a generic type `Tuple<A,B>` that can represent tuples of two elements of arbitrary types `A` and `B`. The definition of the `axiomatic` of the `Tuple` type is presented in Listing 3.8. The essential logical functions for the manipulation of tuples are defined next. The function `couple<A,B>(A x, B y)` acts as a tuple constructor, allowing the creation of a tuple from two elements `x` and `y`. The functions `first<A,B>` and `second<A,B>` are accessors that allow retrieving, respectively, the first and second elements of a given `Tuple<A,B>` t. The complete `axiomatic`, with the axioms used to define the behaviour of each function, is presented in Appendix A.2.

Listing 3.8. Tuple type `axiomatic`.

```
axiomatic Tuple {
    type Tuple<A,B>;
    logic Tuple<A,B> couple<A,B>(A x, B y);
    logic A first<A,B>(Tuple<A,B> t);
    logic B second<A,B>(Tuple<A,B> t);
    ...
```

The types `Set` and `Tuple` are used to define relations as presented next.

3.3   Relation

The relation data structure is a fundamental concept in formal methods that represents a set of ordered pairs (tuples) that define a relationship between elements from two sets. Relations are crucial for modelling complex associations and dependencies between data. Its translation to ACSL involves an `axiomatic` definition that captures the properties and operations of relations. The `axiomatic` presented in Listing 3.9 establishes a generic type `Relation<A,B>` that represents a relation between elements of type `A` and type `B`.

Listing 3.9. Relation type `axiomatic`.

```
axiomatic Relation {
    type Relation<A,B>;
    logic Set< Tuple<A,B> > graph<A,B>(Relation <A,B> r);
    logic Set<integer> dom<A,B>(Relation <A,B> r);
    logic Set<integer> ran<A,B>(Relation <A,B> r);
    logic Relation<A, B> empty_relation<A, B>(Relation<A, B> r);
    ...
```

The `Relation<A,B>` type is defined as a set of ordered pairs, where each pair is a `Tuple<A,B>`. The core of its definition is the function `graph<A,B>`, which returns the set of all tuples that constitute the relation. The functions `dom<A,B>` and `ran<A,B>` define the domain and the range of a relation, respectively. The domain is the set of all the first elements of the pairs in the relation, while the range is the set of all second elements. The function `empty_relation<A, B>` represents an empty relation, which contains no pairs. The complete `axiomatic` with the axioms used to define the behaviour of each function is presented in Appendix A.3

3.4   Function

Functions are a specialised kind of relation where each element in the domain is associated with at most one element in the range. This functional property is fundamental for modelling deterministic mappings and operations. Its translation into ACSL involves a comprehensive `axiomatic` definition that captures the specific characteristics and operations of functions, based on the previously defined `Relation` type. Listing 3.10 presents the `axiomatic` that establishes a generic type `Function<A,B>`, which represents a function mapping elements of type `A` to elements of type B.

Listing 3.10. Function type `axiomatic`.

```
axiomatic Function {
   type Function <A, B>;
   logic  Function <A, B>  relation_to_function <A,B>(Relation <A,B> r);
   logic  Relation <A,B> function_to_relation <A,B>(Function<A, B>  f);
   logic  integer  apply <A,B>(Function <A, B>  f, integer x);
   logic  Function <A, B> empty_function <A, B>(Function <A, B> f);
   logic  Function <A, B>  singleton_function <A,B>(A x, B y);
   ...
```

The `Function<A,B>` type is defined as a specialised `Relation<A,B>` that has the functional property of mapping each element in the domain to a single element in the range. The logical functions `relation_to_function<A,B>` and `function_to_relation<A,B>` provide conversion mechanisms between relations and functions. A relation can be converted to a function only if it is functional, and any function can be viewed as its inherent relation. The `apply<A,B>` function represents the application of a function to an input value `x`, returning the corresponding output. Finally, specialised functions include `empty_function<A, B>`, which represents a function with an empty domain and range, and `singleton_function<A,B>`, which creates a function that maps a single element `x` to y. The complete `axiomatic`, with the axioms used to define the behaviour of each function's operation, is presented in Appendix A.4.

3.5   Sequence

The sequence data structure is a function that maps natural numbers (indices) to elements. Its translation into ACSL involves the use of the ACSL list of type `\list<A>` that represents a sequence of elements of type `A`. To be able to use the type `\list<A>`, as in the type function, the `axiomatic` of this type presents functions to map the type `\list<A>` to the type `Function<integer, A>`. Listing 3.11 presents the list of functions defined for `\list<A>`.

Listing 3.11. Sequence type `axiomatic`.

```
axiomatic Sequence {
   predicate  is_sequence <A,B>(Function <A,B> f);
   logic  \list <A> function_to_list <A>(Function <integer ,A> f);
   logic  Function <integer ,integer >
          list_to_function (\list <integer > l);
   logic  boolean  is_seq_of (\list <integer > l, Set <integer > s);
   logic  Set <integer > ran (\list <integer > l);
   ...
```

The predicate `is_sequence<A,B>` defines what constitutes a valid sequence in this `axiomatic`. The functions `function_to_list<A>` and `list_to_function` are key for interoperability: `function_to_list` transforms a function (representing a sequence) into an ACSL \list and `list_to_function` turns an ACSL \list into its equivalent function representation. The `is_seq_of` operation checks if every element within a given list `l` is also a member of a specified set `s`. Finally, the `ran` operation computes the set of all unique elements present in a list `l`. This is equivalent to the range of the function that represents the list. The whole of the `axiomatic Sequence`, which also contains the axioms used to define its operations, is presented in Appendix A.5.

4 Mapping B Machines to ACSL Specifications

The development using the B-Method starts with an abstract `MACHINE` that uses preconditions, postconditions, and invariants to precisely specify the behaviour of its initialisation and operations. The `MACHINE` can be refined to a more concrete `REFINEMENT`, which can also be refined to an `IMPLEMENTATION`. Finally, using Atelier-B, we can generate the C code from the `IMPLEMENTATION`.

Figure 1 presents the process to build an ACSL specification from the B components (`MACHINE`, `REFINEMENT`, and `IMPLEMENTATION`). Besides the specifi-

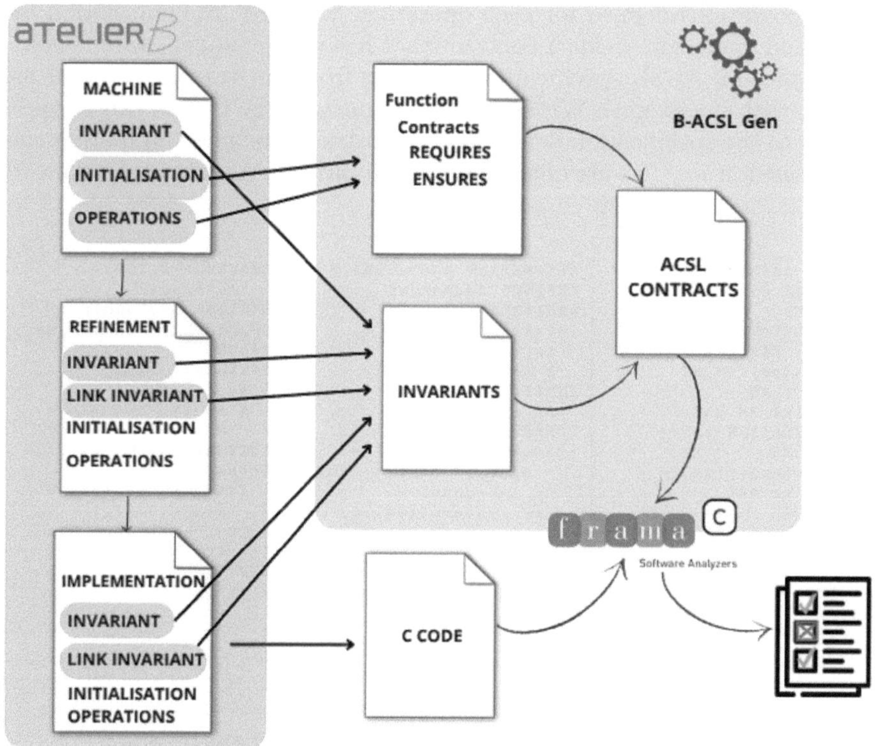

Fig. 1. Mapping process from the B-Method to ACSL

cations of the abstract MACHINE invariant and operations, this process also considers the invariants of eventual SPSVERBa63s and the IMPLEMENTATION. These invariants usually contain a link between the abstract and the more concrete variables (linking invariant). Finally, it creates a connection between the variables of IMPLEMENTATION and the variables of the C code generated by Atelier-B.

The translation of the invariant of each B component yields a separate axiomatic. Each axiomatic contains the axiom that represents the corresponding invariant and the properties of each variable using the functions presented in Sect. 3. Finally, a special axiomatic connects the implementation variables to the C-code variables. Similarly, the translation of the clause PROPERTIES of each B component yields an axiomatic that contains an axiom defining the properties of the CONSTANTS and the SETS of that component.

The variables and constants specified in the B components are translated into logic variables in ACSL. Our translation process yields an axiomatic for each component, which contains the logic variables, representing its variables, respecting their types according to the invariant. The translation of constants also yields an axiomatic that contains a logic variable. The process of translating the operations, including the initialisation, only takes into account the specification of the abstract machine. Our translation process yields contracts for each operation, defining the requires and ensures statements from the pre- and post-conditions defined for each operation. Similarly, the translation of an initialisation operation yields a contract that has only ensures statements.

With the full ACSL specification resulting from our translation, and using Frama-C (with the plugins: WP and ACSL-importer), the C code can be verified according to the specification defined in the abstract machine and its refinement and implementation. The use of these plugins returns to the user each verification

```
MACHINE AddRunner          REFINEMENT AddRunner_r      IMPLEMENTATION
VARIABLES ss               REFINES AddRunner              AddRunner_i
INVARIANT                  VARIABLES ss_r              REFINES AddRunner_r
   ss : POW(NAT)           INVARIANT                   CONCRETE_VARIABLES ss_i
   & ss : FIN(ss)             ss_r : seq(NAT)          VALUES MM = 10
   & card(ss) <= MM          & ss = ran(ss_r)         INVARIANT
CONSTANTS MM               INITIALISATION                 ss_i : NAT
PROPERTIES MM:NAT             ss_r := []                  & ss_i
INITIALISATION ss := {}    OPERATIONS                     = card(ran(ss_r))
OPERATIONS                   AddNewRunner(xx) =       INITIALISATION ss_i := 0
   AddNewRunner(xx) =          ss_r := ss_r <- xx;    OPERATIONS
      PRE xx:NAT            rr <-- count =               AddNewRunner(xx) =
         & xx /: ss           rr := card(ran(ss_r))       ss_i := ss_i + 1;
         & card(ss) < MM   END                          rr <-- count =
      THEN                                                 rr := ss_i
         ss := ss \/ {xx}                              END
      END;
   rr <-- count =
      rr := card(ss)
END
```

Fig. 2. B Components of the AddRunner system.

made to this specification. This process is currently performed manually; the automation of this process is on our near future agenda.

5   Case Study

Our case study is a system that counts the number of participants in a running event. This system has two operations: an operation that adds a new runner and an operation that returns the number of runners. Figure 2 presents a B specification of its abstract `MACHINE`, its `REFINEMENT`, and its `IMPLEMENTATION`. The abstract machine specifies the variable `ss` as a finite set of natural numbers (`NAT`) with its maximum size defined by the constant `MM`. The abstract machine initialises the variable `ss` with the empty set. If the number of runners in `ss` is less than `MM`, the operation `AddNewRunner` receives a natural number `xx` that is not in `ss` and adds it to `ss`. The operation `count` simply returns the cardinality of `ss`. The refinement of `AddRunner` specifies the variable `ss_r` as a sequence of natural numbers whose range equals the set `ss`. Finally, the implementation machine specifies the variable `ss_i` as a natural number equal to the cardinality of the range of `ss_r`. The implementation also defines the value of `MM` as 10.

Following the process described in Sect. 4, the variables and constants of each machine will be translated into SPSVERBa33s that contain logic variables respecting their type, according to the invariant of each machine. In our case study, we have three variables: `ss`, defined as a subset of natural numbers; `ss_r`, defined as a sequence of natural numbers; and `ss_i`, defined as a natural number. In addition to these variables, we also have a constant, named `MM`, that is specified as a natural number. The translation of the abstract machine variable yields the `axiomatic` named `AddRunner_variables`, which contains the logic variable `ss` as a set of integers. The translation of the refinement variable yields the `axiomatic AddRunner_r_variables` with the logic variable `ss_r` as a list of integer numbers. The implementation variable yields `axiomatic AddRunner_i_variables` with the logic variable `ss_i` as an integer number. Furthermore, the constant, defined in the abstract machine, yields the `axiomatic AddRunner_constants`, which contains the logic variable `MM` as an integer. The specification for these SPSVERBa33s is presented in Listing 5.1.

Listing 5.1. Relevant Variables Axioms.

```
axiomatic AddRunner_variables { logic Set<integer> ss; } axiomatic
AddRunner_r_variables { logic \list<integer> ss_r; } axiomatic
AddRunner_i_variables { logic integer ss_i; } axiomatic
AddRunner_constants { logic integer MM; }
```

The abstract machine invariant yields the `axiomatic AddRunner_invariant` that contains the axiom `AddRunner_invariant_ss` defining the variable `ss` as a finite subset of `NAT` with a maximum cardinality `MM`. The refinement's invariant yields the `axiomatic AddRunner_r_invariant`, which has the axiom `AddRunner_invariant_ss_r`, defining the variable `ss_r` as a sequence of natural numbers, and connects the variables `ss_r` to `ss`, specifying that the range of `ss_r` is equal to `ss`. The implementation's invariant yields the `axiomatic` `AddRunner_i_invariant`, which has the axiom `AddRunner_invariant_ss_i` that establishes that the variable `ss_i` belongs to the set `NAT` and connects the variable `ss_i` to the variable `ss_r`, specifying that `ss_i` is equal to the cardinality of the range of the variable `ss_r`. Furthermore, this axiom connects the logic variable `ss_i` to the C program variable `AddRunner__ss_i`. The properties defined in the abstract machine yield the `axiomatic AddRunner_properties`, which has the axiom `AddRunner_properties_MM` defining that the constant `MM` belongs to the set `NAT`. The specification of these SPSVERBa33s is presented in Listing 5.2.

Listing 5.2. Relevant Sequence axioms.

```
axiomatic AddRunner_invariant {
   axiom AddRunner_invariant_ss: inclusion(ss, NAT)
      && is_finite(ss) && card(ss) <= MM;}
axiomatic AddRunner_r_invariant {
   axiom AddRunner_invariant_ss_r: is_seq_of(ss_r, NAT)
      && ss == ran(ss_r);}
axiomatic AddRunner_i_invariant {
   axiom AddRunner_invariant_ss_i: belongs(ss_i, NAT)
      && ss_i == card(ran(ss_r)) && AddRunner__ss_i == ss_i;}
axiomatic AddRunner_properties {
   axiom AddRunner_properties_MM: belongs(MM, NAT);}
```

The initialisation of the abstract `MACHINE` yields the contract of the C function `AddRunner__INITIALISATION`, which has no precondition but ensures that the variable `ss` is equal to the empty set of `NAT`. The `assigns` statement indicates that the concrete variable `AddRunner__ss_i` may be altered in this function. The operation `AddNewRunner` yields the contract of the C function `AddRunner__AddNewRunner`, which `requires` that: (1) the variable `xx` belongs to the set `NAT`; (2) `xx` does not belong to the set `ss`; and (3) the cardinality of `ss` is less than `MM`. Its post-condition establishes that the final value of the set `ss` is the union of the original value of `ss` with the singleton of `xx`. The variable `AddRunner__ss_i` can also be altered in this function. Finally, the operation `count` yields the contract of the function `AddRunner__count`, which does not have preconditions, but ensures that the value of `rr` is the cardinality of `ss`. The statement `assigns` specifies that only the value of `rr` can be altered. The specifications of these contracts are presented in Listing 5.3.

Listing 5.3. Relevant Sequence axioms.

```
function AddRunner__INITIALISATION: contract: ensures ss ==
empty(NAT); assigns AddRunner__ss_i; function
AddRunner__AddNewRunner: contract: requires belongs(xx, NAT);
requires not_belongs(xx, ss);
        requires card(ss) < MM;
        ensures  ss == set_union(\old(ss), singleton(xx));
        assigns  AddRunner__ss_i;
```

```
function AddRunner__count: contract: ensures   *rr == card(ss);
assigns  *rr;
```

Using the Frama-C platform, we were able to verify that the generated C code complies with the contracts derived from the B specification. This verification process used two plugins: ACSL importer, which integrates the formal specification with the corresponding C source code, and WP (Weakest Precondition), which performs the verification of the annotated functions.

Listing 5.4. Frama-C Verification Result.

```
[acsl-importer] Success for spec.acsl [acsl-importer] Done: 1 file.
[wp] Warning: Missing RTE guards [wp] 6 goals scheduled [wp] Proved
goals:   12 / 12
   Terminating:      3
   Unreachable:      3
   Qed:              3 (0.95ms-0.60ms-2ms)
   CVC4 1.8:         3 (115ms-133ms)
```

Listing 5.4 presents the Frama-C output, which was obtained in 2 s on a computer with an AMD Ryzen^{TM} 7 3700U processor with 8 cores, integrated AMD Radeon^{TM} Vega 10 Graphics, 8GB DDR4 RAM, and a 256GB SSD.

6   Related Work

Fürst et al. [15] presented a correct-by-construction approach to generate C code from event-B specifications, proving that a scheduled, refined model refines the original one and thus produces code free of runtime errors. Our work targets the correctness of the code generated by Atelier-B. We start from B-Method machines, automatically derive ACSL contracts, and use Frama-C to deductively verify the actual C code produced by Atelier-B. Therefore, Fürst et al. [15] prove that the generator (and schedule) produces correct code; we prove that the delivered code instance satisfies the properties of the original specification. These approaches are complementary: theirs secures the construction pipeline, ours secures the final artifact against the original contracts and safety requirements.

Beckert et al. [6] connect Java code annotated with (Java Modelling Language) contracts to bounded model checking by transforming contracts into a form suitable for JBMC, the Java Bounded Model Checker. This method enables modular verification within the bounded context of automated model checking. The transformation replaces JML quantifiers with nondeterministic assignments, allowing JBMC to check contract-specified properties within user-defined limits. Our work instead links B-Method machines to ACSL contracts and applies deductive verification in Frama-C on C code actually generated by Atelier-B. Thus, theirs blends modular contracts with bounded model checking on Java; ours carries design-by-contract specs into unbounded (proof-oriented) verification at the C level, preserving the original B abstractions.

Ge et al. [16] translate the final, fully refined Event-B model into an intermediate HLL (High Level Language) representation, and verify extra properties (deadlock/liveness) with the S3 tool set. Then, C code is generated automatically for most system functions, while some are implemented manually based on formal contracts provided in HLL. The process includes an equivalence proof between the HLL model and the generated C code to ensure correctness. Our approach instead starts from B-Method machines across the entire refinement chain, systematically deriving ACSL contracts that mirror those abstractions, and using Frama-C to deductively verify the actual C code produced by Atelier-B.

7 Conclusion

This paper has presented a translation strategy from the B-Method to ACSL, centered on a comprehensive library that maps B-Method data structures—sets, tuples, relations, functions, and sequences—to their corresponding ACSL specifications. The axiomatic definitions and logical predicates preserve the properties of the original structures, enabling formal verification of the C code with the Frama-C toolkit.

The translation process builds on the ACSL library introduced in this paper and is applied to complete B-Method components, covering the abstract, refinement, and implementation levels. At each level, we generate the corresponding ACSL `axiomatic` blocks and contracts, preserving invariants, state variables, and operations contracts in the resulting ACSL specification. Using Frama-C (WP and the acsl-importer), this workflow enables formal verification of the generated C code against the original B specifications.

The viability and effectiveness of the proposed approach were demonstrated through a case study of a simple runner-counting system. The study showed that the methodology preserves traceability from the B specifications to ACSL and supports automated verification with Frama-C. Future work will extend the coverage of B-Method constructs in our ACSL library, automate the translation process, address portability, and evaluate the approach in more complex case studies.

Acknowledgments. We thank NPAD/UFRN for their computing resources. This work is partially funded by INES (https://www.ines.org.br

A   Appendix

A.1   Set

Listing A.1. Set type `axiomatic`.

```
axiomatic set {
    type Set<A>;
```

```
logic Set<A> empty<A>(Set<A> witness);
logic int card<A>(Set<A> ss);
logic Set<integer> singleton<A>(A xx);
logic Set<A> set_union<A>(Set<A> ss, Set<A> tt);
logic Set<A> set_intersection<A>(Set<A> ss, Set<A> tt);
logic Set<A> set_difference<A>(Set<A> s1, Set<A> s2);
predicate is_finite<A>(Set<A> ss);
predicate belongs<A>(A xx, Set<A> ss);
predicate not_belongs<A>(A xx, Set<A> ss);
predicate inclusion<A>(Set<A> ss, Set<A> tt) =
    (\forall A xx; belongs(xx, ss) ==> belongs(xx,tt));
predicate equals<A>(Set<A> ss, Set<A> tt) =
    ( (\forall A xx; belongs(xx, ss) ==> belongs(xx, tt)) &&
      (\forall A yy; belongs(yy, tt) ==> belongs(yy, ss)) );
logic Set<integer> NAT;
logic Set<integer> NAT1;


axiom def_empty_integer:
    \forall Set<integer> S; \forall integer xx;
        not_belongs(xx, empty(S));
axiom def_empty_card: \forall Set<integer> S; card(empty(S)) == 0;
axiom def_inclusion_empty:
    \forall Set<integer> ss; inclusion(empty(NAT), ss);
axiom def_singleton_card:
    \forall integer x; card(singleton(x)) == 1;
axiom singleton_membership:
    \forall integer xx, integer yy;
        belongs(xx, singleton(yy)) <==> xx == yy;
axiom def_singleton_not_belongs:
    \forall integer xx, integer yy;
      xx != yy ==> not_belongs(yy, singleton(xx));
axiom def_card:
    \forall integer xx, Set<integer> ss;
      card(set_union(ss, singleton(xx)))
      == 1 + card(set_difference(ss, singleton(xx)));
axiom union_membership:
    \forall integer xx, Set<integer> ss, Set<integer> tt;
      belongs(xx, set_union(ss, tt))
      <==> belongs(xx, ss) || belongs(xx, tt);
axiom intersection_membership:
    \forall integer xx, Set<integer> ss, Set<integer> tt;
      belongs(xx, set_intersection(ss, tt))
      <==> belongs(xx, ss) && belongs(xx, tt);
axiom difference_membership:
    \forall integer xx, Set<integer> ss, Set<integer> tt;
      belongs(xx, set_difference(ss, tt))
      <==> belongs(xx, ss) && not_belongs(xx, tt);
axiom belongs_not_belongs:
    \forall integer xx, Set<integer> ss;
      not_belongs(xx,ss) <==> !belongs(xx, ss);
axiom is_finite_empty: \forall Set<integer> S; is_finite(empty(S));
axiom is_finite_add:
    \forall integer x, Set<integer> t;
```

```
                is_finite(t) ==> is_finite(set_union(singleton(x),t));
    axiom def_NAT_set:
       \forall integer xx;
          xx >= 0 && xx <= 2147483647 ==> belongs(xx, NAT);
    axiom def_NAT1_set:
       \forall integer xx;
          xx >= 1 && xx <= 2147483647 ==> belongs(xx, NAT1);
}
```

A.2 Tuple

Listing A.2. Tuple type `axiomatic`.

```
axiomatic Tuple {
    type Tuple<A,B>;
    logic Tuple<A,B> couple<A,B>(A x, B y);
    logic A first<A,B>(Tuple<A,B> t);
    logic B second<A,B>(Tuple<A,B> t);
    predicate equals<A,B>(Tuple<A,B> t, Tuple<A,B> s) =
        first(t) == first(s) && second(t) == second(s);

    axiom fst_couple_int_int:
        \forall integer x,y; first(couple(x,y)) == x;
    axiom snd_couple_int_int:
        \forall integer x,y; second(couple(x,y)) == y;
    axiom def_tuple_int_int:
        \forall Tuple<integer,integer> t;
            couple( first(t), second(t) ) == t;
    axiom tuple_extensional_int_int:
        \forall Tuple<integer,integer> u,v;
            first(u) == first(v) && second(u) == second(v) ==> u == v;
    axiom tuple_extensional_int_int_aux:
        \forall Tuple<integer,integer> u,v;
            first(u)
!= first(v) || second(u) != second(v) ==> u != v;
}
```

A.3 Relation

Listing A.3. Relation type `axiomatic`.

```
axiomatic Relation {
    type Relation<A,B>;
    logic Set< Tuple<A,B> > graph<A,B>(Relation<A,B> r);
    logic Set<integer> dom<A,B>(Relation<A,B> r);
    logic Set<integer> ran<A,B>(Relation<A,B> r);
    logic Relation<A, B> empty_relation<A, B>(Relation<A, B> r);
    predicate rel_belongs<A,B>(A x, B y, Relation<A,B> r);
```

```
   axiom equal_relations_definition:
     \forall Relation<integer,integer> r1,
             Relation<integer,integer> r2;
        (\forall Tuple<integer,integer> t;
           belongs(t, graph(r1)) <==> belongs(t, graph(r2)))
           ==> r1 == r2;
   axiom rel_belongs_def:
     \forall integer x, integer y, Relation<integer,integer> r;
        rel_belongs(x, y, r) <==> belongs(couple(x,y),graph(r));
   axiom dom_def:
     \forall integer x, Relation<integer,integer> r;
        belongs(x, dom(r))
        <==> (\exists integer y; rel_belongs(x, y, r));
   axiom dom_empty:
     \forall Relation<integer, integer> r;
        dom(empty_relation(r)) == empty(NAT);
   axiom ran_def:
     \forall integer y, Relation<integer,integer> r;
        belongs(y, ran(r))
        <==> (\exists integer x; rel_belongs(x, y, r));
   axiom ran_empty:
     \forall Relation<integer, integer> r;
        ran(empty_relation(r)) == empty(NAT);
   axiom empty_relation_def:
     \forall Tuple<integer,integer> t, Relation<integer,integer> r;
        not_belongs(t, graph(empty_relation(r)));
   axiom card_empty_relation:
     \forall Relation<integer, integer> r;
        card(graph(empty_relation(r))) == 0;
}
```

A.4   Function

Listing A.4. Function type `axiomatic`.

```
axiomatic Function {
   type Function<A, B>;
   logic Function<A, B>  relation_to_function<A,B>(Relation<A,B> r);
   logic Relation<A,B> function_to_relation<A,B>(Function<A, B>  f);
   logic integer apply<A,B>(Function<A, B>  f, integer x);
   logic Function<A, B> empty_function<A, B>(Function<A, B> f);
   logic Function<A, B>  singleton_function<A,B>(A x, B y);
   predicate is_functional<A,B>(Relation<A,B> r);
   predicate is_injective(Function<integer, integer> f) =
      \forall integer x1, integer x2, integer y;
         rel_belongs(x1, y, function_to_relation(f)) &&
         rel_belongs(x2, y, function_to_relation(f)) ==> x1 == x2;
   predicate is_surjective(Function<integer, integer> f,
                           Set<integer> codomain) =
      \forall integer y;
         belongs(y, codomain) ==>
         (\exists integer x;
```

```
                    rel_belongs(x, y, function_to_relation(f)));
    predicate is_bijective(Function<integer, integer> f,
                           Set<integer> codomain) =
      is_injective(f) && is_surjective(f, codomain);


    axiom is_functional_def:
      \forall Relation<integer, integer> r;
      is_functional(r) <==>
      (\forall integer x, integer y1, integer y2;
        rel_belongs(x,y1,r) && rel_belongs(x,y2,r) ==> y1 == y2);
    axiom relation_to_function_def:
      \forall Relation<integer, integer> r;
        is_functional(r) ==>
          (\forall integer x, integer y;
            rel_belongs(x, y, r)
            <==> rel_belongs(x, y,
                function_to_relation(relation_to_function(r))));
    axiom function_to_relation_def:
      \forall Function<integer,integer> f,integer x,integer y;
        rel_belongs(x, y, function_to_relation(f))
        <==> (belongs(x, dom(function_to_relation(f)))
            && y == apply(f, x));
    axiom apply_def:
      \forall Function<integer, integer> f, integer x, integer y;
        (belongs(x, dom(function_to_relation(f)))
        && rel_belongs(x, y, function_to_relation(f)))
        ==> apply(f, x) == y;
    axiom apply_not_in_dom:
      \forall Function<integer, integer> f, integer x;
        !belongs(x, dom(function_to_relation(f))) ==> apply(f, x) == 0;
    axiom empty_function_def:
      \forall Function<integer,integer> f,Relation<integer,integer> r;
      function_to_relation(empty_function(f)) == empty_relation(r);
    axiom singleton_function_def:
      \forall integer x, integer y, integer a, integer b;
        rel_belongs(a, b,
          function_to_relation(singleton_function(x, y)))
        <==> (a == x && b == y);
}
```

A.5 Sequence

Listing A.5. Sequence type `axiomatic`.

```
axiomatic Sequence {
    predicate is_sequence<A,B>(Function<A,B> f);
    logic \list<A> function_to_list<A>(Function<integer,A> f);
    logic Function<integer,integer>
          list_to_function(\list<integer> l);
    logic boolean is_seq_of(\list<integer> l, Set<integer> s);
    logic Set<integer> ran(\list<integer> l);
    predicate iSeq(\list<integer> l) =
```

```
   is_injective(list_to_function(l));

axiom is_seq_of_nil:
  \forall Set<integer> s; is_seq_of(\Nil, s) == \true;
axiom is_seq_of_cons:
  \forall integer h, \list<integer> t, Set<integer> s;
    is_seq_of(\Cons(h,t), s)
    <==> (belongs(h, s) && is_seq_of(t, s));
axiom ran_nil:
  \forall Set<integer> witness; equals(ran(\Nil), empty(witness));
axiom ran_cons:
  \forall integer h, \list<integer> t;
    equals(ran(\Cons(h,t)),set_union(singleton(h),ran(t)));
axiom is_sequence_def:
  \forall Function<integer, integer> f;
    is_sequence(f) <==>
      (\forall integer i;
        belongs(i, dom(function_to_relation(f))) ==>
          (0 <= i && i < length(f)));
axiom is_sequence_domain_complete:
  \forall Function<integer, integer> f;
    is_sequence(f) ==>
      (\forall integer i; 0 <= i && i < length(f) ==>
        belongs(i, dom(function_to_relation(f))));
axiom function_to_list_empty:
  \forall Function<integer, integer> f;
    function_to_list(empty_function(f)) == \Nil;
axiom function_to_list_cons:
  \forall Function<integer, integer> f;
    is_sequence(f) && length(f) > 0 ==>
      function_to_list(f) ==
      \Cons(apply(f, 0),
          function_to_list(seq_subseq(f, 1, length(f))));
axiom list_to_function_nil:
  \forall Function<integer, integer> f;
    list_to_function(\Nil) == empty_function(f);
axiom list_to_function_cons:
  \forall integer x, \list<integer> l;
    list_to_function(\Cons(x, l)) ==
    seq_concat(singleton_function(0, x),
          seq_shift(list_to_function(l), 1)));
}
```

References

1. Abrial, J.: The B-book - assigning programs to meanings. Cambridge University Press (2005)
2. Acsl importer (2025). https://frama-c.com/fc-plugins/acsl-importer.html
3. Arce, I., et al.: Avoiding the top 10 software security design flaws. IEEE Computer Society Center for Secure Design, Tech. rep. (2014)
4. Barrett, C., et al.: CVC4. In: Gopalakrishnan, G., Qadeer, S. (eds.) CAV 2011. LNCS, vol. 6806, pp. 171–177. Springer, Heidelberg (2011). https://doi.org/10.1007/978-3-642-22110-1_14

5. Baudin, P., et al.: ACSL: ANSI/ISO C Specification Language – Version 1.20. Tech. rep., CEA LIST and INRIA Saclay (March 2009)
6. Beckert, B., Kirsten, M., Klamroth, J., Ulbrich, M.: Modular verification of jml contracts using bounded model checking. In: Leveraging Applications of Formal Methods, Verification and Validation: Verification Principles: 9th International Symposium on Leveraging Applications of Formal Methods, ISoLA 2020, Rhodes, Greece, October 20–30, 2020, Proceedings, Part I 9, pp. 60–80. Springer (2020)
7. Blanchard, A., Bobot, F., Baudin, P., Correnson, L.: Formally verifying that a program does what it should: The wp plug-in. In: Guide to Software Verification with Frama-C: Core Components, Usages, and Applications, pp. 187–261. Springer (2024)
8. Butler, M., Körner, P., Krings, S., Lecomte, T., Leuschel, M., Mejia, L.F., Voisin, L.: The first twenty-five years of industrial use of the b-method. In: ter Beek, M.H., Ničković, D. (eds.) Formal Methods for Industrial Critical Systems, pp. 189–209. Springer International Publishing, Cham (2020)
9. ClearSy: Atelier b. https://www.atelierb.eu/en/ (2025). Accessed 14 July 2025
10. Conchon, S., Coquereau, A., Iguernlala, M., Mebsout, A.: Alt-ergo 2.2. In: SMT Workshop: International Workshop on Satisfiability Modulo Theories (2018)
11. Significant cyber incidents. https://www.csis.org/programs/strategic-technologies-program/significant-cyber-incidents. Accessed 29 July 2023
12. De Moura, L., Bjørner, N.: Z3: An efficient SMT solver. In: International conference on Tools and Algorithms for the Construction and Analysis of Systems, pp. 337–340. Springer (2008)
13. Filliâtre, J.-C., Marché, C.: Multi-prover verification of C programs. In: Davies, J., Schulte, W., Barnett, M. (eds.) ICFEM 2004. LNCS, vol. 3308, pp. 15–29. Springer, Heidelberg (2004). https://doi.org/10.1007/978-3-540-30482-1_10
14. Filliâtre, J.C., Marché, C.: The why/krakatoa/caduceus platform for deductive program verification: (tool paper). In: International Conference on Computer Aided Verification, pp. 173–177. Springer (2007)
15. Fürst, A., Hoang, T.S., Basin, D., Desai, K., Sato, N., Miyazaki, K.: Code generation for event-B. In: Albert, E., Sekerinski, E. (eds.) IFM 2014. LNCS, vol. 8739, pp. 323–338. Springer, Cham (2014). https://doi.org/10.1007/978-3-319-10181-1_20
16. Ge, N., Dieumegard, A., Jenn, E., Voisin, L.: From event-b to verified c via hll. arXiv preprint arXiv:1610.07410 (2016)
17. Hatcliff, J., Leavens, G.T., Leino, K.R.M., Müller, P., Parkinson, M.: Behavioral interface specification languages. ACM Comput. Surv. (CSUR) **44**(3), 1–58 (2012)
18. Hinchey, M., Jackson, M., Cousot, P., Cook, B., Bowen, J.P., Margaria, T.: Software engineering and formal methods. Commun. ACM **51**(9), 54–59 (2008)
19. Kirchner, F., Kosmatov, N., Prevosto, V., Signoles, J., Yakobowski, B.: Frama-c: a software analysis perspective. Formal Aspects Comput. **27**(3), 573–609 (2015)
20. Leavens, G.T., et al.: Jml reference manual (2008)
21. Leroy, X., Blazy, S., Kästner, D., Schommer, B., Pister, M., et al.: Compcert - a formally verified optimizing compiler. In: 2016 ERTS Congress (Embedded Real Time Software and Systems), pp. 1–8. SEE, SEE (January 2016)
22. Martin, D.: 11 of the most costly software errors in history. https://raygun.com/blog/costly-software-errors-history/ (2014)
23. Schneider, S.: The B-Method: An Introduction. Palgrave Macmillan (2001)

A Research Agenda for the Living SysML V2 Blueprint: Toward Executable, Verifiable, and Navigable System Models

Ciprian Teodorov[1,4]([✉]), Lucas Lima[2], Sidney C. Nogueira[2], Sylvain Guerin[3,4], and Loïc Lagadec[1,4]

[1] ENSTA — Institut Polytechnique de Paris, Palaiseau, France
`{ciprian.teodorov,loic.lagadec}@ensta.fr`
[2] Universidade Federal Rural de Pernambuco, Pernambuco, Brazil
`{lucas.albertins,sidney.nogueira}@ufrpe.br`
[3] IMT Atlantique, Nantes, France
`sylvain.guerin@imt-atlantique.fr`
[4] Lab-STICC CNRS UMR 6285, Brest, France
`https://www.ensta.fr` , `https://www.ufrpe.br` , `https://www.imt-atlantique.fr`,
`https://labsticc.fr`

Abstract. Model-Based Systems Engineering (MBSE) has made substantial progress in managing system complexity, yet it still lacks principled support for understanding system behavior during early design. SysML v2 introduces a richer semantics for modeling behavior, but its utility remains limited by a lack of executable semantics, weak interoperability, and the absence of native support for formal verification and design-space exploration. We argue that a paradigm shift is needed, one in which behavioral models become first-class, executable artifacts, navigable within a dynamic design multiverse.

This position paper presents the vision for the Living SysML v2 Blueprint, a next-generation SysML v2 virtual machine that unifies dynamic execution, multiverse exploration, and native formal verification. Central to this vision is the Transparent Execution, Observation, and Control (TEOC) API, enabling accurate semantic inspection and tool interoperability without model transformation. By tolerating incomplete models and exposing structured execution traces, the LivingBlueprint VM empowers system engineers, verification experts, and business strategists to engage with design decisions iteratively, rigorously, and early.

This architecture redefines the semanticsverificationexecution triad at the heart of MBSE, offering new foundations for explainability, trust, and AI-augmented design. This paper outlines the theoretical pillars, practical challenges, and community-wide opportunities of this approach and invites collaborative efforts toward a new class of MBSE platforms centered around behavioral fidelity and multiverse awareness.

Keywords: SysML v2 · Execution Semantics · Formal Verification

M. H. ter Beek and L. Teixeira (Eds.): SBMF 2025, LNCS 16363, pp. 61–81, 2026.
https://doi.org/10.1007/978-3-032-12086-1_4

1   Introduction

System Engineering (SE) has gone through a paradigm shift where traditional document-centric processes are being replaced by model-based initiatives. In this context, Model-based System Engineering (MBSE) has emerged as the *future of SE* given the supposed benefits it provides [27]. MBSE advocates that the "system model" is the unique source of truth, and it reflects the status and state of the system development [39]. It addresses design complexity by using abstract models for formal analysis, overcoming the limitations of document-based methods. It supports earlier Verification and Validation (V&V) of system design through the early and continuous availability of models [11].

The choice of the modeling language to support system engineering processes is crucial because it must sustain not only a common understanding of the system but also allow automated reasoning to optimize engineering tasks. The System Modeling Language (SysML v1) [51] stands out among these languages because it has achieved widespread adoption for large-scale systems in several domains, including automotive, avionics, and medicine [8]. A significant factor for its success was the good quality of tooling support from different vendors, which allowed, in addition to system design, the analysis, simulation, and code generation of those models. In fact, SysML is not only one but a collection of graphical languages that enable the design of different aspects of the system, including structures and behaviors. Despite its recognition by the system engineering community, it has several limitations that prevent it from increasing its reach. Poor semantic consistency, lack of interoperability mechanisms, and complex extension procedures are among its issues. To tackle these challenges, SysML v2 [41] has been proposed in two beta releases (2023 and 2024), promising increased precision, expressiveness, and interoperability, particularly through a new API and its textual language.

SysML v2 is still an evolving language. Its formal semantics is being constantly updated. Since its release, a pilot implementation of the language was made available in both Eclipse and Jupyter notebook environments with basic features [5]. To the best of our knowledge, tooling support for executing and analyzing the behavior of models is not provided by the pilot implementation or any other tool so far. However, we know that this was a relevant aspect that leveraged the adoption of its predecessor. Without an environment where models can be properly executed, simulated, debugged, and analyzed, the SysML v2 language is doomed to fail the community's expectations. Hence, we plan to overcome these challenges by building the Living SysML v2 Blueprint to enact and verify SysML v2 models using state-of-the-art technologies and the work of experts on SysML semantics and tooling development. The Living Blueprint proposes a virtual machine (VM) that would encode the semantics for SysML v2 model elements, especially the ones related to behavior. Interactions with this VM will allow executing and navigating models using refined mechanisms, like multiverse exploration. Furthermore, we envision a verification module to enable the formal verification of properties directly against the model. Finally, we conceive that external communication with this environment can be achieved by a Transparent

Execution, Observation and Control (TEOC) API, facilitating interoperability with users and external tools. Therefore, this paper describes how we expect to concretize the Living SysML v2 Blueprint, describing its main features, principles, and challenges ahead. With this initiative, we envision that the future of MBSE must be execution- and verification-centric, with first-class support for multiverse exploration.

The remainder of this paper is structured as follows. Section 2 describes the current scenario for SysML v1 and v2, and their limitations. Section 3 details our proposal for the Living SysML v2 Blueprint, while Sect. 4 discusses its key principles. Section 5 presents the challenges we foresee in the path ahead, and Sect. 6 discusses the expected impact and opportunities. Finally, Sect. 7 shows research topics for potential collaborators, and Sect. 8 summarizes our vision and concludes.

2   Current State of the Art and Limitations

The adoption and evolution of Systems Modeling Language (SysML) have been shaped by a long-standing community effort to bridge high-level design with rigorous analysis. SysML v1 [51] achieved widespread use in domains like automotive and avionics, largely due to growing interest in MBSE and robust tooling support from various vendors. However, its success was hampered by fundamental limitations: poor semantic consistency, complex extension procedures, and a lack of standardized interoperability. This forced tool vendors to embed their own interpretations to provide analysis and simulation, effectively locking users into proprietary, semantically divergent, ecosystems.

The quest to overcome these limitations has a rich history. Early integrated environments, such as TOPCASED [19, 24], demonstrated the feasibility of federating UML/SysML editors with simulation [13] and formal analysis tools like Tina [6], OBP [16] or CADP [24]. However, this was achieved through intermediate languages and model transformations, which introduced semantic drift and significant maintenance overhead. In parallel, the rCOS Modeler [30] pioneered multi-view modeling with formal contracts and CSP-based consistency checks, advancing refinement reasoning but remaining software-centric and dependent on external provers like FDR.

This lineage of live, executable environments ranges from foundational systems like Smalltalk [25] to domain-specific instances like the *Play-In/Play-Out* approach for scenario specification [26]. Its subsequent evolution, with *Smart Play-Out*, further integrated formal verification and state-space exploration directly into the live environment. LivingBlueprint aims to bring the full power of this paradigm (characterized by transparency, introspection, and direct manipulation) to MBSE, scaling it to the heterogeneous context of SysML v2, making multiverse exploration and native verification first-class capabilities across all its behavioral formalisms.

This lineage reveals a persistent pattern: the reliance on model transformations as the primary means to enable execution and verification. While this strategy made advanced analysis possible, it came at a cost. Each transformation step embeds implicit semantic assumptions that require fragile, labor-intensive, and often unverified equivalence proofs [1,29,50]. This complicates traceability, as counterexamples must be reverse-mapped across encodings, and often degrades property fidelity via semantic mismatches [1]. Furthermore, it creates a high barrier to adoption, as engineers must cope not only with complex domains and SysML itself but also with the intricacies of downstream formal methods tools.

SysML v2 [41] was proposed to overcome these challenges, moving away from a UML profile to a new foundation based on the Kernel Modeling Language (KerML) and its declarative semantics [2]. It introduces a textual notation for improved interoperability and a Systems Modeling API for tool integration. However, while its declarative semantics allows reasoning about model correctness, a standardized operational semantics, defining how the interpretations are executed is not yet available. Consequently, tooling support remains in its infancy. The current SysML v2 toolchain, including the Pilot Implementation[1] and initiatives like SysIDE [53], focuses primarily on model authoring, syntactic checks, and visualization. To the best of our knowledge, no environment supports the direct execution, simulation, or debugging of behavioral models. Recent research, such as the work by Molnár et al. [40], represents a crucial step toward the formal verification of SysML v2 models, but it still relies on a transformation-based pipeline, inheriting the associated challenges of semantic gaps and proof obligations.

This gap is also recognized industrially. While companies like Dassault Systèmes (with CATIA Magic) and initiatives like SysON[2] (Obeo, Eclipse Foundation) and EasyMOD project[3] (IRT Saintexupery) are making strides in methodology, authoring, and usability, they primarily focus on the front-end of the modeling process. Consequently, they lack a native, verification-friendly execution core for SysML v2, ultimately falling back on the transformation-based paradigms that risks to perpetuate the very bottlenecks identified.

The lessons from this lineage are clear. Transformation-based approaches were a necessary stepping stone, but their inherent britleness and complexity limit scalability and rigor. This has catalyzed *transformation-free verification*, a distinct research direction that directly reinforces our proposition [7,29], where verification engines interact directly with model execution semantics rather than relying on intermediate translations. Recent advances in live modeling and integrated verification [18] exemplify this evolution, demonstrating the feasibility of unifying execution and model checking within a single semantics-aware runtime. Prior works on UML [7], AnimUML [28] and industrial BPMN tools [10] has consistently confirmed the value of avoiding translation chains and supporting the execution of partial models. Emerging tools like SysMD [14] further validate

---

[1] https://github.com/Systems-Modeling/SysML-v2-Pilot-Implementation.

[2] https://mbse-syson.org/.

[3] https://www.irt-saintexupery.com/project-easymod/.

this shift by demonstrating the benefits of intuitive, iterative environments that lower the barrier to entry.

Therefore, a critical gap remains unaddressed in the current SysML v2 landscape, specifically: the absence of an environment where its behavioral models can be directly executed, navigated, and formally verified without intermediary transformations. The Living SysML v2 Blueprint vision is conceived to fill this gap. It integrates the lessons of the past by unifying execution, verification, and multiverse exploration within a single semantics-first virtual machine. Rather than maintaining separate proof obligations for every analysis pipeline, we envision a single verified execution substrate that centralizes correctness and enable early, live verification.

3   The Living SysML V2 Blueprint Vision

We envision a paradigm shift in model-based systems engineering: one where behavioral models are no longer passive artifacts, but active, executable structures that support rigorous analysis, early decision-making, and seamless collaboration. At the core of this vision is LivingBlueprint, a next-generation virtual machine for SysML v2 that unifies dynamic execution, multiverse exploration, and native formal verification, without requiring model transformations or syntactic compromises.

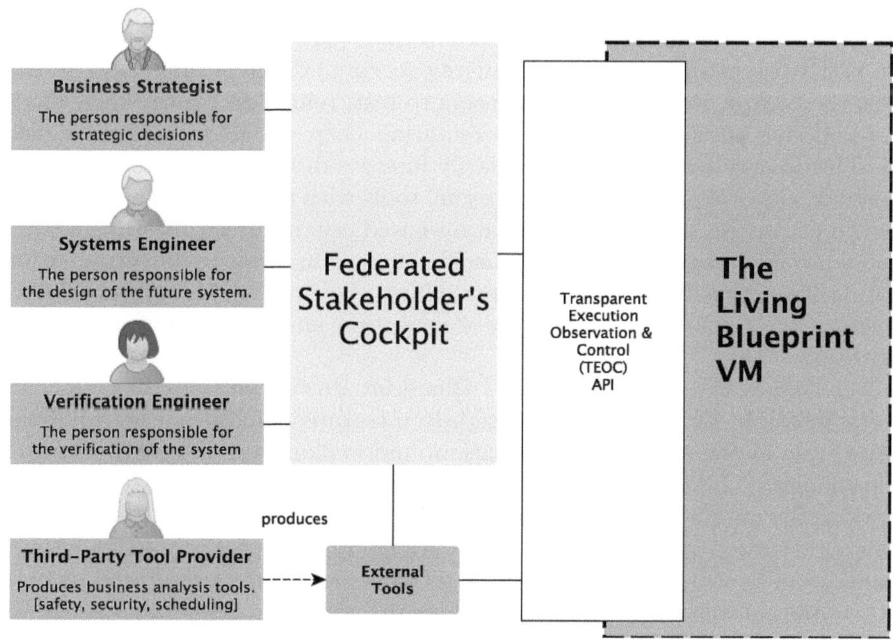

Fig. 1. High-Level Architecture of the Living SysML v2 Blueprint VM.

The high-level architecture of the Living SysML v2 Blueprint VM is shown in Fig. 1. The Living SysML v2 Blueprint VM is designed to serve the needs of four key stakeholder classes (left in Fig. 1), each interacting with the system at different levels of abstraction and with distinct objectives. Business strategists engage with the system at a higher level, using behavioral exploration tools to navigate, query, and analyze the space of possible executions, for scenario-based decision-making and "what-if" analyses that assess design trade-offs. System engineers require an intuitive execution framework that allows them to understand and refine behavioral models as they are being constructed, ensuring that early design decisions align with intended system behaviors. Verification engineers, on the other hand, demand rigorous formal validation capabilities to certify that behavioral specifications conform to logical correctness criteria, captured with temporal logic. Finally, third-party tool providers seek a robust and interoperable execution platform that allows them to integrate advanced analysis tools without relying on syntax-level model transformations or having to reimplement SysML v2's dynamic semantics, thereby lowering the cost and complexity of external tool development.

The Living SysML v2 Blueprint Prototype is designed to offer a structured interaction model tailored to each stakeholder class, ensuring seamless integration with their workflows. System engineers, verification engineers, and business strategists interact with the VM through the Federated Stakeholder's Cockpit (green box in the center of Fig. 1), a user interface built using model federation technology, leveraging the OpenFlexo [4]. This cockpit is designed to act as a bridge between their respective needs (i.e. design validation, behavioral exploration, and formal verification) and the TEOC API of the VM (white box in Fig. 1). By federating models and unifying access to different analytical perspectives, the cockpit would enable engineers to test, refine, and verify their models in a cohesive environment without requiring deep expertise in formal methods. Third-party tool providers primarily interact directly with the TEOC API, bypassing the cockpit to integrate external tools with minimal dependency. However, they can also leverage the federation-based user interface, ensuring a unified experience for integrating domain-specific extensions. This architecture ensures modularity, extensibility, and interoperability, allowing the LivingBlueprint VM to serve as a flexible and future-proof execution and verification platform for SysML v2.

The core of the Living SysML v2 Blueprint Prototype (blue box, right side in Fig. 1) would be built around 3 tightly integrated modules, each fulfilling a critical role in the execution, verification, and exploration of SysML v2 behavioral models. (1) At its foundation lies the Dynamic Semantics Module, which serves as the unique and authoritative source of interpretation for the SysML v2 behavioral subset. It ensures that all executions conform precisely to the intended semantics of SysML v2, avoiding ambiguities or deviations introduced by external transformations. This module provides the execution backbone for the VM, ensuring a faithful and consistent runtime environment. As SysML v2 behavior description is structured on actions and states, we will use our team's expertise on defining semantics for activities [38], state machines [20], and their integration [21] when specifying this module. (2) The Verification Module is intended to embed a customized version of the retargetable OBP2 verification engine [49], enabling formal property validation directly within the VM. By operating at the same semantic level as the execution engine, this module ensures high-fidelity verification results that align tightly with the model's intended behavior. (3) Complementing these, the Multiverse Explorer Module is a high-performance behavior navigation engine built on the pioneering temporal multiverse debugging [42]. This module allows system engineers and business strategists to efficiently navigate, analyze, and query possible execution paths within the behavioral design space. By enabling rapid "what-if" scenario evaluations and behavioral insights, traditional software debugging becomes a structured exploration of specification's behaviors. Together, these three modules form a cohesive, high-fidelity execution environment, making LivingBlueprint a groundbreaking platform for design-space exploration, verification, and behavioral understanding of SysML v2 models.

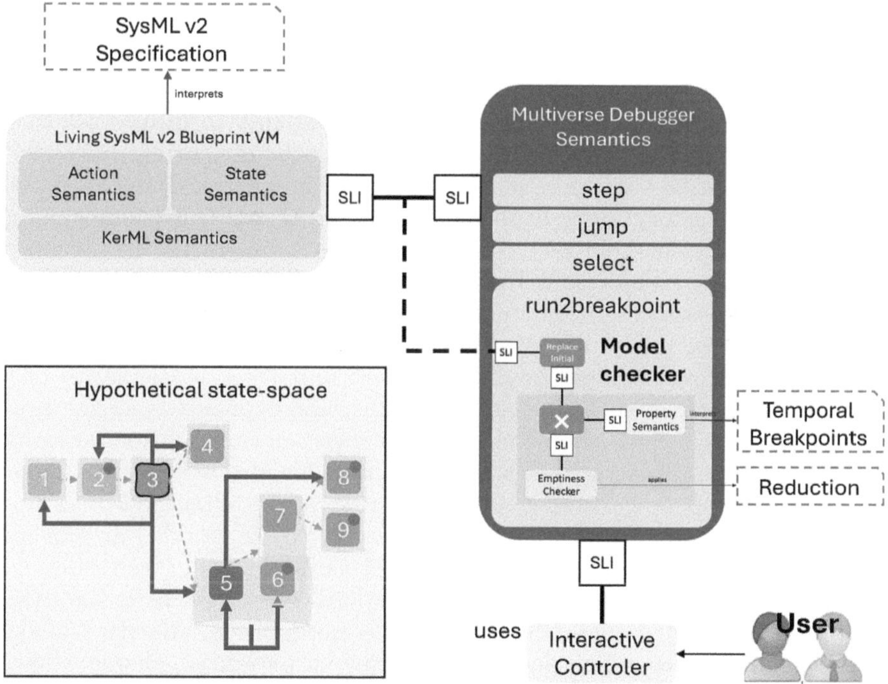

Fig. 2. Internal Architecture of the core of the Living SysML v2 Blueprint Virtual Machine (VM). The VM exposes a Semantic Language Interface through which the pioneering temporal multiverse debugger semantics [42] can be connected to efficiently navigate the possible execution paths. The Hypothetical state space illustrates the navigation capabilities (blue arrows) enabled on a non-deterministic behavior.

The internal architecture of the core of the VM is shown in Fig. 2. The Dynamic Semantics Module composes the actions and state semantics based on the underlying KerML execution model. This module captures the SysML v2 dynamic semantics and exposes a Semantic Language Interface [42] (an essential part of the TEOC API) that offers a semantic bridge to build the analysis tools. The Verification Module and the Multiverse Explorer Module can both be realized by leveraging a state-of-the-art retargetable multiverse debugger [42], which offers a practical and scalable continuum between interactive debugging (interactive exploration of the behavioral state-space) and temporal logic model-checking. This Multiverse Debugger Semantics embeds the OBP2 verification engine [49] natively as well as a highly customizable model-reduction framework able to capture numerous under-approximation strategies. Consider, for instance, the Hypothetical state-space, illustrated in Fig. 2, and suppose that the current state reached during the navigation is state 3 (the orange-filled box). The debug actions exposed to the user are: *(I)* the possibility to interactively **step** through the state space. In this case, the user is presented with a non-deterministic choice between two targets (the state 4, and the cluster $\langle 5, 6 \rangle$), to which he can **step.** Say he steps to the cluster $\langle 5, 6 \rangle$, this cluster (instead of a single target state) represents the potential execution result of a non-deterministic action in the SysML v2 semantics[4], which leads either to state 5 or to state 6; *(II)* the possibility to interactively **select** one of the states in a target cluster, state 5 or 6, when in the cluster $\langle 5, 6 \rangle$; *(III)* the possibility to **jump** back to any previously discovered state, either on the current path (the current universe) or another (an alternative universe that was previously unfolded). The availability of the branching history is one of the particularities of multiverse debugging (as opposed to omniscient debugging, which relies on a linear history structure). *(IV)* the possibility to **run to a breakpoint** (run2breakpoint in Fig. 2), which performs a model-checking reachability query (potentially reduced, using a user-specified **reduction**) driven by the breakpoint semantics (itself captured as an independent semantic component). The second important particularity of the multiverse debugger, used here, stems from the high expressivity of the breakpoints, which range from simple state-based invariants to rich temporal logic formulas. Through this setup, the typical temporal logic model-checking reduces to a run-to-breakpoint action executed in the initial states of the SysML v2 model with the added benefit of having counter-example traces encoded as sequences of native values in the underlying SysML v2 semantic domain (there is no need to transform the counter-examples back to SysML v2 values, as is the case in transformation-based model-checking). Furthermore, the Multiverse Debugger Semantics functions as a high-performance behavior navigation engine, allowing

---

[4] One can argue that the dynamic semantics of SysML v2 should maybe be deterministic, which is definitely possible, however, SysML v2 is a specification language, and as such it should offer abstraction power, allowing non-deterministic execution provides that. Furthermore, the SysML v2 library-based approach to domain-specific language (DSL) embedding definitely opens the door to semantics with non-deterministic execution (consider, for instance, a DSL allowing non-deterministic assignment).

the interactive navigation of the state-space to further the understanding of the behaviors allowed by a SysML v2 specification. This architectural design underscores an innovative proposition of native integration of formal verification and design-space exploration directly within the VM, without introducing semantic brittleness and inconsistencies.

This section demonstrates how the Living SysML v2 BluePrint can potentially fill the gap by providing an environment that enables behavioral models to be directly executed, navigated, and formally verified without intermediary transformations. The SysML v2 virtual machine unifies dynamic execution, multiverse exploration, and native formal verification. The Dynamic Semantics Module would provide a well-defined interpretation of the SysML v2 behavioral subset, serving as a consistent execution environment for SysML v2 models. The Multiverse Explorer Module would offer an engine for exploring, analyzing, and querying possible execution paths within the behavioral design space. The Cockpit would serve as a bridge between behavioral exploration, formal verification, and the TEOC API of the virtual machine, while the TEOC API itself would enable precise semantic inspection and tool interoperability without requiring model transformation.

We strongly believe that building a SysML v2 virtual machine following these design ideas could be a cornerstone in system engineering. The approach we present here is more than a technical solution, it is a statement of intent: that models should live, evolve, and be trusted; that semantics should be explicit and navigable; and that system design should be deeply connected to system understanding. This vision redefines how we think about MBSE tools, not as containers of syntax, but as thinking environments, where design exploration, validation, and traceability emerge naturally from execution.

4   Key Principles

Here we lay down the principles that should guide the development of the Living SysML v2 Blueprint environment.

A Unified Execution and Verification Infrastructure. The central idea behind LivingBlueprint is to provide a semantics-first virtual machine capable of executing the behavioral subset of SysML v2 models directly and faithfully. Rather than treating execution and verification as post-processing steps, they are embedded within the runtime environment itself. This enables temporal logic properties to be checked in situ, supporting the analysis of non-deterministic behaviors, and facilitates early incremental feedback, even in the presence of incomplete or non-conformant models.

Multiverse Exploration as a Modeling Primitive. System engineers often face uncertainty not just in implementation, but in design intent, requirements evolution, and operational assumptions. LivingBlueprint proposes to introduce multiverse exploration as a first-class modeling capability, enabling engineers and business strategists to explore possible execution paths, evaluate alternative scenarios, and understand design implications in a structured and interactive way. Inspired by advances in multiverse debugging and temporal logic model checking [42], this capability transforms debugging from a reactive task into a proactive design-space navigation tool.

The Transparent Execution, Observation, and Control API. A key principle is that LivingBlueprint would expose a Transparent Execution, Observation, and Control (TEOC) API, intended to allow external tools to interact with model execution at the semantic level. This API eliminates the need for brittle model transformations or proprietary hooks, offering a principled interface for integrating AI assistants, runtime monitoring tools, domain-specific verifiers, and federated model environments. It serves as a semantic bridge, not just between tools, but between communities: systems engineers, formal methods researchers, and tool developers.

Executable Semantics for a Continuum of Design. Unlike conventional MBSE platforms that require full specification before execution, LivingBlueprint supports partial and evolving models. This capability empowers engineers to simulate early behaviors, refine them over time, and use the same infrastructure from exploratory modeling to deployment validation. The platform thereby becomes a foundation for semantic-level digital twins, where high-level design models serve as seeds for runtime models linked through refinement mappings to physical implementations. This enables true model continuity, spanning design, analysis, deployment, and adaptation.

5   Scientific and Engineering Challenges

To advance the utility and rigor of SysML v2, several scientific challenges must be addressed. We classify these challenges in three categories: (1) semantic challenges, particularly the formalization and operationalization of the operational semantics; (2) verification challenges, particularly scalability, reuse-based abstract interpretation, heterogeneous refinement, and SysML-level proof engineering; and (3) interoperability.

5.1   Semantic-Level Challenges

High-Performance verification-Ready VM. Building a verification environment that provides results within an acceptable timeframe is crucial to facilitate adoption. This is not an easy task due to the complexity of current systems. The **key scientific challenge** lies in *establishing a formally grounded approach for high-performance operational semantics design.* A guiding promising direction is the Omnisemantics approach [12], which generalizes structural operational semantics to facilitate reasoning about non-determinism. One bridge between this theoretical semantics framework and practical virtual machine design is established through the Semantic Language Interface (SLI) [50], which operationalizes Omnisemantics to integrate execution and formal behavioral analysis. Another venue for addressing this challenge is investing in meta-frameworks like K-framework [46], and Gemoc [55] to reduce their execution overhead and formal verification capabilities. To address the execution overhead, a SysML v2 virtual machine will need to integrate just-in-time code generation [17] and VM implementation techniques that allow for peak performance [34]. Today, it is not necessarily clear how these techniques compose with the needs of formal verification tools. Moreover, the SysML v2 behavioral analysis tools will have to provide the capabilities and performances offered by industry-ready [7,10,23], retargetable verification toolkits like LTSmin [29] or OBP [49]. By leveraging the G$\forall$min$\exists$ SLI [50], as presented in this position paper, we could, as a community, design a state-of-the-art VM for SysML v2 that combines meta-compilation techniques [34] with retargetable verification toolkits [49], all while adhering to a formally grounded approach for operational semantics design [12].

Why Not Transformations. In transformation-centric flows, each step embeds implicit semantic assumptions that must be proved semantics-preserving, proofs that are fragile under language/tool evolution and costly to maintain. They also complicate traceability (counterexamples require reverse mapping across encodings) and often degrade property fidelity via semantic mismatches [1]. By contrast, a single, verified execution substrate avoids duplicated proof obligations and keeps counterexamples and observables natively in the SysML v2 semantic domain.

As discussed in Sect. 2, our design proposes centralizing correctness into a single verified language VM. Any operational semantics introduced for SysML v2 must ultimately be shown correct with respect to the language's formal semantics. However, our proposal aims to minimize the number of such correctness proofs that the ecosystem must maintain. In the current landscape, each model transformation or analysis tool implicitly embeds its own semantic assumptions, requiring separate validation. In contrast, by concentrating the executable meaning of SysML v2 into a single, verified virtual machine (VM), we shift from "many small, unverified transformations" to a single semantics-bearing execution substrate. Once this VM is proved sound and adequate with respect to the formal semantics, all analyses and integrations performed through it inherit that correctness by construction. Thus, the verification effort is centralized and reusable rather than duplicated across tools.

In practice, early versions of the VM may still rely on code generation or interfacing to external simulators for performance reasons. In such cases, the usual translation proof obligations remain; however, in some cases, the effort can be reduced through Pnueli's translation validation technique [44]. Yet the long-term objective is to minimize transformation chains: whenever the VM can execute the model directly, it should, avoiding unnecessary re-encoding of the semantics. For non-software systems, where parts of the specification must still be deployed into the physical world, transformation will remain unavoidable, but it should be treated as a boundary operation, justified and verified only where strictly necessary. Ultimately, proving the VM correct should be a one-time investment that can be maintained alongside its evolution, and potentially, in the future, the VM itself could be extracted from mechanized proofs, following approaches explored in verified compilers [36] and verified interpreters [9,22].

Modular and Heterogeneous Semantic Composition. **Another key challenge** is *enabling modular and heterogeneous semantics design and composition at scale.* SysML v2, as its predecessor, is not one, but a set of several languages employed for different aspects of system engineering. When modeling behavior, it is possible to use both action-based and state-based behavior, and also combine them. Thus, building a semantics for SysML v2 that considers the composition of these two languages for describing behavior is paramount to give enough expressivity for system engineers. Furthermore, the library-based domain-specific language (DSL) embedding proposed in SysML v2 will give birth to a plethora of DSLs, which should compose with SysML v2 and benefit from the underlying SysML v2 execution infrastructure.

5.2   Formal Verification Challenges

Verification Scalability. Scalability is one of the factors that can impact performance, presenting both technical, engineering, and scientific challenges. The previously mentioned complexity of systems impacts the size of the state space to be traversed to check a property. Model checking and dynamic analysis methods often struggle with state-space explosion, making it infeasible to explore these complex systems. Therefore, researching the best methods and techniques to reduce scalability issues must be on the minds of our teams. We believe that not relying on transformations, like most formal methods-based strategies for MBSE verification, is an advantage of the environment presented in this paper. However, this approach should be coupled with model reduction strategies [43], which use under-approximation strategies to improve the scalability. The Living SysML v2 blueprint presented in the previous section integrates the support for a wide range of under-approximations: (1) generic reduction, such as bistate hashing and hash compaction; (2) model-specific reduction, such as predicate abstraction; and (3) language-specific reductions that will be guided by the SysML v2 operational semantics. Nevertheless, *verification scalability* is **another key challenge** that should be addressed systemically in the context of SysML v2, and here we believe that abstract interpretation approaches hold the key.

Among the promising directions, we emphasize the foundational work on abstracting abstract machines [54], which demonstrates a systematic method for deriving static analyses from abstract machines through refactoring and store-allocated continuations. This approach shows how to transform machine semantics into an easily abstractable form to approximate machine behavior. This approach is particularly interesting in the context of SysML v2 due to the language's sheer size, which poses an enormous burden on the implementation of each abstract interpreter. By deriving abstract interpreters directly from the SysML v2 operational semantics, parts of the semantics can be reused to reduce implementation effort. A derived approach dubbed abstracting definitional interpreters [15] highlights the reusability and extensibility of high-level abstract interpreters, particularly when structured with monad transformers, enabling the derivation of various program analyses by composing components. A key insight is the inheritance of properties like "pushdown control flow" from the metalanguage, simplifying complex analyses.

Recently, this approach was applied to WebAssembly to obtain modular definitional interpreters [9], which further demonstrates the ability to decompose the semantics of a complex language into language-independent components that can be instantiated later to obtain a highly configurable interpreter that efficiently offers whole program analysis support with minimal additional code. If we push these ideas further, in the context of SysML v2, we could get to the point where its operational semantics can be seen as a product line, with each variant being a VM geared to a particular usage context. Viewing the language semantics as a product line naturally brings the focus on establishing formal abstraction-refinement relations between the semantic variants.

Heterogeneous Refinement. Having an execution environment for analyzing abstract system specifications leads naturally to another **systemic challenge** *the use of heterogeneous refinement techniques to prove that a system correctly implements the specification.* In this case, the refinement is heterogeneous because the implementation execution infrastructure will not be the SysML v2 virtual machine itself, but an external execution environment that should be bound to the specification by refinement mappings prior to a joint analysis needed to prove the refinement. Working in this direction, implicitly, will offer support for using SysML v2 models as execution monitors and digital twins, even in cases where formal refinements are too difficult to prove or are not a goal of the system designer.

SysML v2 Proof Assistants. Sometimes, automated analysis techniques are not enough to cope with the verification, validation, and certification of complex systems. In these cases interactive proof assistants have been shown to help [35], by allowing the proof engineer to drive the proof efforts. The key challenge that we want to emphasize in this context is understanding the scope of the SysML v2 language and its limitations for proof engineering. In other words, is the SysML v2 library system powerful enough to facilitate the development of domain-specific proof assistants geared towards the system's engineers' needs? Another related challenge is understanding how the SysML v2 operational semantics, captured in a high-performance VM, can be exploited to serve as a bridge for external provers.

5.3   Interoperability

The last two paragraphs in the previous subsection, underlie another **key open challenge**: *how can the SysML v2 VM offer support for effective interoperability with the external world while preserving formal guarantees?* The research efforts around reasoning about the foreign function interfaces of programming languages offer an interesting perspective on this question [52]. In software engineering the interoperability is typically handled through one of 3 approaches [33]: integration, where all components follow a standard structure - imposed by a standard, or an implementation language for instance; unification, where a common meta-level description structures the inter-operating components and their interactions; or federation, where the components are dynamically accommodated through a binding (adapter) model. Given the interoperability problems in systems engineering and the large variability of system analysis tools, we argue that a federation-based interoperability approach is necessary for SysML v2 to achieve a semantic-level interoperability that pushes past the limitations of syntactic-based interoperability (heavily relying on model transformation) and can offer strong correctness guarantees. While many model federation approaches have been proposed [3] (including Vitruvius [31], Epsilon [32], Reactive Links [45], comprehensive systems [47], and OpenFlexo [4]) none has yet considered in depth the rich relations that govern the interoperability of operational semantics (captured through a VM) and the numerous analysis tools in the system engineering toolkit.

We strongly believe that the unified execution and verification infrastructure proposed in this position paper can serve as a real-life experimental framework to help overcome some of these challenges and fuel both the scientific and engineering communities towards a new generation of system engineering tools.

6   Expected Impact and Opportunities

The LivingBlueprint vision holds the potential to reshape the foundations of Model-Based Systems Engineering by embedding execution, verification, and multiverse exploration at the heart of the modeling experience. Its anticipated impacts span scientific, industrial, and methodological domains.

6.1   Scientific Impact

LivingBlueprint redefines the semanticsexecutionverification triad in MBSE by unifying them within a single executable environment. This enables rigorous reasoning on behavioral models without translation or semantic loss. By supporting the execution of incomplete or non-conformant models, it also opens new lines of inquiry into live modeling, behavioral analysis under uncertainty, and early design validation. Moreover, the integration of multiverse exploration introduces a structured way to reason about alternative system trajectories, pushing the boundary of what model execution can offer to engineering science.

An open, interoperable, high-performance virtual machine for SysML v2 presents a transformative opportunity for the scientific community. By enabling early execution, formal analysis, and multiverse exploration of behavioral models, LivingBlueprint provides a unique experimental platform where new ideas in semantics, verification, abstraction refinement, and dynamic system analysis can be tested under realistic conditions. Unlike traditional academic prototypes, this infrastructure is designed for sustained interoperability and extensibility, allowing researchers to embed, evaluate, and scale their contributions within a meaningful systems engineering context. Beyond offering a rigorous foundation for theoretical exploration, LivingBlueprint serves as a direct conduit for scientific impact, enabling researchers to engage with pressing industrial challenges in safety, traceability, automation, and decision support. This dual role (as a research testbed and translational vehicle) positions LivingBlueprint to foster deeper collaborations between formal methods, software engineering, and MBSE communities, accelerating the evolution of system modeling from an abstract design discipline to a continuous, verifiable, and executable science.

6.2 Engineering and Industrial Opportunities

If realized, LivingBlueprint would introduce a transparent and verifiable execution backbone for SysML v2, potentially helping engineers catch specification errors early, explore alternatives systematically, and make decisions with semantic confidence. This improves the quality and agility of system design processes, with direct implications for high-stakes sectors such as aerospace, automotive, defense, and energy. The platform's API-first architecture also lowers the barrier for third-party tool integration, encouraging a modular and interoperable ecosystem rather than monolithic toolchains.

Building on this transparent, semantics-first infrastructure, LivingBlueprint also opens the door to integrating foundation models [48], such as large language or multimodal models, as engineering assistants. Because all observable behaviors and properties are exposed through the TEOC API with explicit semantics, these models can safely operate on verified execution data to support engineers in natural-language querying, automated report generation, or design-space summarization. Rather than replacing formal reasoning, foundation models would amplify it: (1) translating complex traces into explanations, (2) proposing alternative configurations, and (3) assisting in requirements and specification refinement [37]. This combination of formal semantics and adaptive language models could significantly accelerate model comprehension and decision-making in industrial contexts.

6.3 Educational and Methodological Impact

By treating behavioral semantics as an active interface, LivingBlueprint helps demystify formal methods, lowering the learning curve for engineers and students alike. Its stakeholder-oriented cockpit and introspection tools support explainable modeling, making system behavior visible, navigable, and traceable across abstraction levels. This sets the stage for human-in-the-loop verification, collaborative design exploration, and AI-augmented modeling assistants grounded in observable model behavior.

6.4   Long-Term Opportunities

Looking ahead, LivingBlueprint lays the groundwork for a new class of MBSE platforms: *(a)* Semantics-aware development environments, where specifications are immediately executable and verifiable. *(b)* Standardized execution benchmarks, enabling meaningful comparison between SysML v2 tools and fostering open, community-driven validation processes. *(c)* Multiverse-native system design workflows, where exploration and verification are not add-ons, but first-class modeling activities. *(d)* Validation through refinement mappings, establishing traceable links between high-level behavioral models and their corresponding physical implementations, bridging the gap between specification and deployment. *(e)* Semantic-level Digital Twins and model continuity, where executable SysML v2 models become seeds for deploying digital twins. By maintaining refinement-based links across abstraction layers, LivingBlueprint enables continuity between design-time intent and runtime observability, opening new opportunities for system evolution, diagnosis, and predictive maintenance. *(f)* Explainable AI integrations, using structured behavior traces to train models for design synthesis, validation, or anomaly detection.

In essence, LivingBlueprint not only addresses immediate pain points in MBSE practice, it proposes a durable infrastructure for principled, participatory, and verifiable system design in an increasingly complex and interdependent world.

7   Call to Action

The LivingBlueprint vision is more than a proposal for a new tool; it is an invitation to reimagine the foundations of model-based systems engineering. As system complexity grows and trust in digital models becomes critical, we must equip engineers, researchers, and tool developers with infrastructures that are not only rigorous but also exploratory, explainable, and evolvable.

We call on the research community to recognize and contribute to LivingBlueprint as a semantic playground: a high-performance, interoperable execution platform where new ideas in modeling, verification, refinement, and dynamic analysis can be developed, tested, and validated on industrially relevant models. The open and modular architecture encourages contributions from formal methods, programming languages, AI, and MBSE researchers, turning the virtual machine into a shared foundation for cross-disciplinary innovation.

We also invite practitioners and system architects to explore a new kind of modeling workflow: execution-first, verification-aware, and decision-driven. By adopting semantic APIs and transparent behavioral introspection, LivingBlueprint lowers the barriers to early feedback, integration, and collaboration across stakeholder boundaries.

To sustain and expand this vision, we encourage the community to: *(1)* Contribute to the SysML v2 behavioral benchmark, enabling consistent evaluation of execution and verification platforms. *(2)* Experiment with semantic-level model composition approaches, where the models of computation are interconnected natively instead of relying on long and brittle transformation chains. *(3)* Develop and share refinement-based validation strategies, bridging high-level design intent and deployed systems. *(4)* Co-design digital twin workflows grounded in semantic continuity, enabling verification-aware runtime observability. *(5)* Support the evolution of semantically grounded MBSE standards and tooling, advocating for model continuity, traceability, and trustworthy automation.

LivingBlueprint offers not only infrastructure, but direction: a path toward executable systems modeling grounded in science and aligned with engineering reality. We invite researchers, engineers, and toolmakers alike to join in building this path together.

The path toward explainable, evolvable, and trustworthy system models is open, but it must be built collaboratively. Let us not wait for tools to catch up with our ambitions. Let us define the future of MBSE by making its models live, introspective, and multiverse-aware.

8   Conclusion and Future Work

The increasing complexity and interdependence of modern systems demand a new generation of modeling infrastructures, ones that go beyond static diagrams and disconnected tools. LivingBlueprint answers this call by proposing a unified, executable, and verifiable environment for SysML v2 models. By embedding dynamic semantics, native formal verification, and multiverse exploration directly into the virtual machine, it repositions MBSE as a live, introspective, and explainable discipline.

We have argued that modeling must become a continuous act of observation and refinement, where system behavior is not inferred but experienced. The LivingBlueprint architecture, centered on the TEOC API, multiverse navigation, and partial model execution, supports this shift, enabling early feedback, semantic consistency, and stakeholder-inclusive workflows. It also provides the scientific community with a rare opportunity: a high-fidelity platform to explore new ideas in modeling, verification, refinement, and decision support, all grounded in a real engineering context.

LivingBlueprint is a call to reimagine how we think about models: not as passive documents, but as active agents in a larger epistemic and engineering process. By making models executable, traceable, and semantically transparent, we enable not only better systems but better system engineering.

Crucially, Sect. 3 provides an actionable stepping stone, the core internal architecture, that can be realized today, and which will de-risk the endeavor, deliver immediate value, and provide a solid foundation for the community to collaboratively tackle the challenges and incrementally realize the full vision.

The next step is community engagement. We invite researchers, practitioners, and toolmakers to join this effort, starting with this core VM, to help create a modeling ecosystem that is as dynamic, rigorous, and alive as the systems it seeks to build.

References

1. Ab. Rahim, L., Whittle, J.: A survey of approaches for verifying model transformations. Softw. Syst. Model. **14**(2), 1003–1028 (2013). https://doi.org/10.1007/s10270-013-0358-0
2. Almeida, J.a.P.A., Ferreira Pires, L., Guizzardi, G., Wagner, G.: An analysis of the semantic foundation of KerML and SysML v2. In: Conceptual Modeling: 43rd International Conference, ER 2024, Pittsburgh, PA, USA, October 28–31, 2024, Proceedings, pp. 133–151. Springer-Verlag, Berlin, Heidelberg (2024). https://doi.org/10.1007/978-3-031-75872-0_8
3. Amrani, M., et al.: A survey of federative approaches for model management in MBSE. In: Proceedings of the ACM/IEEE 27th International Conference on Model Driven Engineering Languages and Systems, pp. 990–999 (2024)
4. Bach, J.C., Beugnard, A., Champeau, J., Dagnat, F., Guérin, S., Martínez, S.: 10 years of model federation with openflexo: challenges and lessons learned. In: MODELS 2024: ACM/IEEE 27th International Conference on Model Driven Engineering Languages and Systems, pp. 12. ACM, Linz, Austria (Sep 2024). https://doi.org/10.1145/3640310.3674084, best Paper Award, Practice Track
5. Bajaj, M., Friedenthal, S., Seidewitz, E.: Systems modeling language (SysML v2) support for digital engineering. Insight **25**(1), 19–24 (2022)
6. Berthomieu, B., et al.: Fiacre: an Intermediate Language for Model Verification in the Topcased Environment. In: 4th European Congress ERTS Embedded Real Time Software (ERTS 2008), pp. 1–8. SEE : Société de l'électricité, de l'électronique et des technologies de l'information et de la communication and 3AF : Association Aéronautique et Astronautique de France, Toulouse, France (Jan 2008). https://inria.hal.science/inria-00262442
7. Besnard, V., Teodorov, C., Jouault, F., Brun, M., Dhaussy, P.: Unified verification and monitoring of executable UML specifications. Softw. Syst. Model. **20**(6), 1825–1855 (2021). https://doi.org/10.1007/s10270-021-00923-9
8. Bone, M.A., Cloutier, R.J.: The current state of model based systems engineering: results from the OMG^{TM} SysML request for information 2009. In: Proceedings of the 8th Conference on Systems Engineering Research (2010)
9. Brandl, K., Erdweg, S., Keidel, S., Hansen, N.: Modular abstract definitional interpreters for webassembly. In: Ali, K., Salvaneschi, G. (eds.) 37th European Conference on Object-Oriented Programming (ECOOP 2023). Leibniz International Proceedings in Informatics (LIPIcs), vol. 263, pp. 5:1–5:28. Schloss Dagstuhl – Leibniz-Zentrum für Informatik, Dagstuhl, Germany (2023). https://drops.dagstuhl.de/entities/document/10.4230/LIPIcs.ECOOP.2023.5
10. Brumbulli, M., Gaudin, E., Teodorov, C.: Automatic verification of BPMN models. In: 10th European Congress on Embedded Real Time Software and Systems (ERTS 2020). Toulouse, France (Jan 2020). https://hal.science/hal-02441878
11. Cederbladh, J., Cicchetti, A., Suryadevara, J.: Early validation and verification of system behaviour in model-based systems engineering: a systematic literature review. ACM Trans. Softw. Eng. Methodol. (2023). https://doi.org/10.1145/3631976
12. Charguéraud, A., Chlipala, A., Erbsen, A., Gruetter, S.: Omnisemantics: Smooth handling of nondeterminism. ACM Trans. Program. Lang. Syst. **45**(1) (Mar 2023). https://doi.org/10.1145/3579834
13. Combemale, B., Crégut, X., Giacometti, J.P., Michel, P., Pantel, M.: Introducing simulation and model animation in the MDE Topcased Toolkit. In: 4th European

Congress EMBEDDED REAL TIME SOFTWARE (ERTS). http://www.erts2008. org/ Toulouse, France (Jan 2008). https://hal.science/hal-00371596
14. Dalecke, S., Grimm, C.: Sysmd: an inclusive modelling tool. In: 2024 19th Annual System of Systems Engineering Conference (SoSE), pp. 178–183 (2024). https:// doi.org/10.1109/SOSE62659.2024.10620956
15. Darais, D., Labich, N., Nguyen, P.C., Van Horn, D.: Abstracting definitional interpreters (functional pearl). Proc. ACM Program. Lang. **1**(ICFP) (Aug 2017). https://doi.org/10.1145/3110256
16. Dhaussy, P., Roger, J.C., Leroux, L., Boniol, F.: Context aware model exploration with obp tool to improve model-checking. In: ERTS 2012, p. xx. Toulouse, France (Feb 2012). https://ensta.hal.science/hal-00676640
17. Ducasse, Q., Cotret, P., Lagadec, L.: Gigue: A JIT code binary generator for hardware testing. In: Proceedings of the 15th ACM SIGPLAN International Workshop on Virtual Machines and Intermediate Languages, pp. 73–82. VMIL 2023, Association for Computing Machinery, New York, NY, USA (2023). https://doi.org/10. 1145/3623507.3623553
18. Exelmans, J., Teodorov, C., Vangheluwe, H.: Integrating model checking into a live modeling environment. In: Proceedings of the 18th ACM SIGPLAN International Conference on Software Language Engineering, pp. 128–133. SLE '25, Association for Computing Machinery, New York, NY, USA (2025). https://doi.org/10.1145/ 3732771.3742718
19. Farail, P., et al.: The TOPCASED project: a Toolkit in Open source for Critical Aeronautic SystEms Design. In: ERTS 2006 proceedings. Toulouse, France (Jan 2006). https://hal.science/hal-02270461
20. Ferreira, D., Lima, L.: A CSP semantics for UML state machines aiming at hidden formal methods verification. In: Formal Methods: Foundations and Applications: 27th Brazilian Symposium, SBMF 2024, Vitória, Brazil, December 4–6, 2024, Proceedings, pp. 49–67. Springer-Verlag, Berlin, Heidelberg (2024). https://doi.org/ 10.1007/978-3-031-78116-2_4
21. Ferreira, D., Lima, L.: Verifying integrated designs of UML state machines and activities using CSP. In: C. Nogueira, S., Teodorov, C. (eds.) Formal Methods: Foundations and Applications, pp. 68–85. Springer Nature Switzerland, Cham (2025). https://doi.org/10.1007/978-3-031-78116-2_5
22. Franceschino, L., Pichardie, D., Talpin, J.P.: Verified functional programming of an abstract interpreter. In: Drăgoi, C., Mukherjee, S., Namjoshi, K. (eds.) Static Analysis, pp. 124–143. Springer International Publishing, Cham (2021)
23. Gaudin, E., Brunel, E., Brumbulli, M.: Language agnostic model checking for SDL. In: 2023 ACM/IEEE International Conference on Model Driven Engineering Languages and Systems Companion (MODELS-C), pp. 231–240 (2023). https://doi. org/10.1109/MODELS-C59198.2023.00052
24. Gaufillet, P., Farail, P.: TOPCASED results and benefits. In: ERTS 2012 Proceedings. Toulouse, France (Feb 2012). https://hal.science/hal-02192082
25. Goldberg, A., Robson, D.: Smalltalk-80: The Language and its Implementation. Addison-Wesley Longman Publishing Co., Inc, USA (1983)
26. Harel, D., Marelly, R.: Specifying and executing behavioral requirements: the play-in/play-out approach. Softw. Syst. Model. **2**(2), 82–107 (2003). https://doi.org/10. 1007/s10270-002-0015-5
27. Henderson, K., Salado, A.: Value and benefits of model based systems engineering (MBSE): evidence from the literature. Syst. Eng. **24**(1), 51–66 (2021). https://doi. org/10.1002/sys.21566

28. Jouault, F., et al.: AnimUML: A practical tool for partial model animation and analysis. Sci. Comput. Program. **232**(C) (Jan 2024). https://doi.org/10.1016/j.scico.2023.103050

29. Kant, G., Laarman, A., Meijer, J., van de Pol, J., Blom, S., van Dijk, T.: LTSmin: high-performance language-independent model checking. In: Baier, C., Tinelli, C. (eds.) TACAS 2015. LNCS, vol. 9035, pp. 692–707. Springer, Heidelberg (2015). https://doi.org/10.1007/978-3-662-46681-0_61

30. Ke, W., Li, X., Liu, Z., Stolz, V.: rCOS: a formal model-driven engineering method for component-based software. Front. Comput. Sci China **6**(1), 17–39 (2012)

31. Klare, H., Kramer, M.E., Langhammer, M., Werle, D., Burger, E., Reussner, R.: Enabling consistency in view-based system development – the vitruvius approach. J. Syst. Softw. **171**, 110815 (2021). https://doi.org/10.1016/j.jss.2020.110815

32. Kolovos, D., Paige, R., Polack, F.: Detecting and repairing inconsistencies across heterogeneous models. In: International Conference on Software Testing, Verification, and Validation, pp. 356–364 (2008). https://doi.org/10.1109/ICST.2008.23

33. Kosanke, K.: ISO standards for interoperability: a Comparison. In: Konstantas, D., Bourrières, J.P., Léonard, M., Boudjlida, N. (eds.) Interoperability of Enterprise Software and Applications, pp. 55–64. Springer, London, London (2006)

34. Larose, O., Kaleba, S., Burchell, H., Marr, S.: AST vs. Bytecode: interpreters in the age of meta-compilation. Proc. ACM Program. Lang. **7**(OOPSLA2) (Oct 2023). https://doi.org/10.1145/3622808

35. Lecomte, T., Deharbe, D., Prun, E., Mottin, E.: Applying a formal method in industry: a 25-year trajectory. In: Cavalheiro, S., Fiadeiro, J. (eds.) Formal Methods: Foundations and Applications, pp. 70–87. Springer International Publishing, Cham (2017)

36. Leroy, X.: Formal verification of a realistic compiler. Commun. ACM **52**(7), 107–115 (2009). https://doi.org/10.1145/1538788.1538814

37. Leung, M., Murphy, G.: On automated assistants for software development: the role of LLMs. In: 2023 38th IEEE/ACM International Conference on Automated Software Engineering (ASE), pp. 1737–1741 (2023). https://doi.org/10.1109/ASE56229.2023.00035

38. Lima, L., Tavares, A., Nogueira, S.C.: A framework for verifying deadlock and nondeterminism in UML activity diagrams based on CSP. Sci. Comput. Program. **197**, 102497 (2020). https://doi.org/10.1016/j.scico.2020.102497

39. Madni, A.M., Sievers, M.: Model-based systems engineering: Motivation, current status, and needed advances. In: Madni, A.M., Boehm, B., Ghanem, R.G., Erwin, D., Wheaton, M.J. (eds.) Disciplinary Convergence in Systems Engineering Research, pp. 311–325. Springer International Publishing, Cham (2018)

40. Molnár, et al.: Towards the Formal Verification of SysML v2 Models. In: Proceedings of the ACM/IEEE 27th International Conference on Model Driven Engineering Languages and Systems, pp. 1086–1095. MODELS Companion '24, Association for Computing Machinery, New York, NY, USA (2024). https://doi.org/10.1145/3652620.3687820

41. OMG: OMG Systems Modeling Language (SysML v2) - Part 1: Language Specification. https://www.omg.org/spec/SysML/2.0/Beta2/Language/PDF (2024)

42. Pasquier, M., Teodorov, C., Jouault, F., Brun, M., Le Roux, L., Lagadec, L.: Temporal breakpoints for multiverse debugging. In: Proceedings of the 16th ACM SIGPLAN International Conference on Software Language Engineering. pp. 125–137. SLE 2023, Association for Computing Machinery, New York, NY, USA (2023). https://doi.org/10.1145/3623476.3623526

43. Pasquier, M., Teodorov, C., Jouault, F., Brun, M., Roux, L.L., Lagadec, L.: Practical multiverse debugging through user-defined reductions: application to UML models. In: Proceedings of the 25th International Conference on Model Driven Engineering Languages and Systems, pp. 87–97. MODELS '22, Association for Computing Machinery, New York, NY, USA (2022). https://doi.org/10.1145/3550355.3552447

44. Pnneli, A., Shtriehman, O., Siegel, M.: Translation validation for synchronous languages. In: Larsen, K.G., Skyum, S., Winskel, G. (eds.) ICALP 1998. LNCS, vol. 1443, pp. 235–246. Springer, Heidelberg (1998). https://doi.org/10.1007/BFb0055057

45. Raţiu, C.C., Assunção, W.K., Herac, E., Haas, R., Lauwerys, C., Egyed, A.: Using reactive links to propagate changes across engineering models. Softw. Syst. Model. 1–27 (2024)

46. Rosu, G., Serbanuta, T.F.: An overview of the K semantic framework. J. Logic Algebraic Programm. 79(6), 397–434 (2010). https://doi.org/10.1016/j.jlap.2010.03.012, membrane computing and programming

47. Stünkel, P., König, H., Lamo, Y., Rutle, A.: Comprehensive systems: a formal foundation for multi-model consistency management. Formal Aspects Comput. 33(6), 1067–1114 (2021)

48. Sun, J., et al.: A survey of reasoning with foundation models: concepts, methodologies, and outlook. ACM Comput. Surv. 57(11) (Jun 2025). https://doi.org/10.1145/3729218

49. Team, O.R.: OBP2 high-performance, retargetable temporal logic verification engine. http://www.obpcdl.org/ (17 march 2025)

50. Teodorov, C.: G∀min∃: Exploring the Boundary Between Executable Specification Languages and Behavior Analysis Tools. Habilitation à diriger des recherches, Université de Bretagne Occidentale (UBO), Brest (Apr 2023). https://hal.science/tel-04066483

51. The Object Management Group: OMG Systems Modeling Language. Standard 1.7 beta, Object Management Group, Milford, MA, USA (2022). https://www.omg.org/spec/SysML/1.7/Beta1

52. Turcotte, A., Arteca, E., Richards, G.: Reasoning About Foreign Function Interfaces Without Modelling the Foreign Language. In: Donaldson, A.F. (ed.) 33rd European Conference on Object-Oriented Programming (ECOOP 2019). Leibniz International Proceedings in Informatics (LIPIcs), vol. 134, pp. 16:1–16:32. Schloss Dagstuhl – Leibniz-Zentrum für Informatik, Dagstuhl, Germany (2019). https://doi.org/10.4230/LIPIcs.ECOOP.2019.16

53. Vaicenavicius, J., Wiklund, T., Kavolis, D., Draukšas, S., Kalkauskas, A., Vaicenavičius, R.: SysIDE: SysML v2 textual editing and analysis system: overview and applications. CEAS Space J. (02 2025). https://doi.org/10.1007/s12567-025-00595-x

54. Van Horn, D., Might, M.: Abstracting abstract machines. SIGPLAN Not. 45(9), 51–62 (2010). https://doi.org/10.1145/1932681.1863553

55. Zschaler, S., Bousse, E., Deantoni, J., Combemale, B.: A generic framework for representing and analyzing model concurrency. Softw. Syst. Model. 22(4), 1319–1340 (2023). https://doi.org/10.1007/s10270-022-01073-2

Formal Verification of Epistemic States
with Uncertainty in Multi-Agent Systems

Jefferson O. Andrade$^{(\boxtimes)}$

Instituto Federal do Espírito Santo (IFES), Serra, ES, Brazil
`jefferson.andrade@ifes.edu.br`
`https://serra.ifes.edu.br/`

Abstract. Multi-agent systems operating in real-world environments must reason about knowledge and information under uncertainty, with varying degrees of trust and incomplete evidence. While Dynamic Epistemic Logic (DEL) provides a robust framework for modeling knowledge change, its classical binary foundation limits its applicability to scenarios involving gradations of truth and knowledge. The Bilattice Logic of Epistemic Actions and Knowledge (BEAK) addresses this limitation by grounding DEL in bilattice structures, but restricts its semantics to the four-valued bilattice FOUR, limiting expressiveness for complex applications. This paper introduces GEAK (Generalized Bilattice-based Epistemic Logic of Actions and Knowledge), a generalization of BEAK that operates over arbitrary logical bilattices. GEAK preserves the elegant product update mechanism of DEL while extending it to handle multi-valued accessibility relations with custom truth-value structures tailored to specific domains. We present the formal syntax and semantics of GEAK, demonstrate its theoretical properties, and provide a model checker for bilattice-based dynamic epistemic logic. Our contributions are validated through a case study using Ginsberg's seven-valued default logic for multi-agent route planning, where autonomous vehicles coordinate under uncertainty with default assumptions about road conditions. Preliminary results suggest that GEAK offers greater expressiveness than classical approaches while maintaining computational tractability, enabling more realistic modeling and verification of multi-agent systems with sophisticated reasoning patterns involving definite and default information.

Keywords: Dynamic Epistemic Logic · Bilattices · Multi-valued Logic · Model Checking · Multi-agent Systems · Epistemic Actions

1 Introduction

Dynamic Epistemic Logic (DEL) has become a standard framework for analyzing information change in multi-agent systems [6]. However, classical DEL assumes consistent information and logically omniscient agents, limiting its applicability to real-world scenarios where information is often incomplete or contradictory.

© The Author(s), under exclusive license to Springer Nature Switzerland AG 2026
M. H. ter Beek and L. Teixeira (Eds.): SBMF 2025, LNCS 16363, pp. 82–97, 2026.
https://doi.org/10.1007/978-3-032-12086-1_5

To address this, logics based on bilattices-algebraic structures designed to handle such imperfect information—have been proposed [3,10,11].

A significant advancement in this area is the Bilattice Logic of Epistemic Actions and Knowledge (BEAK), which integrates the full power of DEL action models with the four-valued Belnap-Dunn logic (FOUR) [4]. While BEAK successfully models complex epistemic updates in a paraconsistent setting, its semantics are restricted to this single, four-element bilattice. This limits its capacity to model more nuanced scenarios, such as those involving default reasoning or varying degrees of trust, which can be captured by richer bilattice structures.

In this paper, we address this limitation by introducing GEAK (Generalized Bilattice Logic for Epistemic Actions and Knowledge). Our contributions are two-fold:

1. We generalize BEAK by defining its semantics over any logical bilattice, thereby creating a highly flexible framework adaptable to diverse reasoning contexts beyond the four-valued setting. A key aspect is the formalization of multi-valued accessibility relations, allowing for a more fine-grained representation of agent uncertainty.
2. We validate the practical utility of GEAK by presenting an implementation of a direct *explicit-state model checker*. This serves as a proof of concept for the logic and provides a concrete tool for verifying epistemic properties in complex systems.

In parallel to this work, we are developing a *multi-valued bounded model checker* that will incorporate and extend our previous algorithms for bounded model checking over Quasi-Boolean algebras [1,2]. This forthcoming tool will combine GEAK's expressive semantics with the efficiency of bounded verification techniques, paving the way for scalable analysis of multi-agent systems under uncertainty.

The remainder of this paper is organized as follows. Section 2 provides the necessary background on epistemic logic, bilattices, and dynamic epistemic logic. Section 3 positions our work within the broader context of non-classical epistemic logics and model checking approaches. Section 4 presents the formal definition of the GEAK framework, including its syntax, semantics, and key theoretical properties. Section 5 describes our model checking algorithm, its implementation, and a case study. Finally, Sect. 6 summarizes our contributions and outlines directions for future research.

2   Theoretical Background

We review the foundational concepts required for our framework: classical epistemic logic, bilattices, and dynamic epistemic logic.

2.1   Epistemic Logic and Kripke Semantics

Epistemic logic reasons about knowledge using Kripke models [13].

Definition 1 (Kripke Model and Satisfaction). *A Kripke model is structure* $\mathcal{M} = (W, \{R_a\}_{a \in Agt}, V)$ *where* W *is a set of worlds,* Agt *is a finite set of agents,* $R_a \subseteq W \times W$ *is agent* a*'s accessibility relation (typically an equivalence relation for knowledge), and* $V : \mathsf{Prop} \to 2^W$ *maps propositions to worlds where they hold. Satisfaction is defined as:* $\mathcal{M}, w \models p$ *iff* $w \in V(p)$*; Boolean connectives as usual; if* ϕ *is an epistemic formula,* $\mathcal{M}, w \models K_a\phi$ *iff for all* v *such that* $(w, v) \in R_a$*, we have* $\mathcal{M}, v \models \phi$*.*

2.2   Bilattices and Logical Bilattices

Bilattices [10,11] provide a framework for reasoning with incomplete and conflicting information through two partial orders: truth ($\leq_t$) and knowledge ($\leq_k$).

Definition 2 (Bilattice). *A bilattice is a structure* $\mathcal{B} = (B, \leq_t, \leq_k)$ *where* B *is the set of values of the bilattice, and both* $(B, \leq_t)$ *and* $(B, \leq_k)$ *are complete lattices, related by negation* $\neg : B \to B$ *that is an involution, reverses* $\leq_t$*, and preserves* $\leq_k$*.*

Definition 3 (Logical Bilattice). *A logical bilattice is a pair* $(\mathcal{B}, \mathcal{D})$ *where* $\mathcal{B}$ *is a bilattice and* $\mathcal{D} \subseteq B$ *is a prime filter with respect to* $\leq_t$*, called the designated truth values.*

2.3   Dynamic Epistemic Logic (DEL)

Dynamic Epistemic Logic (DEL) extends epistemic logic with modal operators that describe model-transforming actions. The language of DEL is parameterized by action models, which represent the epistemic structure of actions and their effects on agents' knowledge [5,8].

Definition 4 (Language of DEL). *The language* $\mathcal{L}_{\mathsf{DEL}}$ *is defined inductively by the following grammar in BNF:*

$$\phi := p \mid c \mid \neg\phi \mid \phi \wedge \phi \mid \phi \vee \phi \mid \mathbf{K}_j\phi \mid [\alpha, e]\phi$$

where $j \in \mathsf{Agt}$*,* $A \subseteq \mathsf{Agt}$*,* $p \in \mathsf{Prop}$*, and* α *is a pointed action model over* $\mathcal{L}_{\mathsf{DEL}}$ *with* $\alpha = (E, e, \{R_a\}_{a \in \mathsf{Agt}}, \mathrm{pre})$ *where* E *is a finite set of events,* $e \in E$ *is the actual event, each* $R_a \subseteq E \times E$ *is an accessibility relation, and* $\mathrm{pre} : E \to \mathcal{L}_{\mathsf{DEL}}$ *assigns preconditions to events.*

Definition 5 (Action Model and Product Update). *An **action model** is a structure* $\alpha = (E, e, \{R_a\}_{a \in \mathsf{Agt}}, \mathrm{pre})$ *where* E *is a set of action points,* $e \in E$ *is the actual event,* $R_a \subseteq E \times E$ *models agent uncertainty about actions, and* $\mathrm{pre} : E \to \mathcal{L}_{\mathsf{DEL}}$ *gives preconditions. The **product update** is defined as* $\mathcal{M} \otimes \alpha = (W', \{R'_a\}, V')$ *where* $W' = \{(w, e) \in W \times E \mid \mathcal{M}, w \models \mathrm{pre}(e)\}$*,* $R'_a = \{((w, e), (v, f)) \mid (w, v) \in R_a \text{ and } (e, f) \in R_a\}$*, and* $V'(p) = \{(w, e) \in W' \mid w \in V(p)\}$*.*

The semantics for dynamic formulas is given by $\mathcal{M}, w \models [\alpha]\phi$ iff $\mathcal{M}, w \models \mathrm{pre}(k)$ implies $\mathcal{M} \otimes \alpha, (w, k) \models \phi$.

3   Related Work

Our work builds upon several intersecting research areas: bilattice-based epistemic logic, multi-valued model checking, and dynamic epistemic logic verification. We position our contributions within this broader landscape while highlighting the novel aspects of our generalization.

The use of multi-valued logics to represent uncertainty and incomplete information has deep roots in artificial intelligence, with Ginsberg's bilattices [11] providing an elegant algebraic framework that separates truth-values from information states through dual orderings. Belnap's four-valued logic [7] demonstrated the practical utility of this approach for reasoning with inconsistent information. The connection to epistemic logic was explored by Sim [16,17], who proposed multi-valued epistemic logics to address logical omniscience, and by Fitting [9,10], who extensively studied bilattices in logic programming and non-monotonic reasoning. However, these approaches typically focused on static epistemic settings without the dynamic action-based updates central to modern epistemic logic.

The most direct predecessor to our work is the Bilattice Logic of Epistemic Actions and Knowledge (BEAK), introduced by Bakhtiari, van Ditmarsch, and Rivieccio [4]. BEAK was the first framework to successfully integrate bilattice-based semantics with dynamic epistemic logic, defining action semantics over the four-valued bilattice FOUR. This innovation enabled modeling of scenarios with inconsistent or incomplete information while preserving the elegant product update mechanism of DEL. Related work by Rivieccio [14] on Bilattice Public Announcement Logic and Santos [15] on four-valued dynamic epistemic logic demonstrated the feasibility of non-classical foundations for dynamic epistemic reasoning. However, all these approaches remain restricted to specific bilattice structures, limiting their applicability to scenarios requiring different truth-value granularities or domain-specific reasoning patterns.

Our GEAK framework addresses this limitation by generalizing BEAK to arbitrary logical bilattices—i.e., bilattices equipped with designated value sets that define logical consequence. This generalization maintains the theoretical elegance of bilattice-based reasoning while providing the flexibility needed for diverse application domains, from security protocols with multiple trust levels to sensor networks with varying measurement confidence.

The verification of dynamic epistemic logic has evolved from early explicit-state approaches [21] to sophisticated symbolic techniques. Van Benthem et al. [19,20] developed symbolic model checking for DEL using knowledge structures and knowledge transformers, achieving significant scalability improvements through BDD-based representations. However, no model checker—explicit or symbolic—has been developed for bilattice-based dynamic epistemic logics.

Our work also connects to the broader field of multi-valued model checking, where we have previously contributed efficient algorithms for bounded model checking over Quasi-Boolean algebras [1,2]. These earlier works developed novel encoding techniques that avoid the exponential blowup typically associated with multi-valued logic verification, achieving significant performance improvements through compact propositional formula generation rather than naive bit-slicing approaches. The principles and techniques from this previous research form the foundation for our ongoing development of a bilattice-based bounded model checker for GEAK, representing a natural evolution from temporal logic verification to epistemic action verification in multi-valued settings.

The prototype explicit-state model checker presented in this paper serves as both a proof of concept for GEAK's practical applicability and a stepping stone toward more scalable approaches. By demonstrating that bilattice-based dynamic epistemic logic can be effectively implemented and verified, our work opens the door to more sophisticated verification techniques that combine the expressiveness of multi-valued reasoning with the scalability of modern model checking technology.

4   The **GEAK** Framework

The Bilattice Logic of Epistemic Actions and Knowledge (BEAK), as introduced by Bakhtiari et al. [4], provides a powerful framework for reasoning about knowledge change in the presence of inconsistent and incomplete information. However, its semantics are defined exclusively over the four-valued Belnap-Dunn logic (FOUR). While foundational, this choice limits the representation of more nuanced epistemic and doxastic states that arise in many real-world scenarios, such as default reasoning or systems involving multiple levels of trust, which can be elegantly captured by richer bilattices like Ginsberg's DEFAULT [11,18].

GEAK extends BEAK's core principles to a framework that is semantically grounded in *any* logical bilattice, thereby offering greater flexibility and expressive power.

4.1   Multi-valued Accessibility Relations

A key aspect of GEAK is its treatment of the epistemic accessibility relation. In standard Kripke models for DEL, accessibility $R_a \subseteq W \times W$ is a crisp, Boolean concept: a world v is either considered possible from w by agent a, or it is not. This binary view is insufficient for scenarios where an agent's sense of possibility is graded. For instance, an agent might consider a world plausible but with some doubt, or have conflicting evidence regarding its possibility.

To capture this, BEAK defines accessibility not as a simple relation, but as a function mapping pairs of worlds to a value in bilattice FOUR [4]. GEAK follows this definition is inspired by early work on many-valued modal logics [10,12].

Definition 6 (GEAK Model). *A **GEAK** model over a logical bilattice $(\mathcal{B}, \mathcal{D})$ is a tuple $M = (W, \{R_a\}_{a \in \mathsf{Agt}}, V)$, where:*

- *W is a non-empty set of worlds.*
- *For each agent $a \in \mathsf{Agt}$, $R_a : W \times W \to B$ is a multi-valued accessibility relation.*
- *$V : \mathsf{Prop} \to (W \to B)$ is a valuation function mapping atomic propositions to functions from worlds to the bilattice $\mathcal{B}$.*

In Definition 6, the value $R_a(w, v) = b$, where $b \in B$, represents the status of the epistemic link from w to v for agent a. If $\mathcal{B}$ is the bilattice FOUR, $R_a(w, v) = \top$ could model a situation where agent a has contradictory evidence about whether v is a possible alternative to w. Alternatively, if $\mathcal{B}$ is the DEFAULT logic, and $b = \mathsf{dt}$, it could model the situation where agent a believes, *by default*, that v is possible alternative to w, but without evidence.

4.2   Language and Semantics

The language $\mathcal{L}_{\mathsf{GEAK}}$ is almost identical to that of BEAK, except for the fact that Bakhtiari et al. [4, Definition 3], include the for truth-values of FOUR in the language definition, while we assume a more general approach.

Definition 7 (Language of GEAK and Action Models). *Let* $(\mathcal{B}, \mathcal{D})$ *be a designated logical bilattice,* Prop *be a set of propositional variables, and* Agt *be a set of agents. The set* $\mathcal{L}_{\mathsf{GEAK}}$ *of formulas* ϕ *of GEAK is defined as:*

$$\phi := p \mid c \mid \neg\phi \mid \phi \wedge \phi \mid \phi \vee \phi \mid \phi \supset \phi \mid \mathbf{K}_a\phi \mid \langle\alpha\rangle\phi$$

where $p \in$ Prop, $c \in B$, *and* $a \in$ Agt. *We define the* $\mathbf{M}_a\phi \equiv \neg\mathbf{K}_a\neg\phi$.

In the construct $\langle\alpha\rangle\phi$, α *is a bilattice-valued* **action model** *over* $\mathcal{L}_{\mathsf{GEAK}}$, *defined as a tuple* $\alpha = (E, e, \{R_{\alpha,a}\}_{a \in \mathsf{Agt}}, \mathrm{pre})$, *where* E *is a finite set of events with actual event* e, *each* $R_{\alpha,a} : E \times E \to \mathcal{B}$ *is a multi-valued accessibility relation, and* $\mathrm{pre} : E \to \mathcal{L}_{GEAK}$ *assigns a precondition to each event. We write* pre_α *to mean* $\mathrm{pre}(e)$ *for a given action model* α.

Following [4], we also define a number of abbreviations, as shown in Table 1, and call attention to the *strong implication* and the *strong conjunction* (fusion) operations, as they will play an important role later.

Table 1. Abbreviations for logical operators.

Abbreviation	Definition	Description
$x \otimes y$	$(x \wedge \bot) \vee (y \wedge \bot) \vee (x \wedge y)$	knowledge meet
$x \oplus y$	$(x \wedge \top) \vee (y \wedge \top) \vee (x \wedge y)$	knowledge join
$\sim x$	$x \supset \mathsf{f}$	strong negation
$x \to y$	$(x \supset y) \wedge (\neg y \supset \neg x)$	strong implication
$x * y$	$\neg(y \to \neg x)$	fusion/strong conjunction
$x \Leftrightarrow y$	$(x \supset y) \wedge (y \supset x)$	weak equivalence
$x \leftrightarrow y$	$(x \to y) \wedge (y \to x)$	strong equivalence

The semantics, however, are generalized. Let $(\mathcal{B}, \mathcal{D})$ be a designated logical bilattice. The satisfaction relation $M, w \models \varphi$ holds iff the computed value $V(w, \varphi) \in \mathcal{D}$. The valuation V is extended from atomic propositions to all formulas as follows:

- $V(w, p)$ is given by the model for $p \in \mathsf{Prop}$.
- $V(w, \neg\varphi) = \neg V(w, \varphi)$.
- $V(w, \varphi \circ \psi) = V(w, \varphi) \circ V(w, \psi)$, for $\circ \in \{\wedge, \vee, \otimes, \oplus\}$.
- $V(w, K_a\varphi) = \bigwedge_{w' \in W}(R_a(w, w') \to V(w', \varphi))$, where $\bigwedge$ is the infinitary truth-meet in $\mathcal{B}$.
- $V(w, \langle\alpha\rangle\psi)$ is defined via the product update below.

The semantics for the knowledge operator $\mathbf{K}_a$ is the most significant departure from standard DEL. An agent knows φ at world w if, for every world w', the accessibility value of w' from w implies the value of φ at w'. This generalized meet ensures that worlds with non-designated accessibility values (e.g., $\mathbf{f}$ or $\bot$ in FOUR) contribute trivially to the agent's knowledge, while worlds with designated accessibility must support the truth of φ.

Definition 8 (Product Update). *The **product update** $M \otimes \alpha$ yields a new model $M' = (W', \{R'_a\}_{a \in \mathsf{Agt}}, V')$, where:*

- $W' = \{(w, e) \in W \times E \mid M, w \models \mathrm{pre}(e)\}$.
- $R'_a((w, e), (w', e')) = R_a(w, w') \otimes_B R_{\alpha,a}(e, e')$.
- $V'((w, e), p) = V(w, p)$.

The semantics for the dynamic modality is: $M, w \models \langle\alpha\rangle\varphi$ iff $M, w \models \mathrm{pre}(e)$ and $M \otimes \alpha, (w, e) \models \varphi$

Note that the new accessibility relation in the updated model is computed using the knowledge-meet operator $\otimes$. This choice reflects the intuition that the uncertainty about the resulting state is the consensus of the initial uncertainty about the world and the uncertainty about the event that occurred.

4.3 Axiomatization

The proof system for GEAK is a direct generalization of the axiomatic system for BEAK [4]. It includes all axioms and rules for the underlying logical bilattice, along with reduction axioms that provide a recursive analysis of the effects of epistemic actions. The key axioms are presented below.

Atomic Permanence:	$[\alpha]p \leftrightarrow (\mathrm{pre}_\alpha \to p)$
Action and Negation:	$[\alpha]\neg\varphi \leftrightarrow (\mathrm{pre}_\alpha \to \neg[\alpha]\varphi)$
Action and Conjunction:	$[\alpha](\varphi \wedge \psi) \leftrightarrow [\alpha]\varphi \wedge [\alpha]\psi$
Action-Knowledge Axiom:	$[\alpha]K_a\varphi \leftrightarrow (\mathrm{pre}_\alpha \to K_a[\alpha]\varphi)$

The Action-Knowledge axiom remains syntactically simple, but its semantic interpretation is now richer due to the multi-valued nature of the relations and the generalized definition of the $\mathbf{K}_a$ operator. A full proof system would also include axioms for the bilattice connectives and rules for reasoning about the specific properties of the chosen logical bilattice. We have proven the system to be sound for any logical bilattice and conjecture its completeness, with the full proof deferred to an extended version of this paper.

5   Model Checking GEAK

The formalization of GEAK provides a rich framework for specifying properties of multi-agent systems. However, to make this framework practically useful for verification, we need an effective procedure to determine whether a given formula holds in a given model. This is the *model-checking problem* for GEAK. This section presents a practical solution by detailing a direct, explicit-state model-checking algorithm for GEAK. This algorithm serves as the theoretical foundation for our prototype implementation and demonstrates that the logic is decidable for finite models.

Although symbolic methods offer significant performance advantages for large-scale verification, an explicit model checker provides a crucial first step. It serves as a proof of concept, allows for the verification of smaller, intricate scenarios, and establishes a clear semantic benchmark against which future symbolic implementations can be validated.

5.1   The Model-Checking Algorithm

The model-checking problem for GEAK can be stated as follows: given a finite GEAK model M, a world $w \in M$, and a formula φ, determine whether $M, w \models \varphi$. Since truth in GEAK is defined by the valuation of a formula belonging to the set of designated values $\mathcal{D}$, our algorithm must compute the valuation of φ at w, denoted $[\![\varphi]\!]_M(w)$, and then check if this value is in $\mathcal{D}$.

We define a recursive function, EVALUATE(M, φ), which takes a model and a formula and returns a mapping from each world w in the model to the corresponding bilattice value of φ. The algorithm follows the recursive structure of the logic's semantics, as detailed in Algorithm 1. In this algorithm, we assume that all abbreviations will be previously expanded.

The algorithm proceeds bottom-up, first computing the bilattice values for all atomic propositions and constants at every world. It then iteratively computes the values for more complex formulas, using the already-computed values of their subformulaæ.

For the epistemic modality $\mathbf{K}_i\varphi$, since the accessibility relation is multi-values, instead of checking a crisp condition on all accessible worlds, the algorithm now computes a graded value. For each world $v \in W$, it calculates the implication $R_i(w, v) \to [\![\psi_1]\!]_M(v)$. This value represents how the degree of accessibility from w to v supports the truth of ψ_1 at v. The final value of $\mathbf{K}_i\psi_1$ at w is the truth-meet ($\wedge$) of all these implication values across all possible worlds v. This correctly captures the standard algebraic semantics for the box operator in a multi-valued setting.

For the dynamic modality case $[\alpha]\varphi$, it recursively calls itself on the updated model $M \otimes \alpha$. Since each recursive call operates on a strictly smaller subformula or a model update for a subformula, the process is guaranteed to terminate. If the precondition for an action fails, the resulting statement is vacuously true, which corresponds to the top element of the truth-lattice ($\top_t$).

Algorithm 1. The GEAK Model-Checking Algorithm

1: **function** EVALUATE(M, φ)
2:     **Input:** A GEAK model $M = (W, \{R_i\}, V)$ over $(\mathcal{B}, \mathcal{D})$, where $R_i : W \times W \to B$, and a formula φ.
3:     **Output:** A map $Val : W \to B$ where $Val(w) = \llbracket \varphi \rrbracket_M(w)$.
4:     **for all** subformula ψ of φ in increasing order of complexity **do**
5:         **for all** $w \in W$ **do**
6:             **if** ψ is $p \in \mathsf{Prop}$ **then** $Val(w, \psi) \leftarrow V(w)(p)$
7:             **else if** ψ is $c \in B$ **then** $Val(w, \psi) \leftarrow c$
8:             **else if** ψ is $\neg\psi_1$ **then** $Val(w, \psi) \leftarrow \neg Val(w, \psi_1)$
9:             **else if** ψ is $\psi_1 \wedge \psi_2$ **then** $Val(w, \psi) \leftarrow Val(w, \psi_1) \wedge Val(w, \psi_2)$
10:             **else if** ψ is . . . other operators . . . **then** . . . *defined similarly* . . .
11:             **else if** ψ is $\mathbf{K}_i\psi_1$ **then**
12:                 $PartialValues \leftarrow \emptyset$
13:                 **for all** $v \in W$ **do**
14:                     $R_{wv} \leftarrow R_i(w, v)$ $\triangleright$ *Get accessibility value*
15:                     $Val_v \leftarrow Val(v, \psi_1)$ $\triangleright$ *Get subformula value at target world*
16:                     $PartialValues \leftarrow PartialValues \cup \{R_{wv} \supset Val_v\}$
17:                 $Val(w, \psi) \leftarrow \bigwedge\limits_{b \in PartialValues} b$ $\triangleright$ *Truth-meet of all implications*
18:             **else if** ψ is $[\alpha]\psi_1$ **then**
19:                 $M' \leftarrow$ PRODUCTUPDATE(M, α)
20:                 $Val_{\psi_1} \leftarrow$ EVALUATE(M', ψ_1)
21:                 **if** $(w, k) \in W_{M'}$ **then**
22:                     $Val(w, \psi) \leftarrow Val_{\psi_1}(w, k)$
23:                 **else**
24:                     $Val(w, \psi) \leftarrow \top_t$ $\triangleright$ *Or other value for vacuous truth*
25:     **return** $Val(\cdot, \varphi)$

Finally, to solve the model-checking problem for a given world w, we simply run CHECK$(M, w, \varphi) = ($EVALUATE$(M, \varphi)(w) \in \mathcal{D})$.

The dynamic nature of **GEAK** is handled by the PRODUCTUPDATE function. This function takes the current model M and an action model α and computes the new state of the world after an epistemic action occurs by constructing the product model $M \otimes \alpha$, as formally defined in the semantics. A key feature of our generalized framework is that accessibility relations themselves are multi-valued, assigning a value from the bilattice $\mathcal{B}$ to each pair of worlds. The update must, therefore, compute the new multi-valued relations. Algorithm 2 provides a procedural description of this construction.

The PRODUCTUPDATE algorithm operates in two phases:

1. *World Generation (Lines 6–11):* The function first iterates through all possible pairs of worlds and actions (w, k) from the original model M and the action model α. For each pair, it evaluates the precondition of the action, pre(k), in the context of the world w. This is achieved by a call to the main EVALUATE function. If the resulting bilattice value of the precondition is in the set of designated values $\mathcal{D}$, the pair (w, k) becomes a valid world in the

---

Algorithm 2. The Product Update Function for Multi-Valued Relations.

1: **function** PRODUCTUPDATE(M, α)
2:     **Input:** A GEAK model $M = (W, \{R_i\}, V)$ over $(\mathcal{B}, \mathcal{D})$, an action model $\alpha = (K, k, \{\mathbf{R}_i\}, \text{pre})$. Note that $R_i : W \times W \to B$ and $\mathbf{R}_i : K \times K \to B$ are multi-valued.
3:     **Output:** The updated GEAK model $M' = (W', \{R_i'\}, V')$.
4:     $W_{new} \leftarrow \emptyset$
5:     $V_{new} \leftarrow$ new empty map
6:     ▷ *Phase 1: Determine the set of new worlds by checking preconditions.* ◁
7:     **for all** $(w, k) \in W \times K$ **do**
8:         $Val_{pre} \leftarrow$ EVALUATE$(M, \text{pre}(k))$
9:         **if** $Val_{pre}(w) \in \mathcal{D}$ **then**
10:             $W_{new} \leftarrow W_{new} \cup \{(w, k)\}$
11:             $V_{new}((w, k)) \leftarrow V(w)$ ▷ *Copy valuation from the original world.*
12:     ▷ *Phase 2: Construct the new multi-valued accessibility relations.* ◁
13:     **for all** $i \in \mathsf{Agt}$ **do**
14:         $R_i' \leftarrow$ new empty map $(W_{new} \times W_{new}) \to B$
15:         **for all** $(w, k) \in W_{new}$ **do**
16:             **for all** $(v, l) \in W_{new}$ **do**
17:                 $R_i'((w, k), (v, l)) \leftarrow R_i(w, v) * \mathbf{R}_i(k, l)$
18:     **return** $(W_{new}, \{R_i'\}_{i \in \mathsf{Agt}}, V_{new})$

---

new model M'. The valuation for this new world is simply copied from the original world w.

2. *Multi-Valued Relation Construction (Lines 12–18):* After the set of new worlds W' has been determined, the algorithm constructs the new accessibility relations. For each agent i, the new relation R_i' is constructed. The bilattice value assigned to a pair of new worlds, $((w, k), (v, l))$, is computed by taking the fusion $(*)$ of the accessibility value between the original worlds $(R_i(w, v))$ and the accessibility value between the action points $(\mathbf{R}_i(k, l))$.

   This phase directly implements the "no miracles" condition of DEL, ensuring that agents only gain knowledge; they do not forget possibilities they previously considered, unless those possibilities are ruled out by the action's precondition.

   This definition ensures that the degree of possibility between two new states is the "weakest link" between the possibility of the corresponding world-transition and the action-transition. This is the correct and natural generalization of the crisp product update in classical DEL to a fully multi-valued, bilattice-based setting.

   This function is called whenever the main EVALUATE algorithm encounters a dynamic modality $[\alpha]\varphi$. By constructing the updated model, it provides the necessary context in which the subformula φ can be evaluated, thus completing the semantic definition of dynamic actions in a procedural manner.

5.2 Implementation of the Prototype

To demonstrate the practical feasibility of the GEAK framework, we have developed a prototype explicit-state model checker implemented in Scala 3.

Syntax and Parsing. The model checker accepts input in two domain-specific languages: (i) a formula language supporting bilattice connectives ($\wedge, \vee, \rightarrow, \supset, \otimes, \oplus$), epistemic operators ($\mathbf{K}_a\phi$, $\mathbf{M}_a\phi$), dynamic operators ($[\alpha]\phi$, $\langle\alpha\rangle\phi$), and direct bilattice value references (`#value`); (ii) the BEAM Model Syntax for defining complete verification scenarios including bilattice specifications, agent declarations, multi-valued accessibility relations, action models, and verification queries.

Core Data Structures. The implementation employs key abstractions: `Bilattice` (abstract trait with concrete implementations), `TruthValue` (sealed trait hierarchy for bilattice elements), `BeamModel` (case class for BEAM models), `ActionModel` (action model representation), and `Formula` (algebraic data type for GEAK formulas).

Model Checking Engine. The core functionality is implemented through `FormulaEvaluator` (recursive evaluation per Algorithm 1) and `ProductUpdater` (product update construction per Algorithm 2). The model checker supports both individual formula evaluation and batch verification with detailed trace information.

This implementation demonstrates that GEAK can be effectively realized as a practical verification tool. Future work includes symbolic extensions using Multi-Valued Decision Diagrams and a bounded model checking engine building upon our prior work on efficient multi-valued logic verification [1,2].

5.3 Case Study: Default Reasoning in Multi-agent Planning

To demonstrate the expressive power of GEAK beyond the four-valued setting, we present a case study using Ginsberg's seven-valued default logic D7 [11]. This bilattice naturally captures default reasoning scenarios where agents must make decisions based on incomplete information and defeasible assumptions.

Ginsberg's Seven-Valued Default Logic D7. The D7 logic employs seven truth values that distinguish between definite and default information:

- **n** (neither): neither true nor false
- **t** (true): definitely true
- **f** (false): definitely false
- **dt** (default true): true by default
- **df** (default false): false by default
- **db** (default both): both default true and default false
- **b** (both): both definitely true and false (conflict)

Figure 1 shows the Hasse diagram for the bilattice D7, with its truth and knowledge orderings. We designate $\mathcal{D} = \{t, dt, db\}$ as the set of designated values, i.e., the values considered "true enough" for decision-making.

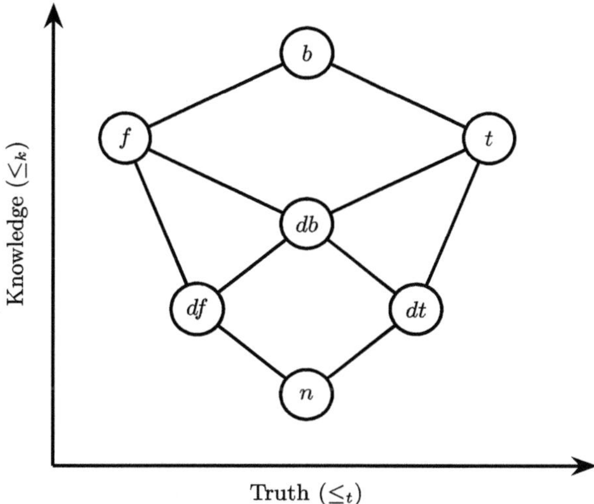

Fig. 1. The D7 bilattice structure for Ginsberg's seven-valued default logic. Values: $\{n, t, f, dt, df, db, b\}$. Designated values: $\{t, dt, db\}$.

Multi-agent Route Planning Scenario. Consider three autonomous vehicles planning routes through a city network where road conditions are uncertain. Each vehicle has sensors providing different quality information about traffic, construction, and weather conditions. The vehicles must coordinate their routes while dealing with default assumptions about road availability. Listing 1, in the appendix, shows the source code modeling this problem.

Analysis and Results. This case study demonstrates several key advantages of GEAK with the bilattice D7:

Default Reasoning: The distinction between definite facts (**#t**, **#f**) and default assumptions (**#dt**, **#df**) allows vehicles to reason with incomplete information while maintaining the ability to revise beliefs when definite information becomes available.

Graduated Uncertainty: The seven-valued structure captures nuanced epistemic states. For example, **#n** represents complete ignorance, **#db** represents conflicting defaults, and **#b** represents definite contradiction.

Multi-valued Accessibility: Each vehicle's accessibility relation reflects its sensor capabilities and information processing quality. Vehicle1 has high confidence in definite reports (**#t**), while Vehicle3 shows more uncertainty (**#n**) about default information.

Dynamic Belief Revision: The sensor update actions demonstrate how default beliefs can be strengthened to definite knowledge or weakened when conflicts arise. The multi-valued accessibility relations capture how different agents process the same information with varying degrees of confidence.

Experimental verification using our prototype model checker confirmed that the coordination protocol successfully enables the vehicles to reach consensus on route selection despite starting with incomplete and potentially conflicting default assumptions. The `decision_quality` property verifies that route choices are based on sufficiently reliable information, while `coordination_success` confirms that at least one vehicle gains definite knowledge about the chosen route.

This example illustrates that GEAK's generalization to arbitrary bilattices enables modeling of sophisticated reasoning patterns that would be impossible with classical binary logic or even the four-valued BEAK framework. The DEFAULT logic's distinction between definite and default information proves particularly valuable for autonomous systems operating under uncertainty.

Experimental Results and Analysis. The route planning case study was executed using our prototype model checker, demonstrating the practical applicability of the GEAK framework with the D7 logic. The verification process successfully validated all specified properties, confirming that the coordination protocol enables effective decision-making under uncertainty.

The experimental results highlight several key advantages of the D7 bilattice structure. The distinction between definite facts (`#t`, `#f`) and default assumptions (`#dt`, `#df`) proved essential for modeling realistic autonomous vehicle scenarios where complete information is rarely available. The intermediate values (`#n`, `#db`, `#b`) captured nuanced epistemic states that would be impossible to represent in classical binary logic or even the four-valued BEAK framework.

The multi-valued accessibility relations demonstrated their crucial role in representing varying sensor capabilities and information processing quality among the three vehicles. Vehicle1's high confidence in definite reports (`#t`) contrasted with Vehicle3's uncertainty (`#n`) about default information, accurately reflecting real-world differences in sensor reliability and data fusion algorithms. The dynamic belief revision process, where default assumptions could be strengthened to definite knowledge or weakened when conflicts arose, showcased the natural way that D7 logic handles information updates.

Performance analysis revealed that the explicit-state model checker handled the seven-valued bilattice efficiently, with verification times remaining tractable even for the complex multi-agent coordination scenario. The designated value set $\{t, dt, db\}$ provided an intuitive threshold for decision-making, allowing vehicles to act on sufficiently reliable information while avoiding decisions based on pure speculation or conflicting evidence.

This case study validates that GEAK's generalization to arbitrary bilattices enables modeling of sophisticated reasoning patterns that extend far beyond classical approaches, while maintaining computational tractability through our explicit-state model checking algorithm. The D7 logic proves particularly valuable for autonomous systems that must operate effectively under uncertainty while maintaining safety and coordination requirements.

6   Conclusion and Future Work

We have presented GEAK, a generalized logic for epistemic actions that extends BEAK beyond its four-valued foundation to any logical bilattice. By incorporating multi-valued accessibility relations in both state and action models, GEAK offers a more expressive framework for reasoning about knowledge dynamics in the presence of inconsistent or incomplete information. We have validated our approach with a prototype explicit-state model checker, demonstrating the logic's practical applicability.

A primary direction for future work is the development of a **bounded model checker** for GEAK. This will leverage SAT/SMT-based techniques to tackle the state explosion problem, extending our previous research on efficient multi-valued bounded model checking for LTL over quasi-boolean algebras [1,2] to the richer context of dynamic epistemic logic. We also plan to explore GEAK's application in verifying security protocols where modeling different levels of trust and deception is crucial.

Acknowledgments. The authors thank IFES, FAPES/UnAC, FAPES Process N° 23158.002093/2025-85) and the UniversidadES system.

A   Route Planning Model

Listing 1. Route Planning with D7 Logic in BEAM Syntax

```
model RouteePlanning {
    bilattice d7;
    agents: vehicle1, vehicle2, vehicle3;
    propositions:
        route_a_clear = #dt,        // Default assumption: Route A is clear
        route_b_clear = #df,        // Default assumption: Route B is blocked
        route_c_clear = #n,         // No information about Route C
        construction_zone = #f,     // Definitely no construction reported
        weather_good = #dt;         // Default assumption: good weather
    accessibility {
        vehicle1: route_a_clear & weather_good;
        vehicle2: route_b_clear | construction_zone;
        vehicle3: weather_good;
    }
    action sensor_update(agent reporter, formula observation) {
        events {
            report_definite: pre: K{reporter}observation;
            report_default:
                pre: ~K{reporter}observation & ~K{reporter}(~observation);
            report_conflict:
                pre: K{reporter}observation & K{reporter}(~observation);
        }
        real: report_default;
        accessibility {
            vehicle1: report_definite <-> report_definite : #t,
                      report_default <-> report_default : #dt,
                      report_conflict <-> report_conflict : #b;
            vehicle2: report_definite <-> report_definite : #dt,
                      report_default <-> report_default : #df,
                      report_conflict <-> report_conflict : #db;
            vehicle3: report_definite <-> report_definite : #dt,
                      report_default <-> report_default : #n,
```

```
                        report_conflict <-> report_conflict : #df;
        }
    }
    action route_decision() {
        events {
            choose_route_a: pre: route_a_clear & ~construction_zone;
            choose_route_b: pre: route_b_clear & weather_good;
            choose_route_c: pre: route_c_clear;
            wait_for_info: pre: ~route_a_clear & ~route_b_clear & ~
                route_c_clear;
        }
        real: choose_route_a;
        accessibility {
            all: choose_route_a <-> choose_route_a : #dt,
                 choose_route_b <-> choose_route_b : #df,
                 choose_route_c <-> choose_route_c : #n,
                 wait_for_info <-> wait_for_info : #db;
        }
    }
    scenario coordination_protocol {
        sensor_update(vehicle1, construction_zone);
        sensor_update(vehicle2, ~route_b_clear);
        sensor_update(vehicle3, ~weather_good);
        route_decision();
    }
    verify {
        initial_defaults: route_a_clear & ~route_b_clear & weather_good;
        after_updates:
            [coordination_protocol](K{vehicle1}construction_zone &
            K{vehicle2}(~route_b_clear) & K{vehicle3}(~weather_good));
        decision_quality: [coordination_protocol]
            (choose_route_a ~> (route_a_clear & ~construction_zone));
        coordination_success:
            [coordination_protocol](K{vehicle1}choose_route_a |
            K{vehicle2}choose_route_a | K{vehicle3}choose_route_a);
    }
}
```

References

1. Andrade, J.O., Kameyama, Y.: A direct algorithm for multi-valued bounded model checking. In: Cha, S.S., Choi, J.-Y., Kim, M., Lee, I., Viswanathan, M. (eds.) ATVA 2008. LNCS, vol. 5311, pp. 80–94. Springer, Heidelberg (2008). https://doi.org/10.1007/978-3-540-88387-6_8. http://www.springerlink.com/index/a130736441w66834.pdf

2. Andrade, J.O., Kameyama, Y.: Efficient multi-valued bounded model checking for LTL over quasi-boolean algebras. IEICE Trans. Inf. Syst. **E95.D**(5), 1355–1364 (2012). https://doi.org/10.1587/transinf.E95.D.1355. http://japanlinkcenter.org/JST.JSTAGE/transinf/E95.D.1355?from=CrossRef&type=abstract

3. Arieli, O., Avron, A.: Reasoning with logical bilattices. J. Logic Lang. Inf. **5**(1) (1996). https://doi.org/10.1007/BF00215626

4. Bakhtiari, Z., van Ditmarsch, H., Rivieccio, U.: Bilattice logic of epistemic actions and knowledge. Ann. Pure Appl. Logic **171**(6), 102790 (2020). https://doi.org/10.1016/j.apal.2020.102790

5. Baltag, A., Moss, L.S., Solecki, S.: The logic of public announcements, common knowledge, and private suspicions. In: Arló-Costa, H., Hendricks, V.F., van Benthem, J. (eds.) Readings in Formal Epistemology. SGTP, vol. 1, pp. 773–812. Springer, Cham (2016). https://doi.org/10.1007/978-3-319-20451-2_38

6. Baltag, A., Renne, B.: Dynamic epistemic logic. In: Zalta, E.N. (ed.) The Stanford Encyclopedia of Philosophy. Metaphysics Research Lab, Stanford University, winter 2016 edn. (2016). https://plato.stanford.edu/archives/win2016/entries/dynamic-epistemic/
7. Belnap, N.D.: A useful four-valued logic. In: Dunn, J.M., Epstein, G. (eds.) Modern Uses of Multiple-Valued Logic, pp. 5–37. Springer, Dordrecht (1977). https://doi.org/10.1007/978-94-010-1161-7_2
8. van Ditmarsch, H., van der Hoek, W., Kooi, B.P.: Dynamic Epistemic Logic. No. v. 337 in Synthese Library, Springer, Dordrecht, Netherlands (2007)
9. Fitting, M.C.: Many-Valued Modal Logics. Fundamenta Informaticae **15**(3-4), 235–254 (1991). http://dblp.uni-trier.de/rec/bibtex/journals/fuin/Fitting91
10. Fitting, M.C.: Bilattices are Nice Things. Self-reference, pp. 53–77 (2006)
11. Ginsberg, M.L.: Multi-valued logics. In: AAAI Proceedings, pp. 243–247 (1986)
12. Jung, A., Rivieccio, U.: Kripke semantics for modal bilattice logic. In: 2013 28th Annual ACM/IEEE Symposium on Logic in Computer Science, New Orleans, LA, USA, pp. 438–447. IEEE (2013). https://doi.org/10.1109/LICS.2013.50. http://ieeexplore.ieee.org/document/6571576/
13. Kripke, S.A.: Semantical considerations on modal logic. Acta Philosophica Fennica **16**, 83–94 (1963)
14. Rivieccio, U.: Bilattice public announcement logic **10**, 459–477 (2014)
15. Santos, Y.D.: A four-valued dynamic epistemic logic. J. Logic Lang. Inform. **29**(4), 451–489 (2020). https://doi.org/10.1007/s10849-020-09313-8
16. Sim, K.M.: Beliefs and bilattices. In: Raś, Z.W., Zemankova, M. (eds.) ISMIS 1994. LNCS, vol. 869, pp. 594–603. Springer, Heidelberg (1994). https://doi.org/10.1007/3-540-58495-1_59
17. Sim, K.M.: Epistemic logic and logical omniscience II: a unifying framework. Int. J. Intell. Syst. **15**(2), 129–152 (2000)
18. Sim, K.M.: Bilattices and reasoning in artificial intelligence: concepts and foundations. Artif. Intell. Rev. **15**(3), 219–240 (2001)
19. van Benthem, J., van Eijck, J., Gattinger, M., Su, K.: Symbolic model checking for dynamic epistemic logic. In: van der Hoek, W., Holliday, W.H., Wang, W. (eds.) LORI 2015. LNCS, vol. 9394, pp. 366–378. Springer, Heidelberg (2015). https://doi.org/10.1007/978-3-662-48561-3_30
20. Van Benthem, J., Van Eijck, J., Gattinger, M., Su, K.: Symbolic model checking for dynamic epistemic logic – S5 and beyond*. J. Log. Comput. **28**(2), 367–402 (2018). https://doi.org/10.1093/logcom/exx038
21. van Eijck, J.: DEMO — a demo of epistemic modelling. In: Interactive Logic: Proceedings of the 7th Augustus de Morgan Workshop, London, pp. 303–362. No. 1 in Texts in Logic and Games, Amsterdam University Press (2007)

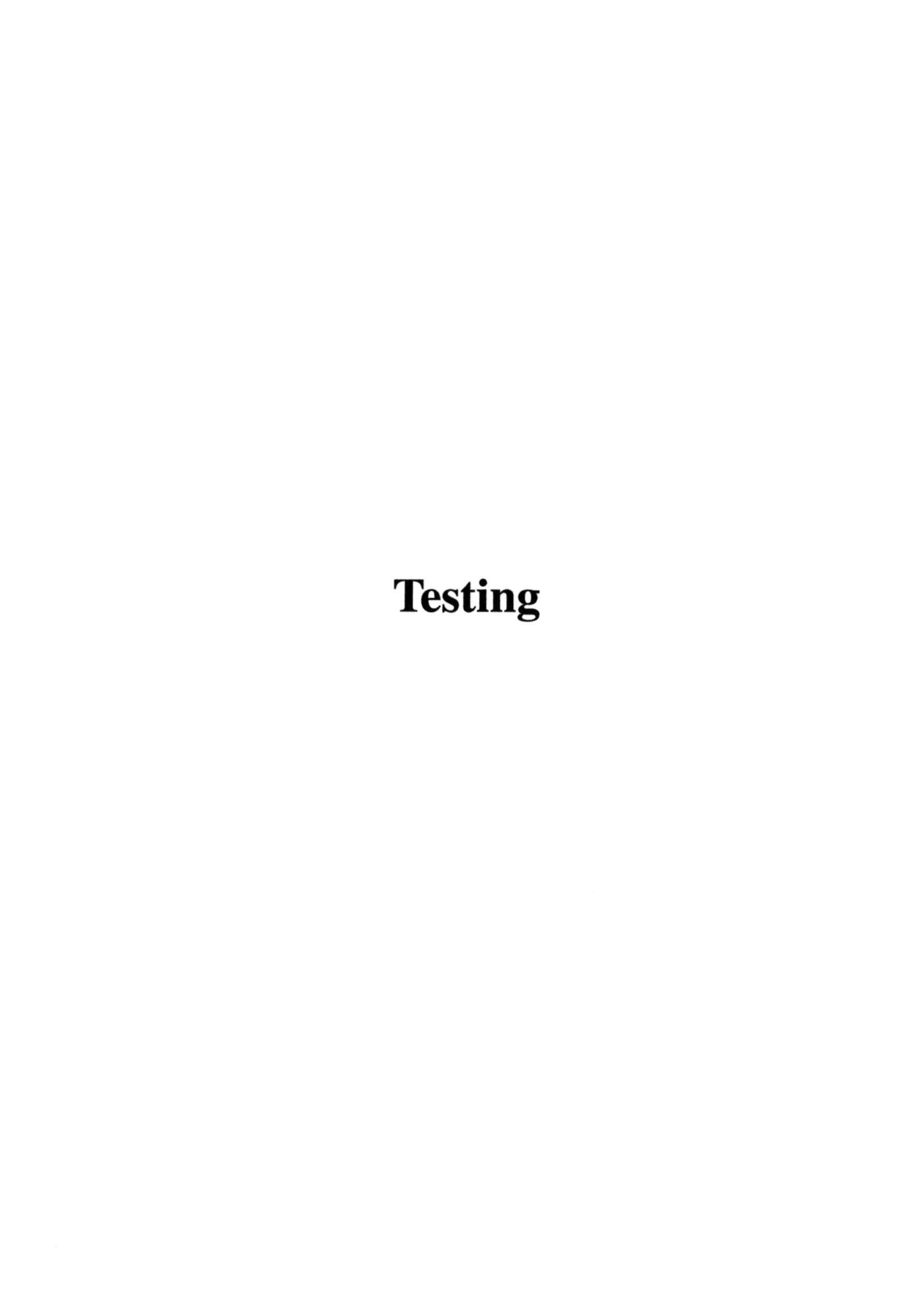

Testing

Deriving Sound Test Scripts
from Requirements Written
in a Controlled Natural Language

Filipe Arruda[1]([⊠]) [iD], Flávia Barros[2] [iD], and Augusto Sampaio[2] [iD]

[1] Centro de Tecnologias Estratégicas do Nordeste, Recife, Brazil
`filipe.arruda@cetene.gov.br`
[2] Centro de Informática, Universidade Federal de Pernambuco, Recife, Brazil
`{fab,acas}@cin.ufpe.br`

Abstract. In an industrial context, ad-hoc/manual testing strategies, using natural language, still seem to be highly prevalent since natural language descriptions are, more likely, easier to understand. Still, the lack of rigor can generate inaccurate tests. Aligned with other modern approaches, we promote the use of natural language descriptions with rigorously defined underlying semantics. As a distinguished feature of our approach, we cover the entire (direct engineering) testing process, from requirements to manual or automated test cases generated automatically. Requirements written in a controlled natural language are parsed, and their semantics are automatically modeled using the CSP process algebra. To address soundness and deal with different abstraction levels, we formalize the concept of a domain model, in which additional information, such as hierarchical composition and a dependence relation among test steps, is defined. Then, sound test cases are generated from the inferred scenarios using the *cspio* conformance relation. These test cases, still expressed in CSP, can then be linearized back to natural language to allow manual execution or directly translated into test scripts for automated execution.

Keywords: Formal Semantics · Controlled Natural Language · Test Case Consistency · Domain Model

1 Introduction

Typically, test cases (TCs) are automated as scripts within a testing framework such as JUnit[1], Pytest[2], or Selenium[3]. They are important resources to verify whether an implementation conforms to the system requirements. The adoption of test automation tools or techniques reduces the cost of test cycles [15]. However, despite this global reduction, the initial implementation cost tends to be

---

[1] https://junit.org/.

[2] https://pytest.org/.

[3] https://www.selenium.dev/.

© The Author(s), under exclusive license to Springer Nature Switzerland AG 2026
M. H. ter Beek and L. Teixeira (Eds.): SBMF 2025, LNCS 16363, pp. 101–118, 2026.
https://doi.org/10.1007/978-3-032-12086-1_6

higher with the use of automation practices, and maintenance can be problematic. Therefore, test scripts should be designed in a way that encourages reuse, becoming easier to maintain and to remain functional despite constant changes on the System Under Test (SUT). In this way, automation becomes an efficient and sustainable solution [10].

The traditional testing process faces several issues: abstraction gap and traceability challenges when linking artifacts like requirements, test cases, and scripts across different abstraction levels and roles; heterogeneous notations that require varied expertise and hinder consistent maintenance; inconsistencies between abstract requirements and concrete tests due to incomplete setups, unmet dependencies, or missing input mappings; inefficiencies in execution time and order when scripts are made self-contained instead of optimizing execution sequences; internationalization problems that introduce ambiguity and misinterpretation, especially with translations; technology lock-in risks from tying the process to specific, fast-changing tools; legibility concerns for novice testers unfamiliar with complex notations; and duplication of artifacts caused by poor traceability.

The aforementioned issues can all be traced back to the lack of a mechanized analysis using precise notations and formal strategies to test case generation and automation. The seminal work of Gaudel [9] argues that testing can be formal, too. From this perspective, there are several test generation strategies and theories based on formal conformance relations, such as *ioco* [19] and *conf* [4]. However, even with a rigorous formal approach, some maintenance issues still arise, such as execution inconsistencies and over-detailed models that need to be updated in every development iteration. Considering this context, the leading question that guides our research is *how to generate sound, consistent and executable test scripts based on requirements written in natural language?* To answer this question, we consider some related challenges: 1) How to process natural language descriptions; 2) How to verify the soundness of derived test cases; and 3) What practical strategy can be used to generate tests that can be interpreted directly by a test driver without demanding over-detailed requirements. The proposed solutions for these challenges are listed next.

- A unified Controlled Natural Language (CNL) to describe requirements, domain model and test cases with a well-defined syntax and precise semantics;
- A denotational semantics in Communicating sequential processes (CSP) for requirements and domain models written in compliance with the CNL.
- A formal support for further specification, *via* domain model, aside from the original requirements, while preserving the underlying behavior.
- Soundness verification by modelling the Implementation Under Test (IUT) as a CSP process, using *CSP Input-Output Conformance (cspio)* [14] as conformance relation.
- A formal definition for test consistency, a property that ensures that test cases, formerly abstract, can be directly executed in an implementation without inconclusive or inconsistent results.
- Tools implementing the direct engineering from requirements, including the automation of the generated test cases.

In the following section, we propose a CNL and present its grammar, parsing rules, and the framework chosen for implementation. Section 3 introduces CSP and the semantic rules for translating a syntactic tree, obtained after parsing requirements and domain model that comply with the CNL, into a CSP model. In Sect. 4, we introduce the *ioco* testing theory, together with its CSP adaptation (cspio). Then, we discuss how to generate sound and consistent test cases by means of CSP refinement assertions. With the resulting traces, we show how to translate them back to natural language and how to map them into automated scripts. Finally, Sect. 5 discusses related work, while Sect. 6 presents our conclusions, summarizes our contributions, and discusses next steps. In particular, future research could explore two integration strategies, both based on Large Language Models (LLMs). One possibility is a mapping approach to infer the frames and slots directly from free-style natural language. An alternative could be translating free-style requirements into grammatically and semantically valid CNL constructs. This would preserve the interpretability and verifiability of the CNL framework while automating its most labor-intensive aspects.

2   Parsing CNL-Compliant Requirements

The pursuit of an integrated testing process eventually has to face the following question: *which notation should be adopted?* As it is further discussed in Sect. 5, there are several proposed frameworks which adopt *ad-hoc* notations to represent the requirements and the generated artifacts. However, one major downfall of adopting such notations is finding (or training) specialists. Thus, the answer to our initial question may indicate the use of a widely known notation: our written natural language since it is ubiquitous and expressive. While natural language is a widely known notation, because of its ambiguous nature, it may not be deterministically interpreted by an algorithm. Then, there is no straightforward way to define a meaningful mapping between textual descriptions and their semantic representations. This lack of precision typically leads to, for instance, an abstract gap between sentences and the actual corresponding execution code. In this light, we propose the use of an CNL, allowing the users to write artifacts in English while certifying that a standard is being followed, leading to a deterministic machine interpretation.

2.1   Frame Structure

We adopted a framework for knowledge representation that allows computer interpretation. The chosen schema is heavily built upon the concept of a *frame*, which is a structure to store data about a stereotyped situation, as defined in [13]. Our work was also inspired by the linguistic approach to semantic representation known as Case Frames [8], which focus on the verb. Each verb defines its own frame, as verb complements may vary.

These frames contain prefixed *slots* that, when filled, represent an instance of a specific situation. Each slot holds a different purpose. Consequently, there

Table 1. Frame example

Required (Static)			Extra (Dynamic)		
Agent	Operation	Patient	Sender	Receiver	Title
(User)	Send	Email Message	filipe.arruda@cetene.gov.br	acas@cin.ufpe.br	Smartest

can be a specific rule (or set of rules) for filling each slot. Because our purpose is to ultimately represent test actions, our frames should convey elements that resemble test steps. In our context, the "agent" slot defaults to the user, since our frames aim to describe how a user (tester) can interact with the SUT. The verb slot is named as 'operation', and its immediate complement is always the 'patient' (see Table 1). We also adapted the Frame theory by dividing the slots into two categories: Required and Extra. The former must be present in every frame, acting as a unique identifier. The latter, instead, does not define the action intention, but all other dynamic properties and modifiers of a situation. This separation allows us to use the required slots as unique identifiers (when mapping to script methods) and pass the dynamic slot values as arguments.

2.2   Syntax

Our main goal when designing the CNL is to write any test artifact using the same subset of natural language, following the same rules. To provide a general idea of which sentences comply with our CNL, we present in [3] an overview of the grammar (excerpt) using the Extended Backus-Naur Form (EBNF) notation.

To simplify the presentation of the syntax, we begin by illustrating a simple sentence that complies with intermediate production rules. For instance, the production rule for Actions states that it is required to have an Operation and a Patient. Thus, the following basic sentence would be successfully recognized: *A message is sent.* The word "message" would be the Patient while "send" would be the Operation. Additionally, an action can have Agent, Modality, Polarity and a Predicative Qualifier. For illustration, a sentence containing all these slots is: *The user must not send a message early.* In this case, we incremented the initial sentence by adding the "user" as Agent, a Required Modality (represented by the modal verb "must"), the Negative Polarity and a Predicative Qualifier (adjective "early"). Also, the patient slot can be further incremented. For instance, we could add an anaphoric reference by replacing "message" for the pronoun "it". Also, we could add an attributive adjective for the object in question, or even a quantifier. Finally, we could use coordinating conjunctions to join two patients and form a more complex one (noun phrase coordination).

To describe requirements, sentences may have a Circumstance, which can be a Single (or recurrent) Event or a Condition. Each Circumstance has a corresponding preceding conjunction, namely "when", "if" and "until" (and their synonyms). For instance, the following sentence has a circumstance: *When the button is pressed then a message is sent.* Ultimately, both Circumstances and

Statements are described by means of Actions, allowing us to use a single structure for conditions and tasks, More complex configurations can be found by exploring the other production rules, but the above examples represent the core language we defined. Implementation details are discussed next.

2.3   CNL Implementation

The CNL requirements and Backus-Naur Form (BNF) both give an idea of what sentences comply with our standard. However, other technical and functional issues arise when implementing these constraints.

To implement the parser, we used The Grammatical Framework (GF). It is both a theoretical framework and a special-purpose programming language for the description of natural languages [2]. It was designed to have an out-of-the-box support for the complexities found in natural languages [16]. Every GF grammar is composed of one abstract syntax and one or more concrete syntaxes. Abstract syntaxes model a specific application domain (similarly to ontologies), whereas concrete syntaxes are language-dependent and thus the latter encode a particular idiom. Because there is a separation between the syntaxes, the abstract one can be used as interlingua between multiple concrete languages [2].

The development of domain-specific application grammars, such as the one defined in this work, usually reuses a subset of the natural language syntax and lexicon to reduce ambiguity. To ease this burden, GF provides a Resource Grammar Library (RGL), which covers comprehensive morphologies and syntactic structures from more than 20 languages [11]. In this light, instead of defining from scratch the inner workings of a natural language, we can reuse the mature syntactic and morphologic paradigms, detailed by specialists, already present in the RGL. For instance, to create a full-fledged sentence using RGL, we could use the mkS function with the following signature: $mkS\ (Tense) \rightarrow (Ant) \rightarrow (Pol) \rightarrow Cl \rightarrow S$. This function must receive a tense (conditional, future, past or present), an anteriority (anterior or simultaneous), polarity (positive or negative), and a declarative clause to be adapted.

In our scenario, not only do we need to parse a sentence but also to manipulate the parse tree in order to linearize it in different ways. For instance, a test step must always be in the imperative mood, while requirements may be presented in the indicative mood. Even though the action (identified by its frame slots) remains the same, its linearization may differ depending on the artifact.

3   Formal Semantics for CNL-Compliant Specifications

We define a formal semantics for compliant requirement models via mapping into CSP models. More specifically, we map actions and circumstances into CSP events and processes. We then use the FDR model checking tool to automate conformance verification and Test Case (TC) generation, via process refinement checking. A distinguishing feature of using a process algebra like CSP for this purpose is abstraction. Since test generation is expressed in terms of counterexamples obtained from refinement checking using FDR, rather than by defining ad-hoc algorithms for each modeling formalism [14], we reason at a purely process algebraic level, agnostic to the structure of a particular model. As a result, there is no need for manipulation of state spaces or control flow, which are typical in algorithmic test generation approaches based on operational models such as Labelled Transition System (LTS) or Finite-State Machine (FSM). Also, in a process algebraic context, it is possible to extend an approach that consider ony control flow with data and timed aspects, for instance.

Communicating Sequential Processes (CSP) is a formal notation for modeling concurrent systems using algebraic, denotational, and operational approaches. Its core abstractions are processes and events. An event is a basic modeling unit representing any given situation. The abstraction level depends on which behaviors are relevant to the model. The other basic elements of CSP are the fundamental processes *Stop* and *Skip*, which model the absence of communication (deadlock) and successful termination, respectively. In addition to those core elements, one can use a rich repertoire of algebraic operators [17].

3.1 Semantics of Requirements

Because we aim to define a formal semantics for the proposed CNL requirements in CSP, in order to be able to reason about soundness and consistency we must adopt an appropriate mapping that reflects the dynamics of interacting with a SUT to observe its responses. In this light, we represent the requirements in terms of input and output events. The testing theory is discussed in Sect. 4.

Test actions are the building blocks of test steps, domain models and requirements. Then, since all artifacts are just different kinds of compositions of these actions, we provide a mapping between the test action elements and CSP processes. Due to the testing theory we adopt, there must be a distinction between input and output events in a specification. The intuition for interpreting a requirement is simple: every action from a requirement circumstance is mapped to an input event, while the actions within a statement are translated into outputs.

Here we present the initial semantic rule that translates the specifications into CSP processes and events. All semantic rules are detailed in the extended version [3]. It is worth mentioning that, for simplicity, we assume that all necessary channels and auxiliary sets are declared. The initial and more abstract artifact is the feature document, in which the requirements are listed. Each requirement, in turn, can be represented by one or more normalized sentences. The metalanguage expressions used to define the semantic rules are underlined and highlighted with a different color (gray). We also use meta keywords to define auxiliary and local functions (*let...within*) and other variables (*where*). The symbol $\widehat{=}$ denotes a function definition.

Rule 1. Feature $[\![$ feature: Feature $]\!]$ =

$$
\begin{aligned}
&\underline{\text{let }} \text{list(current, remaining)} \;\hat{=} \\
&\quad \underline{\text{if }} \#\text{remaining} = 0 \\
&\qquad [\![\, \text{current} \,]\!] \\
&\quad \underline{\text{else}} \\
&\qquad [\![\, \text{current} \,]\!] \; [+ \; \alpha_{current} \cap \alpha_{head\ remaining} \; +] \; \text{list(head remaining, tail remaining)} \\
&\underline{\text{within}} \\
&\quad REQ = \text{list(head sentences, tail sentences)} \\
&\underline{\text{where}} \\
&\quad \text{sentences} = \text{normalize(feature.sentences)}
\end{aligned}
$$

Rule 1 shows that a feature is composed of a sequence of sentences. Each sentence is then semantically interpreted in a separate rule. Finally, the final specification, called REQ, is defined by using the synchronizing external choice operator between all individual sentences. Each sentence usually represents a single requirement, but there are cases where it can represent more than one. This is why we have to normalize them by searching the sentence for disjunctions.

Each normalized sentence (by splitting disjunctions when necessary) is mapped to a CSP process by converting its circumstances (inputs) and statements (outputs) into event sequences. This conversion also assigns a unique identifier to each action by concatenating its slot values, and prefixes it with $i\_$ or $o\_$ according to whether it represents an input or an output event. The result is a precise event trace for each sentence, which the FEATURE rule then composes using the synchronizing external choice operator to form the complete specification. To illustrate these semantic rules presented in the previous section, consider the feature: *i) A message must be sent after the option is enabled. ii) When the option is enabled the main screen should be shown.* By applying Rule 1, assuming that $sentences = [sentence_i, sentence_{ii}]$, REQ is defined as the resulting process of applying the synchronizing external choice operator over both processes, as shown below:

Example 1. REQ = i_enableoption $\rightarrow$ o_sendmessage $\rightarrow$ *Skip*
$\quad [+ \{i\_enableoption\} +]$
$\quad$ i_enableoption $\rightarrow$ o_showmainscreen $\rightarrow$ *Skip*

3.2   Semantics of Domain Models

While requirements describe what should be implemented and tested, domain models give details on how. It is especially relevant for test engineers to give concrete implementation details when creating test cases so manual testers and the automation team can execute the tests without guessing undocumented behaviors. These concrete details can be expressed through associations between actions which together form a domain model.

The following description presents a sample domain model related to "Sending a message". There is a well-known *dependency* between "Send a message" and "Activate a connection", requiring the connection to be activated before sending a message. Conversely, "Activating the Airplane Mode" *cancels* any action of "Activating a connection". Thus, if airplane mode is activated after the connection, the connection must be activated again before attempting to send a message. The *instantiation* relation represents concrete and alternative ways to execute an action; for instance, to "Activate a connection", one can "Activate the WiFi" or "Activate the 4G". Finally, "Open the app", "Write a message", and "Submit the message" describe the ordered steps to "Send a message", and these actions can also be further detailed.

Rule 2 gives an overview of the main events and processes used to model the domain. We define the *DOMAIN* process that uses a replicated external choice operator over all main inputs, followed by a recursive call. *domain_main_inputs* includes only the main inputs, i.e., the first (source) input event of a relation. For instance, by envisioning the domain model as a graph, a dependency between two actions could be represented by the edge $i\_sendmessage \rightarrow i\_turnwifion$ ("send message" depends on "turning the wifi on"), in which the first node would be the main input.

Rule 2. Domain ⟦ domain: Domain ⟧ =

```
DOMAIN = [] main_input: domain_main_inputs @ EXECUTE(main_input);
DOMAIN
   EXECUTE(x) = (INJECT(x) [] NOTINJECT(x)); CANCELS(x)
   INJECT(x) = DEP(x); COMPOSITE(x); INJECTED(x)
   COMPOSITE(x) = execute.x -> INSTANTIATE(x); x -> executed.x -> SKIP
   ⟦ domain.dependencies ⟧
   ⟦ domain.cancellations ⟧
   ⟦ domain.details ⟧
   ⟦ domain.instantiations ⟧
   ⟦ domain.consistencyChoices ⟧
```

Then, we have the definition of *EXECUTE* which, in words, describes the steps of how to consistently execute an action by considering its details. Its definition begins by presenting a choice between two distinct parameterized processes *INJECT* and *NOTINJECT*. It introduces the possibility of modeling what happens when the execution is consistent and when it is not. The latter is especially important when testing for setup error scenarios. By diving on the *INJECT* definition, we identify a sequential composition of *DEP*, *COMPOSITE* and INJECTED. The processes *DEP* and INJECTED are placeholders for describing what should be executed before and after any given action. *DEP* is only defined for actions that have dependencies. In its definition, discussed in Rule 3, the actions that should be executed before x will be declared. *COMPOSITE* is a process for detailing how to execute the input x. Its definition shows the auxiliary events *execute* and *executed*, to mark exactly before and after the action execution. Other processes can add events related to the execution of x by synchronizing with these auxiliary marks. If x is an abstract input, for instance, the concrete actions will be recursively listed. It is worth mentioning that, between these auxiliary events, instead of just synchronizing with x we call the process *INSTANTIATE* which is a placeholder for the cases when an abstract action can be executed in different but equivalent ways.

After the definition of these core processes, we have the characterization of all actual dependencies, cancellations, details, instantiations and consistency choices. Rule 3 shows that, for all dependencies present on the domain model, we define an "instance" of *DEP*, pattern matching with the given event *main*. The definition of *DEP* shows that there are two alternatives: the setup is already executed or it should be executed. We rely on the FDR analysis mechanism to give the shortest trace, thus not including re-execution of dependencies when it is not necessary. The *VERIFY_DEP* makes clear that if the dependency was already executed (via *EXECUTE*) then it will synchronize with the auxiliary event *isexecuted*. Finally, *DEP(_)* is defined for all the other cases when an action does not have dependencies.

Rule 3. Dependencies ⟦ dependencies: DependencyList ⟧ =

```
for main, deps @ dependencies
   DEP(main.id) = for dep in deps
     (VERIFY_DEP(dep.id) [] EXECUTE(dep.id));
DEP(_) = SKIP
VERIFY_DEP(x) = isexecuted.x -> SKIP
```

While all rules are detailed in an extended version [3], we give a brief description of the remaining rules next. *Cancellations* describe which events must be re-executed when a given main action is performed, covering incompatible actions (e.g., logging out cancels a previous login). *Details* specify the concrete steps to execute an abstract action as a sequence of sub-actions, inspired by the composite design pattern. *Instantiations* are similar, but define an action in terms of equivalent alternatives, allowing flexibility in execution (e.g., activating WiFi or 4G to establish a connection). Consistency choices model both success scenarios and what should happen when setup actions are missing, enabling the specification of explicit behaviors for inconsistent executions and reducing inconclusive analysis results.

To illustrate the semantic rules for domain models presented above, we get the partial CSP model as follows:

$DEP(i\_sendmessage) = (VERIFY\_DEP(i\_activatedata) ~[]~ EXECUTE(i\_activatedata))$

$DEP(\_) = Skip$

$CANCELS(i\_activateairplanemode) = cancels.i\_activateconnection \rightarrow Skip$

$CANCELS(\_) = Skip$

$DETAILS(i\_sendmessage) = EXECUTE(i\_openapp);~ EXECUTE(i\_writemessage);$
$$EXECUTE(i\_submitmessage)$$

$DETAILS(\_) = Skip$

$INSTANTIATE(i\_activateconnection) = EXECUTE(i\_activatewifi)$
$$[]~ EXECUTE(i\_activatefourg)$$

$INSTANTIATE(x) = DETAILS(x)$

Since the domain model and requirements are defined in terms of CSP processes, we can now leverage generation mechanisms built upon refinement checkers to generate sound and consistent tests. A fitting generation mechanism is discussed in the next section.

4   Sound and Consistent TC Generation and Automation

Because test completeness is not feasible, we can not assume that a System Under Test (SUT) is correct only because some test cases passed. However, if we guarantee that whenever a test fails, then the SUT is not conformant to the requirements, we say that this particular test is sound. The approach to generate sound test cases is to define a formal conformance relation between implementation and specification, from which we derive valid test cases.

4.1   Test Generation

Based on a conformance relation, test cases can be automatically generated from the input test model using algorithms which ensure that the generated tests satisfy relevant properties, such as *soundness*. Informally, soundness means that if an IUT fails a test case, then the IUT does not conform to the model from which the test was generated. The *ioco* (Input-Output Conformance) [19] is one of the most widely used conformance relations. It is based on Input-Output LTS (LTS) that in turn are a special class of Labelled Transition System (LTS). IOLTS events, unlike LTS, are partitioned into input and output events.

Definition 1 (ioco).
$$i ~ioco~ s \stackrel{\frown}{=} \forall \sigma \in straces(s) \bullet out(\Delta_i, \sigma) \subseteq out(\Delta_s, \sigma)$$
$$where ~ out(X, \sigma) = \{e : O_\delta \mid \sigma ^\frown \langle e \rangle \in straces(X)\}$$

Definition 1 states that an implementation i conforms to a given specification Δ_s when the set of observed outputs after "performing" any suspension trace (σ) in i is a subset of the observed outputs after the same trace (σ) in Δ_s. Suspension traces, in addition to the original concept of traces, include the observation of quiescence [6]. The symbol Δ_x, where x is any LTS, represents x behavior after adding δ in every state that manifests quiescence. Likewise, the symbol δ annotated on the set O indicates that it includes quiescence. Quiescence represents the lack of observable behavior, as in deadlocks, livelocks, and output locks. Considering this definition, we can establish that *iolts2* ioco *iolts1* but the opposite is not true, since *o_dialog* is not an output observable in *iolts2* after the trace $\langle i\_send \rangle$: $out(iolts1, \langle i\_send \rangle) \not\subseteq out(iolts2, \langle i\_send \rangle)$

To allow an automated conformance verification and further test case generation via model checking, without relying on ad-hoc algorithms, we will use a process algebraic characterization of the ioco relation in CSP called *CSP Input-Output Conformance (cspio)*. This new relation also assumes that the events are partitioned into inputs and outputs and that the Implementation Under Test (IUT) can be modelled as a CSP process. Similar to *ioco*, any given IUT conforms to a specification S if, after performing the same available traces, the outputs from IUT are a subset of the S outputs. To automate the verification of this conformance relation, it is encoded as the following CSP refinement check:

Definition 2 (cspio   verification). $S \quad \sqsubseteq_T \quad (S \quad \triangle \quad ANY(\Sigma_{Io},$ $Stop)) \, |[\, \Sigma_{IUT} \,]| \, IUT$

The intuition of the right-hand side of the refinement check (Definition 2) is to offer all possible specification traces for the implementation to synchronize and verify the outputs. The direct comparison between S and IUT would not work, since IUT can have, by definition, traces not present in S, because it can accept extra inputs or offer additional outputs after a trace that does not belong to S [6]. Then, $(S \triangle ANY(\Sigma_{Io}, Stop)) \, |[\, \Sigma_{IUT} \,]| \, IUT$ masks IUT traces that should not be verified by *cspio*. It blocks inputs not accepted by S, and the interruption of S on $ANY(\Sigma_{Io}, Stop)$ allows synchronization of output events from IUT that S does not produce, terminating the process. If this interruption happens, then the refinement would be false, as expected. If the resulting process does not produce different outputs from the same inputs, then the refinement is valid and IUT cspio S.

The Abstract Test Generator (ATG) provides guided test generation based on the *cspio* conformance relation [14] and CSP traces semantics. Its core idea is to exercise a specification, obtain relevant scenarios as counterexamples of refinement verification, and generate sound test cases from them. From a specification S, traces satisfying a given property can be extracted, with optional selection criteria expressed as test purpose (partial specifications), also defined as CSP processes, that describe the desired aspects for generated tests. A common mechanism involves adding marker events $(MARK = accept.n)$ to S to obtain S', then using refinement checking on $S \sqsubseteq_T S'$; counterexamples of the form $ts \smallfrown \langle m \rangle$ yield the scenarios.

A test case (Test Case (TC)) is a CSP process that interacts with the implementation (IUT) through parallel composition, with verdict events *pass*, *fail*, or *inco* indicating the outcome. Test case alphabets are dual to those of the *IUT*: test outputs are *IUT* inputs, and *IUT* outputs are test inputs. An important property that should be pursued when generating test cases is that these TCs should not generate false fails. This property, known as soundness, guarantees that when a test execution reaches a fail verdict then the implementation, for sure, does not conform to the specification. The Definition 3 formally defines a sound test case in CSP:

Definition 3 (Soundness).
$$\langle fail \rangle \in traces(EXEC \setminus (\Sigma_{I_{IUT}} \cup \Sigma_{O_{IUT}})) \Rightarrow \neg(IUT \ cspio \ S)$$

To build a sound test case from a test scenario, we have to make sure that it records all output events that the specification communicates at each step of the given scenario. The process of building the sound test case is iterative and begins with a default annotated trace *atrace* with the format $\langle (ev_i, out_i) ^\frown (accept.n, \{\}) \rangle \bullet 1 <= i <= \#ts$ where ev_i is the ith element of *ts* and out_i the corresponding set of output events after performing the trace until ev_{i-1}.

Consistency Analysis. The domain is modeled with CSP events and processes. However, the actual processes that carry out the consistency analysis are discussed next. The core idea is to combine the original requirements in parallel with the domain to build a more detailed specification, which is then used to generate test cases that are consistent in that there are no missing steps necessary for their executions by a test driver.

For a test case to be consistent, all rules expressed in the associated domain model must be satisfied. As presented in Sect. 3.2, these rules can encompass dependencies, compositions, and other relations.

To keep track of which actions are active at each step, we define the process *EXECUTION_HISTORY*, which allows other processes to synchronize with it to check whether an input is currently active. For instance, when evaluating the dependencies of *i_submitmessage*, it could detect that *i_activatedata* was already executed and, therefore, skip its execution. The *EXECUTION_HISTORY* process applies the replicated interleave operator to parametrize a process *LOOP* with all events that may occur from the domain model. The *LOOP* process maintains the record of which actions were executed, synchronizing with the markers *execute* and *executed* whenever an input event is performed on the *REQ* process or by the *DOMAIN* itself.

Listing 1.1 presents the augmented specification that is used to generate concrete test cases: the resulting process of putting the requirements, domain model, and execution history together. The first process, *CONSISTENCY_ANALYZER*, is the result of combining the *DOMAIN* from Sect. 3.2 with the *EXECUTION_HISTORY* process discussed above. With this process, it is possible to reason about consistency since we combine the effects of the rules from the domain model with the expected execution progress. *REQ_MARKED*, in turn, is another intermediate process that adds information about consistency choices directly on the original requirements. Finally,

Listing 1.1. Consistent specification

```
CONSISTENCY_ANALYZER = DOMAIN  [| aux_domain_events |]
    ↪ EXECUTION_HISTORY
REQ_MARKED = REQ [+ inter(req_events, choice_events) +]
    ↪ CHOICES
SPEC = (REQ_MARKED [| union(inter(req_events, domain_events),
    ↪ consistency_success_events) |] CONSISTENCY_ANALYZER)   \
    ↪ all_aux_events
assert REQ* [T= SPEC*
assert SPEC* [T= REQ*
```

SPEC is the process used later as the specification for test case generation. Instead of capturing only the original and abstract requirements, it now holds more detailed events to generate concrete and consistent test cases.

Since we add behavior to the initial requirements, we must ensure that the original behavior is still preserved. It is important to have a guarantee that any information about the domain does not interfere with the core behavior. While it could be valuable for other scenarios, it is important in our industrial context to ensure that any information added by test analysts (or any other stakeholders) does not tamper with, for instance, third party requirements or critical functionalities. The assertions guarantee not only that the new specification is a refinement of the original requirement, but also that they are in fact equivalent. The refinement, in both directions, is checked after hiding the extra and auxiliary events from both processes.

A test scenario is built from the counterexample produced by checking the model against a specific test purpose. The scenario is then annotated to include all possible outputs for each step. This annotation is important to mark inconclusive results, i.e., outputs that are not relevant for the current scenario, but are possible outcomes defined in the specification [18]. The annotated trace is then supplied to *TC_BUILDER* to build a sound test case. Since the process *TC_BUILDER* is sound [18], the resulting test case is always sound and can then be linearized back to natural language. Each input event becomes a test step, while the corresponding output event is the expected result. We can trace back the action using the *id* from the trace. With its corresponding syntactic structure, we can linearize the action back to English, as seen in Sect. 2.

The total number of scenarios depends on the number of circumstances in the original requirement. It can be calculated by the combination $\binom{n}{k}$ with n as the number of circumstances and $k = 2$, since a circumstance has only two states: it either happens or it does not. There are some cases in which the additional requirements are too obvious or trivial, or even do not make sense. In these cases, the analysts can remove the test cases from the selection after generation.

4.2 Test Case Automation

The output of the proposed test generation strategy is sound and consistent test cases that comply with our CNL. Because these test cases are already consistent, there is no need to insert supplementary setup or reorganize the script since all dependencies and details defined in the domain model are already resolved. Only the mapping to execution methods (which the test adapter recognizes) is lacking. For this matter, we present here a straightforward strategy: direct code mapping.

This straightforward strategy consists of mapping CNL-compliant sentences into their corresponding scripts. This direct association is possible due to the action representation parsed from the sentence. Following the frame theory, we can assign a unique identifier to the fixed frame slots (such as operation and patient) and then map each singular frame to the corresponding script method. We implemented this mapping mechanism using a proprietary framework adopted within the industrial context of our research. Because it is not publicly available, we instead present an analogous implementation using the Java programming language and the UIAutomator framework [1] for Android UI Testing. Listing 1.2 shows an example of this sentence-to-script mapping.

Listing 1.2. Sample Java script mapping

```
@Smartest("press_a_button")
public void pressButton(String identifier, String description, String
    ↪ text) {
...
  mDevice.findObject(selector).click();
}
```

In Listing 1.2, Line 2, we have a method declaration that is mapped to a sentence by the annotation in Line 1. The parameters have the same name as the slots the associated frame can have. Line 4 shows a method call on the variable *mDevice* that holds the API access to functions related to user interactions with the connected device. The API for the interaction with a device may differ from one automation framework to another.

Because the sentences are CNL-compliant, it does not matter how they were written since they will always be mapped to their corresponding method and the arguments. This mapping must be made for all atomic actions. Since all other actions are compositions of these basic actions, the automation effort is kept at a minimum. The choice of which actions should be atomic is entirely dictated by the team. In our scenario, there is a 1:1 mapping from each API native method available to a single action described in text. Then, assuming that the atomic actions are mapped considering the domain model described above, we can generate a code script that, when executed, gives a pass/fail result.

5 Related Work

Although the related work presented here share some features with ours, particularly considering that the inputs are textual documents in natural language, they do have some fundamental differences that are summarized next.

DASE [23], NAT2TEST [5], TaRGeT [7], UMTG [21], and RTCM [25] provide no reuse of specification/test artifacts. Cucumber [24] allows a simple form of reuse when the step is shared among test scenarios. Our work, instead, addresses reuse to a much larger extent. For instance, in our approach, a test case can be a step of a more elaborate test case, whereas a scenario is not qualified as a possible step for reuse in Cucumber.

A recent work [12] leverages pre-trained Natural Language Processing (NLP) models to generate test scripts by matching natural language descriptions with test methods that locate Graphical User Interface (GUI) elements. Because a pre-trained NLP model is applied, there is a considerable error rate while matching, even though only simple and atomic descriptions are used. In our context, using a CNL for requirements and domain model allows us to create accurate matches, define abstract actions on-the-fly, and ensure soundness and consistency.

The aforementioned strategies that generate test scripts adopt specifications that either match the implementation abstraction level or annotate the abstract model with low-level details. Because our strategy proposes a compositional domain model, details can be further added according to the organization's roles and processes. Besides, because the semantics are formally defined to the atomic level, generated test scripts are verified to be sound and consistent. Most of the above-mentioned approaches focus on generation instead of automation of existing test cases. These approaches rely on formal and well-documented requirements from which they can generate TCs. Unfortunately, up-to-date requirements are seldom available in the non-critical software industry. In addition, to allow a fully mechanized generation of automated test cases, the requirements need to be specified at a lower level of abstraction. None of these approaches provide a (bottom-up) alternative to building a domain model from manually generated TCs and allow consistency checks as we propose here.

None of the cited approaches address test step sequence consistency and dependency notions, with an associated verification mechanism; this is a distinguishing contribution of our approach.

Despite the large scope of our work, we do not support some elements featured in other tools or strategies. For instance, even though we support passing data through parameters, we do not generate test input data. We also do not model timed-based behaviors. Finally, the generation mechanism is tied to the cspio relation and cannot be instantiated in other formalisms as easily as in NAT2TEST, which has an intermediate and hidden formalism.

6 Conclusions

In this work, we present a strategy to generate and automate test cases from requirements written in natural language. Our main contribution is to allow testing teams, that are also involved in a similar industrial perspective, to generate sound and consistent test cases automatically while still writing specifications in natural language (whose meaning is automatically obtained using an underlying, and hidden, formal semantics in CSP). Additionally, with the help of a dynamically evolving domain model, test teams are not compelled to specify the entire functionality in a single take, allowing them to postpone more concrete descriptions for other roles down the line or when the feature is mature enough to be tested.

In summary, the scope of this work encompasses requirement and domain model specifications, and the generation of test scripts, including the necessary artifacts in between. Specification, verification, and generation are supported. Because the semantics are formally defined and mechanically verified by custom tools, we ensure two important properties automatically: soundness and consistency. While the former property is well-known and regarded in the literature for test generation, the latter is a major contribution of our work, which ensures that the generated test cases can be executed on a concrete implementation. This consistency notion is derived from the information present in the domain model (dependencies, cancellations, details, etc.) while the generation mechanism ensures that these relations do not change the behavior specified by the requirements. Another major contribution is the definition of a CNL flexible enough for describing both requirements and the corresponding test cases.

6.1 Ongoing and Future Work

Regarding ongoing and future work, it is not uncommon to find teams that do not follow the traditional specification phase and skip it until they need to write test cases. Because of this, there are no requirements to rely on, which blocks test design teams from using established strategies that generate test cases while ensuring soundness. In this situation, the only relevant artifacts are the existing test cases or scripts. Therefore, a possible alternative is to apply a reverse engineering process: the existing scripts can be used to abstract test case descriptions in a CNL, from which use cases can also be derived, and ultimately, into high-level requirements.

While the use of a CNL allows us to precisely define parsing rules and formal semantics, authoring requirements that fully comply with CNL syntactic and semantic constraints remains a non-trivial task. Even though the proposed editor assists users by highlighting errors and providing autocomplete suggestions, some users still find the process cumbersome or restrictive compared to their accustomed modes of expression. This usability challenge represents a key barrier to broader industrial adoption.

In this context, we propose investigating the use of Large Language Models (LLMs) [20, 22] to interpret freestyle natural language descriptions extracted from unstructured requirement documents and transform them into structured representations in the form of *frames* and *slots*. Instead of relying solely on a constrained input format, LLMs could automatically derive the structured information that underpins formal reasoning. While such automatic mappings cannot guarantee complete unambiguity, they hold the potential to significantly enhance productivity and reduce the cognitive overhead associated with CNL authoring. Moreover, this capability would enable the parsing of legacy requirement descriptions.

Then, future research could explore two integration strategies. First, a *direct mapping approach* could aim to use LLMs to infer the frames and slots directly from uncontrolled natural language. Second, an *indirect approach* could leverage LLMs as CNL translators, converting informal requirement sentences into grammatically and semantically valid CNL constructs. This would preserve the interpretability and verifiability of the CNL framework while automating its most labor-intensive aspects.

Acknowledgments. We thank Motorola Mobility, a Lenovo company, for the long-term partnership and for the financial support that has allowed the applicability of research results on test case generation and automation in an industrial context.

References

1. Android: Android uiautomator description (2015). http://developer.android.com/tools/help/uiautomator/index.html. Accessed 25 Mar 2015
2. Angelov, K.: The Mechanics of the Grammatical Framework. Chalmers Tekniska Hogskola (Sweden) (2011)
3. Arruda, F., Barros, F., Sampaio, A.: Extended version: deriving sound test scripts from requirements written in a controlled natural language. https://github.com/fmca/sbmf2025 (2025)
4. Brinksma, E.: A theory for the derivation of tests. In: Proceedings of the 8th International Conference Protocol Specification, Testing and Verification, pp. 63–74. North-Holland (1988)
5. Carvalho, G., et al.: NAT2TESTSCR: test case generation from natural language requirements based on SCR specifications. Sci. Comput. Program. **95**, 275–297 (2014)
6. Cavalcanti, A., Hierons, R.M., Nogueira, S., Sampaio, A.: A suspension-trace semantics for CSP. In: 10th International Symposium on Theoretical Aspects of Software Engineering, TASE 2016, Shanghai, China, July 17–19, 2016, pp. 3–13 (2016). https://doi.org/10.1109/TASE.2016.9
7. Ferreira, F., Neves, L., Silva, M., Borba, P.: Target: a model based product line testing tool. Tools Session of CBSoft (2010)
8. Fillmore, C.J.: The case for case'in bach & harms (eds.) universals in linguistic theory. Holt, Rinehart, and Winston (1968)
9. Gaudel, M.-C.: Testing can be formal, too. In: Mosses, P.D., Nielsen, M., Schwartzbach, M.I. (eds.) CAAP 1995. LNCS, vol. 915, pp. 82–96. Springer, Heidelberg (1995). https://doi.org/10.1007/3-540-59293-8_188
10. Grechanik, M., Xie, Q., Fu, C.: Maintaining and evolving GUI-directed test scripts. In: Proceedings of the 31st International Conference on Software Engineering, ICSE 2009, pp. 408–418. IEEE Computer Society, Washington, DC, USA (2009). https://doi.org/10.1109/ICSE.2009.5070540
11. Gruzitis, N., Paikens, P., Barzdins, G.: Framenet resource grammar library for GF. In: International Workshop on Controlled Natural Language, pp. 121–137. Springer (2012)
12. Li, C.: Mobile GUI test script generation from natural language descriptions using pre-trained model. In: 2022 IEEE/ACM 9th International Conference on Mobile Software Engineering and Systems (MobileSoft), pp. 112–113. IEEE (2022)

13. Minsky, M.: A framework for representing knowledge. The Psychology of Computer Vision (1975)
14. Nogueira, S., Sampaio, A., Mota, A.: Test generation from state based use case models. Formal Asp. Comput. **26**(3), 441–490 (2014)
15. Rafi, D.M., Moses, K.R.K., Petersen, K., Mäntylä, M.V.: Benefits and limitations of automated software testing: Systematic literature review and practitioner survey. In: 2012 7th International Workshop on Automation of Software Test (AST), pp. 36–42. IEEE (2012)
16. Ranta, A.: Grammatical framework: Programming with multilingual grammars, vol. 173. CSLI Publications, Center for the Study of Language and Information Stanford (2011)
17. Roscoe, B.: An operational semantics for CSP (1986)
18. Sampaio, A., Nogueira, S., Mota, A., Isobe, Y.: Sound and mechanised compositional verification of input-output conformance. Softw. Test., Verif. Reliab. **24**(4), 289–319 (2014). https://doi.org/10.1002/stvr.1498
19. Tretmans, J.: Test generation with inputs, outputs and repetitive quiescence. Softw. Concepts Tools **17**(3), 103–120 (1996)
20. Vaswani, A., et al.: Attention is all you need. In: Advances in Neural Information Processing Systems, vol. 30 (2017)
21. Wang, C., Pastore, F., Goknil, A., Briand, L.C., Iqbal, Z.: UMTG: A toolset to automatically generate system test cases from use case specifications. In: Proceedings of the 2015 10th Joint Meeting on Foundations of Software Engineering, pp. 942–945. ESEC/FSE 2015, ACM, New York, NY, USA (2015).https://doi.org/10. 1145/2786805.2803187
22. Wang, J., Huang, Y., Chen, C., Liu, Z., Wang, S., Wang, Q.: Software testing with large language models: survey, landscape, and vision. IEEE Trans. Softw. Eng. **50**(4), 911–936 (2024)
23. Wong, E., Zhang, L., Wang, S., Liu, T., Tan, L.: Dase: document-assisted symbolic execution for improving automated software testing. In: 2015 IEEE/ACM 37th IEEE International Conference on Software Engineeringm vol. 1, pp. 620–631. IEEE (2015)
24. Wynne, M., Hellesoy, A.: The cucumber book: behaviour-driven development for testers and developers. Pragmatic Bookshelf (2012)
25. Yue, T., Ali, S., Zhang, M.: RTCM: a natural language based, automated, and practical test case generation framework. In: Proceedings of the 2015 International Symposium on Software Testing and Analysis, pp. 397–408. ISSTA 2015, ACM, New York, NY, USA (2015). https://doi.org/10.1145/2771783.2771799

Executable Conformance Testing Theories: From Theory to Practice and Back

Gustavo Carvalho[(✉)] [iD], Lucas Santana, Fábio Sobral, and Beatriz Souza

Centro de Informática, Universidade Federal de Pernambuco, 50.740-560 Recife, PE, Brazil
{ghpc,lvcs,fnps,babs}@cin.ufpe.br

Abstract. The presence of software is pervasive in the society, and, due to its impact on our routines, the concern about its quality and reliability is a matter of utmost importance, especially when it comes to critical systems. Although software testing is a crucial step in software production, it is typically associated with some risks and elevated costs, particularly, when carried out manually. Model-based testing (MBT) tools are capable of changing this scenario, enabling automatic test design and execution. However, assessing the correctness of these tools, which are also software developed by humans, is a valid concern too. To alleviate this concern, formal testing approaches are proposed, encompassing a well-defined conformance relation, along with test generation and execution strategies. Moreover, it is typically expected a proof of the soundness of the proposed approach. Unfortunately, many of the devised conformance relations are only theoretically defined, or are associated with disconnected implementations, that is, with no rigorous guarantees that the proposed theory is implemented correctly. Here, we show how an industrial-strength interactive theorem prover (Rocq) can be used to simultaneously formalise and provide a correct mechanisation of conformance testing theories; bridging the gap between theory and practice.

Keywords: Rocq · reactive systems · conformance testing · ioco

1 Introduction

In today's society, the influence of software on human life is evident, pervasive in almost everything from simple everyday activities to the more complex and critical ones. In this context, identifying potential software flaws has become increasingly important, which is typically achieved via testing. In addition to increasing software quality, finding a flaw in the early development stages can significantly reduce the costs of correcting it [13].

Testing is often performed manually. Tests created and executed manually are subject to human error. To ensure higher software quality and reliability, tools capable of automatically generating and executing tests are perceived as a more effective option for the software verification stage.

M. H. ter Beek and L. Teixeira (Eds.): SBMF 2025, LNCS 16363, pp. 119–137, 2026.
https://doi.org/10.1007/978-3-032-12086-1_7

In this context, Model-Based Testing (MBT) techniques are particularly relevant. This technique allows for the automated creation of large numbers of test cases using a model specification of the system to be tested as a starting point. However, the quality of these tools, which are also human-made software, is also a matter of concern, as they are similarly subject to failures that can result in the identification of a nonexistent faults (false positives) or the failure to identify existing faults (false negatives).

The aforementioned problems can be minimised by the use of formal methods, since testing can be formal, too; as emphasised by the title of the seminal paper by Gaudel [6]. In this paper, the author defines the notion of formal testing strategies, with the purpose of demonstrating that the automated generation and execution of tests can be proven correct (*sound*). Particularly, this ensures that any implementation that fails the generated tests does not actually conform to the system specification.

Since the seminal paper by Gaudel, many formal testing theories have been devised, aiming at the verification of different properties, and types of systems. For instance, in [14], we have a testing strategy based on the conformance relation `ioco`. This relation distinguishes input actions from output actions, allowing for a more realistic approach to testing reactive systems. In [7], the authors propose `tioco`, an extension of `ioco` that takes into account time.

Leveraging `ioco` to cope with hybrid systems (i.e., systems that exhibit both discrete and continuous behaviour) is investigated in [10], where a hybrid version of `ioco` is proposed: `hioco`. A different notion of hybrid conformance is considered in [1], which takes into account explicit time and data error bounds. In [8,11], the theory of conformance is further extended to address stochastic cyber-physical systems.

Unfortunately, many of the devised conformance relations are only theoretically defined (i.e., with no concrete implementations, with no supporting software), or are associated with disconnected implementations (i.e., with no guarantees that the implementation reflects the theoretical definition). Motivated by the disconnection between conformance testing theories and their mechanisations, when available, the overall goal of this paper is to show how an industrial-strength interactive theorem prover (Rocq[1] [2] – previously known as Coq) can be used to bridge this gap.

Therefore, in this paper, considering the `ioco` relation as an example, we show how to bridge the gap between the theory and practice of formal conformance testing, simultaneously formalising and providing a correct mechanisation of conformance testing theories. Moreover, we exemplify how moving from the theory to the practice aids in identifying shortcomings of the theory. The main contributions of this work are as follows.

- Formalisation (syntax/semantics) of a language for reactive systems;
- Correct mechanisation for producing the semantics from specifications;
- Graphical visualisations of generated semantics using Graphviz;

---

[1] Link: https://rocq-prover.org/.

– Mechanisation of the `ioco` testing theory for reactive systems;
– Definition of tactics that automates various parts of this work.

This paper is structured in the following sections. Section 2 presents background information necessary to understand this work; particularly, conformance testing based on `ioco`, and the interactive theorem prover Rocq. Section 3 shows how Rocq can be used to both formally specify and provide mechanisation for the definition of models of specifications and implementations, besides checking their conformance. Afterwards, in Sect. 4, we present how to create models of test cases, and check conformance via testing. Finally, Sect. 5 provides our concluding remarks, besides addressing related and future work.

2 Background

First, we discuss the notion of conformance testing based on formal testing theories (Sect. 2.1). Then, we present an overview of Rocq (Sect. 2.2).

2.1 Conformance Testing

Here, we provide an overview of conformance testing, and the foundational work by Tretmans [14] for testing reactive systems with the separation between inputs and outputs. Further details are presented in the following sections, interleaved with our characterisation in Rocq.

Models of Specifications and Implementations. Model-based testing is a testing technique in which tests are generated from models that describe the expected behaviour of the system. These tests are then used to verify that an Implementation Under Test (IUT) satisfies the expected behaviour. These behaviours can be described in terms of a sequence of inputs, actions, outputs, states, and other aspects. Therefore, a starting point consists of defining models of specifications; adopting a modelling notation that is expressive enough to describe the intended behaviour.

Labelled Transition Systems (LTSs) is a notation commonly used to specify the behaviour of reactive systems and, thus, in [14], the authors use LTSs to describe models of specifications, but also of IUTs. An LTS is defined as a structure formed by labeled states and transitions. The states represent the possible states of the system, and the labeled transitions describe actions the system can perform from that state.

Formally speaking, an LTS is a quadruple (Q, L, T, q_0), such that: Q represents the enumerable and non-empty set of states of the system; L is the enumerable set of labels describing system actions; T is the set of transitions given by $T \subseteq Q \times (L \cup \{\tau\}) \times Q$, where $\tau \notin L$; and q_0 is the initial state, where $q_0 \in Q$. It is important to highlight that τ is a special label to characterize the internal actions of the system, that is, actions that are not observable from an external interface.

122   G. Carvalho et al.

Figure 1a, replicated from [14], shows an LTS, named r, represented by a graph. It models a candy machine with an interacting button (but) that dispenses chocolate ($choq$) and liquorice (liq). An arrow highlights the initial state r_0, $Q = \{r_0, r_1, r_2, r_3, r_4, r_5\}$, $L = \{but, liq, choc\}$, and the set of transitions T is $\{(r_0, but, r_1), (r_0, but, r_2), (r_1, liq, r_3), (r_2, but, r_4), (r_4, choc, r_5)\}$.

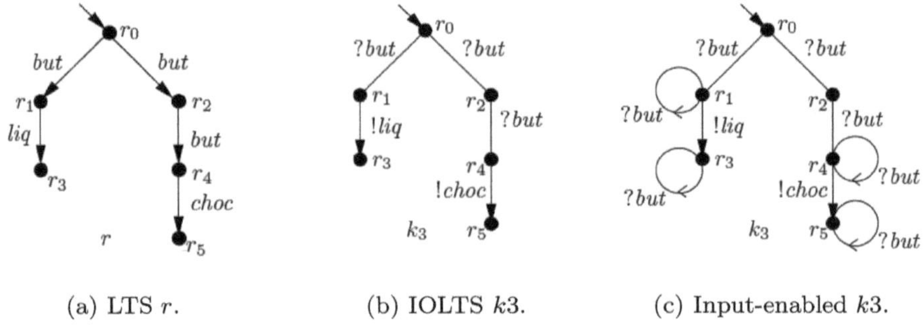

(a) LTS r.   (b) IOLTS $k3$.   (c) Input-enabled $k3$.

Fig. 1. Examples of LTS, IOLTS, and IOTS [14].

Although transition labels explicitly indicate the possible actions that can be performed in the system, the above definitions abstract away whether the actions represent inputs or outputs. To distinguish between input and output labels, in [14], the authors define a new class of LTSs, LTSs with inputs and outputs, where the set of labels L is divided into two new sets: L_I, denoting input actions; and L_U, denoting output actions. This new class is represented by the quintuple (Q, L_I, L_U, T, q_0), where $L_I \cap L_U = \emptyset$, and is equivalent to an LTS $(Q, L_I \cup L_U, T, q_0)$. For ease of visualization, input labels are prefixed with a "?" and output labels with "!"; see Fig. 1b.

Although this nomenclature is not used in [14], here an LTS with inputs and outputs is referred to as an IOLTS. It is important not to confuse this term with an IOTS. An Input-Output Transition Systems (IOTS) models systems where outputs are actions initiated by the system and never rejected by the environment; analogously, inputs are actions initiated by the environment, and never rejected by the system. Consequently, an IOTS is an LTS with inputs and outputs, where, for all reachable states of the system, there are transitions that start from these states with each of the labels of L_I. Therefore, an IOTS can be seen as an input-enabled IOLTS; see Fig. 1c.

Finally, there is a special treatment to cases where the system performs no output actions. In these cases, the lack of response is observed by a special output action called quiescence (δ). A state without output actions is called quiescent. Annotating an LTS with quiescence produces a special class of LTSs.

Although an LTS is a powerful semantic model for representing system implementations and specifications, real systems can contain thousands of states, making their graphical representation or the quadruple (Q, L, T, q_0) impractical. To solve this limitation, it is common to introduce a language such that each expression in this language characterises an LTS. Thus, it is possible to specify more complex systems using language operators that combine simpler systems (expressions). In [14], such a language is called *Behaviour Expressions* (BE). Further details about this language are given later.

Conformance Relation. There are several ways to define whether an implementation is correct relative to a specification. In [14], the authors base their theory on the conformance relation `ioco` (*input-output-conformance*). The work assumes that the implementations to be tested can always be represented by IOTSs, which have input and output sets equal to those in the specification.

Informally, for an implementation i and a specification s, we say i `ioco` s if, and only if, for every possible sequence of labels from s (known as a trace), executing it on i yields an output that is predicted in s. The absence of outputs is also considered; if quiescence is observed at i, then quiescence should be predicted at s.

Models of Test Cases, Test Generation and Execution. Although the conformance relation provides the foundation to assert whether an implementation is correct, it is typically not possible to check its behaviour exhaustively (for every possible sequence of labels). Therefore, we need strategies for testing implementations for correctness. Considering this, in [14], we also have models for describing test cases. Roughly speaking, transitions systems augmented with verdicts (*pass*, *fail*) that synchronise with models of implementations. Outputs of test cases are taken as inputs by the implementations, conversely, the outputs produced by the implementation are received as inputs by the test cases to reach verdicts. To conclude the formalisation of the testing theory, it is also necessary to define an algorithmic way of generating models of test cases from models of specifications; besides formalising the notion of test execution.

Soundness and Completeness. The final step of defining a formal testing theory is to argue about its soundness and completeness. The theory is sound if, and only if, whenever an implementation i fails a test suite T (comprising test cases generated from a specification s), this implementation is necessarily non-conforming with respect to the specification s; that is, $\neg(i$ `ioco` $s)$. A theory is said to be complete if, and only if, it is possible to generate a test suite T such that, if i passes T, than $(i$ `ioco` $s)$. Although theoretically relevant, such a test suite is typically large enough to be feasible in practice.

2.2   Rocq

Rocq, whose previous name was Coq, is a proof assistant (also known as an interactive theorem prover) designed to assist in the creation of formal definitions, algorithms, and mathematical assertions. It is based on the theory of Calculus of Constructions [4], and provides Gallina as a native functional programming language. Every valid computable definition in Gallina must terminate. This way, the language avoids infinite loops and the halting problem. In addition to Gallina, it has a set of predefined tactics that aid in the construction of proofs, as well as a language for defining new tactics (Ltac).

Types, Functions, and Registers. Gallina standard library includes Boolean, numeric, and other common data structures. New types are introduced using the `Inductive` keyword. Types are defined by constructors, which may or may not receive arguments. The definition *nat_list* exemplifies this syntax defining a type comprising lists of natural numbers. There are two constructors: *nil*, representing an empty list, and *cons*, representing a list whose first element is the natural number n followed by a list of natural numbers l.

```
Inductive nat_list : Type :=      Fixpoint app (l1 l2 : nat_list) : nat_list :=
  | nil                             match l1 with
  | cons (n : nat) (l : nat_list).  | nil ⇒ l2
                                    | cons h t ⇒ cons h (app t l2)
                                    end.
```

Non-recursive functions are defined with the `Definition` keyword. Pattern matching (`match`) is often used to describe the body of a function. Recursive functions are typically defined with the `Fixpoint` keyword. The *app* function computes the concatenation of two lists of natural numbers. Note that the first argument always decreases in size with each recursive call to the function; this ensures function termination.

Logical propositions are represented by the `Prop` type. Function *nat_is_even* returns a logical proposition characterising the parity of a number n based on the existence of a natural number k such that $n = 2 * k$.

```
Definition nat_is_even       Inductive Forall :
(n : nat) : Prop :=          (nat → Prop) → nat_list → Prop :=
  ∃ (k : nat), n = 2 × k.       | Forall_nil (P : nat → Prop) : Forall P nil
                                | Forall_cons (P : nat → Prop) (n : nat)
                                  (l : nat_list) : P n → Forall P l →
                                    Forall P (cons n l).
```

Logical propositions can also be defined inductively. In this case, the constructors determine rules for constructing valid propositions. For example, *Forall* relates a list of natural numbers (*nat_list*) and a property on natural numbers (*nat →* `Prop`). Given a proposition P and a list l, the proposition *Forall P l* is true if, and only if, all elements of the list l satisfy the property P. This automatically holds for empty lists (rule *Forall_nil*). Rule *Forall_cons* provides the inductive argument: if P n, and *Forall P l*, then P holds for all elements of the list (*cons n l*).

In Gallina, we also have records. Differently from typical programming languages, a `Record` creates types that group data (variables/attributes) and properties. To create instances, it is necessary to provide values for the variables along with proofs of the defined properties. Definition *even_nat_list* is the type of lists of even natural numbers; (*l*) is its only attribute, and the property (*all_nat_in_l_are_even*) determines that the list *l* contains only even natural numbers.

```
Record even_nat_list : Type := mkEvenNatList {
    l : nat_list ;
    all_nat_in_l_are_even : Forall nat_is_even l
}.
```

Proofs and Theorems. As a proof assistant, one can also propose `Theorem`, and employ proof tactics to demonstrate that the theorem statement holds. Rocq also offers proof automation features. Moreover, in addition to the predefined tactics, one can create new and custom tactics employing an integrated proof language called `Ltac`.

3   Models of Specifications and Implementations

Now, considering the `ioco` conformance testing theory, we show how an interactive theorem prover, such as Rocq, can be used to simultaneously formalise and provide mechanisation for formal testing theories. By doing this, we achieve a mechanisation tightly connected to the theory, bridging the gap to the practice. Also, this aids in identifying shortcomings of the formalisation, as discussed later. Although we illustrate this considering the `ioco` conformance testing theory, the same argument applies to conformance testing based on other relations.

All definitions, theorems, proofs, automation tactics, and examples developed in this work are publicly available in a permanent repository [3]. The general structure of our formalisation is as follows.

- `LTS_*.v` and `IOTS.v` files: provide the foundations by formalising the notion of LTSs, IOLTSs, and IOTSs, which are used as models of specifications and implementations. More details in Sect 3.2.
- `BE_*.v` files: define the syntax and semantics of a process language for specifying reactive systems. More details in Sect 3.1.
- `graphviz.v`: enables graphical visualisation of the models proposed in this work via an integration with Graphviz. More details in Section 3.3.
- `IOCO.v`: formalises the `ioco` conformance relation and associated definitions. More details in Sect 3.4.
- `TTS.v`: formalises models of test cases, besides the notion of test execution. More details in Sect 4.
- Files such as `list_helper.v` and `ltacs.v` provide auxiliary definitions; for instance, the former provides lemmas related to list manipulation, and the latter provides custom tactics developed for assisting the mechanisation of conformance testing theories.

This formalisation comprises more than 4,000 lines of Rocq code. Additional 1,000 lines of code are provided with examples for the developed definitions. Despite the focus on `ioco`, parts of our formalisation can be reused and extended for different purposes. For example, one can use the definitions in `LTS_*.v` to formalise other conformance relations that are not based on `ioco`; similarly, the contents of `BE_*.v` aid the mechanisation of other process languages.

3.1 A Description Language

In [14], the language of Behaviour Expressions (BE) is defined by the following grammar, where a is a label; B is an expression of the language; $\mathcal{B}$ is a set of expressions; G is a set of labels; and P is a process name.

$$B ::= a \; ; B \mid \mathbf{i} \; ; B \mid \Sigma \, \mathcal{B} \mid B \, |[\, G \,]| \, B \mid \mathbf{hide} \; G \; \mathbf{in} \; B \mid P$$

In the language, $a \; ; \; B$ represents the prefix operation, that is, the system performs a (i.e., the action represented by a), and then behaves as B. The same applies to $\mathbf{i} \; ; B$, where $\mathbf{i}$ represents the internal action, whose label is τ. The choice operation is represented by Σ where one of the behaviours from $\mathcal{B}$ is chosen through the actions performed by the system. This operation can also be represented by the operator $\Box$, so that $B_1 \; \Box \; B_2 \; \Box \; B_3$ is equivalent to $\Sigma\{B_1, B_2, B_3\}$.

In $B \, |[\, G \,]| \, B$, two processes execute in parallel, and the actions whose labels are contained in G are executed synchronously, while the others are executed asynchronously. The syntactic sugars $\|$ and $\|\|$ are used to represent, respectively, $|[\, L \,]|$ and $|[\, \emptyset \,]|$, where L is the complete set of labels of the system.

In turn, $\mathbf{hide} \; G \; \mathbf{in} \; B$ represents the behaviour of B by replacing the label actions contained in G with internal actions (τ). Finally, it is possible to use the operator $:: =$ to associate an expression with a name, as in $P :: = \; B$, associating the behaviour B with the process named P. Processes can be referenced in behaviours through their name. Thus, assuming there is a process named P defined, the expression P functions as a reference to the behaviour of the process named P, that is, to the behaviour B. For those familiar with process languages, such as CSP [12], it can be seen that the language considered in [14] is a simple yet representative one.

In Rocq, this language is formalised via *ProcessBehaviour*. We have one constructor for each syntactic construction of the language, and the formalisation closely follows the above grammar. *Event* is an inductive type that represents both external and internal ($\mathbf{i}$) actions, thus, allowing for both types of prefix operations.

```
Inductive ProcessBehaviour :=
  | Prefix : Event → ProcessBehaviour → ProcessBehaviour
  | Choice : ChoiceSet → ProcessBehaviour
  | Parallel : ProcessBehaviour → set EventName → ProcessBehaviour →
              ProcessBehaviour
  | Hide : ProcessBehaviour → set EventName → ProcessBehaviour
  | ProcessInstantiation : ProcessName → ProcessBehaviour
with ChoiceSet :=
      | Values : set ProcessBehaviour → ChoiceSet.
```

Additionally, the type *ProcessDefinition* associates a *ProcessName* (a string) with a *ProcessBehaviour*. Finally, *BehaviourExpressions* comprises a list of *ProcessDefinition*, along with necessary well-formedness conditions (e.g., the processes have unique names).

Using `Notation`, we also define a concrete syntax for the language, which allows us to write specifications as *fig1_r_BE*. It declares, using Behaviour Expressions, the LTS previously shown in Fig. 1a; *STOP* denotes the choice between an empty set of behaviours (also known as a deadlock, a state with no outgoing transitions).

```
Definition fig1_r_BE : BehaviourExpressions.
Proof.
    create_behaviour_expressions
      ["fig1_r" ::= "but";; "liq";; STOP [] "but";; "but";; "choc";; STOP].
```

It worth noting that *create_behaviour_expressions* is an auxiliary definition (see the excerpt below) that proves automatically the associated well-formedness conditions. First, this custom tactic refines the current proof goal, and then applies a specific decision procedure to each generated subgoal; the symbol | separates such procedures. For example, in the first one, it verifies whether process definitions are associated with unique names. Proving the second subgoal ensures that there are no references to undefined process names.

```
Ltac create_behaviour_expressions expressions :=
    refine (mkBehaviourExpressions expressions _ _ _ _);
    [ list_has_no_dup_with_error
      ltac:(fun x ⇒ fail 0 "The process" x "is defined twice")
    | simpl; repeat split; (elem_in_list ||
        match goal with
        | ⊢ _ = ?x ∨ _ ⇒ fail 0 "Invalid reference to" x
        end)
    | ... ].
```

The semantics of the language is described through a Structural Operational Semantics (SOS). An SOS defines the meaning of a language element by formalising what computation will be induced from that element. In the case of BE, we have rules associated with each syntactic operator.

In Roqc, the semantics is formalised through the relation *sosR*, an inductive definition where each SOS rule is represented by one or more constructors. The inductive type relates two elements of *ProcessBehaviour* and an *Event*. For the elements of the relation, it means that, there is a transition from one behaviour, which can be seen as a state, to another with a label represented by the event.

In our work, we define a function *create_LTS_from_BE* to automatically compute the LTS from a given specification in the language BE. Furthermore, we prove that our function is correct, which means that for any obtained LTS, it follows precisely from the SOS, and its well-formedness conditions also hold. It is worth noting that here we take advantage of the possibility of defining functions in proof mode, which means that, at the same time, we define how to compute an LTS from a Behaviour Expression, and prove that the obtained LTS is correct (i.e., all associated well-formedness conditions hold) by construction. We comment on some of these conditions in the following section. These "create" functions (*create_behaviour_expressions* and *create_LTS_from_BE*) are defined in the file `ltacs.v`.

By doing this, we enable the creation of tools to inspect, analyse, and test transition systems from behaviour expressions with the guarantee that the computation is correct, and strictly follows the semantics defined. In what follows, we illustrate the application of this function to definition *fig1_r_BE* in order to obtain the LTS shown in Fig. 1a. The number 6 consists in a user-defined computation (recursion) upper bound. This is necessary since from a Behaviour Expression, it is possible to express an LTS with an infinite number of states. If the provided bound is not sufficient to finish the construction of the LTS, an error is signaled to the user.

> **Definition** *fig1_r* : *LTS*.
> **Proof.** *create_LTS_from_BE* *fig1_r_BE* "fig1_r" 6. **Defined.**

It is important to say that, when formalising this part of the theory, at first, we were not able to prove the termination of *create_LTS_from_BE*. After careful analysis, we noticed that this could only be proved by admitting an additional well-formedness condition for the language BE. As discussed in detail in [12, p. 100], the combination of hiding with recursion does not always form constructive expressions, preventing us from reaching a unique fix point.

Consider the expression shown below. It defines a process P that initially communicates a, followed by a recursive call, however, hiding further communications of a. In the theory of process algebras, the behaviour introduced by this recursive call is known as divergence: an infinite unbroken sequence of internal actions. Although the underlying semantics could capture such a behaviour by defining a state with a self-loop labelled with a τ, the absence of a unique fix point prevents the direct application of the SOS rules from generating a finite number of states.

$$P ::= a \; ; \; \textbf{hide } a \textbf{ in } P$$

When mechanising a theory, this is an important aspect to consider, and, thus, tools like FDR^2, a refinement checker for the CSP process algebra, prohibit such types of recursions. Instead, one could capture the same behaviour by communicating a followed by P'', whose events are hidden (see the definition of P').

$$P' :: = a \ ; \ \textbf{hide} \ a \ \textbf{in} \ P''$$
$$P'' :: = a \ ; \ P''$$

This result emphasises how bridging the gap between theory and practice gets back to the theory, highlighting missing discussions that are relevant when constructing tools to enable practical applications of the theory.

3.2   Transition Systems

Our Rocq characterisation of `ioco` conformance testing defines types for the needed formalisms of transitions systems (e.g., LTSs, IOLTSs, and IOTSs). We use records to promote cohesion between the constituents attributes, and associated well-formedness conditions. For instance, in what follows, we show part of the record LTS.

```
Record LTS : Type := mkLTS {
      Q : set state
    ; L : set label
    ; T : set transition
    ; q0 : state

    ; Q_non_empty : Q ≠ []
    ; q0_in_Q : In q0 Q
    ; valid_transitions : each_transition_is_valid T Q L
    ; ...
}.
```

The first four attributes (Q, L, T, and $q0$) follow from its theoretical definition (see Sect. 2.1). Then, we also formalise the associated well-formedness conditions; for example, Q cannot be empty (property Q_non_empty), $q0$ is an element of Q (property $q0\_in\_Q$). The property $valid\_transitions$ states that each transition in T must relate states in Q by means of labels in L, this is ensured by the auxiliary definition $each\_transition\_is\_valid$.

As mentioned before, when creating instances of such types, one needs to provide values to the attributes, but also prove that the properties hold for them. In our formalisation, we also provide the user with custom tactics for automatically discharging these proofs. For example, the tactic $solve\_LTS\_rules$, after informing the `Record` instance data through the `apply` command, uses pattern matching to invoke other auxiliary tactics; e.g., $elem\_in\_list$ checks whether an

---

[2] Link: https://cocotec.io/fdr/.

element belongs to a list.

```
Ltac solve_LTS_rules Q L T q0 := apply (mkLTS Q L T q0) ;
  repeat (
    match goal with
    | ⊢ In _ _ ⇒ elem_in_list
    | ⊢ _ ≠ nil ⇒ solve_list_not_empty
    | ⊢ each_transition_is_valid _ _ _ ⇒ solve_transition_valid
    | ⊢ NoDup _ ⇒ list_has_no_dup
    end
  ) ; fail "One or more contextual rules were not fulfilled".
```

With this tactic (*solve_LTS_rules*), it is possible to define an LTS in a straight-forward way. For example, the LTS shown previously in Fig. 1acan also be defined in Rocq as follows. The tactic receives four arguments, which correspond to the respective attributes of the *LTS* record.

```
Definition fig1_r' : LTS.
Proof. solve_LTS_rules
          [0;1;2;3;4;5]
          ["but";"liq";"choc"]
          [(0, event "but", 1);(1, event "liq", 3);
           (0, event "but", 2);(2, event "but", 4);(4, event "choc", 5)]
          0.
Defined.
```

Similar results to the previous ones are available for other types of transition systems in the theory, such as input-output LTSs (IOLTS), and input-enabled IOLTS (IOTS). To illustrate one of these, see definition *IOLTS*.

```
Record IOLTS : Type := mkIOLTS {
      lts : LTS
    ; L_i : list label
    ; L_u : list label

    ; disjoint_input_output_labels : is_disjoint L_i L_u
    ; ...
  }.
```

It comprises an *LTS*, the set of input (L_i) and output (L_u) labels, besides new well-formedness conditions (e.g., *disjoint_input_output_labels*, which ensures that L_i and L_u are disjoint).

The records and tactics developed in this work can be reused when extending or adapting the results for different conformance testing theories. For example, when formalising `tioco`, an extension of `ioco` for timed systems, one can extend the record *IOLTS*, and its associated tactic, to deal with the additional information (i.e., time).

3.3   Graphviz Integration

Visualisation plays an important role when validating specification models. It is not always straightforward to formally capture the intended behaviour, particularly, when dealing with parallel processes. In such situations, being able to visualise a graphical representation of the model (or at least part of it, when the complete one is too large) enables inspection and, thus, detection of modelling errors.

In this work, graphical visualisation of different types of transition systems is achieved via Graphviz. It is an open-source graph visualization software, which allows the creation of diagrams in useful formats, such as SVG and JPEG, through a graph description written in a textual language (DOT).

The first step to graphically represent the structures of this work is to describe each structure in DOT. To this end, functions are defined to convert different types of structures (e.g., Behaviour Expressions, LTS, IOLTS, etc.) into its *string* representation in DOT; the functions *generate_dot_behaviour_expressions* and *generate_dot_lts* produce DOT representations for Behaviour Expressions and LTSs, respectively. All details about these functions can be found in the file `graphviz.v`.

For example, by executing the commands below, and with the support of Graphviz, we obtain the graphical representations of *fig1_r_BE* and *fig1_r*, as shown in Fig. 2. As expected, both commands render the same visualisation, since *fig1_r* is the LTS obtained from *fig1_r_BE*.

```
Compute (generate_dot_behaviour_expressions "fig1_r" fig1_r_BE 6).
Compute (generate_dot_lts fig1_r).
```

It is important to highlight that, unlike the example presented in [14] (see Fig. 1a), the generated graphical representation has fewer states (at the bottom). This happens because the formal representation in Rocq unifies states that describe the same behaviour; in the case of Fig. 2, STOP. Therefore, both representations are semantically equivalent.

Actually, this highlights once again the benefits of bridging the gap between the theory and the associated mechanisation. The transition systems shown in Fig. 1 were extracted from [14]. We believe that the representations shown in Fig. 2 are more accurate. They were not drawn by hand, but automatically generated from the defined semantics, and, thus, unify states with the same behaviour, as dictated by the underlying Structural Operational Semantics.

3.4   The Conformance Relation

As seen in Sect. 2.1, an implementation i is said to be `ioco`-conforming to a specification s if, for every trace of the specification, the set of outputs observed in i after executing this same trace is a subset of the outputs predicted in s. In Rocq, we provide an inductive characterization of `ioco` (*ind_ioco*), which formalises this intuition.

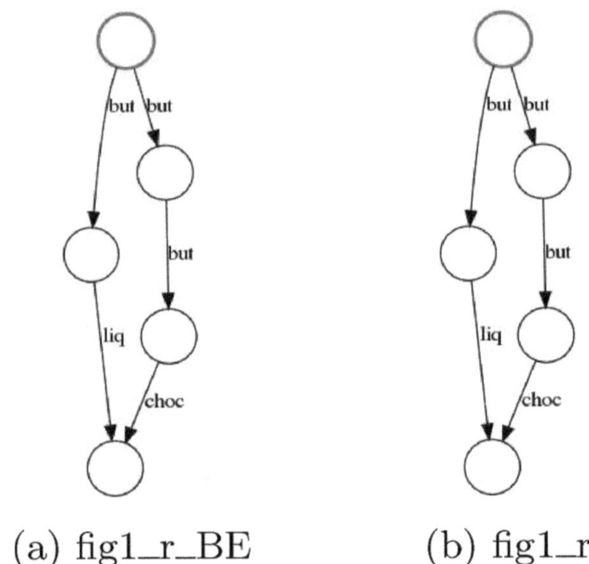

(a) fig1_r_BE   (b) fig1_r

Fig. 2. Graphical visualisations obtained with Graphviz.

Definition *ind_ioco* ($i : IOTS$) ($s : IOLTS$) : **Prop** :=
  $\forall$ ($Qi\ Qs$: **set** *state*) (t : *list s_label*) ($out\_i\ out\_s$: **set** *s_label*),
  ind_s_traces_LTS t (*create_s_IOLTS* s) $\rightarrow$
  ind_s_after_IOLTS t Qi (*create_s_IOLTS* $i.(embedded\_iolts)$)) $\rightarrow$
  ind_s_after_IOLTS t Qs (*create_s_IOLTS* s) $\rightarrow$
  ind_out Qi *out_i* (*create_s_IOLTS* $i.(embedded\_iolts)$)) $\rightarrow$
  ind_out Qs *out_s* (*create_s_IOLTS* s) $\rightarrow$
  incl out_i out_s.

The Rocq characterisation of **ioco** relies on some auxiliary definitions, as we describe now. The function *create_s_IOLTS* annotates an IOLTS with quiescence information; this is also called a suspended IOLTS. When applying this function to the implementation i, we need to retrieve the embedded IOLTS. Recall that an implementation is an IOTS, a restricted form of an IOLTS, which is input-enabled.

The inductive definition *ind_s_traces_LTS* ensures that t is a trace of the specification s. Similarly, *ind_s_after_IOLTS* inductively defines that Qi and Qs are the states reached by the implementation and specification, respectively, after the trace t. Finally, *ind_out* is used to formalise that out_i and out_s are the outputs observed at the implementation and specification, respectively, from the reached states Qi and Qs.

Considering these definitions, conformance is defined as follows. Let s be an IOLTS, then i is said to be **ioco**-conform s if, and only if, for every trace t of s (annotated with quiescence), the outputs observed at i after t (out_i- obtained by considering the outputs of the states Qi reached at i after t) are contained in the outputs observed at s after the same t (out_s- obtained by considering the outputs of the states Qs reached at s after t).

In the directory **examples** [3], one can find examples (see their names below) proving that this relation holds (or does not hold) for some of the examples presented originally in [14]. Therefore, we have mechanised in Rocq some of the proofs whose intuitions were presented in the original paper about **ioco**.

Example *i1_ioco_s1* : *ind_ioco imp_i1 spec_s1_IOLTS*.

Example *i1_not_ioco_s3* : ¬ (*ind_ioco imp_i1 spec_s3_IOLTS*).

4 Testing

In order to formalise testing, we first need to define the notion of models of test cases, then of test case executions. The following sections address these aspects.

4.1 Models of Test Cases

The record *TTS* shown in the following code snippet formalises the notion of a Test Transition System (TTS) in Rocq. In essence, a TTS is an IOTS with *fail* and *pass* states, besides an additional special symbol (*theta–* θ). In a test, θ indicates the detection of quiescence (i.e., the implementation produces no outputs).

```
Record TTS : Type := mkTTS {
      iots : IOTS
    ; fail_state : state
    ; pass_state : state
    ; theta : label


    ; ...
    ; imp_Li := set_remove string_dec theta iots.(embedded_iolts).(L_u)
    ; imp_Lu := iots.(embedded_iolts).(L_i)
    ; is_deterministic : ind_deterministic iots.(embedded_iolts).(sc_lts).(lts)
    ; pass_fail_diff : pass_state ≠ fail_state
    ; ...
  }.
```

Various well-formedness conditions need to hold such that a TTS is considered valid. Here, we comment on just a few of them. The values *imp_Li* and *imp_Lu* represent, respectively, the set of input and output labels of the implementation to be tested. From the test's point of view, the outputs of the implementation are inputs to the test, while the inputs of the implementation are outputs of the test. However, to avoid confusion, for terminology purposes, the implementation is considered as the reference. Therefore, these sets are referenced as inputs and outputs of the implementation.

Also shown above, a TTS needs to be a deterministic IOTS (*is_deterministic*). Additionally, the pass and fail states need to be different ones (*pass_fail_diff*). Finally, as we have done for other definitions, we provide a custom tactic that aids in the creation of TTSs, as shown in the code snippet below. Given the size of this tactic, only its signature is shown here. The full definition is available in the provided artefact [3] (see the file `TTS.v`).

> `Ltac` *create_TTS iots pass_state fail_state theta.*

From the received arguments (i.e., the IOTS used to construct this TTS, the states *pass_state* and *fail_state*, and the special label *theta*), an instance of a TTS is created, proving all associated well-formedness properties automatically. In Fig. 3, we show an example of a TTS. It first provides `?but` to the implementation, and then expects to receive `!liq`, followed by the detection of quiescence. Any other reaction from the implementation leads to the `fail` state.

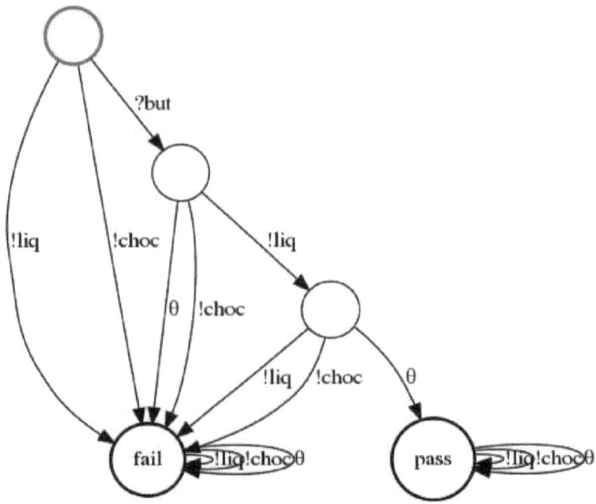

Fig. 3. Graphical visualisation of a TTS generated with Graphviz.

4.2   Test Execution

Informally, a test execution works as follows. If there is an internal transition (τ) in the implementation, the test execution evolves while maintaining the test state, but updating the implementation state from the internal transition. If there is a transition labeled with $a \in L_I \cup L_U$ in both the implementation and the test case, the test execution evolves synchronising the execution of these transitions, reaching the target states of these transitions. Finally, if the implementation is in a quiescent state, the test, upon observing this quiescence, evolves to the state reached by its transition labeled with θ.

Definition *ind_test_run* formalises a test execution, which is characterised by a trace (list of labels) that takes the test to the state *pass* or *fail*. Definition *ind_passes* formalises when an implementation passes a test case; this happens if, and only if, for every possible execution of the test, the state reached is never a failed state.

Definition *ind_test_run* (*sigma* : *list label*)
(*test* : *TTS*) (*imp* : *IOTS*) : **Prop** :=
   $\exists$ (*i'* : *state*),
      ind_test_execution_trace sigma test.(pass_state) i' test imp $\vee$
      ind_test_execution_trace sigma test.(fail_state) i' test imp.

Definition *ind_passes* (*imp* : *IOTS*) (*test* : *TTS*) : **Prop** :=
   $\forall$ (*ll* : *list label*) (*i'* : *state*),
      ind_test_run ll test imp $\rightarrow$
      $\neg$ *ind_test_execution_trace ll test.(fail_state) i' test imp.*

Finally, definitions *ind_passes_set* and *ind_fails_set* define when an implementation passes or fails a test suite, respectively. To pass a test suite, the implementation must pass all test cases that make up the suite. This notion is captured inductively. Any implementation passes an empty test suite (*passes_set_r1*). If an implementation passes a test *test*, and a test suite *tests*, then it passes this test suite augment with this test (i.e., *test:: tests*). To fail, it is sufficient for there to be one test in the suite that the implementation fails.

Inductive *ind_passes_set* : *IOTS* $\rightarrow$ **set** *TTS* $\rightarrow$ **Prop** :=
  | *passes_set_r1* (*imp* : *IOTS*) :
      ind_passes_set imp []
  | *passes_set_r2* (*test* : *TTS*) (*tests* : **set** *TTS*) (*imp* : *IOTS*) :
      ind_passes imp test $\rightarrow$
      ind_passes_set imp tests $\rightarrow$
      ind_passes_set imp (*test* :: *tests*).

Definition *ind_fails_set* (*imp* : *IOTS*) (*tests* : **set** *TTS*) : **Prop** :=
   $\exists$ (*test* : *TTS*), *In test tests* $\wedge$ $\neg$ *ind_passes imp test.*

5   Conclusion

In this work, we revisit the `ioco` conformance testing theory using the interactive theorem prover Rocq. In such an exercise, we formalise models of specifications, implementations, and test cases, besides precisely defining the notion of conformance and test execution. Despite considering a specific testing theory, some contributions (models and custom tactics) can be reused by other studies, since they comprise typical structures, for instance, Labelled Transition Systems (LTSs), and Input-Output Transition Systems (IOLTSs).

Here, we also highlight the benefits of mechanising formal testing theories in interactive theorem provers. Besides providing tool support tightly linked to the theory, it aids in revealing missing discussions in the theory.

Related work. To the best of our knowledge, we are not aware of the formalisation of formal testing theories in the Rocq universe. Differently, there are some initiatives reported in the literature using Isabelle/HOL [9]. In [15], the authors develop a theory for incremental conformance testing of timed state machines. In [5], the authors revisit the *Circus* [17] testing theory. *Circus* is a language that promotes the description of complex data and behaviour specifications via the integration of Z [16] and CSP [12] with a refinement calculus.

Therefore, this work distinguishes itself by the following aspects. (1) It addresses a different testing theory: conformance testing based on `ioco`. (2) Providing semantically equivalent logical and executable characterisations, thus, bridging the gap between theory and practice. (3) Bringing to the Rocq university the development of formal conformance testing.

Future work. As future work, we envisage the following opportunities. (1) Prove that some auxiliary functional definitions, which are not part of the main results reported here, reflect their inductive counterparts. (2) Define more automation tactics. Despite the many custom tactics defined, others can be devised; for instance, to show that a LTS is strongly convergent, and to show that a given implementation is `ioco`-conform to a specification. (3) Formalise test generation algorithms, as the one proposed in [14]. (4) Mechanise in Rocq the proof that the `ioco` testing theory is sound. As a by-product, provide custom tactics for proving soundness of formal testing theories. (5) Improve the documentation of our Rocq formalisation to foster its reuse.

Disclosure of Interests. The authors have no competing interests to declare that are relevant to the content of this article.

References

1. Araujo, H., Carvalho, G., Mohaqeqi, M., Mousavi, M.R., Sampaio, A.: Sound conformance testing for cyber-physical systems: theory and implementation. Sci. Comput. Program. **162**, 35–54 (2018). https://doi.org/10.1016/j.scico.2017.07.002. Special Issue on TASE 2016
2. Bertot, Y., Castran, P.: Interactive Theorem Proving and Program Development: Coq'Art The Calculus of Inductive Constructions, 1st edn. Springer Publishing Company, Incorporated (2004)

3. Carvalho, G., Santana, L., Sobral, F., Souza, B.: Rocq Formalisation of IOCO Test. Theor. (2025). https://doi.org/10.5281/zenodo.16885107
4. Coquand, T., Huet, G.: The calculus of constructions. Inf. Comput. **76**(2), 95–120 (1988). https://doi.org/10.1016/0890-5401(88)90005-3
5. Feliachi, A., Gaudel, M.C., Wenzel, M., Wolff, B.: The circus testing theory revisited in Isabelle/HOL. In: Groves, L., Sun, J. (eds.) Formal Methods and Software Engineering, pp. 131–147. Springer, Berlin Heidelberg, Berlin, Heidelberg (2013)
6. Gaudel, M.-C.: Testing can be formal, too. In: Mosses, P.D., Nielsen, M., Schwartzbach, M.I. (eds.) CAAP 1995. LNCS, vol. 915, pp. 82–96. Springer, Heidelberg (1995). https://doi.org/10.1007/3-540-59293-8_188
7. Krichen, M., Tripakis, S.: Interesting properties of the real-time conformance relation tioco. In: Barkaoui, K., Cavalcanti, A., Cerone, A. (eds.) ICTAC 2006. LNCS, vol. 4281, pp. 317–331. Springer, Heidelberg (2006). https://doi.org/10.1007/11921240_22
8. Leemans, S.J.J., Syring, A.F., van der Aalst, W.M.P.: Earth movers' stochastic conformance checking. In: Hildebrandt, T., van Dongen, B.F., Röglinger, M., Mendling, J. (eds.) Business Process Management Forum, pp. 127–143. Springer International Publishing, Cham (2019)
9. Nipkow, T., Wenzel, M., Paulson, L.C.: Isabelle/HOL: A Proof Assistant for Higher-order Logic. Springer-Verlag, Berlin, Heidelberg (2002)
10. Osch, M.: Hybrid input-output conformance and test generation. In: Havelund, K., Núñez, M., Roşu, G., Wolff, B. (eds.) FATES/RV -2006. LNCS, vol. 4262, pp. 70–84. Springer, Heidelberg (2006). https://doi.org/10.1007/11940197_5
11. Qin, X., Hashemi, N., Lindemann, L., Deshmukh, J.V.: Conformance testing for stochastic cyber-physical systems. In: 2023 Formal Methods in Computer-Aided Design (FMCAD), pp. 294–305 (2023). https://doi.org/10.34727/2023/isbn.978-3-85448-060-0_38
12. Roscoe, A.W.: Understanding Concurrent Systems. Springer, London (2010)
13. RTI International: the economic impacts of inadequate infrastructure for software testing. Nat. Inst. Stand. Technol. p. 1 (2002)
14. Tretmans, J.: Model based testing with labelled transition systems. In: Formal methods and testing, pp. 1–38. Springer (2008)
15. Tvardovskii, A., El-Fakih, K., Yevtushenko, N.: Testing and incremental conformance testing of timed state machines. Sci. Comput. Program. **233**, 103053 (2024). https://doi.org/10.1016/j.scico.2023.103053
16. Woodcock, J., Davies, J.: Using Z: Specification, Refinement, and Proof. Prentice-Hall international series in computer science, Prentice Hall (1996). https://books.google.com.br/books?id=ua1QAAAAMAAJ
17. Woodcock, J., Cavalcanti, A.: The Semantics of circus. In: Bert, D., Bowen, J.P., Henson, M.C., Robinson, K. (eds.) ZB 2002. LNCS, vol. 2272, pp. 184 203. Springer, Heidelberg (2002). https://doi.org/10.1007/3-540-45648-1_10

Availability and Contracts

Availability Model and Evaluation of Bus Rapid Transit Surveillance System

Raquel F. Trajano[1], Carlos Melo[2,3], and Jamilson Dantas[1(✉)]

[1] Universidade Federal de Pernambuco, Recife, Pernambuco, Brazil
`{rft,jrd}@cin.ufpe.br`
[2] Universidade de Pernambuco, Garanhuns, Pernambuco, Brazil
`carlos.melo@upe.br`
[3] Universidade Federal de Sergipe, Aracaju, Sergipe, Brazil

Abstract. The integration of Information and Communication Technologies (ICT) has become essential to enhancing urban infrastructure and addressing challenges in modern cities, particularly in urban mobility. Bus Rapid Transit (BRT) systems are crucial for enhancing mobility, but they require robust monitoring to ensure safety and service quality, particularly at high-traffic stations. This paper presents a hierarchical availability model for monitoring systems in BRT stations, combining Reliability Block Diagrams (RBDs) to represent the system structure and Continuous-Time Markov Chains (CTMCs) to model the dynamic behavior of Edge Computing components. The proposed approach supports the evaluation of system availability and informs decision-making in the design and planning of smart urban infrastructure. A case study demonstrates the model's applicability in a realistic IoT-enabled BRT environment, highlighting its effectiveness in estimating availability metrics and improving service resilience. Evaluation results indicated a baseline system availability of 99.70%, translating to nearly 26 h of annual downtime. Sensitivity analysis revealed the Edge computing unit as the most critical component, and implementing warm standby redundancy for this unit substantially improved system availability, reducing annual downtime by up to 76% in evaluated scenarios.

1   Introduction

Information and Communication Technologies (ICT) have emerged as key enablers for transforming cities into more efficient, resilient, and connected environments. These technologies support the digitalization of urban infrastructure and the modernization of public services, enabling more effective resource management and improved service delivery to citizens [13]. Smart cities arise from the strategic use of ICT to address the complex demands of contemporary urbanization [22].

Urban mobility remains a challenge for modern cities [1]. High-capacity public transportation systems, such as Bus Rapid Transit (BRT), play a central role in addressing this issue [7]. However, the efficient operation of BRT systems requires continuous monitoring to ensure safety, passenger flow, and service quality, especially at stations, which are critical nodes concentrating large passenger volumes.

Technologies such as the Internet of Things (IoT) and Edge Computing are increasingly integrated into transportation infrastructures. IoT enables real-time data collection through devices that monitor environmental conditions, occupancy, safety, and operational status. Presence sensors, air quality monitors, temperature sensors, smoke detectors, and surveillance cameras are examples of devices that may be employed to monitor BRT stations [23,24].

Edge Computing complements IoT usage by enabling data processing directly at the data source, close to or inside the station. This approach reduces cloud dependency, lowers latency, and improves system resilience for applications that require rapid response, anomaly detection, passenger flow management, and emergency response [21].

Due to the operational complexity of BRT stations, public administrators must evaluate and ensure the effectiveness of the service provided through monitoring systems that aid in the decision-making process. Analytical modeling techniques are appropriate for this purpose, as they enable the simulation of operational behaviors, potential failure modes, and recovery processes at lower costs than other evaluation methods without disrupting the real-world environment [7,16].

This paper proposes a hierarchical availability model for a monitoring system deployed in a BRT station. The proposed approach combines Reliability Block Diagrams (RBD) models to represent the system's static structure with Continuous-Time Markov Chains (CTMC) to capture the dynamic behavior of failures and repairs of Edge components. This approach enables the estimation of quantitative availability metrics to support the planning, sizing, and improvement of urban infrastructure. The main contributions of this paper are summarized below:

- A hierarchical availability model for monitoring systems in BRT stations.
- A quantitative availability evaluation method to support decision-making for the design, planning, and improvement of urban infrastructure.
- A case study that applies the proposed model to a realistic urban mobility scenario involving IoT-based sensing and Edge Computing architectures.

The remainder of this paper is organized as follows: Sect. 2 presents related work. Section 3 introduces the background and key concepts. Section 4 details the proposed methodology. Section 5 presents the availability modeling approach based on RBDs and CTMCs. Section 6 presents the case studies used to demonstrate the feasibility of the proposed models. Finally, Sect. 7 summarizes the conclusions and outlines directions for future work.

2   Related Work

The deployment of intelligent systems in urban environments, especially for public transportation services such as Bus Rapid Transit (BRT) and IoT-Edge continuous integration, has motivated several studies on dependability evaluation. Prior research explores the intersection of IoT, Edge Computing, and stochastic modeling techniques to evaluate such systems. This section reviews these studies and highlights how the present work differs, with a focus on the availability of monitoring sensors and surveillance of BRT stations.

Araújo et al. [2] present a Stochastic Petri Net (SPN) model to evaluate the availability of intelligent systems, considering sensor and Edge failure and repair rates, which will be used as input parameters to the models proposed in this paper. While their approach effectively captures system dynamics, the current work differs in employing a hierarchical modeling framework that combines RBDs with CTMCs. This enables a finer-grained assessment of the BRT station's infrastructure, including IoT sensors and Edge devices.

Dantas et al. [6–8] investigate the performability of BRT systems and Medium Priority Transport Systems (STUMP) using CTMC and SPN models. Their studies focus on operational metrics such as vehicle arrival probabilities, travel time under failures, and queue dynamics. Some works optimize fleet size and headway for service availability [7], while others assess reliability over mission times [6]. These contributions target the transport service itself. In contrast, the present study models the availability of the technological infrastructure that supports station monitoring and management independent of vehicle operations.

Oliveira et al. [17] analyze the dependability of an agricultural monitoring system using a cloud-fog-edge architecture. Their quantitative model assesses availability while discussing trade-offs between latency and reliability. Although methodologically similar, their focus is on the agricultural Internet of Things (IoT). At the same time, the current work addresses an urban application characterized by distinct failure modes and operational constraints involving presence sensors, environmental monitors, and Edge computing units.

Lins et al. [15] evaluate the reliability and availability of drone-based surveillance systems using stochastic Petri net (SPN) models, emphasizing energy redundancy through the use of spare batteries. Their focus on mobile aerial video surveillance differs significantly from this work, which addresses stationary, ground-based monitoring infrastructure within BRT stations. However, both models capture a set of dependencies, component interactions, and failure behaviors characteristic of IoT-Edge deployments and surveillance systems.

Borges et al. [4] propose RBD and SPN models to assess the availability of distributed video surveillance systems with redundant storage strategies. Their study includes real testbed validation and explores hot and cold standby configurations. The obtained values will also serve as input parameters for the models proposed in this paper once both approaches utilize hierarchical stochastic models that encompass an integrated set of IoT devices (presence and environmental sensors) and Edge processors, thereby providing a broader availability assessment.

3   Background

This section outlines the technologies used in the BRT station monitoring system and provides an overview of the availability modeling and sensitivity analysis needed for understanding this work.

3.1   IoT and Smart Devices

The Internet of Things (IoT) is defined as a global network of interconnected objects and devices capable of uniquely identifying themselves and communicating with each other using standardized communication protocols [11]. In urban environments, sensors are key IoT components employed for real-time data collection, supporting applications related to mobility, safety, and environmental monitoring [18].

A typical IoT architecture consists of multiple layers. The perception layer includes sensors and physical devices responsible for data acquisition, while the network layer handles the transmission of this data to processing and analysis platforms [24].

Data generated by sensors are stored in databases and used to support intelligent decision-making systems in domains such as smart cities, public health, safety, and sustainability. In the context of BRT stations, IoT-based solutions support operational planning and management, enhancing user comfort, safety, and service efficiency.

3.2   Edge Computing

Edge Computing is defined according to the location of computing resources, the technologies involved, or the specific requirements of the application [12]. This flexibility allows edge computing to adapt to the operational needs of distributed systems, such as intelligent urban infrastructures.

An edge architecture consists of edge servers, IoT devices, sensors, and a communication infrastructure that enables data processing close to the data source. It can be categorized based on factors such as context-awareness, resource management, resilience, sustainability, and real-time responsiveness, focusing on low latency, local autonomy, and efficient node-to-node communication [21].

Edge computing can process data at the source without relying on constant connectivity to remote cloud servers [12]. This close-to-end device relationship is particularly relevant for scenarios such as BRT station monitoring, where environmental sensors, cameras, and passenger counting devices generate real-time data. Edge computing enables immediate responses, such as adjusting lighting, triggering alerts, or notifying operators about crowding conditions. While processing sensitive information locally also enhances privacy and energy efficiency in smart city applications [5].

3.3 Availability Modeling

Availability evaluation is a fundamental aspect of system dependability analysis. Dependability refers to a system's ability to deliver specified services continuously and correctly despite component failures [3]. It encompasses multiple attributes, including availability, safety, reliability, integrity, and maintainability.

Availability is defined as the probability that a system is operational at a given time, taking into account both failures and repairs. The steady-state availability, applicable when the system reaches stable behavior over time, is given by [16]:

$$A = \frac{MTTF}{MTTF + MTTR} \tag{1}$$

where MTTF stands for the Mean Time To Failure and MTTR for the Mean Time To Repair.

This equation assumes that the mean time to system failure is significantly greater than the mean recovery time, which is typically the case for most systems, such as intelligent urban mobility infrastructure. Derived metrics include unavailability, UA = 1 - A, and downtime over a period T, computed as DT = UA $\times$ T.

The **Reliability Block Diagram (RBD)** is commonly used for reliability and availability evaluation due to its clarity in representing structural relationships among system components [16]. The RBD structure formally describes system states using logical or structural functions that define the operational conditions [16]. Common configurations include series systems, where a single component failure causes the system to fail, and parallel systems, where the system remains operational as long as at least one component is functioning [16].

Redundant systems can also be modeled using the **K-out-of-N (KooN)** structure [14]. In these systems, proper operation is ensured if at least K out of N components are functional. This characteristic generalizes series (NooN) and parallel (1ooN) configurations [14]. The steady-state availability for a KooN system is given by Eq. 2.

$$A = \sum_{i=K}^{N} \binom{N}{i} A_c^i \times (1 - A_c)^{N-i} \tag{2}$$

Continuous-Time Markov Chains (CTMC) are also used to represent systems where transitions between states, such as failures and repairs, occur continuously over time [16]. In this approach, system behavior is modeled by states (e.g., operational, failed, under repair), with transitions governed by failure and repair rates, typically assumed to follow exponential distributions. For a single-component repairable system, for instance, the states "Up" and "Down" are connected through failure rate (λ) and repair rate (μ), enabling the calculation of the steady-state availability based on the probability of being in the "up" state.

3.4 Sensitivity Analysis

Sensitivity analysis assesses how variations in input parameters affect system availability through failure rates (λ), repair rates (μ), MTTF, and MTTR [9]. A typical approach applied to this paper involves computing partial derivatives of the availability function with respect to these parameters or applying finite variation methods.

For example, considering the steady-state availability, the sensitivity of availability with respect to the failure rate λ is calculated as:

$$\frac{\partial A}{\partial \lambda} = -\frac{\mu}{(\lambda + \mu)^2} \tag{3}$$

Sensitivity analysis can also be extended to more complex systems, including those modeled with Reliability Block Diagrams (RBD) and Continuous-Time Markov Chains (CTMC), where it assists in identifying critical components or processes that most affect system availability [14,16].

By quantifying the influence of a parameter over the system availability, a sensitivity technique may support maintenance planning, redundancy decisions, and investment prioritization, contributing to more resilient and dependable system designs [9,20].

4 Proposed Architecture

This section describes the physical and functional architecture of the intelligent monitoring system designed for Bus Rapid Transit (BRT) stations. The system integrates environmental sensors, surveillance cameras, and Edge Computing units to support continuous monitoring and decision-making by public authorities.

4.1 System Overview

The proposed system is intended for medium-sized BRT stations, such as those found in Recife, Pernambuco, Brazil. These stations typically have a rectangular layout covering an area of approximately 340 square meters. Figure 1 shows a high-level schematic representation of the evaluated environment.

The monitoring system consists of three main subsystems: **Environmental Sensing Subsystem**, **Video Surveillance Subsystem**, and **Edge Computing Subsystem**. Each subsystem is described in the following subsections.

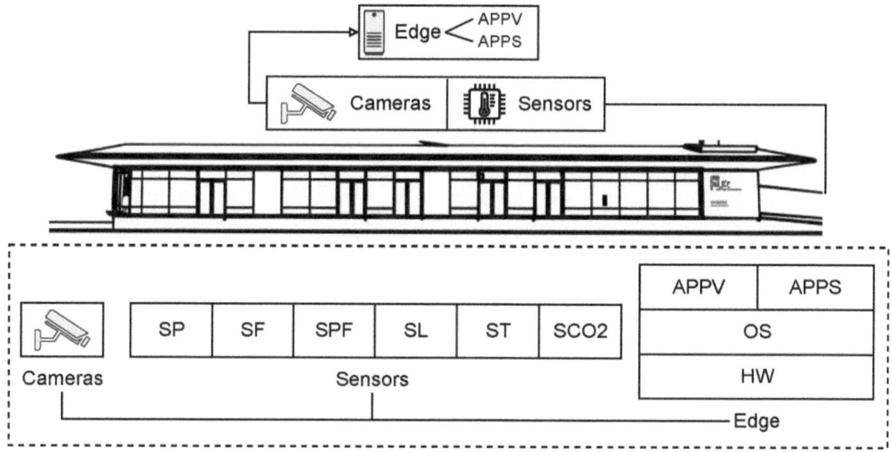

Fig. 1. High-Level View of the Evaluated Environment

4.2 Environmental Sensing Subsystem

This subsystem includes a diverse set of IoT sensors designed to monitor environmental and operational conditions inside the station. Table 1 lists the types of sensors and their monitored variables.

Table 1. Sensor types and monitored variables.

ID	Sensor	Monitored Variable / Purpose
SP	SE-10 PIR	Detects human presence in restricted areas or crowds; supports passenger counting
SP	PMS5003	Measures fine particulate matter (PM 2.5)
SL	OPT3001	Measures visible light intensity; supports environmental control and passenger comfort
SF	Smoke Detector	Detects smoke; supports fire safety
ST	BME280	Measures temperature, pressure, and humidity
SCO2	MG811	Detects carbon dioxide (CO_2) concentration

These sensors are deployed in strategic positions within the station to ensure effective monitoring of environmental quality and operational safety.

4.3 Video Surveillance Subsystem

The surveillance system is composed of digital cameras positioned to provide full coverage of the station. These cameras support functionalities such as facial recognition, detection of abandoned objects, and crowd flow analysis.

Camera placement is optimized using the approach proposed by Erdem and Sclaroff [10], which formulates the deployment as a Set Cover Problem (SCP). This problem is solved using Integer Linear Programming (ILP), allowing the selection of camera positions and focal lengths (35 mm and 50 mm) to maximize coverage and minimize redundancy.

4.4 Edge Computing Subsystem

The Edge Computing unit serves as the local processing hub of the monitoring system. It is responsible for collecting, storing, and processing data from both the environmental sensors and surveillance cameras. The Edge unit operates autonomously, reducing dependence on cloud resources and enabling real-time decision-making.

This subsystem consists of four main components:

- **Hardware (HW)**: physical processing unit with sufficient computing and storage capacity;
- **Operating System (OS)**: software platform managing the execution of services;
- **Video Surveillance Application (APPV)**: handles processing of video streams;
- **Sensor Monitoring Application (APPS)**: processes data collected from sensors.

Together, these subsystems form an integrated and intelligent architecture capable of supporting continuous monitoring, anomaly detection, and efficient incident response in public transportation stations.

5 Availability Modeling Approach

This section presents the modeling strategy adopted to evaluate the availability of the intelligent monitoring architecture described in Sect. 4. The approach is based on a hierarchical modeling technique that combines Reliability Block Diagrams (RBDs) for structural modeling and Continuous-Time Markov Chains (CTMCs) for dynamic behavior representation.

5.1 Structural Modeling with RBDs

Reliability Block Diagrams (RBDs) are used to model the static configuration of the system components, capturing the logical arrangement of sensors, cameras, and the Edge computing unit. Each subsystem is represented as a series of blocks, and the overall availability is computed as the product of the availability of individual components:

$$A_{\mathsf{S}} = A_{\mathsf{HW}} \times A_{\mathsf{OS}} \times A_{\mathsf{APPV}} \times A_{\mathsf{APPS}} \tag{4}$$

Redundancy with K-out-of-N Structures For the environmental sensors and surveillance cameras, a K-out-of-N (KooN) redundancy scheme is adopted. In this configuration, a subsystem remains operational as long as at least K out of N identical components are functioning.

The availability A_{KooN} of such a redundant group is given by Eq. 2 described earlier.

This modeling approach allows capturing the impact of both replication and failure tolerance within sensor and camera groups, enabling a more realistic evaluation of the system's structural robustness.

5.2 Dynamic Modeling with CTMCs

To model the dynamic behavior of the Edge subsystem, particularly under redundancy configurations, a Continuous-Time Markov Chain (CTMC) is employed. The CTMC captures failure, repair, activation, and common-cause failure events for a warm standby configuration with two Edge units.

Figure 2 illustrates the CTMC model. Table 2 summarizes the states, while Table 3 provides the description of transition rates.

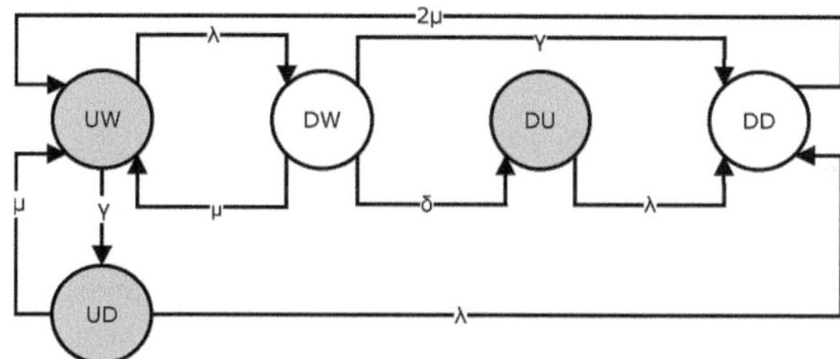

Fig. 2. CTMC model of the Edge system under warm standby redundancy. Shaded states represent operational configurations contributing to system availability.

Table 2. CTMC for the Edge Redundant Model

State	Description
UW	Both Ed1 and Ed2 are operational; Ed1 is active, Ed2 is in standby
DW	Ed1 has failed; Ed2 remains operational in standby mode
DU	Ed1 remains down; Ed2 transitions to active mode
DD	Both Ed1 and Ed2 are down (system failure)
UD	Ed1 is repaired and becomes active; Ed2 remains down

The infinitesimal generator matrix Q for the CTMC is expressed as:

$$Q = \begin{bmatrix} -(\lambda + \gamma) & \lambda & 0 & 0 & \gamma \\ \mu & -(\mu + \gamma + \delta) & \delta & \gamma & 0 \\ \mu & 0 & -(\mu + \lambda) & \lambda & 0 \\ 2\mu & 0 & 0 & -2\mu & 0 \\ \mu & 0 & 0 & \lambda & -(\mu + \lambda) \end{bmatrix}$$

Table 3. CTMC Transition Rates and Descriptions

Rate	Description
λ	Failure rate of Ed1 (when Ed2 is standby or Ed2 has failed)
μ	Repair rate of Ed1 (when Ed2 is operational or failed)
γ	Common-cause failure rate affecting Ed1 and Ed2 simultaneously
δ	Activation rate of Ed2 upon Ed1 failure (standby to active)
2μ	Accelerated repair when both Ed1 and Ed2 are down (parallel repair)

System availability A is defined as the sum of the probabilities of the operational states:

$$A = \pi_{\mathrm{UW}} + \pi_{\mathrm{DU}} + \pi_{\mathrm{UD}}$$

Solving the balance equations yields the following closed-form expression:

$$A = \frac{2\mu \left(\delta\gamma + \delta\lambda + \gamma^2 + \gamma\mu + \lambda^2 + \lambda\mu \right)}{\lambda\gamma\delta + 2\delta\gamma\mu + \delta\lambda^2 + 4\delta\lambda\mu + \lambda\gamma^2 + 2\gamma^2\mu + 4\gamma\lambda\mu + 4\gamma\mu^2 + 2\lambda^2\mu + 4\lambda\mu^2 + 2\mu^2\delta + 2\mu^3} \tag{5}$$

This equation allows the estimation of steady-state availability considering both independent and common-cause failures in a warm standby configuration.

5.3 Evaluation Tools and Metrics

All models were implemented and simulated using the Mercury tool [19]. Availability metrics such as Mean Time To Failure (MTTF), Mean Time To Repair (MTTR), and steady-state availability were computed based on the system structure and parameter values obtained from the literature.

These modeling approaches enable public administrators and system designers to evaluate the impact of architectural decisions, redundancy strategies, and component reliability on overall system availability in urban monitoring environments.

6   Case Studies

This section presents four case studies that evaluate the availability of the intelligent monitoring system described in Sect. 4, based on the modeling approaches detailed in Sect. 5. The scenarios explore baseline performance, architectural variations, sensitivity analysis, and the impact of redundancy strategies.

6.1   Case Study I: Baseline Model Evaluation

This study evaluates the system's availability in its initial configuration, consisting of one unit of each sensor, one camera, and a single Edge computing unit.

Table 4. Availability Metrics for Baseline Architecture

Parameter	Value
MTTF (h)	188.90
MTTR (h)	0.55
Availability (%)	99.70
Annual Uptime (h)	8,739.94
Annual Downtime (h)	25.86

The system is modeled using RBDs, and the results are obtained through the Mercury tool (Table 4).

The baseline configuration achieves an availability of 99.70%, which results in nearly 26 h of expected downtime per year. This highlights the need to explore enhancements, particularly for critical components like the Edge unit.

6.2   Case Study II: Architectural Variations

To evaluate how system scaling affects availability, four configurations were analyzed with increasing numbers of sensors and cameras. Table 5 summarizes the K-out-of-N settings for each variant.

Table 5. System Architectures with Redundancy Levels

Architecture	SP	SF	SPF	SL	ST	SCo2	Cameras (35 + 50 mm)
I	2 of 17	2 of 6	2 of 4	2 of 4	2 of 4	2 of 4	2 of 7
II	4 of 17	3 of 6	3 of 4	3 of 4	3 of 4	3 of 4	3 of 7
III	6 of 17	4 of 6	4 of 4	4 of 4	4 of 4	4 of 4	4 of 7
IV	10 of 17	5 of 6	3 of 4	2 of 4	1 of 4	1 of 4	4 of 7

Figure 3 presents the availability results. The baseline architecture outperforms some redundant configurations, demonstrating that redundancy alone does not guarantee higher availability—especially when the required operational components (K) increase.

Naive replication can introduce constraints that increase vulnerability to failure. More components may result in longer repair times and more complex recovery processes. Thus, effective redundancy planning must consider both failure tolerance and maintainability.

6.3   Case Study III: Sensitivity Analysis

This analysis identifies components with the greatest influence on system availability. A differential sensitivity method was applied by varying the MTTF and MTTR of each component by ±50% (Fig. 4).

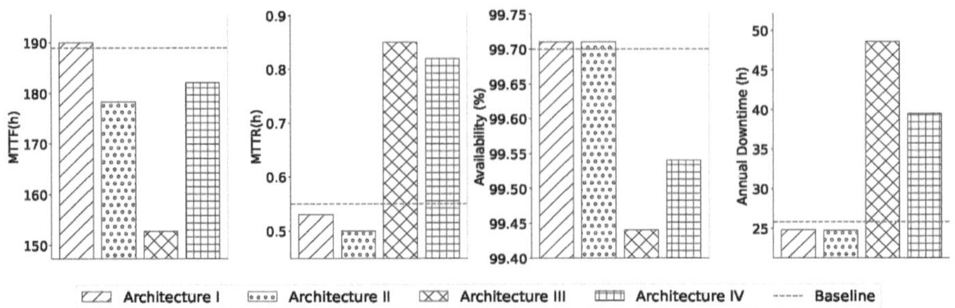

Fig. 3. Availability Comparison Among Architectures

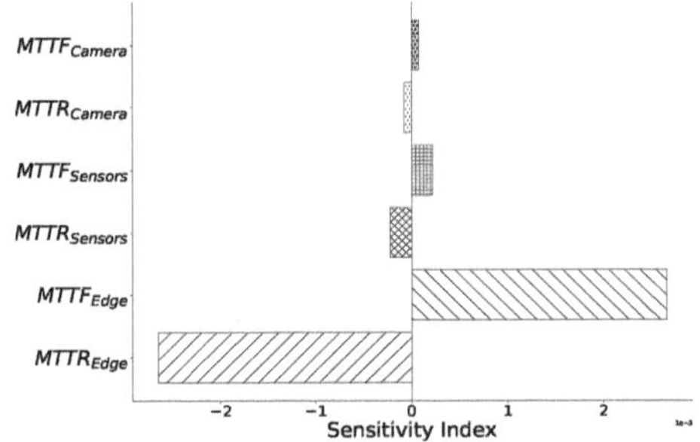

Fig. 4. Sensitivity Index for Each Parameter

Results show that the Edge unit has the highest impact on system availability. Improving the MTTF or MTTR of this component significantly increases overall system reliability. Figure 5 shows the impact of varying the Edge's MTTF.

6.4   Case Study IV: Edge Redundancy Analysis

Based on the sensitivity results, a warm standby redundancy mechanism was implemented for the Edge subsystem, modeled through the CTMC structure described in Sect. 5. The same four architectures from Case Study II were re-evaluated with this redundancy in place (Fig. 6).

The inclusion of redundancy significantly increases the system's MTTF and reduces the annual downtime across all configurations. For example, in Architecture II, annual downtime is reduced from over 180 h to just 1 h and 35 min. These results validate the effectiveness of targeted redundancy for critical subsystems and demonstrate the advantage of integrating structural and behavioral modeling in availability assessments.

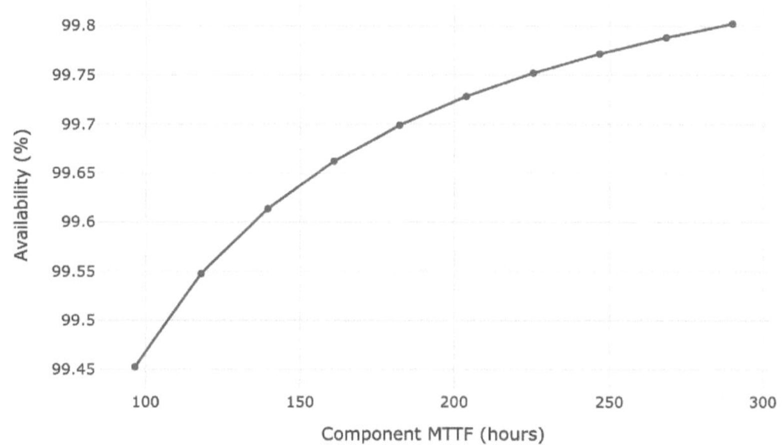

Fig. 5. Impact of Edge's MTTF on System Availability

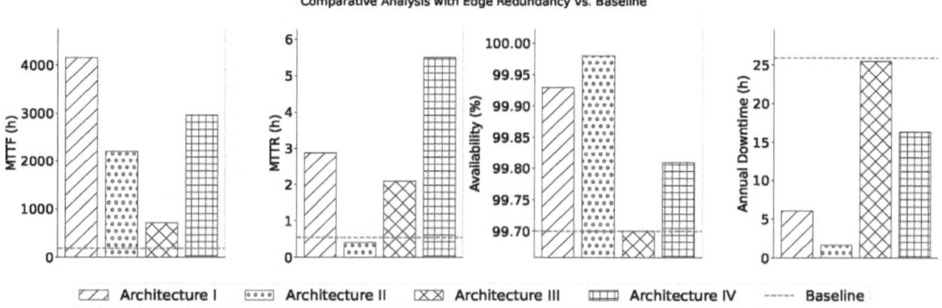

Fig. 6. Availability Comparison with Edge Redundancy

7   Conclusion and Future Works

This paper proposes and evaluates the feasibility of an intelligent monitoring system architecture for BRT public transport stations, utilizing environmental sensors, surveillance cameras, and Edge Computing processing. The main objective was not only to quantify the availability of a baseline configuration but also to identify components with a higher impact on availability and investigate the effect of redundancy strategies on improving system availability through a generalizable and parameterizable approach based on stochastic modeling and evaluation.

To achieve these objectives, a set of RBDs is used to represent the compositional structure of the sensors, cameras, and Edge subsystems, including K-out-of-N configurations. A CTMC is employed to analyze the dynamic failure and repair behavior in a scenario with a redundant Edge environment, utilizing a warm standby strategy.

The evaluation results for the baseline system indicated an availability of 99.70%, which implies an annual downtime of approximately 26 h. This value may directly impact public transportation operations, as passengers may be in danger due to a series of factors related to surveillance unavailability or smoke sensors that fail to detect a fire at the station. We conducted a differential sensitivity analysis, which revealed that the Edge unit has the most significant impact on overall system availability, considerably outweighing the influence of the sensors and camera subsystems. Consequently, case studies showed that increasing redundancy in sensing subsystems without addressing Edge resilience results in only marginal improvements in total availability.

The effectiveness of introducing warm standby redundancy for the Edge Computing unit resulted in a substantial increase in system availability, with annual downtime reduced by up to 76% in one of the evaluated architectures compared to the evaluated baseline scenario, which had less than two hours of downtime, versus 26 h in the latter.

As future work, the model should be extended to include the investigation of other redundancy strategies, incorporating new system components such as Fog and Cloud layers, and an analysis of different maintenance and repair policies. Additionally, incorporating a cost-benefit analysis for the various availability enhancement strategies could provide a more comprehensive perspective to support informed decision-making by public administrators.

References

1. Albertsen, N., Diken, B.: Mobility, justification, and the city. NA **14**(1) (2013)
2. Araujo, E., Dantas, J., Matos, R., Pereira, P., Maciel, P.: Dependability evaluation of an IoT system: A hierarchical modelling approach. In: 2019 IEEE International Conference on Systems, Man and Cybernetics (SMC), pp. 2121–2126. IEEE (2019)
3. Avizienis, A., Laprie, J.C., Randell, B., Landwehr, C.: Basic concepts and taxonomy of dependable and secure computing. IEEE Trans. Dependable Secure Comput. **1**(1), 11–33 (2004)
4. Borges, I., Andrade, E., Silva, F.A., Callou, G.: Availability evaluation of a video surveillance system with distributed storage. Clust. Comput. **28**(4), 273 (2025)
5. Bukhsh, M., Abdullah, S., Bajwa, I.S.: A decentralized edge computing latency-aware task management method with high availability for IoT applications. IEEE Access **9**, 138994–139008 (2021)
6. Dantas, R., Dantas, J., Melo, C., Maciel, P.: Performance evaluation in brt systems: An analysis to predict the brt systems planning. Case Stud. Transp. Policy **9**(3), 1141–1150 (2021)
7. Dantas, R., Dantas, J., Melo, C., Oliveira, D., Maciel, P.: Sensitivity analysis in a brt system. In: 2019 IEEE International Systems Conference (SysCon), pp. 1–8. IEEE (2019)
8. Dantas, R.C.D.S.P., Avelino, J.A.P.F., Dantas, J.R., Maciel, P.R.M., Melo, C.: Performability model for the medium priority transport systems. In: 2023 18th Iberian Conference on Information Systems and Technologies (CISTI), pp. 1–6. IEEE (2023)

9. Ebeling, C.E.: An introduction to reliability and maintainability engineering. Waveland Press (2019)
10. Erdem, U.M., Sclaroff, S.: Automated camera layout to satisfy task-specific and floor plan-specific coverage requirements. Comput. Vis. Image Underst. **103**(3), 156–169 (2006)
11. Gubbi, J., Buyya, R., Marusic, S., Palaniswami, M.: Internet of things (IoT): A vision, architectural elements, and future directions. Futur. Gener. Comput. Syst. **29**(7), 1645–1660 (2013)
12. Khan, L.U., Yaqoob, I., Tran, N.H., Kazmi, S.A., Dang, T.N., Hong, C.S.: Edge-computing-enabled smart cities: a comprehensive survey. IEEE Internet Things J. **7**(10), 10200–10232 (2020)
13. Kondepudi, S., et al.: Smart sustainable cities analysis of definitions. The ITU-T focus group for smart sustainable cities (2014)
14. Kuo, W., Zuo, M.J.: Optimal reliability modeling: principles and applications. John Wiley & Sons (2003)
15. Lins, L., Nascimento, E., Dantas, J., Araujo, J., Maciel, P.: Stochastic modeling for assessing the reliability and availability of drone-based surveillance systems. In: 2024 IEEE International Systems Conference (SysCon), pp. 1–8. IEEE (2024)
16. Maciel, P.R.M.: Performance, reliability, and availability evaluation of computational systems, Volume 2: Reliability, availability modeling, measuring, and data analysis. Chapman and Hall/CRC (2023)
17. Oliveira, F., Pereira, P., Dantas, J., Araujo, J., Maciel, P.: Dependability evaluation of a smart poultry house: addressing availability issues through the edge, fog, and cloud computing. IEEE Trans. Industr. Inf. **20**(2), 1304–1312 (2023)
18. Perera, C., Zaslavsky, A., Christen, P., Georgakopoulos, D.: Context aware computing for the internet of things: a survey. IEEE Commun. Surv. Tutorials **16**(1), 414–454 (2013)
19. Pinheiro, T., et al.: The mercury environment: a modeling tool for performance and dependability evaluation. In: Intelligent Environments 2021, pp. 16–25. IOS Press (2021)
20. Saltelli, A., Tarantola, S., Campolongo, F., Ratto, M., et al.: Sensitivity analysis in practice: a guide to assessing scientific models, vol. 1. Wiley Online Library (2004)
21. Trigka, M., Dritsas, E.: Edge and cloud computing in smart cities. Future Internet **17**(3), 118 (2025)
22. Trindade, E.P., Hinnig, M.P.F., da Costa, E.M., Marques, J.S., Bastos, R.C., Yigitcanlar, T.: Sustainable development of smart cities: a systematic review of the literature. J. Open Innov. Technol. Market Compl. **3**(3), 1–14 (2017)
23. Valencia-Arias, A., et al.: Research trends in the use of the internet of things in sustainability practices: a systematic review. Sustainability **16**(7), 2663 (2024)
24. Zeng, F., Pang, C., Tang, H.: Sensors on internet of things systems for the sustainable development of smart cities: a systematic literature review. Sensors **24**(7), 2074 (2024)

Resource Contracts for Active Objects

Charaf Eddine Dridi⬤, Violet Ka I Pun(✉)⬤, and Volker Stolz⬤

Western Norway University of Applied Sciences, Bergen, Norway
`{Charaf.Eddine.Dridi,Violet.Ka.I.Pun,Volker.Stolz}@hvl.no`

Abstract. Workflows coordinate tasks across departments or organisations, where correct execution depends not only on control dependencies but also on the availability of shared resources. This paper presents ReAct, a resource-aware active object language for workflow modelling. In ReAct, method declarations serve as contracts: they specify alternative resource profiles in their signatures, giving methods multiple execution options when resources are limited. Methods can be invoked only once their dependency conditions are satisfied; at activation, a feasible resource profile is then selected and allocated. We encode the language in Maude and show how workflows can be executed, simulated, and verified against their declared dependencies and resource requirements.

Keywords: Active objects · Resource allocation · Contracts · Maude · Workflow Models

1 Introduction

A business process is a collection of structured tasks to fulfil a certain goal within an organisation [1], and a workflow [21] describes the arrangement of tasks and resources within a business process. Workflows can sometimes span across multiple departments or even organisations, with multiple workflows running concurrently. These workflows may share resources while one or more tasks in a workflow local in an organisation are depending on the completion of tasks in the concurrent workflows running in different organisations. Planning this kind of workflows is challenging as it requires specific knowledge from multiple domains to have an overview of how resources are shared across multiple workflows as well as how tasks depend on each other.

Therefore, while there exists tools, e.g., Workflow Management Systems (WMS), that are used to model and automate business processes across heterogeneous tasks while enforcing the intended business logic [8,20], the support for capturing the aforementioned concerns for cross-organisational workflows is limited and inflexible [19].

To address this, we proposed in our earlier work [18] a core language, based on [3], that supports specifying the dependency between tasks (modelled as methods) in method declarations. This allows workflow models to be statically checked, using a type system, to ensure that method invocations respect the declared dependencies.

M. H. ter Beek and L. Teixeira (Eds.): SBMF 2025, LNCS 16363, pp. 156–175, 2026.
https://doi.org/10.1007/978-3-032-12086-1_9

This paper extends the core language in [18], by allowing resource requirements to be specified in the method declaration. Here, resources are referred to discrete and reusable entities (not consumable or continuous quantities), such as doctors, cars, equipment, required for executing a task. The extended language, called ReAct, enables workflow planners to specify not only one, but multiple alternative sets of resources (each alternative is referred to as a resource profile). Such alternative resource profiles can enhance flexibility of method execution when resources are limited as well as enable decision support in selecting resources based on the metrics that need to be optimised.

With this extension, method declarations in our language can be considered as a form of *contracts* that have to be fulfilled before a method can be invoked: methods can start executing only when all the depending tasks have been completed, and at least one of the required resource profiles is available. Such contracts can potentially facilitate workflow planning by automating the coordination of tasks and resources based on the constraints on execution order and required resources provided by domain experts.

We also provide an *original* implementation of a Maude framework, which gives our language a generic, executable operational semantics well suited to workflow execution. The framework captures the behaviour of workflows modelled in our language, and allows us to check if one or all executions respect the conditions specified in the method declaration.

The rest of the paper is organised as follows: Sect. 2 presents the syntax and operational semantics of ReAct, extending the core language introduced in [18] with explicit resource declarations and resource-aware rules. Section 3 provides a brief overview of rewriting logic and Maude, and introduces a novel executable specification of the extended semantics in Maude. Section 4 shows the execution and simulation results of an example workflow, illustrating how resources and dependencies are managed and how Maude's search functionality supports verification of behavioural properties. Section 5 discusses related work, and Sect. 6 concludes the paper with future work.

2 Core Language

In this section, we introduce our core language, ReAct, that allows specifying resource requirements for individual tasks in a workflow model. The language is based on active objects [4], which uses the actor model of concurrency and cooperative scheduling. It is an extension of our earlier work [18] enforcing task dependency in workflows. We first present the syntax with an illustrative example and then discuss the relevant semantic rules.

2.1 Syntax

Figure 1 shows the abstract syntax of ReAct, which extends the core language defined in [18] by having the notion of global resources R and by allowing specifying resources required RP to execute a task in a workflow at the level of method declaration.

A ReAct program P consists of a resource pool R, class declarations $\overline{CD}$ and a main method. The resource pool is a multiset of pairs $(t, \mathcal{A})$ representing a resource of type t with uninterpreted attributes $\mathcal{A}$. A class declaration has a name C, fields $\overline{x}$ of types $\overline{T}$ and methods $\overline{M}$. A method M is defined by its signature Sg, specifying its name m and return type T, formal parameters $\overline{x}$ of types $\overline{T}$, the task dependencies DP, and the resource requirement RP of method m, where DP and RP are optional, indicated by square brackets $[\,]$. A method body consists of local variables $\overline{x}$ of types $\overline{T}$ and a sequence of statements s.

$$
\begin{array}{rcl}
P & ::= & R \ \overline{CD} \ \{\overline{T \ x} \ ; \ s\} \\
R & ::= & \emptyset \mid \{(t, \mathcal{A})\} \cup R \\
CD & ::= & \textbf{class} \ C \ \{\overline{T \ x} \ ; \ \overline{M}\} \\
M & ::= & Sg \ \{\overline{T \ x} \ ; \ s\} \\
Sg & ::= & T \ m(\overline{T \ x}) \ [DP] \ [RP] \\
T & ::= & B \mid \textbf{Fut}\langle B\rangle \\
B & ::= & C \mid \textsf{Bool} \mid \textsf{Int} \mid \textsf{Unit} \mid \dots \\
DP & ::= & dp \mid DP \vee DP \\
RP & ::= & rp \mid RP \vee RP
\end{array}
\qquad
\begin{array}{rcl}
s & ::= & x = rhs \mid \textbf{skip} \mid \textbf{if} \ e \ \textbf{then} \ s \ \textbf{else} \ s \\
& \mid & \textbf{await} \ f? \mid \textbf{return} \ e \mid s \ ; \ s \\
rhs & ::= & e \mid \textbf{new} \ C \mid f.\textbf{get} \\
& \mid & e.m(\overline{e}) \ \textbf{after} \ fs \mid e!m(\overline{e}) \ \textbf{after} \ fs \\
e & ::= & x \mid b \mid fs \mid \textbf{this} \\
fs & ::= & \textbf{True} \mid fts \mid fs \vee fs \\
fts & ::= & f? \mid fts \wedge fts \\
dp & ::= & C.m \mid dp \wedge dp \\
rp & ::= & (t, n, \mathcal{A}) \mid rp \wedge rp
\end{array}
$$

Fig. 1. Abstract syntax.

Task dependencies DP specified in the method signature are in disjunctive normal form (DNF) and need to be completed prior to invoking method m. We use $C.m$ to denote a depending method m of class C. We model resource requirements RP similarly, where each rp denoted as $(t, n, \mathcal{A})$, indicating the quantity n of resources of type t with attributes $\mathcal{A}$, where $n \in \mathbb{N}^+$. The signature of methods that do not depend on any other task and not require any resource is written as $T \ m(\overline{T \ x})$.

Example 1. Let $DP = DP_1 \vee DP_2$, $RP = RP_1 \vee RP_2$, where $DP_1 = C_1.m_1$, $DP_2 = C_2.m_2 \wedge C_2'.m_2'$, $RP_1 = (t_1, n_1, \mathcal{A}_1)$ and $RP_2 = (t_2, n_2, \mathcal{A}_2) \wedge (t_2', n_2', \mathcal{A}_2')$. The signature $T \ m(\overline{T \ x}) \ DP \ RP$ specifies the constraints on tasks dependency and the resource requirements of method m. Precisely, the signature states that method m is depending on the completion of method m_1 of class C_1 or method m_2 of class C_2 *and* method m_2' of class C_2'; and indicates that the method requires either n_1 resources of type t_1 with attributes $\mathcal{A}_1$ or n_2 resources of type t_2 with attributes $\mathcal{A}_2$ as well as n_2' resources of type t_2 with $\mathcal{A}_2'$.

Consequently, one can consider the signature of a method as a contract specifying the completion of certain tasks and the requirements of resources that needs to be fulfilled prior to executing the method.

Types are standard, where $\textbf{Fut}\langle B\rangle$ is a future type with values of type B. Statements, as well as the right-hand side of an assignment, are similar to those in typical active object languages, except for method invocations. Each method

```
 1  { (Intern, A_1), (Intern, A_2), (SeniorNurse, A_3),
 2    (JuniorNurse, A_4), (JuniorNurse, A_5), (SeniorResident, A_6),
 3    (LabTechnician, A_7)
 4      ... }
 5
 6   class Hospital {
 7     Unit registerPatient()
 8       req (Intern,1,...) ∨ (JuniorNurse,1,...) { ... }
 9
10     Unit startTreatmentPlan()
11       dep RadiologyUnit.imagingScan ∧ LaboratoryUnit.bloodTest
12       req (Intern,1,...) ∧ (JuniorNurse,2,...) { ... } }
13
14   class CardiologyUnit {
15     Unit assessPatient()
16       dep Hospital.registerPatient
17       req (SeniorResident,1,...) ∧ (SeniorNurse,1,...) { ... } }
18
19   class RadiologyUnit {
20     Unit imagingScan()
21       dep CardiologyUnit.assessPatient
22       req (JuniorResident,1,...) ∨ (SeniorNurse,1,...) { ... } }
23
24   class LaboratoryUnit {
25     Unit bloodTest()
26       dep CardiologyUnit.assessPatient
27       req (LabTechnician,1,...) ∨ (Intern,1,...) { ... } }
28
29  { Hospital h = new Hospital();
30    CardiologyUnit cu = new CardiologyUnit();
31    RadiologyUnit ru = new RadiologyUnit();
32    LaboratoryUnit lab = new LaboratoryUnit();
33
34    Fut<Unit> f1 = h!registerPatient();
35    Fut<Unit> f2 = cu!assessPatient() after f1?;
36    Fut<Unit> f3 = lab!bloodTest() after f2?;
37    Fut<Unit> f4 = ru!imagingScan() after f2?;
38    Fut<Unit> f5 = h!startTreatmentPlan() after f3? ∧ f4?;
39  }
```

Fig. 2. Illustrative example.

invocation is associated to a future f, and we use **await** f? to suspend a process until the associated method returns, i.e., f? is evaluated to *true*, and f.**get** to retrieve the value store in f. Methods can be, either synchronously or asynchronously, invoked only after a (possibly empty) set of methods have completed.

To specify the depending methods, we use an **after** clause containing fs that is in DNF. To invoke a method, either at least one conjunction fts in fs is evaluated to true or fs is True, i.e., no depending method is specified. Remark that both DP and fs are required to type check whether methods are invoked conforming to the task dependency specified in the method definition and we refer the interested readers to [18] for the details.

We illustrate the syntax with the simple workflow model presented in Fig. 2, which consist of four classes and a main method. For the clarity of the code, we prepend a keyword **dep** to the task dependency and **req** to the resource requirements in the method declaration.

The resource pool is specified in Lines 1–4. The four classes are defined in Lines 6–27, while the main method is defined in Lines 29–38, which first creates the objects of the four classes. The workflow then starts with registering a patient at the hospital (Line 34), which does not have any task dependency, but requires either an `Intern` *or* a `JuniorNurse`, as reflected in the method signature in Lines 7–8. Note that the specific attributes of the resources are omitted here. After the registration, the patient is assessed by the `CardiologyUnit` (Line 35), which requires one `SeniorResident` *and* one `SeniorNurse` (Lines 15–17). Only after the patient is assessed, two tasks can proceed in parallel: a blood test (Line 36) in the `LaboratoryUnit`, requiring a `LabTechnician` *or* an `Intern`, and an imaging scan (Line 37) in the `RadiologyUnit`, requiring a `JuniorResident` *or* a `SeniorNurse` (Lines 20–22), as shown in the method signatures in (Lines 25–27) and (Lines 20–22), respectively. Finally, once both the blood test and the imaging scan complete, the patient can start the treatment plan at the hospital (Line 38), which requires an `Intern` *and* two `JuniorNurse`, as specified in Lines (10–12).

$$
\begin{aligned}
cn &::= \epsilon \mid obj \mid invoc \mid res \mid F \mid cn \; cn & p &::= \mathbf{idle} \mid \{l \mid s\} \\
obj &::= o(a, p, q) & q &::= \emptyset \mid \{l \mid s\} \mid q \\
invoc &::= invoc(o, f, m, \overline{v}) & val &::= v \mid \bot \\
res &::= \emptyset \mid \{(t, \mathcal{A})\} \cup res & v &::= o \mid f \mid b \mid k \\
F &::= fut(f, val) & s &::= \mathbf{cont}(f) \mid \mathbf{suspend} \mid \dots \\
a, l &::= \epsilon \mid [\dots, x \mapsto v, \dots] & rhs &::= e.m(\overline{e}) \mid e!m(\overline{e}) \mid \dots
\end{aligned}
$$

Fig. 3. Runtime syntax.

2.2 Semantics

We present in the following first the syntax of the runtime configuration of *ReAct*, and then proceed to the semantics that manages the task dependency and resource requirements for method invocations in the core language.

Runtime Syntax. The runtime syntax is defined in Fig. 3. A runtime configuration *cn* consists of objects, invocation messages, a global resource pool and futures, denoted as *obj*, *invoc*, *res* and *F*, respectively. Each element in the configuration is separated by space. An empty configuration is written as ϵ. An object comprises an object identifier o, a map a associating object fields to values, a running process p and a pool q of processes waiting to run on the object. A process $\{l \mid s\}$ consists of a map l binding local variables to values and a sequence of statements s, or can also be `idle`.

An invocation message $invoc(o, f, m, \overline{v})$ includes the identity of the callee o, the associated future f, the invoked method m, and its actual parameters $\overline{v}$. A future $fut(f, val)$ consists of its identifier f and a value val which is v if the future is resolved or $\perp$ otherwise. The resource pool res is a multiset of pairs $(t, \mathcal{A})$, each of which indicates the type t and attributes $\mathcal{A}$ of a resource.

The statements are extended with $\mathbf{cont}(f)$ to return control to the caller process and $\mathbf{suspend}$ to move a running process into the pool of pending processes, while the right hand side of an assignment is extended with method invocations without the $\mathbf{after}$ clause.

$$\text{(Async-Call-After)}$$
$$o(a, \{l \mid x = e!m(\overline{e}) \text{ after } fs \; ; \; s\}, q)$$
$$\rightarrow o(a, \{l \mid \text{if } fs \; \{x = e!m(\overline{e}) \; ; \; s\} \text{ else } \{\text{suspend} \; ; \; x = e!m(\overline{e}) \text{ after } fs \; ; \; s\}\}, q)$$

$$\text{(Sync-Call-After)}$$
$$o(a, \{l \mid x = e.m(\overline{e}) \text{ after } fs \; ; \; s\}, q)$$
$$\rightarrow o(a, \{l \mid \text{if } fs \; \{x = e.m(\overline{e}) \; ; \; s\} \text{ else } \{\text{suspend} \; ; \; x = e.m(\overline{e}) \text{ after } fs \; ; \; s\}\}, q)$$

$$\text{(Async-Call)}$$
$$\frac{o' = [\![e]\!]_{aol} \quad \overline{v} = [\![\overline{e}]\!]_{aol} \quad f \text{ fresh}}{\begin{array}{c} o(a, \{l \mid x = e \, ! \, m(\overline{e}) \; ; \; s\}, q) \\ \rightarrow \; o(a, \{l \mid x = f \mid s\}, q) \quad invoc(o', f, m, \overline{v}) \quad fut(f, \perp) \end{array}}$$

$$\text{(Sync-Call)} \qquad\qquad \text{(Invoc)}$$
$$\frac{o' = [\![e]\!]_{aol} \quad o \neq o' \quad f \text{ fresh}}{\begin{array}{c} o(a, \{l \mid x = e.m(\overline{e}) \; ; \; s\}, q) \\ \rightarrow \; o(a, \{l \mid f = e!m(\overline{e}) \; ; \; x = f.\mathbf{get} \; ; \; s\}, q) \end{array}} \qquad \frac{\{l \mid s\} = \text{bind}(o, f, m, \overline{v}, \text{class}(o))}{\begin{array}{c} o(a, p, q) \quad invoc(o, f, m, \overline{v}) \\ \rightarrow \; o(a, p, q \cup \{l \mid s\}) \end{array}}$$

Fig. 4. Semantics – part I [18].

Operational Semantics. A selection of representative semantic rules is presented in Figs. 4 and 5. The remaining rules are standard and can be found in Fig. 8 in the appendix. For clarity, the semantic rules only show the components in a runtime configuration that are affected by the reduction steps. Figure 4 shows the rules defined in [18] that handle method invocations based on task dependency. Rules Async-Call-After and Sync-Call-After handle asynchronous and synchronous method invocations, respectively, where task dependency has to be taken into account, by rewriting the invocation to a conditional statement checking the evaluation of fs in the $\mathbf{after}$ clause. If it returns $\mathtt{True}$, the invocation is reduced to one without task dependency; otherwise, a $\mathbf{suspend}$ statement is prepended to the invocation so that the process will be moved to the pool of pending processes. The evaluation of fs has been defined in [18] and can be found in Fig. 9 in the appendix.

While task dependencies in method calls are checked explicitly at the point of invocation, resource requirements are handled implicitly only when activating the invocation at the callee object (see later in Fig. 5). Thus, method calls without task dependency are handled as usual, as shown in rules ASYNC-CALL and SYNC-CALL, emitting a message $invoc(o, f, m, \overline{v})$, which in turn is used to create a process through a binding process by rule INVOC. For a method m defined as $T\ m(\overline{T\ x})\ DP\ RP\ \{\overline{T\ y}\ ;\ s\}$ in class C, we define:

$$\text{bind}(o,\ f,\ m,\ \overline{v},\ C)\ =\ \{\ destiny \mapsto f,\ rr \mapsto RP,\ \overline{x} \mapsto \overline{v},\ ar \mapsto \bot,\ \overline{y} \mapsto \bot\ |\ s[o\backslash\mathbf{this}]\ \}$$

that returns a process executing method m by binding its local variable $destiny$, required resource profiles rr and formal parameters $\overline{x}$ to future f, RP and $\overline{v}$, respectively, while the allocated resources ar and local variables $\overline{y}$ remain undefined. Remark that DP is not required in the function, and in the case RP is not specified, i.e., no resource is required, rr is mapped to $\emptyset$. Note also that the local variables $destiny$, rr and ar are reserved keywords.

$$\text{(SELF-SYNC-CALL)}$$
$$\frac{o = [\![e]\!]_{aol} \quad \overline{v} = [\![\overline{e}]\!]_{aol} \quad f' \text{ fresh} \quad f = l(destiny) \qquad \{l'\ |\ s'\} = \text{bind}(o, f', m, \overline{v}, \text{class}(o)) \quad ares = \text{fpr}(l'(rr), res) \neq \emptyset}{\begin{array}{l} o(a, \{l\ |\ x = e.m(\overline{e})\ ;\ s\}, q) \quad res \\ \rightarrow\ o(a, \{l'[ar \mapsto ares]\ |\ s'\ ;\ \mathbf{cont}(f)\}, q \cup \{l\ |\ x = f'.\mathbf{get}\ ;\ s\}) \quad res\backslash ares \quad fut(f', \bot) \end{array}}$$

$$\begin{array}{cc} \text{(ACTIVATE-NoRESREQ)} & \text{(ACTIVATE-RESALLOC)} \\[4pt] \dfrac{l(rr) = \emptyset}{\begin{array}{l} o(a, \mathtt{idle}, q \cup \{l\ |\ s\}) \\ \rightarrow\ o(a, \{l\ |\ s\}, q) \end{array}} & \dfrac{l(ar) \neq \bot}{\begin{array}{l} o(a, \mathtt{idle}, q \cup \{l\ |\ s\}) \\ \rightarrow\ o(a, \{l\ |\ s\}, q) \end{array}} \end{array}$$

$$\text{(ACTIVATE-ToALLOC)}$$
$$\frac{l(rr) \neq \emptyset \quad l(ar) = \bot \quad ares = \text{fpr}(l(rr), res) \neq \emptyset}{\begin{array}{l} o(a, \mathtt{idle}, q \cup \{l\ |\ s\}) \quad res \\ \rightarrow\ o(a, \{l[ar \mapsto ares]\ |\ s\}, q) \quad res\backslash ares \end{array}}$$

$$\begin{array}{cc} \text{(RETURN)} & \text{(SELF-SYNC-RETURN)} \\[4pt] \dfrac{v = [\![e]\!]_{aol} \quad f = l(destiny)}{\begin{array}{l} o(a, \{l\ |\ \mathbf{return}\ e\ ;\ s\}, q) \quad fut(f, \bot)\ res \\ \rightarrow\ o(a, \{l\ |\ s\}, q) \quad fut(f, v)\ res \cup l(ar) \end{array}} & \dfrac{f = l(destiny)}{\begin{array}{l} o(a, \{l'\ |\ \mathbf{cont}(f)\}, q \cup \{l\ |\ s\})\ res \\ \rightarrow\ o(a, \{l\ |\ s\}, q)\ res \cup l(ar) \end{array}} \end{array}$$

Fig. 5. Semantics – part II. Resource-aware extensions of operational rules.

Figure 5 presents the rules that we extend from those in [18] to manage resources in ReAct. Resource allocation is handled implicitly through activating a process residing in the pending pool, which is controlled by the three ACTIVATE rules. To allocate resources to a process, rule ACTIVATE-ToALLOC first checks if the process has been granted any resources and if any of the required resource profile is available in the resource pool. Then, it allocates the resources specified in the available profile, by updating the local variable ar, and removes them from the pool. In other words, resource allocation will only take place when the process first becomes active in the callee object.

$$\mathrm{fpr}(RP, \mathit{res}) = \begin{cases} \mathrm{fpr}(\mathit{rp}, \mathit{res}) & \text{if } RP = \mathit{rp} \\ AR & \text{if } RP = RP' \vee \mathit{rp} \text{ and } AR = \mathrm{fpr}(\mathit{rp}, \mathit{res}) \neq \emptyset \\ \mathrm{fpr}(RP', \mathit{res}) & \text{if } RP = RP' \vee \mathit{rp} \text{ and } \mathrm{fpr}(\mathit{rp}, \mathit{res}) = \emptyset \end{cases}$$

$$\mathrm{fpr}(\mathit{rp}, \mathit{res}) = \begin{cases} \mathrm{fpr}((t, n, \mathcal{A}), \mathit{res}) & \text{if } \mathit{rp} = (t, n, \mathcal{A}) \\ AR \cup \mathrm{fpr}(\mathit{rp}', \mathit{res} \setminus AR) & \text{if } \mathit{rp} = \mathit{rp}' \wedge (t, n, \mathcal{A}) \\ & \quad \text{and } AR = \mathrm{fpr}((t, n, \mathcal{A}), \mathit{res}) \neq \emptyset \\ \emptyset & \text{if } \mathit{rp} = \mathit{rp}' \wedge (t, n, \mathcal{A}) \\ & \quad \text{and } \mathrm{fpr}((t, n, \mathcal{A}), \mathit{res}) = \emptyset \end{cases}$$

$$\mathrm{fpr}((t, n, \mathcal{A}), \mathit{res}) = \begin{cases} \{(t, \mathcal{A})\} & \text{if } (t, \mathcal{A}) \in \mathit{res} \text{ and } n = 1 \\ \{(t, \mathcal{A})\} \cup AR & \text{if } (t, \mathcal{A}) \in \mathit{res} \text{ and } n > 1 \\ & \quad \text{and } AR = \mathrm{fpr}((t, n-1, \mathcal{A}), \mathit{res} \setminus \{(t, \mathcal{A})\}) \neq \emptyset \\ \emptyset & \text{otherwise.} \end{cases}$$

Fig. 6. Definition of $\mathrm{fpr}(RP, \mathit{res})$.

The evaluation of the set of required resources is handled by the auxiliary function $\mathrm{fpr}(l'(\mathit{rr}), \mathit{res})$ ("feasible profile") as shown in Fig. 6, which returns the (multi)set of selected resources to be allocated *ares*. Activating processes that do not require any resource or have already been granted the required resources is carried out by ACTIVATE-NORESREQ and ACTIVATE-RESALLOC.

Resource allocation for synchronous self-calls are handled when the methods are invoked, as shown in rule SELF-SYNC-CALL. To make a synchronous self-call, the rule first checks if any of the resource profiles required by the method is available in the resource pool. Then, it allocates the available required resources to the newly created process and appends statement **cont**(f) to the sequence of statements s', which is later used to return control to the caller process. Finally, the allocated resources are removed from the resource pool. Allocated resources will only be returned when the corresponding method returns, as seen in rule RETURN and SELF-SYNC-RETURN.

As we can see from the semantics, methods can only be executed if two conditions hold. Firstly, invoking a method needs to fulfil the task dependency. Therefore, to successfully invoke a method, one of the conjunctions in *fs* must be evaluated to true, i.e., all the futures in a conjunction are resolved. Secondly, an invoked method can only start execution if one of the profiles specified in its resource requirements (if any) is satisfied, given a global resource pool.

3 Formalising Active Objects in Maude

Achieving an executable formal specification along with automatic verification is a complex task. As seen in Sect. 2, the language encompasses three main aspects. Firstly, we define the syntax of ReAct to identify all the entities of the language that constitute its grammar. Secondly, we specify the runtime configuration to capture how these entities are structured during execution. Lastly, we provide the operational semantics that governs the behaviour and describes how the configuration is evolving.

Correspondingly, we need a formal language and toolset capable of expressing rich structures, composing conditional behaviours, and directly executing their specifications. These considerations led us to choose the Maude language [6], as an implementation of rewriting logic that satisfies our requirements. We choose this language for several reasons: (i) it is expressive enough to encode ReAct's static entities and their relationships; (ii) its equational theory provides the necessary predicate logic for defining equations, computational constraints and feasibility checks; (iii) its executable rewriting logic semantics allow rule application to depend on complex guards such as resource availability or future resolution; and (iv) it includes built-in search and model checking facilities that enable automated verification of properties.

3.1 Maude and Rewriting Logic

The Maude language is a high performance language and tool set based on rewriting logic that supports formal specification, execution, and analysis of systems. Its integration of equational logic with rewrite rules enables concise modelling of system behaviour and rigorous reasoning about system properties [5,6]. Formally, a rewrite logic theory is a tuple $(\Sigma, E \cup A, R)$, where $(\Sigma, E \cup A)$ is a membership equation logic theory: Σ is the signature that specifies sorts, subsorts, operators and messages, E a set of (possibly conditional) equations, A a set of equational attributes for operators (e.g., associative, commutative), and R a collection of (possibly conditional) rewrite rules.

The different modules in Maude can be implemented using an object-oriented specification that encompasses objects, messages, classes, and inheritance. An object is represented as $\langle O : C \mid a_1 : v_1, \ldots, a_n : v_n \rangle$ where O is the object name, C is an instance of class, a_i are attribute identifiers, and v_i are their corresponding values for $i = 1 \ldots n$. Concurrent states in object-oriented modules are modelled as multisets of objects and messages, and interactions between objects are governed by rewrite rules:

$$\text{crl } [l] : \langle O_1 : C_1 \mid a_{s_1} \rangle \ldots \langle O_n : C_n \mid a_{s_n} \rangle M_1 \ldots M_m$$
$$\implies \langle O_{i_1} : C'_{i_1} \mid a'_{s_{i_1}} \rangle \ldots \langle O_{i_k} : C'_{i_k} \mid a'_{s_{i_k}} \rangle M'_1 \ldots M'_q \quad \text{if Cond.}$$

3.2 Execution Semantics

In this section, we show how we employ a Maude-based rewrite theory to define the language and the semantics of ReAct. The executable artefact (code and example) is archived in [9]. Formally, the operational semantics of ReAct is implemented in Maude as:

$$\text{def}_{ReAct} = \{\Sigma_{ReAct}, (E \cup A)_{ReAct}, R_{ReAct}\}$$

Table 1. Correspondence between ReAct and Maude

<table>
<tr><th colspan="2">ReAct</th><th>Maude</th></tr>
<tr><td rowspan="20">Syntax</td><td>Object</td><td><code>class OBJECT | id : Oid, fields : Int,
    proc : ProcessState, suspended : ProcessPool .</code></td></tr>
<tr><td>Method</td><td><code>class METHOD | sig : Oid, body : Oid .</code></td></tr>
<tr><td>Signature</td><td><code>class SIGNATURE | ret : Int, name : MethodName,
    params : ParamList, dp : DP, requires : ResourceProfile .</code></td></tr>
<tr><td>Resource</td><td><code>class RESOURCE | type : String, attrs : AttrSet,
    state : ResState, ResCost : Int .</code></td></tr>
<tr><td>Resource
Profile</td><td><code>sort ResourceProfile .

op noneProfile : -> ResourceProfile .
op needs : String Int AttrSet -> ResourceProfile [ctor] .
op _and_ : ResourceProfile ResourceProfile ->
    ResourceProfile [ctor assoc comm id: noneProfile] .
op _or_ : ResourceProfile ResourceProfile ->
    ResourceProfile [ctor assoc comm id: noneProfile] .</code></td></tr>
<tr><td>Statement</td><td><code>sort Statement .
op _=_!_(_) : Object Expr Oid Args -> Statement [ctor] .
op _=_._(_) : Object Expr Oid Args -> Statement [ctor] .
op _=_!_(_)after_ : Object Expr Oid Args Object ->
    Statement [ctor] .
op _=_._(_)after_ : Object Expr Oid Args Object ->
    Statement [ctor] .
sort Statement .

ops skip eos suspend : -> Statement [ctor] .
op await : Oid -> Statement [ctor] .</code></td></tr>
<tr><td>Process</td><td><code>sort ProcessState .</code></td></tr>
<tr><td>State</td><td><code>ops idle : -> ProcessState .
op { _ | _ } : LocalVarList Statement -> ProcessState [ctor] .</code></td></tr>
<tr><td>Future</td><td><code>sort FutureState .
class Future | value : ValueOption, state : FutureState .
ops unresolved resolved : -> FutureState [ctor] .</code></td></tr>
<tr><td rowspan="4">Semantics</td><td>Equations</td><td><code>**Equations:** clauseSatisfied(FS), bind(O,F,...), get(F),
    feasibleProfile(RP, RS)</code></td></tr>
<tr><td>Messages</td><td><code>**Messages:** op invoc(O,F,M,A) :
    Oid FutureOid Oid Args -> Msg [ctor] .</code></td></tr>
<tr><td>Semantics
rules</td><td><code>**Rewrite Rules:**
crl [rewrite-rule-name] : State => State' if Equation .</code></td></tr>
<tr><td>Properties</td><td><code>**Model Checking:** search [[n, m]] in ModId : initial-state =>*
pattern [such that cond] .</code></td></tr>
</table>

where Σ_{ReAct} defines the structure and data types for the main entities of *ReAct* (objects, processes, method signatures, invocations, resources, etc.); $(E \cup A)_{ReAct}$ specifies the language's equational theory, specifying computations such as message construction, future binding, and the equational properties of resources; and R_{ReAct} defines the dynamic semantics via a set of rewrite rules that capture operational behaviour. These rules include method invocation, process creation and suspension, and resource allocation and release.

The encoding of ReAct into executable and analysable Maude specifications without loss of information is based on the mappings shown in Table 1. The specifications of the grammar is implemented in an object-oriented module named **REACT-SYNTAX**. The operational semantics of the language is encoded as a set of conditional rewrite rules in another object-oriented module called REACT-SEMANTICS. These modules enable us to perform simulation of the behaviour using rewrite engine of Maude.

Table 1 summarises the main sorts, classes, and operators defining ReAct. The class METHOD associates a method body with its SIGNATURE. The latter captures task dependencies dp and required resource profiles requires—both are required for method execution—using the sort ResourceProfile and its constructors (noneProfile, needs, _and_, _or_) to define alternative resource combinations. Statements comprising method bodies are represented by the sort Statement, defined by operators including asynchronous _= _!_(_) and synchronous method calls _= _._(_), method invocations with dependencies after, and control-flow instructions such as skip, return, suspend, and await, etc.

The runtime configuration consists of floating entities i.e., objects, messages, resources, and futures. Each object is an instance of OBJECT whose process state is built with the sort ProcessState and the operator {_ | _}, which binds destiny, method parameters, and the resource binding to a LocalVarList and pairs them with the statement sequence. Invocation messages invoc(...) float in the configuration and when consumed by the INVOC rule, create a process that is placed in the ProcessPool to await resources or dependency resolution. Method results are represented by Future objects (with value and FutureState = resolved/unresolved). The global pool of resources is modelled by a set of objects instances of class RESOURCE within RESOURCE-POOL.

The operational semantics leverages Maude's rewriting engine: sorts, classes, operators, equations, messages, and (possibly conditional) rewrite rules. Together, they form a rewrite theory whose executions are driven by pattern matching and equational evaluation representing the auxiliary equations. Rules have the shape crl [name] : State => State' if Condition .. The left-hand side matches entities in the global configuration; the condition is simplified by the auxiliary equations (e.g., resource feasibility or future resolution); the right-hand side updates object fields, futures, process pools, and the resource pool, possibly emitting or consuming coordination messages. Messages (invoc(...), releaseRes(...), etc.) serve as coordination artefacts: one rule can emit a message to signal a request, and another rule consumes it to advance execution.

As an example, Fig. 7 presents the conditional rewrite rule ACTIVATE-ALLOC. When activation requires resources (recorded in rr) and none have yet been allocated (ar == noneProfile), the ACTIVATE-ALLOC rule computes a feasible profile via feasibleProfile(...), updates the pool, moves the process to execution, and stores the chosen profile in ar. The application condition of the rule indicates that the process must have resources requested but not allocated.

Since rules operate within an associative-commutative multiset, the rewrite engine of Maude explores them nondeterministically, so the same initial configuration may evolve along multiple interleaving paths, producing a branching execution tree from any given initial configuration. For example, after an invoc(...) message is emitted, Maude may immediately apply the Invoc rule

```
crl [activate-alloc] :
  < RP : RESOURCE-POOL | pool : ResS >
  < O : OBJECT | id : OCid, fields : Fld,
  proc : idle, suspended : { LVL ; (rr :== RP) ; ( ar :== noneProfile )
    | S } ; Q >
=>
  < RP : RESOURCE-POOL | pool : reserveResources(feasibleProfile(RP,
    ResS), ResS) >
  < O : OBJECT | id : OCid, fields : Fld,
  proc : { LVL ; (rr :== RP) ; (ar :== feasibleProfile(RP, ResS)) | S },
  suspended : Q >
if RP =/= noneProfile.
```

Fig. 7. Rewrite rule ACTIVATE-ALLOC

to suspend the callee's process or postpone it in favour of other available rewrites. Similarly, `activate-alloc` only fires when its guard conditions are satisfied (i.e., when resources become available), competing nondeterministically with other enabled rules for execution.

Maude's rewrite engine serves as the core executor of ReAct operational semantics. It continuously scans the global configuration—composed of objects, messages, and resource pools—matching the left-hand side patterns of conditional rewrite rules, evaluating guard conditions via the underlying equational theory, and applying the corresponding state transformations. Messages such as `invoc(...)` act as explicit staging points, enabling one rule to emit a message that another rule can subsequently consume. Auxiliary equations (e.g., `bind(...)` and `releaseRes(...)`) handle process creation setup and resource release, while rewrite rules directly update object fields, process states, and resource allocations within an executable framework. This inherent concurrency and interleaving of invocation, suspension, resource-aware activation, and execution is precisely what Maude's built-in search and model checking tools can potentially exhaustively analyse. We hence have tool support to ensure that ReAct correctness properties hold across all possible execution paths.

4   Simulation and Analysis

This section presents an executable Maude example, which integrates resource consumption and release with the semantics of method calls, to show correct allocation and termination behaviour. To this end, we revisit the example from Fig. 2 inspired by coordination in a hospital emergency department. The workflow models asynchronous medical tasks across different units, subject to both task dependencies and resource constraints.

4.1   Example

The workflow comprises five asynchronous tasks: `registerPatient`, `assess-Patient`, `bloodTest`, `imagingScan`, and `startTreatmentPlan`. The workflow starts with `registerPatient` on the `Hospital` object. Once registration completes, `assessPatient` on `CardiologyUnit` is triggered with explicit `after` clauses. Similarly, only after `assessPatient` completes, both `bloodTest` on `LaboratoryUnit` and `imagingScan` on `RadiologyUnit` are triggered and these two tasks run concurrently. When both tasks `bloodTest` and `imagingScan` complete, `startTreatmentPlan` is initiated at `Hospital`.

Each method invocation is an asynchronous task whose activation is delayed until its `after` dependencies are resolved. In addition, each method declares a required resource profile via `requires`, allowing alternatives through `and`/`or` combinators. These contracts are used to test feasibility at activation time; if sufficient matching resources are available, they are allocated atomically and the process moves from `suspended` to `active`.

All methods draw from a shared `RESOURCE-POOL` containing limited personnel with roles and attributes. Each `RESOURCE` specifies a type (e.g., `"Resident"`, `"Intern"`), and their attributes like `(years(5) ; shift("day"))`. We recall that the pool is modelled as a multiset; the attributes are uninterpreted constants, whose only role is exact matching. We use the following initial resource pool:

```
(Intern, (years(2) ; shift("day"))), (JuniorResident, (years(5) ; shift("day"))),
(SeniorResident, (years(10) ; shift("day"))), (Nurse, (years(5) ; shift("day"))),
(JuniorNurse, (years(5) ; shift("day"))), (JuniorNurse, (years(5) ; shift("day"))),
(SeniorNurse, (years(10) ; shift("day"))), (SeniorNurse, (years(10) ; shift("day"))),
(LabTechnician, (years(5) ; shift("day")))
```

4.2   Execution

Using Maude's rewrite command `rewrite in ACTIVE-OBJ-RESOURCE-TEST : init`, the Maude engine performs iterative applications of the operational semantics rules until no further rewrites are possible. Execution completes almost instantly after 453 rewrites, and the system reaches a stable, terminating state, indicating successful execution and resource handling: every object in the final configuration has reached an idle state and no rule of the operational semantics is enabled. Inspection of the final configuration shows that:

1. **All tasks completed with correct resource discipline:** the `RESOURCE-POOL` in the final state is identical to the one in the initial state. Thus, every allocation obtained during execution has been returned to the pool, leaving it ready for subsequent tasks.
2. **All futures resolved:** every declared method call in our example has finished execution, i.e., all associated futures have been resolved and received a value.
3. **No pending invocations or suspended processes:** There are no *invoc* messages in the configuration, and every object has `proc : idle` with no suspended calls. With no calls in progress, all guards satisfied, and no rules enabled, the system has reached termination.

Next, we discuss how Maude's search mechanism allows us to check all possible executions of our system, as the asynchronous method calls give naturally rise to non-determinism.

4.3   Reachability Analysis

We use Maude's `search` to systematically explore the state space of ReAct (specified as a rewrite theory). By selecting the search arrow `=>!` (canonical final states), we can target terminating configurations. Pattern matching over futures, resource states, and objects lets us pose precise queries that reveal liveness issues related to resource consumption, leading to deadlocks, that a single rewrite trace might miss.

All Futures Resolved. To check liveness, we searched for final states where all four futures that we declare in the code (`fregRecord`, `fcardioAssess`, `fimagingScan`, `fbloodTest` and `finitiateTreatment`) were resolved:

```
search in ACTIVE-OBJ-RESOURCE-TEST : init =>!
  < fregRecord         : Future | state : resolved >
  < fcardioAssess      : Future | state : resolved >
  < fimagingScan       : Future | state : resolved >
  < fbloodTest         : Future | state : resolved >
  < finitiateTreatment : Future | state : resolved >
  C:Configuration .
```

This query returned 345 solutions, showing that from the initial configuration all futures resolve in canonical final states (`=>!`) across many interleavings. The number of solutions emerges from intermediate rewriting sequence (e.g., message handling and resource release) that produce syntactically distinct but observationally equivalent configurations with respect to futures and resource availability. Note that this is a program-specific property here, and not necessarily true for ReAct programs in general.

Resource Release. Similarly, we use the canonical state arrow `=>!` to check that specific resources are *available* in all terminating states:

```
search in ACTIVE-OBJ-RESOURCE-TEST : init =>!
  < resourcePool | pool :
     (< r4 : RESOURCE | type : "Junior Resident",
                      state : available > : _) >
  C:Configuration .
```

This query succeeds and shows that the Junior Resident (identified by `r4` in the Maude model) is always released at termination. Conversely, searching with `state : consumed` produced no solutions, thus verifying that no resource leaks occur in terminating states.

Global Pool Restoration. To show that *all* terminating states restore the resource pool to exactly what it was in the initial state, we define an observer `poolOf : Configuration -> ResourceSet` that extracts the pool from any configuration, and a predicate `samePool(C)` that checks `poolOf(C) == poolOf(init)` (equality is checked up to the ACU multiset operator of the pool, so order does not matter). We then ask Maude to explore all *final states* reachable from `init` and return only those that *violate* the invariant. Any solution to the query below would be a counterexample:

```
search in ACTIVE-OBJ-RESOURCE-TEST : init =>!
  C:Configuration
  such that not samePool(C) .
```

This search returned *No solution* meaning Maude found no terminating state with a different pool. Therefore, in every terminating run, all reserved resources are released and the final pool is identical to the initial one.

As a separate sanity check, we also requested at least one final state where the invariant holds *and* nontrivial activity occurred (some future resolved and at least one asynchronous call was issued):

```
search [1] in ACTIVE-OBJ-RESOURCE-TEST : init =>!
  < fm : FUTMON | resolved : RF >
  < counter : COUNTER | count : N >  C:Configuration
  such that samePool(C) and (RF =/= noneF) and (N > 1) .
```

Together, these two searches demonstrate that every terminating execution restores the resource pool exactly to its initial multiset.

5 Related Work

Extensive work has been carried out for workflow modelling and numerous formal approaches have been proposed to analyse workflow behaviour as well as resource management.

UML Activity Diagrams [10] are competitive with WMS notations and provide a powerful notation for modelling control and data flows, they also allow limited communications. However, they lack explicit constructs for modelling inter-workflow message exchanges, making cross-organisational workflows difficult to capture precisely. Both BPEL [17] and BPMN [16] offer rich control-flow constructs for modelling workflows; however, the former lacks inter-workflow messaging, and although the latter supports message exchanges, the dependencies between concurrent workflows are not captured, which prevents reasoning about global workflow consistency and dependencies.

Coloured Petri Nets [13] and YAWL [2] are generally comparable in expressivity to many workflow languages, but control-flow modelling for multiple instances and advanced synchronisation remains limited, and inter-workflow communication is partially supported via hierarchical models in CPN-based approaches. Across all these notations resources remain annotations (lanes/roles or tokens) rather than contracts: there is no built-in notion of a resource profile with feasibility, and disciplined release tied to method activation/return.

BPMN-based resource provisioning strategies by Durán *et al.* [11] focus on dynamic allocation at the business process level. Although they provide executable semantics in Maude, resources are not part of the program syntax:

resource requirements are not declared in language artefacts, but parameterise scheduling policies at the process level. Similar to this paper, $\mathcal{R}$PL [3] targets cross-organisational workflows and supports explicit notion of the dependency of task execution order at the level of method invocation. Compared to $\mathcal{R}$PL, ReAct not only models task dependency at the level of method invocation, but also allows specifying at the level of method definition, which makes it possible to verify that the workflow behaviour complies with the required execution order. While resources are explicitly handled, i.e., acquired and released, in $\mathcal{R}$PL, resources in ReAct are managed implicitly when methods are activated and return according to the requirement specified in the method definition. Resources in Real-Time ABS [14] are capacity provided by deployment components that are consumed explicitly using cost/deadline annotations and recovered when time advances, which are quite from how resources are modelled and handled in ReAct.

Cooperative contracts by Kamburjan *et al.* [15] specify a method's pre/post conditions, frames, and overlap-at-suspension clauses, backed by a denotational trace semantics for an active object language. The focus is on deductive specification and verification of contracts around **await** and **get**, not on resource-aware execution, and the scheduling of the underlying language is unaffected.

Certification of time as a resource through type systems has been addressed by Crary *et al.* [7], where a virtual clock is threaded through types to enforce constant or input-dependent step bounds at compile time. In these approaches, running time is abstracted into a consumable quantity (steps or ticks), and the type checker provides verified bounds on this abstract resource. However, they do so by ignoring runtime dynamics: there are no shared pools, no alternative resource profiles, and no allocateâĂŞrelease discipline responsive to feasibility. Moreover, the work does not address the coordination and communication of concurrent workflows.

fBPMN [12] assigns a first-order logic semantics to BPMN, allowing tasks, events, and gateways to be translated into logical formulas for reasoning about control-flow properties such as consistency and soundness. However, it remains focused on branching and sequencing and does not provide an operational account of communication or synchronisation between concurrent processes. In particular, operational semantics for allocation, suspension, activation, and release of resources lie outside the scope of fBPMN's logic-based formalisation.

In contrast, ReAct is a resource-aware active object language that places resource requirements in method declarations and treats them as interface contracts. The latter are enforced by the operational rules during execution; i.e., at activation, the rules check feasibility, select and consume a concrete set of resources, and at return they release exactly that set. Dependencies are expressed as future-based guards and checked before a call proceeds, enabling correct ordering within the workflow under concurrency. Finally, the semantics and runtime are executable in Maude, its rewriting logic supports systematic search to demonstrate workflow termination, respect of dependencies, and absence of resource leaks across all interleavings.

6 Conclusion

In this paper, we present a resource-aware active object language, ReAct, for workflow modelling. The language extends the core language introduced in [18], which focuses on handling task dependency, by allowing specifying resource requirements in method signatures. By stating these two components at the level of method declaration, the method signatures can be seen as contracts that have to be fulfilled prior to execution; specifically, only when the specified depending tasks have completed and when the required resources are available. ReAct allows specifying alternative resource profiles in the method signature, which consequently increases the flexibility of method execution when resources are limited while keeping call sites free of resource details. Thus, such specification in method declarations can potentially contribute to automated workflow planning, where the specifications are provided by domain experts, and we believe that ReAct fills a gap in workflow modelling.

The operational semantics enforces an allocate-at-activation discipline: a method can only be invoked only when its dependency-guards (when present) hold, and the invoked method can only be activated if a feasible set of available resources exists. The selected resources are allocated atomically on activation and released on return. In addition, we develop an *original*, executable Maude semantics which allows us to analyse the behaviour of workflows modelled in ReAct. Using Maude's search functionality on our example, we demonstrated workflow termination and absence of resource leaks.

Future Work. As mentioned, ReAct is an extension of the core language introduced in [18], where a type system is proposed to verify that the behaviour of a workflow respects the task dependency specified in the method signature. Therefore, another possible extension would be to integrate this type system in our presented Maude framework to enrich its functionality. Our interest in a type system is also the reason why we are not yet focusing on more dynamic resource consumption, e.g., through parameters, computation, or transformation: while this is trivial to support in the runtime system, it has implications for static analysis where an upper bound has to be derivable.

We are also planning to introduce a priority-aware scheduler that leverages (i) priority levels declared in method definition (e.g., emergency vs. routine), and (ii) attributes of available resources (e.g., cost, availability, usage time) to decide which process should be activated and which concrete resources to consume. The scheduler can use a scoring function that balances priority, resource attributes, and estimated waiting time in the suspended queue while still giving precedence to methods with higher-priority.

Finally, we plan to investigate in how far Maude's built-in temporal logic model checking can be used to verify other behavioural properties of ReAct workflows, such as verifying that at the start of every recursive or iterative execution, the global resource pool has been restored to its initial configuration, in other words, resources are released between iterations and not held indefinitely.

Acknowledgements. This work is part of the CROFLOW project: Enabling Highly Automated Cross-Organisational Workflow Planning, funded by the Research Council of Norway (grant no. 326249).

A   Appendix

In this appendix, we present semantics omitted from Figs. 4 and 5 and the definition of the evaluation $[\![fs]\!]_F$ in Fig. 9.

$$
\begin{array}{c}
\text{(IF-TRUE)} \\
[\![e]\!]_{a\,ol,F} = \textbf{True} \\
\hline
o(a, \{l \mid \textbf{if } e \textbf{ then } s_1 \textbf{ else } s_2 \; ; \; s\}, q) \; F \\
\rightarrow o(a, \{l \mid s_1 \; ; \; s\}, q) \; F
\end{array}
\qquad
\begin{array}{c}
\text{(IF-FALSE)} \\
[\![e]\!]_{a\,ol,F} = \textbf{False} \\
\hline
o(a, \{l \mid \textbf{if } e \textbf{ then } s_1 \textbf{ else } s_2 \; ; \; s\}, q) \; F \\
\rightarrow o(a, \{l \mid s_2 \; ; \; s\}, q) \; F
\end{array}
$$

$$
\begin{array}{c}
\text{(AWAIT-TRUE)} \\
v \neq \bot \\
\hline
o(a, \{l \mid \textbf{await } f? \; ; \; s\}, q) \; \mathit{fut}(f, v) \\
\rightarrow o(a, \{l \mid s\}, q) \; \mathit{fut}(f, v)
\end{array}
\qquad
\begin{array}{c}
\text{(AWAIT-FALSE)} \\
v = \bot \\
\hline
o(a, \{l \mid \textbf{await } f? \; ; \; s\}, q) \; \mathit{fut}(f, v) \\
\rightarrow o(a, \textbf{idle}, q \cup \{l \mid \textbf{await } f? \; ; \; s\}) \; \mathit{fut}(f, v)
\end{array}
$$

$$
\begin{array}{c}
\text{(GET)} \\
v \neq \bot \\
\hline
o(a, \{l \mid x = f.\textbf{get} \; ; \; s\}, q) \; \mathit{fut}(f, v) \\
\rightarrow o(a, \{l \mid x = v \; ; \; s\}, q) \; \mathit{fut}(f, v)
\end{array}
\qquad
\begin{array}{c}
\text{(NEW)} \\
o' = \text{fresh} \quad a' = \text{atts}(C, o') \\
\hline
o(a, \{l \mid x = \textbf{new } C \; ; \; s\}, q) \\
\rightarrow o(a, \{l \mid x = o' \; ; \; s\}, q) \; o'(a', \textbf{idle}, \emptyset)
\end{array}
$$

$$
\begin{array}{c}
\text{(CONTEXT)} \\
cn \rightarrow cn' \\
\hline
cn \; cn'' \rightarrow cn' \; cn''
\end{array}
\qquad
\begin{array}{c}
\text{(SKIP)} \\
o(a, \{l \mid \textbf{skip} \; ; \; s\}, q) \\
\rightarrow o(a, \{l \mid s\}, q)
\end{array}
\qquad
\begin{array}{c}
\text{(SUSPEND)} \\
o(a, \{l \mid \textbf{suspend} \; ; \; s\}, q) \\
\rightarrow o(a, \textbf{idle}, q \cup \{l \mid s\})
\end{array}
$$

Fig. 8. Semantic rules [18] omitted from Figs. 4 and 5. Assignments for fields and local variables are typical and omitted). The auxiliary function atts(C, o') returns the default values of the fields of class C and o' is the value for **this**.

$$
[\![fs]\!]_F = \begin{cases} [\![fs']\!]_F \vee [\![fts]\!]_F & \text{if } fs = fs' \vee fts \\ [\![fts]\!]_F & \text{if } fs = fts \end{cases}
$$

$$
[\![fts]\!]_F = \begin{cases} [\![fts']\!]_F \wedge [\![f?]\!]_F & \text{if } fts = fts' \wedge f? \\ [\![f?]\!]_F & \text{if } fts = f? \end{cases}
$$

$$
[\![f?]\!]_F = \begin{cases} \textbf{True} & \text{if } \mathit{fut}(f, v) \in F \wedge v \neq \bot \\ \textbf{False} & \text{otherwise.} \end{cases}
$$

Fig. 9. Definition of the evaluation $[\![fs]\!]_F$ [18], with minor adjustment due to updated syntax.

References

1. van der Aalst, W.M.P.: Exploring the process dimension of workflow management, Computing Science Reports, vol. 97/13. Technische Universiteit Eindhoven (1997)
2. van der Aalst, W.M.P., ter Hofstede, A.H.: YAWL: yet another workflow language. Inf. Syst. **30**(4), 245–275 (2005)
3. Ali, M.R., Lamo, Y., I Pun, V.K.: Cost analysis for a resource sensitive workflow modelling language. Sci. Comput. Program. **225**, 102896 (2023)
4. de Boer, F., et al.: A survey of active object languages. ACM Comput. Surv. **50**(5), 76:1–76:39 (2017). https://doi.org/10.1145/3122848
5. Clavel, M., et al.: Maude manual (version 3.1). SRI International (2020)
6. Clavel, M., et al. (eds.): All About Maude - A High-Performance Logical Framework, How to Specify, Program and Verify Systems in Rewriting Logic. LNCS, vol. 4350. Springer, Heidelberg (2007). https://doi.org/10.1007/978-3-540-71999-1
7. Crary, K., Weirich, S.: Resource bound certification. In: Proceedings of the 27th ACM SIGPLAN-SIGACT Symposium on Principles of Programming Languages, pp. 184–198 (2000)
8. Dourish, P.: Process descriptions as organisational accounting devices: the dual use of workflow technologies. In: Proceedings of the 2001 ACM International Conference on Supporting Group Work, pp. 52–60 (2001)
9. Dridi, C.E., I Pun, V.K., Stolz, V.: Resource contracts for active objects, October 2025. Source code: https://github.com/selabhvl/maude-active-objects. https://doi.org/10.5281/zenodo.17305152
10. Dumas, M., ter Hofstede, A.H.M.: UML activity diagrams as a workflow specification language. In: Gogolla, M., Kobryn, C. (eds.) <<UML>> 2001. LNCS, vol. 2185, pp. 76–90. Springer, Heidelberg (2001). https://doi.org/10.1007/3-540-45441-1_7
11. Durán, F., Rocha, C., Salaün, G.: Resource provisioning strategies for BPMN processes: specification and analysis using Maude. J. Logical Algebraic Meth. Program. **123**, 100711 (2021)
12. Houhou, S., Baarir, S., Poizat, P., Quéinnec, P., Kahloul, L.: A first-order logic verification framework for communication-parametric and time-aware BPMN collaborations. Inf. Syst. **104**, 101765 (2022)
13. Jensen, K., Kristensen, L.M.: Coloured Petri Nets – Modelling and Validation of Concurrent Systems. Springer, Heidelberg (2009). https://doi.org/10.1007/B95112
14. Johnsen, E.B., Schlatte, R., Tapia Tarifa, S.L.: Integrating deployment architectures and resource consumption in timed object-oriented models. J. Logical Algebraic Meth. Program. **84**(1), 67–91 (2015)
15. Kamburjan, E., Din, C.C., Hähnle, R., Johnsen, E.B.: Behavioral contracts for cooperative scheduling. In: Ahrendt, W., Beckert, B., Bubel, R., Hähnle, R., Ulbrich, M. (eds.) Deductive Software Verification: Future Perspectives. LNCS, vol. 12345, pp. 85–121. Springer, Cham (2020). https://doi.org/10.1007/978-3-030-64354-6_4
16. Michele, C., Alberto, T.: BPMN: an introduction to the standard. Comput. Stand. Interfaces **34**, 124–134 (2012)
17. Ouyang, C., Dumas, M., ter Hofstede, A.H., van der Aalst, W.M.P.: From BPMN process models to BPEL web services. In: Proceedings of 2006 IEEE International Conference on Web Services, ICWS 2006, pp. 285–292. IEEE (2006)

18. I Pun, V.K., Stolz, V.: Enforced dependencies for active objects. In: Active Object Languages: Current Research Trends, LNCS, vol. 14360, pp. 359–374. Springer (2024)
19. Reichert, M., Weber, B.: Enabling Flexibility in Process-Aware Information Systems – Challenges, Methods, Technologies. Springer, Heidelberg (2012). https://doi.org/10.1007/978-3-642-30409-5
20. Senkul, P., Toroslu, I.H.: An architecture for workflow scheduling under resource allocation constraints. Inf. Syst. **30**(5), 399–422 (2005)
21. Workflow Management Coalition: Workflow Management Coalition Terminology & Glossary (1999). https://wfmc.org/wp-content/uploads/2022/09/TC-1011_term_glossary_v3.pdf

Formal Methods and AI

Inference of Deterministic Finite Automata via Q-Learning

Elaheh Hosseinkhani$^{(\boxtimes)}$ [iD] and Martin Leucker [iD]

Universität zu Lübeck, Lübeck, Germany
`{Elaheh.Hosseinkhani,leucker}@isp.uni-luebeck.de`

Abstract. Traditional approaches to inference of deterministic finite-state automata (DFA) stem from symbolic AI, including both active learning methods (e.g., Angluin's L* algorithm and its variants) and passive techniques (e.g., Biermann and Feldman's method, RPNI). Meanwhile, sub-symbolic AI, particularly machine learning, offers alternative paradigms for learning from data, such as supervised, unsupervised, and reinforcement learning (RL). This paper investigates the use of *Q-learning*, a well-known reinforcement learning algorithm, for the passive inference of deterministic finite automata. It builds on the core insight that the learned Q-function, which maps state-action pairs to rewards, can be reinterpreted as the transition function of a DFA over a finite domain. This provides a novel bridge between sub-symbolic learning and symbolic representations. The paper demonstrates how Q-learning can be adapted for automaton inference and provides an evaluation on several examples.

Keywords: Automata Learning · Q-Learning · Reinforcement Learning · Symbolic and Sub-symbolic AI Integration

1 Introduction

Many interactive systems can be effectively modeled as automata, allowing for structured analysis and understanding of their behavior. Beyond system modeling, automata have broad applications in fields such as software verification, natural language processing, and network protocol analysis. As a result, automata learning–the process of automatically constructing automata from observations is a compelling area of research with practical relevance across multiple domains.

One of the most commonly used and well-studied machine models is that of deterministic finite-state automata (DFA)–and we focus on DFA also in this paper. The problem of learning such automata is addressed within the field of grammatical inference, which has received considerable attention in recent years. There are two principle ways to learn an automaton: learn an automaton from a black-box system itself, i.e., *active learning*, or learn an automaton directly from observational data, i.e., *passive learning*. The active learning setting has been the most studied in the literature [3,15]. In that setting, the process of

M. H. ter Beek and L. Teixeira (Eds.): SBMF 2025, LNCS 16363, pp. 179–195, 2026.
https://doi.org/10.1007/978-3-032-12086-1_10

learning an automaton consists of querying the black-box system with two types of queries: *membership queries*, to check if a specific sequence of observational data is accepted by the system, and *equivalence queries*, to check if the language accepted by the automaton corresponds to the ones described by the system. A key research direction involves extending the learning process to more expressive classes of automata, like non-deterministic finite automata [6] and various classes of data automata [7,8]. Many of the algorithms for active learning elaborate on the Nerode's right congruence classes which characterize a minimal DFA uniquely. To this end, a characteristic set that uniquely identifies the automaton is eventually obtained [4] by queries and storing the results in a clever way. Roughly, a characteristic set consists of strings leading to states as well as strings distinguishing states.

Active learning has several limitations. For instance, it may require many interactions with the black-box system, which can be prohibitively costly. This drawback is exacerbated by the fact that the equivalence queries can often be done only statistically and therefore may entail heavy testing, if one requires a high accuracy. In addition, the numerous interactions also suppose a potentially unlimited access to the black-box system, which in real-world situations would often not be possible. Another drawback of active learning is that it completely leaves out all the available observational data, a resource that is often abundantly available.[1] By contrast, passive learning is data-driven: an automaton is learned directly from the data without interaction with the black-box system.

Until now, the study of automata passive learning dealt with DFA (deterministic finite automaton) and NFA (non-deterministic finite automaton), and several techniques have been used to handle this learning problem. Since learning (minimal) automata is NP-complete in general [9], a popular method is constraint-solving, which consists in encoding the passive learning problem as a set of constraints over integers [5]. A solution over the numbers 1 to k exists iff there is a corresponding automaton with k states. Such constraint problem may be translated into a satisfiability problem of propositional logic, which can be solved using a SAT solver [10]. Regular Positive and Negative Inference (RPNI) [12] is a further classic algorithm for learning deterministic finite automata (DFA) from labeled examples. It starts by building a prefix tree acceptor and then merges states while ensuring consistency with both positive and negative examples. RPNI is efficient in practice but in general, no minimal automaton is obtained.

All mentioned learning algorithms are part of so-called symbolic AI, the field that, in simple words, uses explicit symbols and rules to represent knowledge and logic and corresponding algorithms. Sub-symbolic AI, on the other hand, refers to AI approaches that do not use explicit, symbolic representations of knowledge but often numerical methods to process and learn from data. Especially sub-symbolic AI has gained a lot of attention in recent years and our main research

---

[1] Admittedly, existing observational data, e.g. previously recorded traces in form of log files can easily be integrated in the initial phase of typical active learning algorithms like Angluin's L* [3].

question in this paper is to find out whether one of the techniques of sub-symbolic AI is usable for learning automata.

In general, one may distinguish three different kinds of subsymbolic learning techniques: *Supervised Learning*, which relies on labeled data, where each input has a corresponding correct output. The model, often different forms of neural networks, learns to map inputs to outputs based on these explicit examples. *Unsupervised Learning* deals with unlabeled data, aiming to find patterns, structures, or relationships within the data without predefined outcomes. In *Reinforcement Learning (RL)*, an *agent* learns to make sequential decisions by interacting with an *environment*. The agent receives *rewards* or *penalties* for its actions, and its goal is to maximize the cumulative reward over time.

One of the first works using sub-symbolic techniques for (passively) learning an automaton was [2], which used supervised learning for estimating a recurrent neural network which is subsequently turned into an automaton. In this paper, we investigate whether reinforcement learning can be used for obtaining DFAs. More precisely, we use Q-learning for learning a strategy eventually representing the transition function of the automaton in question.

As a prototypical model-free RL, Q-Learning [13] enables agents to learn through trial and error, without requiring explicit knowledge of the environment. The agent explores a finite set of *states* that represent different configurations of the environment. A corresponding set of actions defines the options available in each state. Upon taking an action, the agent receives feedback in the form of a reward. Over time, it gradually improves its decisions using a process known as *temporal-difference learning*.

For automata inference (see Sect. 3), we adapt the Q-function as a symbolic structure encoding transitions over a finite input domain. More precisely, the states in the sense of Q-learning are automaton states plus input letter and the action that the agent may choose and which is optimized is the automaton successor state for the given state and input letter–the transition. A further difficulty arises as, potentially, each (automaton) successor state may be an accepting (final) or a non-accepting(non-final) state.

In summary, we address the question of whether Q-learning can be applied to passive automata learning. We answer this question positively by introducing the algorithm Q-PAI which stands for Q-learning-based passive automata interference. We give a detailed comparison to the work in [2] and to RPNI, showing that Q-learning often outperforms the other approaches on the considered benchmarks. This paper is organized as follows: Sect. 2 introduces the necessary preliminaries, including fundamental concepts of automata, automata learning, the motivation for our approach, and an overview of Q-learning. Section 3 presents our method for using Q-learning to infer automata. Section 4 reports the evaluation, including the experimental setup and results. Section 5 concludes the paper and outlines directions for future work.

2   Preliminaries

2.1   Automata

Let $\mathbb{N}$ denote the natural numbers, and, for $n \in \mathbb{N}$, let $[n] := \{1, \ldots, n\}$. For the rest of this section, we fix an alphabet Σ. A *deterministic finite automaton* (DFA) $\mathcal{A} = (S, s_0, \delta, S^+)$ over Σ consists of a finite set of *states* S, an *initial state* $s_0 \in S$, a *transition function* $\delta : S \times \Sigma \to S$, and a set $S^+ \subseteq S$ of *accepting states*. A *run* of $\mathcal{A}$ is a sequence $s_0 \xrightarrow{\sigma_1} s_1 \xrightarrow{\sigma_2} \ldots \xrightarrow{\sigma_n} s_n$ such that $\sigma_i \in \Sigma$, $s_i \in S$ and $\delta(s_{i-1}, \sigma_i) = s_i$ for all $i \in [n]$. It is called *accepting* iff $s_n \in S^+$. The *language* accepted by $\mathcal{A}$, denoted by $\mathcal{L}(\mathcal{A})$, is the set of strings $u \in \Sigma^*$ for which an accepting run exists. Since the automaton is deterministic, it is reasonable to call the states $S \setminus S^+$ also *rejecting states*, denoted by S^-. We extend δ to strings as usual by $\delta(s, \epsilon) = s$ and $\delta(s, u\sigma) = \delta(\delta(s, u), \sigma)$ for all $s \in S$, $u \in \Sigma^*$, and $\sigma \in \Sigma$. The size of $\mathcal{A}$, denoted by $|\mathcal{A}|$, is the number of its states S, denoted by $|S|$. A language is *regular* iff it is accepted by some DFA. A language L is called *prefix closed* iff for all $u\sigma \in L$ also $u \in L$. We call an automaton prefix closed iff its accepted language is prefix closed.

2.2   Automata Learning

A *sample* is a set of strings that, by the language in question, should either be accepted, denoted by $+$, or rejected, denoted by $-$. For technical reasons, it is convenient to work with prefix-closed samples. As the samples given to us are not necessarily prefix closed we introduce the value *maybe*, denoted by ?. Formally, a *sample* is a partial function $O : \Sigma^* \to \{+, -, ?\}$ with finite, prefix-closed domain $\mathcal{D}(O)$. That is, $O(u)$ is defined only for finitely many $u \in \Sigma^*$ and is defined for $u \in \Sigma^*$ whenever it is defined for some ua, for $a \in \Sigma$. For a string u the sample O yields whether u should be *accepted*, *rejected*, or we do not know (or do not care). For strings u and u', we say that O *disagrees* on u and u' if $O(u) \neq ?$, $O(u') \neq ?$, and $O(u) \neq O(u')$. Sometimes it is convenient to identify O with a (finite) set of observations $O = \{(u, +) \mid O(u) = +\} \cup \{(u, -) \mid O(u) = -\}$ and the context identifies when we consider O as function or as a set. An automaton $\mathcal{A}$ is said to *conform* with a sample O, if whenever O is defined for u we have $O(u) = +$ implies $u \in \mathcal{L}(\mathcal{A})$ and $O(u) = -$ implies $u \notin \mathcal{L}(\mathcal{A})$.

Definition 1 (Passive Learning Problem). *Given a sample O, the concept of passive learning is the task to obtain a minimal DFA $\mathcal{A}$ that conforms to O.*

2.3   Q-Learning

Reinforcement Learning (RL) [1] is a framework for sequential decision-making in which an agent interacts with an environment to learn a policy that maximizes cumulative reward. The learning process is driven by state transitions and delayed feedback, without requiring an explicit model of the environment. In contrast to supervised learning, RL does not rely on labeled input-output pairs

---

Algorithm 1. Generic Q-Learning Procedure

1: Initialize the Q-table $\mathcal{Q}(q,a)$ for all $q \in Q$, $a \in A$
2: **for** each episode **do**
3:     Select a random initial state q
4:     **while** goal not reached **do**
5:         Choose action a using an exploration strategy (e.g., ϵ-greedy)
6:         Execute action a
7:         Observe reward $r \leftarrow R(q,a)$ and next Q-learning State q'
8:         Update Q-function: $\mathcal{Q}(q,a) \leftarrow \mathcal{Q}(q,a) + \alpha \left[r + \gamma \cdot \max_{a' \in A} \mathcal{Q}(q',a') - \mathcal{Q}(q,a) \right]$
9:         Set $q \leftarrow q'$
10:     **end while**
11: **end for**

---

but instead discovers behavior through exploration and reward signals. This generality makes RL particularly appealing for tasks in which the system's structure is unknown or only partially observable.

Q-Learning is a foundational model-free RL algorithm. It assumes that a finite set of *states* Q is given, representing possible states of the environment the agent may be in. The set of *actions* A denotes the possible actions the agent may pick in each state. A *reward function* $R : Q \times A \to \mathbb{R}$ provides the direct reward when choosing an action a in a state q. In the Q-learning algorithm an agent incrementally constructs a value function $Q : Q \times A \to \mathbb{R}$ that estimates the utility of executing action $a \in A$ in state $q \in Q$. The update rule adjusts Q based on observed rewards (R) and the estimated value of successor states, following the principle of temporal difference learning. Notably, Q-Learning is off-policy, enabling the agent to evaluate the optimal policy independently of the current exploration strategy. In the context of automata inference (see Sect. 3), we reinterpret the Q-function as a symbolic structure encoding transitions over a finite input domain, thereby connecting statistical learning with the formal construction of DFA [13]. The generic form of Q-learning is defined in Algorithm 1.

Once the Q-table is initialized arbitrarily (line 1), the Q-function is updated (line 8) a fixed number of times (line 2). Hereby, one may update either the values for all q or only for those for reaching a certain goal (line 4). The update of the Q-function is weighted based on the so-called *learning rate* $\alpha \in (0,1]$ and the *discount factor* for future rewards $\gamma \in [0,1]$. For choosing the next action a to explore (line 5), several strategies may be chosen, some of which depend on a so-called exploration rate $\epsilon \in [0,1]$.

Strategy. Our learning strategy is based on trajectory exploration followed by reward-based Q-value updates. For each word, the agent builds a path through abstract states using either exploration (random transitions) or exploitation (choosing the best-known transition). The Q-table is updated twice: once based on the label of the terminal state, and once based on whether the constructed DFA accepts the word correctly. This double-reward structure helps the agent learn transitions that are both locally and globally correct.

3   Using Q-Learning for Learning Automata

We are now ready to present our Q-learning-based approach for passively inferring a DFA from a given sample O. As described in Sect. 2.3, Q-learning operates on states and actions, estimating the best action to take in a given state. In our context, the goal is to learn the transitions of a DFA–that is, to determine the successor state given a current automaton state and the input letter to be read. Simply put, we aim to learn, for each automaton state and input symbol, which state the transition should lead to. As such, the states in the sense of Q-learning are pairs of automaton states and input letters. The actions in the sense of Q-learning are the (automaton) states. Notably, each potential successor state appears in two variants: accepting (final) and non-accepting (non-final). Therefore, the Q-learning function must estimate both the target state and whether it should be accepting or rejecting.

To prevent confusion between the Q-learning process and the resulting DFA, we explicitly distinguish between their respective representations. Consider we are estimating a DFA $\mathcal{A} = (S, s_o, \delta, S^+)$ over the alphabet Σ. Then we define the learning space as follows: $Q = S \times \Sigma$ is the set of states for Q-learning, $F = \{+, -\}$ indicates automata states to be final $(+)$ or non-final $(-)$, $A = S \times F$ is the set of actions the Q-learning algorithm may choose from. Each Q-value is defined via the function $\mathcal{Q} : Q \times A \to \mathbb{R}$ which is in fact a function $\mathcal{Q} : S \times \Sigma \times S \times F \to \mathbb{R}$. The value $\mathcal{Q}(s, \sigma, s', f) \in \mathbb{R}$ represents the learned utility of taking transition $s \xrightarrow{\sigma} s'$, where s' has acceptance status f. We organize the learned Q-values in a structured Q-table, with row labels ranging over pairs of automata states and input labels and column labels ranging over the automata states paired with $+$ and $-$. Then, the Q-table maps each transition—defined by a state, input symbol, next state, and acceptance status—to a corresponding utility value. Note that the Q-table has shape of $n \times |\Sigma|$ rows and $2n$ columns for a DFA of n states in question.

The general Q-learning algorithm (Algorithm 1) is then instantiated to a specialized version for passively learning automata resulting in Algorithm 2. Here, we use the notation summarized in Table 1.

Let us explain the algorithm in detail: While in the general Q-learning algorithms, each update of the Q-table improves it, this is not the case here, as we explain below. Therefore, we operate with two Q-tables $\mathcal{Q}$ and $\mathcal{Q}^*$ where $\mathcal{Q}$ is our working table while $\mathcal{Q}^*$ keeps the currently best table. Moreover, we work with both, the Q-table as well as a direct representation of it as an automaton. The Q-table is used for updating Q-values while the automaton representation is used to evaluate the Q-table in terms of an automaton. Again, we work with two automata representations $\mathcal{A}$ and $\mathcal{A}^*$ with an initial state s_0, again using $\mathcal{A}$ for temporary updates while keeping the so-far best version in $\mathcal{A}^*$. In lines 2 and 3, we initialize the two Q-tables as well as the automata. We learn for $\mathcal{E}$ episodes, line 4. Each episode consists of processing each sample, line 5, letter by letter (line 8), building-up a path from the initial state s_0 (line 6) and choosing the successor state according to the Q-table (line 10) and appending it to the current trace τ (line 11). The selection of the action to choose next (i.e., the successor

---

Algorithm 2. Q-PAI – Q-learning-based Passive Automata Inference

---

Require: Global Constants α, γ, ϵ_{min}, r

1: **function** Q-PAI$(\Sigma, O, n, \mathcal{E})$
2:     Initialize Q-tables $\mathcal{Q}$, $\mathcal{Q}^*$ $\leftarrow$ zero matrices of dimension $(n \cdot |\Sigma|) \times (2n)$
3:     Initialize DFAs $\mathcal{A}$ and $\mathcal{A}^*$ with initial state s_0
4:     **for** episode $= 1$ to $\mathcal{E}$ **do**
5:         **for** each sample $(w = \sigma_1 \dots \sigma_k, y) \in O$ **do**
6:             Set $s \leftarrow s_0$, $\tau \leftarrow [\,]$, $\chi \leftarrow 0$
7:             **while** $\chi = 0$ **do**
8:                 **for** $i = 1$ to $|w|$ **do**
9:                     $q \leftarrow (s, \sigma_i)$
10:                    $a = (s', f) \leftarrow$ ExploreOrExploit$(\mathcal{Q}, q, i)$
11:                    Append (s, σ_i, s', f) to τ; set $s \leftarrow s'$
12:                **end for**
13:                $\mathcal{Q}, \mathcal{A}, \chi, \mathcal{Q}^*, \mathcal{A}^* \leftarrow$ EvaluateAndUpdate$(\mathcal{Q}, \mathcal{Q}^*, O, \tau, w, y, \chi)$
14:                **if** $\chi = 2$ **then**
15:                    **return** Inferred DFA $\mathcal{A}^*$
16:                **end if**
17:            **end while**
18:        **end for**
19:    **end for**
20:    **return** Inferred DFA $\mathcal{A}^*$
21: **end function**

---

state of the automaton to explore) is determined via function ExploreOrExploit (line 10). When the whole word w has been processed, the Q-tables and automata are reevaluated and updated based on the whole trace τ via function EvaluateAndUpdate. Depending on the reevaluation, the word w is processed again ($\chi = 0$) or the next word in the sample is considered ($\chi = 1$). Eventually, all samples have been processed $\mathcal{E}$ times and the algorithm returns the learned automaton $\mathcal{A}^*$ (line 20). If during learning an automaton is found that conforms to the observed behavior, the goal of the algorithm is reached and the resulting automaton $\mathcal{A}^*$ is returned (line 15).

Let us now turn our attention to the two subroutines ExploreOrExploit and EvaluateAndUpdate, which explore the best action (successor state) and update the Q-tables/automata, respectively.

Adaptive Exploration Based on Q-Value Variance. Let us start with explaining ExploreOrExploit$(\mathcal{Q}, q, i)$, see Algorithm 3. It takes the current Q-table, the current state (automaton state and letter σ), and the current position in the word considered. Its goal is to either pick the best action according to the current Q-table (line 7) or to pick one randomly, line 5. The latter is done to address the issue of premature convergence to suboptimal policies. We implemented an adaptive exploration strategy that dynamically adjusts the exploration probability based on the statistical variance of Q-values in a given state. This mechanism

Table 1. Notation for Q-Learning

k: The index of the current symbol in the input word. This value is often used to modulate exploration intensity (e.g., more exploration early in the word, more exploitation later).

ϵ: The current exploration probability—the likelihood of choosing a random action rather than the best known one.

$\epsilon_{\min}$: A minimum bound on ϵ, used to ensure that the agent never completely stops exploring.

α: The **learning rate**, determining how much new information overrides the existing Q-values. A typical value lies in $(0, 1)$.

γ: The **discount factor**, specifying how much future rewards are taken into account. When $\gamma = 0$, the agent only considers immediate rewards; when $\gamma \to 1$, it prioritizes long-term rewards.

τ: The **transition trajectory**, a list of state-action-state triples (s_i, σ_k, s_j) recorded during the processing of a sample word w. It captures the agent's path through abstract learning states $\mathcal{Q}$.

O: The **observation** , a finite set of labeled strings: $O = \{(w_1, y_1), \ldots, (w_n, y_n)\}$, where $w_i \in \Sigma^*$ and $y_i \in \{+, -\}$ indicates acceptance by the target language.

$\mathcal{Q}$: The **Q-table**, a function $\mathcal{Q} : S \times \Sigma \times S \times F \to \mathbb{R}$ storing utility values for transitions in the learning space.

$\mathcal{Q}^*$: The **best Q-table** encountered during training, based on DFA accuracy.

$\mathcal{A}$: The **current DFA** constructed from the current Q-table via a greedy policy.

$\mathcal{A}^*$: The **best DFA** discovered so far during training, according to evaluation on data samples O.

χ: An integer flag that controls processing of the current word: $\chi = 0$ means reprocess the word, $\chi = 1$ means skip it, and $\chi = 2$ terminates the Q-learning procedure.

allows the agent to explore more in uncertain or under-trained regions of the state-action space.

The core idea is to compute an adaptive ϵ from the variance of Q-values at the current state (lines 2,3). A higher variance suggests greater uncertainty in action quality and thus warrants more exploration. Concretely, the dynamic threshold builds on the variance of the values in the row of q (line 2), amplified by the position i of the letter to consider and compared to 1.0 and $\epsilon_{\min}$, lines 2–3. The choice of whether to explore randomly or deterministically depends on randomly choosing a value and comparing it to the dynamic threshold ϵ, line 4.

Evaluate and Updating the Q-table. Let us now turn our attention towards the function EVALUATEANDUPDATE($\mathcal{Q}$, $\mathcal{Q}^*$, O, τ, w, y, χ), see Algorithm 4. The main task of this function is to update the Q-table. This is less obvious as in the general Q-learning algorithm (Algorithm 1) as the Q-table holds two versions of each automaton state, once as final state, once as non-final state. Clearly, any automaton has each state either as final or non-final state. Therefore, we

---

Algorithm 3. Explore and Exploit Subroutine

1: **Subroutine** EXPLOREANDEXPLOIT($\mathcal{Q}, q = (s, \sigma), i$)
2:     $\mathcal{V} \leftarrow \mathrm{Var}(\mathcal{Q}[s, \sigma, \cdot, \cdot])$
3:     $\epsilon \leftarrow \max(\epsilon_{\min}, \min(1.0, i \cdot \mathcal{V}))$
4:     **if** $\mathrm{rand}() < \epsilon$ **then**
5:        Randomly sample (s', f) from $\mathcal{Q}[s, \sigma, \cdot, \cdot]$
6:     **else**
7:        $(s', f) \leftarrow \arg\max_{(s'', f')} \mathcal{Q}[s, \sigma, s'', f']$
8:     **end if**
9:     **return** (s', f)
10: **End Subroutine**

---

roughly do the following: We compute rewards according to the Q-table and update it correspondingly (lines 3,4). Moreover, we translate the Q-table into an automaton (line 5), hereby choosing each automaton state to be final or non-final. We also use the resulting automaton to compute a reward and use it for updating the Q-table (line 8).

Thus, the Q-table is updated twice, once by general means according to Q-learning, once by interpreting the table as an automaton. If this results in an automaton that conforms to the sample, we are done (lines 12,13). If not, we check whether the current automaton $\mathcal{A}$ fits better to the sample than the previously best automaton $\mathcal{A}^*$. If so, we take it, otherwise we ignore the update of the Q-table and the resulting automaton. Moreover, if the classification of the word w under consideration as final/non-final state compared with that in the automaton does not match, the word is re-considered for further processing.

Q-table Update. The Q-table is updated exactly as in the general case for Q-learning (Algorithm 1, line 8), applied for each letter in the considered state sequence τ, resulting in Algorithm 5.

DFA Construction from Q-table. Given a learned Q-table $\mathcal{Q}$, we aim to construct a deterministic finite automaton (DFA) that captures the policy embedded in $\mathcal{Q}$. This process involves three main steps: extracting optimal actions, pruning transitions, and identifying final states (see Algorithm 8). First, lines 2–4, we compute the optimal policy π^* by selecting the action (s', f) that maximizes the Q-value for each state-symbol pair (s, σ), formally: $\pi^*[s, \sigma] = \arg\max_{(s', f)} \mathcal{Q}[s, \sigma, s', f]$. Next, we prune the state-action graph using only the positively labeled trajectories in the observation set O^+. For each accepted word $w = \sigma_1 \ldots \sigma_k$, we simulate the path from the initial state s_0 by following the optimal actions in π^*. The corresponding transitions $\delta(s, \sigma_i) = s'$ are added, and the set of visited states is updated accordingly, lines 6–13. During this process, if the target label f of any optimal action is $+$, the target state s' is added to the final state set $\mathcal{S}^+$ (line 15). This ensures that the DFA accurately reflects the terminal predictions encoded in the Q-table. Finally, we construct the DFA as a tuple: $\mathcal{A} = (\mathcal{S}, s_0, \delta, \mathcal{S}^+)$ where $\mathcal{S}$ is the set of all visited states, s_0 is the initial state, δ is the transition function, and $\mathcal{S}^+$ is the set of final (accepting) states.

Algorithm 4. EVALUATE AND UPDATE SUBROUTINE

1: **Subroutine** EVALUATEANDUPDATE($\mathcal{Q}, \mathcal{Q}^*, O, \tau, w, y, \chi$)
2:      $(\_, \_, \_, \hat{y}_1) \leftarrow$ last element of τ
3:      $r_1 \leftarrow$ COMPUTEREWARDFROMQTABLE($\hat{y}_1, y$)
4:      $\mathcal{Q} \leftarrow$ UPDATEQTABLE($\mathcal{Q}, \tau, r_1$)
5:      $\mathcal{A} \leftarrow$ DFAFROMQ($\mathcal{Q}$)
6:      $\hat{y}_2 \leftarrow \mathcal{A}(w)$
7:      $r_2 \leftarrow$ COMPUTEREWARDFROMDFA($\hat{y}_2, y$)
8:      $\mathcal{Q} \leftarrow$ UPDATEQTABLE($\mathcal{Q}, \tau, r_2$)
9:      $\mathcal{A} \leftarrow$ DFAFROMQ($\mathcal{Q}$)
10:      $\hat{y}_2 \leftarrow \mathcal{A}(w)$
11:      $\chi \leftarrow 1$ **if** $\hat{y}_2 = y$
12:      **if** Accuracy($\mathcal{A}, O$) $= 1$ **then**
13:          $\mathcal{Q}^* \leftarrow \mathcal{Q}; \quad \mathcal{A}^* \leftarrow \mathcal{A}; \chi \leftarrow 2$
14:      **else**
15:          **if** ACCURACY($\mathcal{A}, O$) $>$ ACCURACY($\mathcal{A}^*, O$) **then**
16:              $\mathcal{Q}^* \leftarrow \mathcal{Q}; \mathcal{A}^* \leftarrow \mathcal{A}$
17:          **end if**
18:      **end if**
19:      **return** $\mathcal{Q}, \mathcal{A}, \chi, \mathcal{Q}^*, \mathcal{A}^*$
20: **End Subroutine**

Algorithm 5. UPDATE QTABLE SUBROUTINE

1: **Subroutine** UPDATE Q-TABLE($\mathcal{Q}, \tau, r$)
2:      **for** each $(s, \sigma, s', f) \in \tau$ **do**
3:          $\mathcal{Q}[s, \sigma, s', f] \leftarrow \mathcal{Q}[s, \sigma, s', f]$

$$+ \alpha \cdot \left[r + \gamma \cdot \max_{(s'', f') \in \mathcal{S} \times F} \mathcal{Q}[s, \sigma, s'', f'] - \mathcal{Q}[s, \sigma, s', f] \right]$$

4:      **end for**
5:      **return** $\mathcal{Q}$
6: **End Subroutine**

DFA Completion with Sink State. To ensure that the transition function δ of the DFA is total for all $s \in \mathcal{S}, a \in \Sigma$, we introduce a *Sink* state ($\bot$) that adds ($\bot$) if not already present, redirects all undefined transitions (s, σ) to ($\bot$) and append $\delta(\bot, \sigma) \leftarrow \bot$ for all $\sigma \in \Sigma$.

Accuracy($\mathcal{A}, O$). The accuracy of an automaton $\mathcal{A}$ with respect to a given sample O is defined as the proportion of words in O that are classified correctly (as accepted or non-accepted) by $\mathcal{A}$. Formally:

$$\text{Accuracy}(\mathcal{A}, O) = \frac{|\{(w, y) \in O \mid \mathcal{A}(w) = y\}|}{|O|}$$

where $\mathcal{A}(w)$ denotes the classification of w by $\mathcal{A}$.

Algorithm 6. REWARD COMPUTATION FROM Q-TABLE SUBROUTINES

1: **Subroutine** COMPUTEREWARDFROMQTABLE($\hat{y}, y$)
2:     **if** $y = \hat{y}$ **then**
3:         **if** $Label = 0$ **then**
4:             $R \leftarrow 2 \times r$
5:         **else**
6:             $R \leftarrow 4 \times r$
7:         **end if**
8:     **else**
9:         $R \leftarrow -r/2$
10:     **end if**
11:     **return** R
12: **End Subroutine**

Algorithm 7. REWARD COMPUTATION FROM DFA SUBROUTINE

1: **Subroutine** COMPUTEREWARDFROMDFA($\hat{y}, y$)
2:     **if** $\hat{y} = y$ **then**
3:         $R \leftarrow r$
4:     **else**
5:         $R \leftarrow -r/2$
6:     **end if**
7:     **return** R
8: **End Subroutine**

Reward Computation. The reward is computed by checking whether the suggested state (final/non-final) coincides with the samples classification, giving more weight to positive labels. Moreover, the main reward is given for the Q-table, while less reward is applied when the DFA is considered. The exact numerical values have been tuned empirically based on the experimental section. Formally, let $y \in \{+, -\}$ be the sample label and $\hat{y}$ the predicted label for a given word. Then:

$$R_{\text{DFA}}(y, \hat{y}) = \begin{cases} r & \text{if } \hat{y} = y \ \wedge \ y = + \\ 0 & \text{if } \hat{y} = y \ \wedge \ y = - \\ -\dfrac{r}{2} & \text{otherwise} \end{cases} \qquad R_{\text{Qtable}}(y, \hat{y}) = \begin{cases} 4r & \text{if } \hat{y} = y \ \wedge \ y = + \\ 2r & \text{if } \hat{y} = y \ \wedge \ y = - \\ -\dfrac{r}{2} & \text{otherwise} \end{cases}$$

Here, the R_{Qtable} corresponds to the reward assigned after processing an entire word. In this, a correct classification of a negative label yields $2r$, correct classification of a positive label yields $4r$, and any mismatch results in a penalty of $-r/2$. R_{DFA} corresponds to the reward assigned after verifying the DFA's final/non-final state prediction for the current word, where a reward of r is given only when the prediction matches a positive label ($y = +$), a penalty of $-r/2$ is applied for any mismatch, and zero reward is given for correctly classified

---

Algorithm 8. DFA FROM Q SUBROUTINE

1: **Subroutine** DFAFROMQ($\mathcal{Q}, O, \Sigma$)
2:     Initialize $\pi^* \leftarrow \{\}, \delta \leftarrow \{\}, \mathcal{S} \leftarrow \{s_0\}, \mathcal{S}^+ \leftarrow \{\}$
3:     **for** each state s and symbol σ in $\mathcal{Q}$ **do**
4:         $\pi^*[s, \sigma] \leftarrow \arg\max_{(s', f)} \mathcal{Q}[s, \sigma, s', f]$
5:     **end for**
6:     **for** each $(w, y) \in O$ **do**
7:         **if** $y = +$ **then**
8:             $s \leftarrow s_0$
9:             **for** each symbol σ_i in w **do**
10:                 $(s', f) \leftarrow \pi^*[s, \sigma_i]$
11:                 $\delta(s, \sigma_i) \leftarrow s'$
12:                 $\mathcal{S} \leftarrow \mathcal{S} \cup \{s'\}$
13:                 $s \leftarrow s'$
14:                 **if** $f = +$ **then**
15:                     $\mathcal{S}^+ \leftarrow \mathcal{S}^+ \cup \{s'\}$
16:                 **end if**
17:             **end for**
18:         **end if**
19:     **end for**
20:     $\mathcal{A} \leftarrow$ COMPLETEDFAWITHSINK$(\mathcal{S}, s_0, \delta, \mathcal{S}^+)$
21:     **return** $\mathcal{A}$
22: **End Subroutine**

---

negative labels. The exact numerical values of these weights $(r, 2r, 4r, -r/2)$ have been tuned empirically, as described in the experimental section.

This concludes the description of our inference algorithm Q-PAI. Putting a bound on the while-loop, our algorithm will always terminate. It is formally unclear, whether the algorithm will provide a conforming automaton if one exists. That said, if the algorithm does not terminate with a conforming example, one might re-execute Q-PAI with a larger n for the target automaton size. Note that a conforming automaton always exists with n matching the size of the sample. As in many applications of reinforcement learning, we do not have strong formal guarantees of the algorithm but in practice it performs well. So, we continue with the evaluation of Q-PAI evaluation in the next section.

4   Evaluation

Data Sets. To evaluate the applicability of Q-learning for automata inference, we employed two types of benchmark datasets: Tomita grammars [14] and the BLE communication traces collected by [2] which represent real-world data from the Bluetooth Low Energy protocol. The Tomita grammars are a standard benchmark of seven regular languages over $\{0,1\}$, each defined by a minimal DFA with varying complexity. As a practical case study, we use BLE traces from real devices containing three system on the chips (SoCs) CYBLE-416045-02 (3 states), nRF52832 (5 states), CC2650 (5 states), each representing symbolic input sequences of full protocol sessions. In this dataset the whole input alphabet was considered. For each dataset, we employ three types of training sets to evaluate learning performance under different input conditions: [(1)] Characteristic set, minimal set of samples sufficient for identifying the target DFA. [(2)] AAL-Generated Data, samples generated via the AALpy framework [11], simulating active learning interactions such as membership and equivalence queries; and [(3)] Random Data, samples drawn randomly from the input space to reflect unstructured or naturalistic behavior. These datasets pose greater challenges due to larger alphabets and behavioral variability, allowing us to evaluate the scalability and robustness of the approach.

During training, we make no assumptions about the total number of states. The initial number of states is set to $|w|_{\min}$, the length of the shortest word in the sample set. If no automaton can be found that correctly matches the observations, the number of states is incremented by one, and the procedure is repeated. Our experiments aim to answer the following core questions: [(1)] Can Q-learning, in a passive setting, recover the correct structure of the target DFA given sufficiently informative samples? [(2)] How does the learned automaton behave under variations in the input data, such as characteristic sets, AAL-generated samples, and randomly sampled inputs? [(3)] How does the method compare to existing symbolic learners with respect to accuracy, robustness, and sample efficiency?

Experimental Setup. All experiments were conducted on a MacBook Pro (Model Identifier: `Mac14,7`) equipped with an Apple M2 chip featuring 8 cores (4 performance and 4 efficiency), 16 GB unified memory, and macOS. The experiments were executed in a Python 3.10 environment using a custom implementation of the Q-learning framework. Each Q-learning model was trained over a maximum of $\mathcal{E} = 200$ episodes, with adaptive exploration controlled by a variance-based ϵ-strategy (see Algorithm 3). We applied a fixed learning rate $\alpha = 0.1$ and discount factor $\gamma = 0.9$. Through empirical tuning, we observed that a reward parameter of r = 1 led to improved convergence behavior and higher accuracy across our experiments. For each grammar, the learner is trained on labeled strings and evaluated on a disjoint test set. Metrics include learning accuracy, inferred automaton size, number of episodes and learning time. DFA extraction follows the convergence of the Q-table, after which pruning and final state determination are applied.

Results. Table 2 and Table 3 highlight the comparative analysis of Q-Learning, RNN, and RPNI across a variety of automata inference tasks. Q-learning effectively inferred minimal DFAs with high accuracy, particularly when characteristic datasets were provided. In most Tomita grammars, Q-learning achieved 100% accuracy with minimal standard deviation. Even in more complex cases such as Tomita 5 and Tomita 7, accuracy remained high (e.g., $95.0 \pm 7.02\%$ and $89.0 \pm 4.14\%$, respectively), while still ensuring minimal state representations. These results confirm that Q-learning consistently identifies the correct number of DFA states, as expected from the target languages, and exhibits reliable convergence behavior. Q-learning also demonstrated stable and efficient runtime characteristics. Training durations remained under one minute for simpler grammars and scaled reasonably for more complex cases (e.g., approximately 17 min for Tomita 5 and 3.55 min for Tomita 7).

On BLE datasets, Q-learning maintained accuracy above 90% in all scenarios, achieving $95.45 \pm 7.12\%$ and $90.05 \pm 2.87\%$ on 'nRF52832' and $95.09 \pm 2.67\%$ on 'cc2650'. Additionally, the inferred DFAs matched the expected sizes for each device, confirming the method's robustness in real-world protocol modeling. Overall, Q-learning provides a reliable, scalable, and interpretable framework for automaton learning, delivering both minimality and accuracy without significant computational overhead. In comparison to other approaches, Q-learning consistently yielded more compact models than RNNs, which tend to overestimate the number of states. While RPNI is theoretically grounded, its performance was found to be highly sensitive to the dataset structure and often failed to produce minimal or accurate DFAs across complex or real-world inputs. These findings highlight Q-learning's advantage in balancing interpretability, minimality, and predictive performance across both synthetic and practical domains. However, unlike formal methods such as RPNI, Q-learning lacks theoretical guarantees of convergence to the correct minimal DFA. Accuracy slightly declines in more complex scenarios–for instance, Tomita 5 and Tomita 7 achieve $95.0 \pm 7.02\%$ and $89.0 \pm 4.14\%$ accuracy, respectively, indicating difficulty in generalizing to grammars with more intricate structure. Training time also increases substantially with dataset complexity, reaching up to 17 min for Tomita 5 and over 47 min for certain BLE datasets (e.g., nRF52832). In summary, our evaluation is promising though further evaluations are beneficial.

5   Conclusion

This paper introduced Q-PAI, a Q-learning-based algorithm for passively inferring an automaton given a finite sample. With Q-learning being a sub-symbolic learning mechanism to derive symbolic structures, we effectively link model-free learning with formal automata representations. Our approach demonstrates strong empirical performance in both accuracy and generalization. Its ability to infer compact, minimal DFAs across diverse dataset types, including characteristic sets, random traces, and AAL-generated samples—makes it a promising candidate for practical formal language learning tasks.

However, this approach also presents several challenges. First, it is highly sensitive to the design of the reward function, which must be carefully tuned to reflect learning objectives and class balance. Second, the choice of exploration strategy can introduce inefficiencies in large or sparse state-action spaces, potentially leading to slower convergence. As the size of the target DFA increases, the scalability of the Q-table is expected to become a limiting factor due to higher memory and computational demands. Moreover, unlike formal algorithms such as RPNI, Q-learning lacks theoretical guarantees for convergence and minimality, relying instead on empirical performance and heuristic tuning. These limitations indicate that while Q-learning is effective and practical in many settings,

Table 2. Evaluation results of Q-Learning, RNN, and RPNI on Tomita grammars.

Dataset	Auto. Size	Dataset Type	#Samples {avg, std}	# Hypothesis States		# Learned DFA's States		Learned min%			Iteration (avg)		Accuracy (%) {avg;std}		Time(min:sec)	
				Q	RNN	Q	RPNI	Q	RNN	RPNI	Q	RNN	Q	RNN	Q	RNN
Tomita1	1	Characteristic	2	1	–	1	2	100	–	0	1	–	100	–	0:3 ±0:0.27	–
		AAL	364	1	207	1	207	100	100	0	1	2	100	100	0:3 ±0:0.92	36:0 ± 33:0
		Random	44±7.25	2	44	1	44	100	100	0	1	2.2	100 ± 0	100	0:3± 0:0.6	4:0±2:0
Tomita2	2	Characteristic	5	2	–	2	3	100	–	0	1	–	100	–	0:2± 0:0.31	–
		AAL	693	2	390	2	418	100	100	0	1	2	100	100	0:2±0:0.7	02:18:0±1:22
		Random	224 ±15.26	2	227	2	270	100	100	0	2	2	100 ± 0	100	0:1.50±0:0.2	0:45±0:43
Tomita3	4	Characteristic	19	4	–	4	4	100	–	100	12	–	100	–	1:01±0:6.37	–
		AAL	1149	4	545	4	584	100	100	0	1	2	100	90	0:46.18	43:28± 23:15
		Random	737±8.63	4	740	4	1006	100	100	0	20	2	94.80±1.52	100	1:04±0:38	43:01±37:01
Tomita4	3	Characteristic	14	3	–	3	4	100	–	0	3	–	100	–	0:1±0:0.23	–
		AAL	866	3	459	3	484	100	100	0	2	2	100	80	0:12± 0:4	20:33± 39:28
		Random	134±7.23	3	135	3	154	100	100	0	20	2	100 ± 0	80	1:0.3 ±0:59	05:27±3:31
Tomita5	4	Characteristic	18	4	–	4	4	100	–	100	3	–	100	–	0:1±0:1	–
		AAL	1149	4	436	4	469	100	100	0	15	2	100	10	29:36± 5:43	3:42 ±0
		Random	133.67±7.13	5	135	4	154	100	100	0	20	2	95±7.02	100	17:04 ±18:22	4:42 ±3:29
Tomita6	3	Characteristic	10	3	–	3	3	100	–	100	1	–	100	–	0:1±0:0.52	–
		AAL	585	3	308	3	333	100	100	0	1	2	100	100	0:15± 0:9	2:03 ±1:50
		Random	69±7.63	3	70	3	76	100	100	0	20	2	100 ± 0	100	1:10±0:20	24 :0 ± 20:0
Tomita7	4	Characteristic	24	7	–	4	5	100	–	0	1	–	100	–	5:17± 2:30	–
		AAL	1193	5	564	4	606	100	100	0	7	2	100	60	2:0 ± 1:27	3:35 ±12:30
		Random	134.20 ± 5.54	4	135	4	195	100	100	0	20	2	89±4.14	80	3:55 ± 0:50	3:51 ±2:28

Table 3. Evaluation results of Q-Learning, RNN, and RPNI on BLE devices.

Dataset	Auto. Size	Dataset Type	#Samples {avg, std}	# Hypothesis States		# Learned DFA's States		Learned min%			Iteration (avg)		Accuracy (%) {avg;std}		Time(min:sec)	
				Q	RNN	Q	RPNI	Q	RNN	RPNI	Q	RNN	Q	RNN	Q	RNN
cyble-416045-02	3	Characteristic	30	3	–	3	31	100	–	0	1	–	100	–	0:4.04s ± 0:3.07	–
		AAL	546	3	547	3	547	100	100	0	2	2.4	100	100	1:34 ± 0:28	1:30 ±31:00
		Random	942±72	3	946	3	943±72	100	67	0	1	2.6	92.19 ± 1.92	90	14: 14 ± 16:02	24:30 ±36:35
cc2650	5	Characteristic	50	5	–	5	51	100	–	0	1	–	100	–	0:14.31s ± 0:5.07	–
		AAL	1179	5	1180	5	1180	100	10	0	1	3.3	95.09± 2.67	100	29:50 ± 1:21:29	57:08 ±1:06:56
		Random	957±172	5	9564	5	958±172	100	78	0	1	2.6	85.61±3.71	90	34:01±01:10	13:02:51 ± 11:22:21
nRF52832	5	Characteristic	50	5	–	5	51	100	–	0	1	–	100	–	0:15 ±0: 4.74	–
		AAL	895	5	896	5	896	100	100	0	1	2.7	95.45 ± 7.12	100	47:05 ± 1:49:11	6:09 ± 4:00
		Random	14245 ±141	5	14109	5	14246 ±141	100	100	0	1	21	90.05 ± 2.87	100	18:12 ± 0:8.06	3:58:09 ± 2:37:52

future work should address its scalability, efficiency, and theoretical grounding
to strengthen its applicability.

References

1. Robotica **17**(2), 229–235 (1999). https://doi.org/10.1017/S0263574799271172
2. Aichernig, B.K., König, S., Mateis, C., Pferscher, A., Tappler, M.: Learning minimal automata with recurrent neural networks. Softw. Syst. Model. **23**(3), 625–655 (2024). https://doi.org/10.1007/s10270-024-01160-6
3. Angluin, D.: Learning regular sets from queries and counterexamples. Inf. Comput. **75**(2), 87–106 (1987)
4. Berg, T., Grinchtein, O., Jonsson, B., Leucker, M., Raffelt, H., Steffen, B.: On the correspondence between conformance testing and regular inference. In: Cerioli, M. (ed.) FASE 2005. LNCS, vol. 3442, pp. 175–189. Springer, Heidelberg (2005). https://doi.org/10.1007/978-3-540-31984-9_14
5. Biermann, A.W., Feldman, J.A.: On the synthesis of finite-state machines from samples of their behavior. IEEE Trans. Comput. **21**(6), 592–597 (1972). https://doi.org/10.1109/TC.1972.5009015
6. Bollig, B., Habermehl, P., Kern, C., Leucker, M.: Angluin-style learning of NFA. In: Boutilier, C. (ed.) IJCAI 2009, Proceedings of the 21st International Joint Conference on Artificial Intelligence, Pasadena, California, USA, 11–17 July 2009, pp. 1004–1009 (2009). http://ijcai.org/Proceedings/09/Papers/170.pdf
7. Bollig, B., Habermehl, P., Leucker, M., Monmege, B.: A robust class of data languages and an application to learning. Log. Methods Comput. Sci. **10**(4) (2014). https://doi.org/10.2168/LMCS-10(4:19)2014
8. Decker, N., Habermehl, P., Leucker, M., Thoma, D.: Learning transparent data automata. In: Ciardo, G., Kindler, E. (eds.) PETRI NETS 2014. LNCS, vol. 8489, pp. 130–149. Springer, Cham (2014). https://doi.org/10.1007/978-3-319-07734-5_8
9. Gold, E.M.: Language identification in the limit. Inf. Control **10**(5), 447–474 (1967). https://doi.org/10.1016/S0019-9958(67)91165-5
10. Grinchtein, O., Leucker, M., Piterman, N.: Inferring network invariants automatically. In: Furbach, U., Shankar, N. (eds.) IJCAR 2006. LNCS (LNAI), vol. 4130, pp. 483–497. Springer, Heidelberg (2006). https://doi.org/10.1007/11814771_40
11. Muškardin, E., Aichernig, B.K., Pill, I., Pferscher, A., Tappler, M.: AALpy: an active automata learning library. In: Hou, Z., Ganesh, V. (eds.) ATVA 2021. LNCS, vol. 12971, pp. 67–73. Springer, Cham (2021). https://doi.org/10.1007/978-3-030-88885-5_5
12. Oncina, J., Garc a, P.: Inferring regular languages in polynomial update time. World Scientific (1992).https://doi.org/10.1142/9789812797902_0004
13. Russell, S.J., Norvig, P.: Artificial Intelligence: A Modern Approach, Global Edition 4e. Pearson (2021)
14. Tomita, M.: Dynamic construction of finite-state automata from examples using hill-climbing. In: Proceedings of the Fourth Annual Conference of the Cognitive Science Society, Ann Arbor, MI, USA, pp. 105–108 (1982). https://apps.dtic.mil/sti/pdfs/ADA120123.pdf
15. Vaandrager, F.W.: Model learning. Commun. ACM **60**(2), 86–95 (2017)

Formal Development of a Safety Controller for Machine Learning Outputs in Vital Railway Systems

Thierry Lecomte[(✉)]

CLEARSY, Aix en Provence, France
`thierry.lecomte@clearsy.com`

Abstract. The integration of machine learning (ML) into safety-critical railway systems raises significant challenges for certification, as current safety standards require transparent, fully specified system designs, whereas ML models are inherently opaque after training. This short paper presents an on-going work where a proof-of-concept architecture is explored, in which ML outputs are validated by an independently implemented safety controller. The controller is developed using the B method and deployed on a safety-grade computing platform, focusing on free track detection as the application scenario. In this setup, a convolutional neural network proposes a candidate track path, and the safety controller verifies its consistency with physical and geometric constraints. The work illustrates how formal specification and proof can be applied to the safety component in order to constrain the influence of ML, without addressing the full certification process. This proof-of-concept highlights the potential for combining formally developed safety logic with advanced perception modules in railway applications, while acknowledging that further work is required for industrial deployment.

Keywords: formal methods · safety critical · software development · railway

1 Introduction

Safety-critical systems, such as those in the railway [3,8], aerospace, and medical sectors, demand the highest levels of reliability, availability, and integrity [2,5, 11,13]. Historically, innovation in such systems has been constrained by the preference for mature, well-understood technologies [4,9]. While this approach minimizes risks, it can also lead to outdated or unsupported systems, limiting available functionalities.

The emergence of advanced computing paradigms—cloud computing, Internet of Things (IoT), sensor fusion, distributed architectures, and notably AI/ML—promises significant performance enhancements. However, these technologies challenge established safety demonstration methodologies. Machine learning (ML), in particular, operates as a black box, generating decision criteria

M. H. ter Beek and L. Teixeira (Eds.): SBMF 2025, LNCS 16363, pp. 196–206, 2026.
https://doi.org/10.1007/978-3-032-12086-1_11

through training rather than explicit design. This makes compliance with safety standards difficult, especially when system design traceability is mandatory.

In 2022, the UIC[1] initiated a project called "NMSD: New Methods for Safety Demonstrations" fully subcontracted to CLEARSY. The project is aimed at facilitating the adoption of new technologies for the construction of safe systems by providing safety reasoning and demonstration elements, as it is not feasible to restrict systems to "known solutions" or to limit the amount of embedded innovations. Following this work, the UIC would issue global recommendations that enable exchanges between worldwide railway operators and manufacturers. Railway standards may evolve as a result.

The work presented in this paper corresponds to one ongoing action item of this project NMSD related to the use of AI and ML for safety functions. It explores an architecture enabling the integration of ML into vital systems without compromising safety, by constraining ML outputs to verifiable forms and validating them through deterministic safety controllers formally developed and executed on specific redundant hardware.

This paper is organised as follows. Section 2 explains why using ML with railways safety standards is a challenge. Section 3 introduces an approach based on certified control. Section 4 presents a proof of concept by applying this approach to free track detection function, before concluding.

2   Safety Standards and the Machine Learning Challenge

The European railway safety standards EN 50126, EN 50128 (EN 50716), and EN 50129 define a rigorous framework for the lifecycle of safety-related systems.

EN 50126 addresses the overall lifecycle of railway systems, from concept through decommissioning, with a strong emphasis on systematically managing safety at every stage. It requires that safety is not treated as an afterthought but as an integral part of the design process, supported by documented analyses, hazard identification, and risk assessment. The standard insists on a controlled and traceable process, meaning that every design decision, requirement, and verification activity must be justified and linked to specific safety objectives. This traceability ensures that safety arguments can be reconstructed and verified, and that changes in requirements or design can be assessed for their impact on the overall safety case.

EN 50129 focuses on the safety demonstration for railway signalling and control systems, requiring the production of a safety case that convincingly shows the system meets its safety objectives. This involves providing evidence that both systematic errors—arising from specification mistakes, design flaws, or implementation defects—and random hardware failures have been identified, analysed, and either eliminated or adequately mitigated. The standard structures the safety case into clear arguments supported by verifiable evidence, ensuring that safety is demonstrated through objective proof rather than assumption. It

---

[1] International Union of Railways, Paris, https://uic.org.

also requires that any residual risks are explicitly stated, justified, and accepted by the relevant stakeholders, reinforcing the transparency and accountability of the safety assurance process.

EN 50128 (and its updated version EN 50716) governs the development of software for railway control and protection systems, with a central requirement that every software component must conform exactly to its approved specification. This means that functional behaviour, performance characteristics, and interface definitions must be fully described and verified against the specification at each development stage. The standard prescribes rigorous development processes, including formal specification methods, structured code reviews, and verification activities such as static analysis, unit testing, and integration testing. By enforcing strict traceability between requirements, design, implementation, and verification, EN 50128/EN 50716 aims to ensure that no unintended functionality is introduced and that the implemented system behaves predictably under all defined operating conditions.

ML disrupts this framework. In traditional systems, algorithms are fully specified before implementation, allowing formal proofs and exhaustive verification. In ML-based systems, the algorithm is effectively defined by the training process, which produces weights and decision boundaries that are not (yet) human-interpretable. Thus, while testing may reveal functional adequacy, it cannot guarantee the absence of systematic errors, as the internal logic remains unknown. As such, these standards classify ML techniques as "Not Recommended" for SIL3 and SIL4 software-based applications[2].

The integration of ML into safety-critical systems, such as railways, offers both opportunities and risks. ML modules excel in perception tasks (e.g., image segmentation for track detection) where explicit algorithmic solutions are prohibitively complex. Their strength lies in quickly proposing candidate solutions, which can then be independently verified. This property makes ML useful in contexts where checking a solution is easier than computing one from first principles. However, risks arise because ML models are inherently opaque and cannot guarantee predictable behavior under all operating conditions. Key dangers include:

- Invalid outputs: An ML module may produce spurious or inconsistent results (e.g., mis-segmented track boundaries), which, if used directly, could reduce safety or operational availability.
- False positives/false negatives: An overly conservative safety mechanism could trigger emergency braking unnecessarily (false positive), affecting service reliability. Conversely, undetected hazards (false negatives) could compromise safety.
- Dataset limitations: Insufficiently diverse or imbalanced training data may impair generalization, leading to systematic biases in outputs.
- Environmental variability: Performance may degrade under rare but safety-relevant conditions (e.g., adverse weather, unusual track geometry).

---

[2] SIL3 and SIL4 are the highest Safety Integrity Levels defined by the railways standards. A failure of a SIL3/SIL4 system could lead to injury or death.

To mitigate these risks, the proposed architecture constrains ML to a proposer role while delegating final safety decisions to a formally verified controller. This ensures that ML outputs never directly trigger safety functions; instead, they are validated against deterministic physical and geometric constraints.

3   Proposed Approach: Verifiable ML Outputs and Safety Controllers

The method experimented with in this project draws inspiration from the MIT concept of Certified Control [10], in which a ML module is trained not only to produce task-specific results but also to generate outputs in a form that can be checked by an independent verification component. In our adaptation, the architecture consists of two clearly separated parts (Fig. 1):

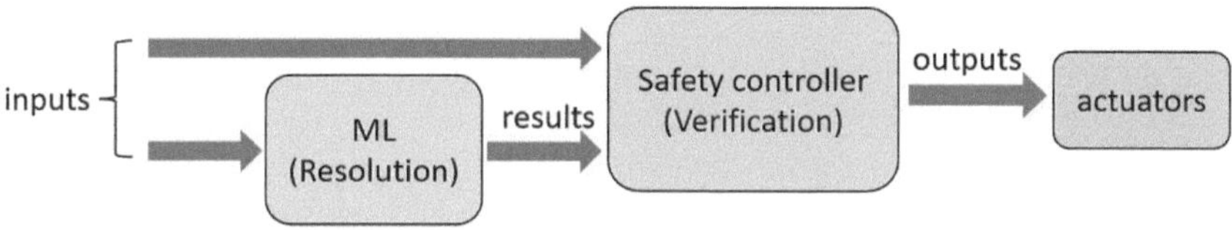

Fig. 1. ML with verifiable results + safety controller.

In our adaptation, the architecture consists of two clearly separated parts: a ML module and a safety controller. The ML Module is optimized for task performance, potentially using advanced models such as convolutional neural networks (CNNs) for perception tasks. Its role is to propose a candidate solution to a given problem. a deterministic, independently developed component that receives the same inputs as the ML module and applies explicit, verifiable rules to assess the validity of the ML's proposal.

This approach is particularly suited to problems for which verifying a proposed solution is substantially easier than solving the problem from first principles. In such cases, the ML module serves as a high-performance but unverifiable proposer, and the safety controller acts as the gatekeeper, allowing only outputs that can be confirmed against predefined safety properties.

An alternative architecture sometimes considered in safety-critical domains is diverse redundancy. In this alternative, the architecture would consist of two independently developed ML modules—potentially produced by separate teams, employing distinct development tools and trained on different datasets—whose outputs are evaluated by a voter component. A permissive action is taken only if both modules produce compatible results. While this strategy can reduce the likelihood of coincident errors, it does not eliminate the fundamental opacity of ML models. In practice, without the ability to fully understand or explain the internal decision-making of either ML module, it remains impossible to guarantee that agreement between them implies correctness. Consequently, the verification-based architecture presented here offers a more direct and auditable path to safety assurance in contexts where the behaviour of ML components cannot be exhaustively analysed.

4   Proof-of-Concept: Free Track Detection

To validate the concept, a proof-of-concept (PoC) was developed for free track detection in a railway context. Free track detection refers to the ability of a railway system to determine the length of unobstructed track ahead of a train, within which safe operation is possible. The process involves identifying the physical limits of the track—usually defined by the rails themselves—and detecting any obstacles or discontinuities along the path. In the context of onboard perception, this requires processing sensor data (e.g., camera images) to locate the rails, verify their geometry, and confirm that no objects intrude into the space between them up to a certain distance. The resulting free track distance is then used to determine whether the train can continue at its current speed or needs to brake in order to stop before an obstacle. In safety-critical implementations, free track detection is used to initiate emergency braking whenever the available clear track ahead falls below the distance required for safe stopping.

4.1   Functional Principle

The architecture is in two parts (Fig. 2). The ML module identifies the free track path ahead of the train from a primary camera image. The safety controller then uses a secondary camera to verify that the identified path is bounded by visible rails on both sides of the path. It confirms that rail geometry matches standard gauge (1435 mm spaced parallel rails), with compatible turns and slopes. Finally it computes the free track distance to the next obstacle using pinhole camera geometry.

In the considered scenario, only a genuine free track can appear as two parallel lines spaced 1435 mm apart in front of the train. This geometric property ensures that the verification function remains valid regardless of the ML module's behaviour, provided that the safety controller itself is correct. Furthermore, consistency between the paths derived from both cameras is achieved only if the cameras, including their alignment and orientation, are functioning correctly.

The key safety property for this function is defined as follows:

P1: The reported free track distance must always be less than or equal to the actual free distance to the first obstacle. This ensures that braking can occur safely before collision.

The presence of multiple tracks—whether parallel, crossing, diverging, or converging—introduces additional complexity for free track detection, as the system must correctly identify which track segment is relevant to the train's movement. Handling such situations may require supplementary information from

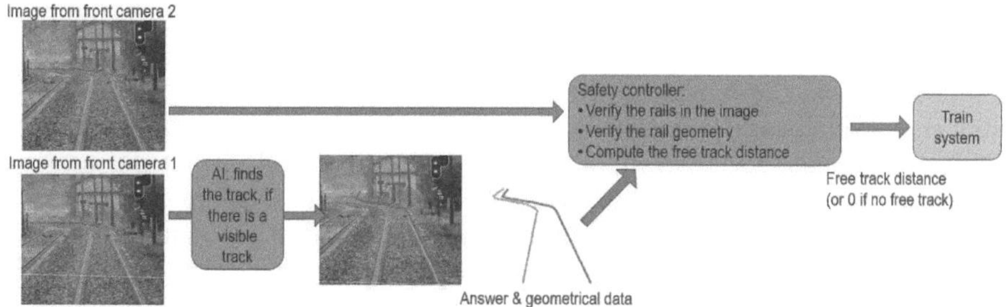

Fig. 2. Proof of concept: free track detection.

trackside infrastructure, such as the position and state of switches. These scenarios are beyond the scope of the present proof of concept and are not addressed in the current implementation.

4.2   Machine Learning Implementation

A U-Net model [14] was chosen as the ML architecture for the image segmentation task, owing to its proven effectiveness in delineating object boundaries in complex visual scenes. The model was trained from scratch using a synthetic dataset generated via a train simulation game, which allowed full control over scene composition, camera placement, and environmental parameters. The resulting dataset contained 650 imagepath pairs, each consisting of a raw camera view and a corresponding ground-truth segmentation mask representing the track path. Training was performed over 10 epochs, yielding an accuracy of approximately 90%.

While these initial results are encouraging, the relatively small size and imbalance of the dataset—both in terms of environmental diversity and distribution of track geometries—likely limit the model's generalization performance. It is expected that expanding the dataset to include more varied lighting conditions, weather patterns, and track configurations, as well as balancing the representation of straight and curved sections, would lead to improved robustness and accuracy.

In the proposed architecture, the ML model's sole function is to generate a candidate path for further evaluation. It is not required to achieve perfect segmentation, as the downstream safety controller performs independent verification of the candidate against strict geometric and physical constraints. This separation of concerns ensures that occasional inaccuracies in the ML output do not compromise overall system safety, provided that the safety controller itself is correct.

4.3   Safety Controller Implementation Functional

In the initial stage of the project, the work focused exclusively on implementing the functional logic of the safety controller and evaluating its behaviour in an offline setting. The processing chain begins with the application of edge detection to the regions of interest identified by the ML module, isolating the rail boundaries in the camera images. From these detected edges, the controller validates that the spacing between the rails corresponds to the standard gauge of 1,435 mm, allowing for tolerances due to perspective and curvature, and confirms that the rails are approximately parallel. Once these geometric checks are satisfied, the controller applies a pinhole camera model to compute the distance from the train to the end of the detected clear track segment. This calculated free track distance is then compared with the train's braking curves—computed for service braking and taking into account the current speed, the minimum guaranteed braking capacity, and the topographical characteristics of the track. If the available free track is shorter than the safe stopping distance, the controller would, in a real deployment, trigger an emergency braking request[3].

For this proof-of-concept, the controller was developed in Python, using the image processing capabilities of the OpenCV library for tasks such as edge detection, line fitting, and geometric transformation. The evaluation was conducted entirely offline, using a dataset separate from the ML training set, composed of synthetic images generated from a 3D railway simulation game. The dataset included a variety of scenarios, both with unobstructed track and with obstacles present, enabling the validation of the controller's decision logic under controlled conditions.

The offline experiments demonstrated that the functional chain could reject unsafe ML outputs and provide conservative free track distance estimates, even when the ML segmentation was imperfect. These encouraging results motivate the next stage of the project: the development of a safety-grade implementation of the controller capable of real-time processing on certified hardware.

This decomposition continues until all leaf properties are either proven by design or allocated to external safety conditions.

4.4 Safety Controller Implementation Safety-Critical

This stage of the project is ongoing and is expected to continue until 2026.

Following the principle that "safety is by design", the work begins with a formal, property-oriented safety demonstration of the system [6,7,15,16]. The top-level safety property, P1, is progressively refined through successive iterations. The first refinement step yields:

- $P2$: A path validated by the controller corresponds to a genuine free track.
- $P2_{th}$: The geometric formulas used to compute the free track distance are mathematically correct.
- $P2_{code}$: These formulas are correctly implemented in code, free of defects.
- P_{hard}: The computing platform guarantees safe execution of the controller.

---

[3] This safety function is commonly referred to as Automatic Train Protection (ATP).

This refinement process is repeated until all properties are decomposed into leaf properties that can be either guaranteed by design or identified as exported safety-related application conditions.

To address $P2_{code}$, the controller is formally specified and verified using the B method [1], ensuring that the implemented decision logic conforms exactly to its formal specification.

To address P_{hard}, the controller is deployed entirely within a safety-critical execution environment [12], providing immunity to transient hardware faults. The implementation targets the CLEARSY Safety Platform (Fig. 3), which supports the execution of safety-critical applications written in B and C at Safety Integrity Level 4 (SIL4), while managing systematic and random failures. Compliance is ensured provided that a set of Safety-Related Application Conditions, covering software, hardware, and the development lifecycle, are met. In the current design, image processing primitives are implemented in C, while decision functions are specified in B. The B specifications are compiled into replicated binaries, generated using different compilers from the same formal model, to further mitigate the risk of systematic software errors.

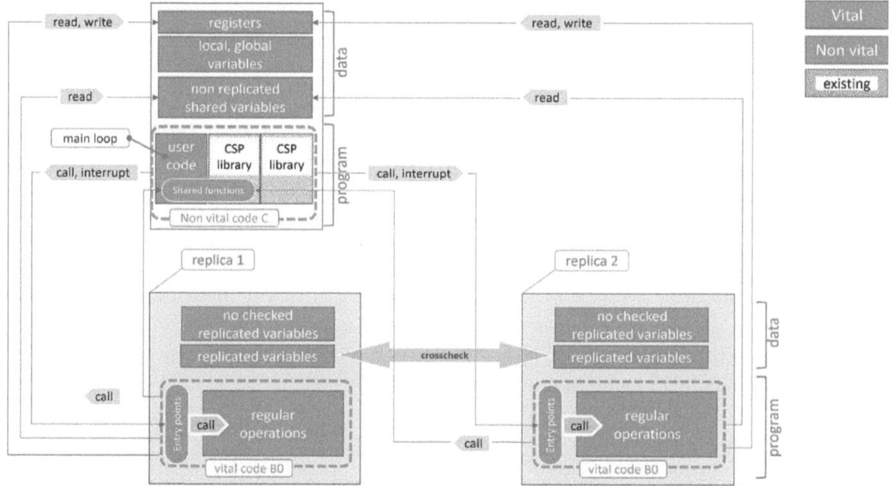

Fig. 3. CLEARSY Safety Platform: software architecture. An application is composed of non-replicated C functions (green) and of replicated B operations (orange). The code of compiled operations and related memory spaces are controlled frequently to detect divergent behaviour. (Color figure online)

Once the formal development is complete, a real-time prototype will be deployed on the safety platform and tested under operational conditions. Data will be collected from a host train operating on real tracks, with the system observing but not exerting any control over train movement. These tests will serve to assess the performance, robustness, and integration feasibility of the approach under realistic railway scenarios.

5 Conclusion and Perspectives

This work has presented a proof-of-concept architecture for integrating ML into safety-critical railway functions without compromising certification requirements. The proposed approach deliberately separates performance-oriented perception (ML module) from safety assurance (formally developed safety controller), enabling the exploitation of advanced perception capabilities while preserving deterministic, verifiable safety logic.

In the free track detection scenario, the ML module reduces the complexity of the verification problem by proposing a candidate path, while the safety controller independently validates its geometric and physical consistency against stringent safety properties. This division of responsibilities ensures that system safety is not contingent on the internal correctness of the ML component.

The systematic use of formal methods, and in particular the B method, both for the safety analysis and for the software development of the safety controller, could become a key contribution when the project is completed with success. The top-level safety property is refined into verifiable sub-properties, which are formally specified and mathematically proven. The resulting implementation is deployed on the CLEARSY Safety Platform, achieving a credible pathway toward Safety Integrity Level 4 (SIL4) compliance. This rigorous, proof-based approach guarantees traceability from safety requirements to executable code, and ensures that the decision logic conforms exactly to its formal specification.

By constraining ML outputs to verifiable forms and embedding them within formally proven safety architectures, this work demonstrates a credible pathway, using formal methods, for the trustworthy adoption of AI in domains where certification has historically excluded opaque, data-driven technologies. The PoC results confirm the feasibility of this dual-layer architecture, even when ML outputs are imperfect, by enforcing conservative decisions that maintain operational safety.

In the context of the UIC "New Methods for Safety Demonstration" initiative, UIC members will evaluate the results obtained in this project and assess whether this architecture can be reused or extended to other safety-critical functions. Such adoption would reinforce the prominent role of formal methods—particularly the B method—in shaping future safety assurance strategies for the railway sector.

Future work could address above limitations by integrating multi-sensor data sources, expanding verification strategies to more complex operational contexts, and validating performance under realistic environmental variability. At a broader level, scaling this approach to other ML-based railway applications will require the definition of standardized architectural patterns and corresponding safety argumentation frameworks, potentially influencing the evolution of railway safety standards.

Acknowledgements. The work and results described in this article were mostly funded by the project P734 NMSD "New Methods for Safety Demonstration" managed by UIC (International Union of Railways, Paris, https://uic.org.

References

1. Abrial, J.: The B-book - Assigning Programs to Meanings. Cambridge University Press (2005)
2. ter Beek, M.H., et al.: Formal methods in industry. Form. Asp. Comput. **37**(1) (2024). https://doi.org/10.1145/3689374
3. Behm, P., Benoit, P., Faivre, A., Meynadier, J.: Météor: a successful application of B in a large project. In: Wing, J.M., Woodcock, J., Davies, J. (eds.) Formal Methods, World Congress on Formal Methods in the Development of Computing Systems, FM'99, Toulouse, France, 20–24 September 1999, Proceedings, Volume I. LNCS, vol. 1708, pp. 369–387. Springer, Heidelberg (1999). https://doi.org/10.1007/3-540-48119-2_22
4. Boulanger, J.: Safety of Computer Architectures. Wiley (2010)
5. Butler, M., et al.: The first twenty-five years of industrial use of the b-method. In: ter Beek, M.H., Ničković, D. (eds.) Formal Methods for Industrial Critical Systems, pp. 189–209. Springer, Cham (2020)
6. Comptier, M., Deharbe, D., Perez, J.M., Mussat, L., Pierre, T., Sabatier, D.: Safety analysis of a CBTC system: a rigorous approach with event-B. In: Fantechi, A., Lecomte, T., Romanovsky, A. (eds.) Reliability, Safety, and Security of Railway Systems. Modelling, Analysis, Verification, and Certification, RSSRail 2017. LNCS, vol, 10598. Springer, Cham (2017). https://doi.org/10.1007/978-3-319-68499-4_10
7. Comptier, M., Leuschel, M., Mejia, L.F., Perez, J., Mutz, M.: Property-Based Modelling and Validation of a CBTC Zone Controller in Event-B, pp. 202–212, January (2019)
8. Dolle, D.: Les logiciels de s curit de trainguard mt cbtc. Le Rail **136**, 34–39 (2007)
9. Forin, P.: Vital coded microprocessor principles and application for various transit systems. IFAC Proceedings Volumes **23**(2), 79–84 (1990). iFAC/IFIP/IFORS Symposium on Control, Computers, Communications in Transportation, Paris, France, 19-21 September. http://www.sciencedirect.com/science/article/pii/S1474667017526531
10. Jackson, D., et al.: Certified control: an architecture for verifiable safety of autonomous vehicles (2021). https://arxiv.org/abs/2104.06178
11. Lecomte, T.: Applying a formal method in industry: a 15-year trajectory. In: Alpuente, M., Cook, B., Joubert, C. (eds.) FMICS 2009. LNCS, vol. 5825, pp. 26–34. Springer, Heidelberg (2009). https://doi.org/10.1007/978-3-642-04570-7_3
12. Lecomte, T., Deharbe, D., Fournier, P., Oliveira, M.: The CLEARSY safety platform: 5 years of research, development and deployment. Sci. Comput. Program. **199**, 102524 (2020)
13. Lecomte, T., Déharbe, D., Prun, É., Mottin, E.: Applying a formal method in industry: a 25-year trajectory. In: da Costa Cavalheiro, S.A., Fiadeiro, J.L. (eds.) Formal Methods: Foundations and Applications - 20th Brazilian Symposium, Proceedings, SBMF 2017, Recife, Brazil, 29 November–1 December 2017. LNCS, vol. 10623, pp. 70–87. Springer, Heidelberg (2017). https://doi.org/10.1007/978-3-319-70848-5_6

14. Ronneberger, O., Fischer, P., Brox, T.: U-Net: convolutional networks for biomedical image segmentation (2015). https://arxiv.org/abs/1505.04597
15. Sabatier, D.: Using formal proof and b method at system level for industrial projects, pp. 20–31, June 2016
16. Sabatier, D., Burdy, L., Requet, A., Guéry, J.: Formal proofs for the NYCT line 7 (flushing) modernization project. In: Derrick, J., et al. (eds.) ABZ 2012. LNCS, vol. 7316, pp. 369–372. Springer, Heidelberg (2012). https://doi.org/10.1007/978-3-642-30885-7_34

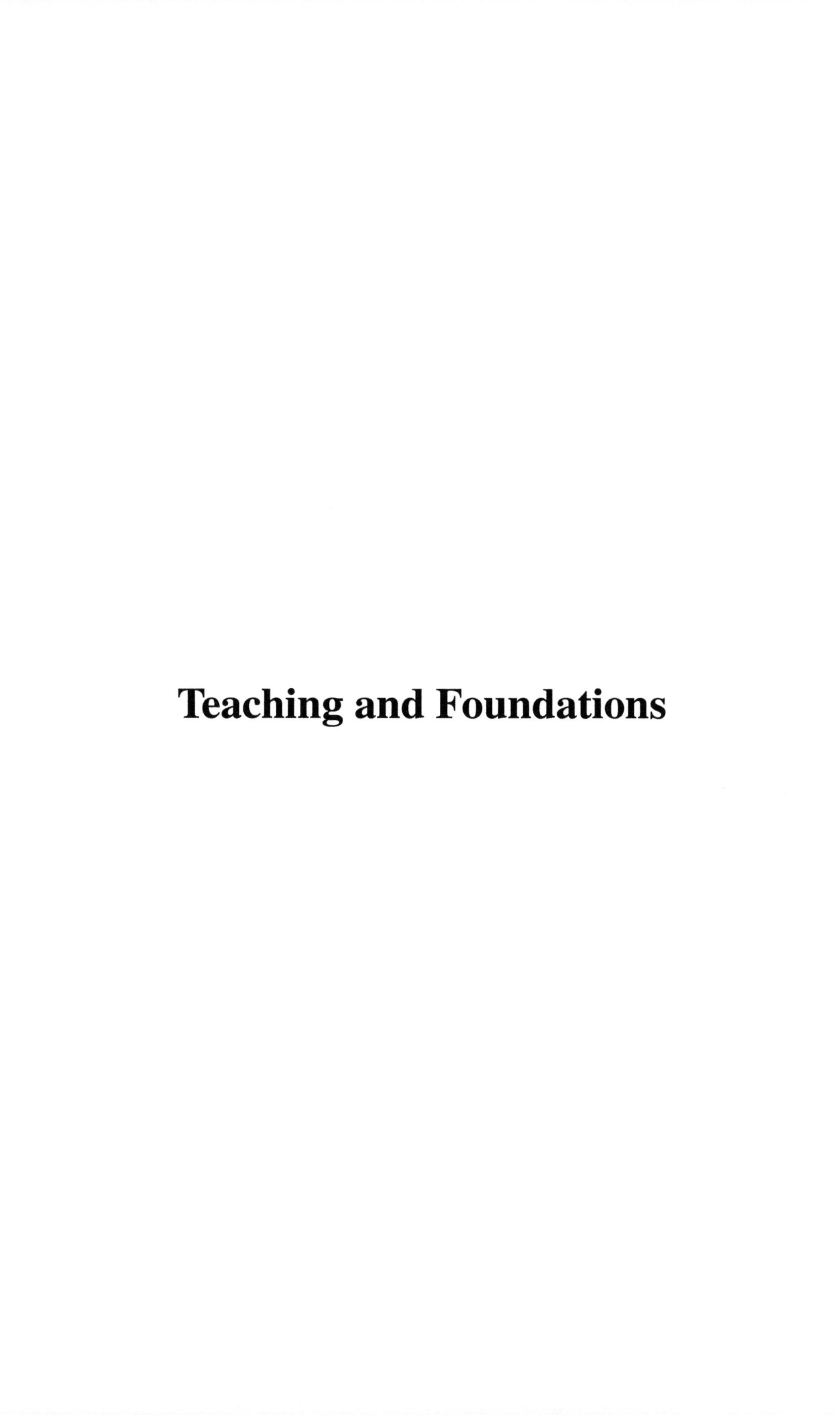

Teaching and Foundations

The Turner 2-Strings Machines

Rafael Dueire Lins[1,2](✉) (iD)

[1] Depto. de Computação, Universidade Federal Rural de Pernambuco, Recife, Brazil
`rafael.dueirelins@ufrpe.be,rdl@cin.ufpe.br`
[2] Centro de Informática, Universidade Federal de Pernambuco, Recife, Brazil

Abstract. This paper presents an abstract machine that can be easily used to teach intermediate and source code optimization, fundamental issues in a course on compiler construction techniques, bringing together theory and practice of computer science in a simple way.

Keywords: Reports on teaching formal methods · Abstract machines · Intermediate code optimization · Source code optimization · code performance · benchmarking

1 Introduction

Teaching compiler construction techniques is a challenging task as students often assume that in such a course they will learn how to build compilers, a task they are unlikely to undertake, which can lead to an immediate loss of motivation for enrolling in the course. In a strict "classical" view of a compiler it is a program that takes as input a program written in a high-level language and produces as output its equivalent in machine code.

In a modern course on compiler construction techniques it is fundamental to teach students to program better, as they will have a deeper understanding of what is behind a compiler, allowing them to develop code that is not only more maintainable but overall more efficient in time, space, or time and space. Besides that, students and CS professionals must understand that code co-pilots and AI-based systems are a reality now and the programming task itself is losing importance. Today, computer science professionals must have a deeper understanding of the features of the code to be developed. Such knowledge will enable them to provide the correct prompts to AI-based systems resulting in code that correctly meets the system requirements. Such a course is the place of convergence between theory of computation, programming language evolution, operating systems, and computer architecture, providing an integral view of computer science as an experimental science.

A compiler must be seen as any tool that takes a program file as input and yields another file as output with semantic equivalence. According to such a wide view, a LaTex environment such as Overleaf is a compiler, which takes a file of LaTex commands and ouputs a formatted document.

No doubt, a compiler is a complex software. The analysis-synthesis model [5] depicted in Figure 02 presents the phases involved in compilation. Abstract

M. H. ter Beek and L. Teixeira (Eds.): SBMF 2025, LNCS 16363, pp. 209–224, 2026.
https://doi.org/10.1007/978-3-032-12086-1_12

machines enable the step-by-step execution of programs, eliminating the numerous details of real (hardware) machines. Thus, they provide an intermediate language stage for compilation, bridging the gap between the high-level of a programming language and the low-level machine code. Reference [13] teaches that

"... abstract machines their use as an intermediate language for compilation is an essential feature. As a result the implementation of a programming language consists of two stages. The implementation of the compiler and the implementation of the abstract machine. This is a typical divide-and-conquer approach. From a pedagogical point of view, this simplifies the presentation and teaching of the principles of programming language implementations. From a software engineering point of view, the introduction of layers of abstraction increases maintainability and portability and it allows for design-by-contract."

Figure 1 presents the analysis-synthesis model with an abstract machine.

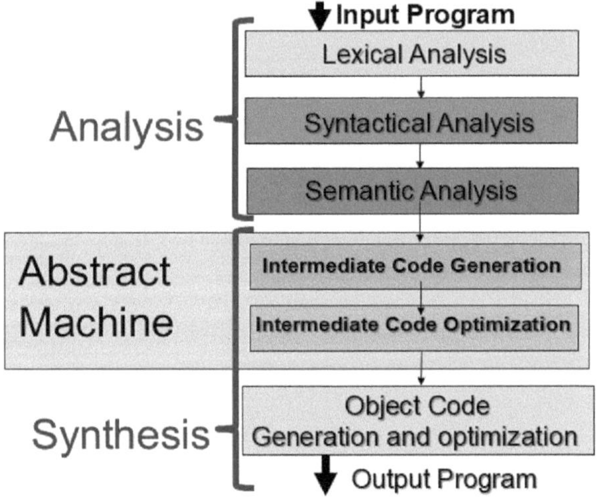

Fig. 1. Analysis-Synthesis Compilation Model with Abstract Machine

This paper presents a simple abstract machine that professors can easily use to teach students about intermediate and source code optimization techniques. Such a machine embodies the full power of *effective computability*, showing students that theory and practice are deeply associated. The machine presented here permits easy comparison not only the impact of different CPUs processing the code, but also allows one to see the impact of different sizes of RAM, operating systems, as well as versions of GCC, the Gnu C Compiler.

The first version of the machine is explained in the very first class of the undergraduate course on Compiler Construction Techniques and the students receive the source code in C together with a test program. The first task performed by the students is to study the code (presented below) and to execute it, putting the execution-time of the test program, together with the features of their hardware, the operating system, and the version of the GNU-C in a spreadsheet shared by all class. Every week, an optimization is explained and the students can immediately see its impact on processing time. Such a machine has been used with success in the last six years, and was used in over fifteen semestral courses with an average of forty students per course. The theoretical part of the course justifies all the optimization steps performed, showing that theory and practice meet perfectly.

2   Combinatory Logic

Combinatory Logic was developed by Moses Schönfinkel, a Jewish Russian mathematician. From 1914 to 1924, Schönfinkel was a member of David Hilbert's group at the University of Göttingen in Germany [2]. On 7 December 1920 he delivered a talk entitled Elemente der Logik ("Elements of Logic") to the group where he outlined the concept of combinatory logic, a system equivalent to First-Order Logic. Heinrich Behmann, a member of Hilbert's group, later revised the text and published it in 1924 [1]. Unfortunately, Schönfinkel was persuaded by the Stalinist propaganda of "Building a Socialist Russia" and went back to Russia. Possibly due to his dissident political views, in 1927 Schönfinkel was sent to a Gulag, a mental hospital (actually a labor camp) and died in 1942. Schönfinkel pioneered the idea that the concept of *function* was more general than the concept of *number* and showed that only two *combinators* were enough to represent all functions in first-order logic:

- K a b $\Rightarrow$ a   (projection)
- S a b c $\Rightarrow$ ac (b c)   (composition)

In 1927, while an instructor at Princeton University, Haskell B. Curry rediscovered the work of Moses Schönfinkel in the field of Combinatory Logic. Schönfinkel's work had anticipated much of Curry's own research, and as a consequence, he moved to University of Göttingen where he could work with Heinrich Behmann and Paul Bernays, who were familiar with Schönfinkel's work. Curry was supervised by David Hilbert and worked closely with Bernays, receiving a Ph.D. in 1930 with a dissertation on combinatory logic [4]. Curry introduced several new combinators.

David Hilbert's 10th problem was still open, however: the determination of the solvability of a Diophantine equation. Actually, that problem, the *Entscheidungsproblem* was the main research objective of Schönfinkel's work. Paul Bernays in 1927 wrote a paper with their ideas entitled "Zum Entscheidungsproblem der mathematischen Logik" ("On the Decision Problem of Mathematical Logic"). Solomon Feferman [7] explains the *Entscheidungsproblem* as "the question whether there exists an effective method to decide, given any well-formed formula of the pure first-order predicate calculus, whether or not it is valid in all possible interpretations".

In the early 1930s, Alonzo Church developed the λ-Calculus, which according to Feferman [7] is "a fragment of a quite general formalism for the foundation of mathematics, whose fundamental notion is that of arbitrary functions rather than arbitrary sets". Eventually, it was shown that Combinatory Logic, the λ-Calculus, Herbrand-Gödel general recursiveness, and the Turing machine were equivalent and solved Hilbert's *Entscheidungsproblem.*

Gödel's 1931 incompleteness theorem showed that no formal system for arithmetic would be complete, consistent, and have a finite number of axioms, putting an end to the Peano-Russell Logicist School.

Two decades later, programmable computers became a reality. Programming with the language of mathematics became a dream of the computer science community. Konrad Zuze pioneered such an initiative with his language Planlkalkul [11] (1944–1945), a language that was completely ignored. In 1960, ALGOL [10] and LISP [9] got closer to that purpose. LISP was the first programming language to encompass an interpreter for λ-expressions.

In 1972, David Turner implemented SASL [3] (St Andrews Static Language) a purely functional programming language, based on the applicative subset of ISWIM. In 1976, Turner redesigned and reimplemented it as a non-strict (lazy) language. A real revolution in implementation happened in 1978, when David Turner used an extended set of combinators [12] to re-implement SASL using a graph-reduction machine [6]. Unfortunately, Turner Graph Reduction Machine is too complex to be used in a first Compiler Construction Course to illustrate the fundamental issues of intermediate and source code optimization.

3   The Turner 2-Strings of Characters Machine

This simple machine utilizes two arrays of strings of characters. Initially, the string (program) to be executed is the input array and the output array is empty. The machine scans the "code" from left-to-right of the input array and writes the result in the output array. After each rewritting step, the two arrays exchange roles. The rewritting sequence stops whenever there is no possible rewritting. The sequence of steps in rewriting the program K(SK)(KK)SK is presented:

```
I_Array_1: K(SK)(KK)SK          O_Array_2:
```

Scanning from left-to-right the input array, one finds the leftmost combinator K and its arguments are a=(SK) and b=(KK). Reducing the K and placing the result in the output string O_Array_2, one gets:

```
I_Array_1: K(SK)(KK)SK          O_Array_2: (SK)SK
```

Now, the two arrays swap roles: Array_2 becomes the input array and Array_1 becomes the output array.

```
O_Array_1: K(SK)(KK)SK          I_Array_2: (SK)SK
```

Now, the leftmost symbol is " (" which has to be discarded yielding:

```
O_Array_1: SKSK                     I_Array_2: (SK)SK
```

The arrays swap roles: **Array_1** becomes the input and **Array_2** the output.

```
I_Array_1: SKSK                     O_Array_2: (SK)SK
```

The leftmost combinator is S and the resulting expression is written in **Array_2**.

```
I_Array_1: SKSK                     O_Array_2: KK(SK)
```

Now, the arrays swap roles. **Array_2** is the input and **Array_1** the output array.

```
O_Array_1: SKSK                     I_Array_2: KK(SK)
```

The leftmost combinator is K and the resulting expression is written in **Array_1**.

```
O_Array_1: K                        I_Array_2: KK(SK)
```

Array_1 becomes now the input array and **Array_2** becomes the output array.

```
I_Array_1: K                        O_Array_2: KK(SK)
```

The leftmost combinator is K. There are no arguments, thus execution stops.

Once the way the machine works is explained to the students, in the very first day of a Compiler Construction Techniques course, in the second part of the first class, the C-code implementation is presented. It is emphasized that the KS-Machine has all the power of effective computability, and that will be shown in the theoretical part of the course.

3.1 Machine Implementation

The language C is the perfect language to analyse the performance of programs and their optimization, not only for its outstanding performance, but also because of its the associated tools (debugger, profiler, etc.). The students are presented to the C-code of the machine in the first practical class and receive it via Google Classroom. The **main** routine presents the kernel of the 2-Strings of Characters Machine:

```c
int main() {
    char* array1 = input; char* array2 = output; char* array3;
    while (array1[1] != '\0') {
        switch (array1[0]) {
            case 'K': reduceK(array1,array2); break;
            case 'S': reduceS(array1,array2); break;
            case '(': disParenthesis(array1); array2[0] = 'X'; break;
            default: break;}
        array3 = array1; array1 = array2; array2 = array3;}
    int i;
    for (i = 0; array1[i] != '\0'; i++) {printf("%c", array1[i]);}
    printf("\n");
    printf("Time = %lf", (double)(clock()/CLOCKS_PER_SEC));
    return 0;}
```

The students also receive via Google Classroom several ancillary functions. The
`reduceK` routine that implements the "K" combinator (K a b => a) is:

```c
void reduceK(char* array1, char* array2) {
    int A, nA; int n = 1; A = n;
    find_argument(array1,&n); nA = n-1;
    find_argument(array1,&n); int k = 0; int i;
    for (i = A; i <= nA; i++) {array2[k] array1[i]; k++; }
    for (n = n; array1[n] != '\0'; n++) {array2[k] = array1[n]; k++;}
    array2[k] = '\0';}
```

The "S" combinator (S a b c => ac(bc)) is reduced by the `reduceS` function:

```c
void reduceS(char* array1, char* array2) {int A, nA; int B, nB;
    int C, nC; int n=1; A=n;
    find_argument(array1,&n); nA=n-1; B=n;
    find_argument(array1,&n); nB=n-1; C=n;
    find_argument(array1,&n); nC=n-1;
    int k=0; int i;
    for(i=A; i<=nA; i++) {array2[k] = array1[i]; k++;}
    for (i=C; i<= nC; i++) {array2[k] array1[i]; k++;}
    array2[k] = '('; k++;
    for (i=B; i<= nB; i++) {array2[k]=array1[i]; k++;}
    for (i=C; i<=nC; i++) {array2[k] array1[i]; k++;}
    array2[k] =')'; k++;
    for (n=n; array1[n]!='\0'; n++) {array2[k]=array1[n]; k++;}
    array2[k]='\0';}
```

Whenever a parenthesis "(" reaches the leftmost part of the code in the input
array it should be discarded together with the closing parenthesis ")".

```c
void disParenthesis(char* array1, int* p) {
    int paren = 1; int c = *p;
    while (paren != 0) {
        switch (array1[c]) {
            case '(': paren++; c++; break;
            case ')': paren--; c++; break;
            default: c++; }}
```

The matching parenthesis is found by:

```c
void m_parentesis(char* array1, int* p) {
    int paren = 1; int c = *p;
    while (paren != 0) {
        switch (array1[c]) {
            case '(': paren++; c++; break;
            case ')': paren--; c++; break;
            default: c++;}}
    *p = c;}
```

The ancillary procedure `find_argument` finds the arguments of a combinator.

```
void find_argument(char* array1, int* p) {
    int c = *p;
    if (array1[c]=='('){c++; m_parentesis(array1,&c);} else {c++;}
    *p=c;}
```

3.2   The KS-Benchmark

Together with the source code, the students receive the test KS-program, and instructions on how to run it. (such as, disconnect the machine from the web, kill all processes, and re-boot the machine), as well as the link to a shared spreadsheet in which the student should input the features of their PC, the version of the operating system and the GCC compiler. Students with dual-boot machines are told to include both versions of the results. Table 1 presents the results for the 2-Strings of Characters Machine. The results for the KS-program appear in the **KS** column.

After the execution of each benchmark, the students are invited to analyze the table of results and try to draw conclusions comparing the different architectures, operating systems, and versions of the GCC. For instance, the first four lines in Table 1 are from an Apple M2-8 GB RAM. For the sort of benchmarks executed here, it seems that the MacOS 15.0.1 operating system is more efficient than Sonoma 14.4.1, as its times are consistently smaller. It is also interesting to notice that the performance ranking may change as optimizations are performed. That sort of benchmarking clearly demonstrates to students that, whenever developing a program, they need to see how it behaves in the target architecture, and that there are no "all-time-winner" solution.

3.3   The KSI-Benchmark

In his work [1], Schönfinkel also introduced a simplification to combinator expressions with the *I combinator*, showing by extensionality that $I = S\ K\ K$:

- I a $\Rightarrow$ a   (identity)

The first optimization the students should perform is to modify the `case`-switch of the `main` program to encompass the I-combinator and to develop the `reduceI` procedure. The students receive the KSI-program and feed their results to the shared spreadsheet. This simple intermediate-code optimization brings yields a time performance gain of around 25%, as shown in the **KSI** column of Table 1.

3.4   Introducing Curry-Combinators

Curry [4] introduced two combinators important to language implementation:

- B f g x $\Rightarrow$ f (g x)
- C f g x $\Rightarrow$ f x g

216   R. D. Lins

The second intermediate-code optimization that the students must perform is to introduce the B and C combinators. The students receive the KSIBC version of the test program and execute it following the same instructions. The performance gain of such a simple intermediate-code optimization is enormous, as can be seen in the **Cur** column of Table 1.

Table 1. Table presenting the top 20 results ordered by KS execution time in seconds (**Cur** is the Curry Combinator machine, **Tur** is the Turner Combinator machine, **Pro** is the Turner Combinator machine with the case switch ordered by the greatest to the smallest number of calls provided by the profiler, and **-Ox** is the Turner combinator machine, with the case switch ordered by the profiler compiled with the optimization flag **x** set up. [1] Apple M2-8 GB RAM, [2] AMD R7 5700X@3.40 GHz-16GB RAM, [3] i5-1235U@1.30 GHz-8GB RAM, [4] I7-11880h@3.20Ghz-16GB RAM, [5] i7-9700K@3.60Ghz-16GB RAM, [6] i5-9400F@2.90GHz-16GB RAM, [7] i5-10210U@1.60GHz-8GB RAM, [8] AMD R7 5700u@1.8Ghz-8GB RAM, [9] i7-8565U@1.80GHz-16GB RAM, [10] i5-10210Ux8@4.20Ghz-20GB RAM, [11] i5-1135G7@2.40GHz-8GB RAM, [12] i5-10210Ux8@4.20Ghz-20GB RAM, [13] i5-10210U@2.11 GHz-20GB RAM, [14] i5-7300HQ@2.50GHz-16GB RAM, [15] i5-2400@3.10 GHz-8GB RAM, [16] AMD R5 3600@4.0GHz -16GB RAM, [17] i7-10510U@1.80GHz-16GB RAM.

Machine with 2-Strings of Characters											
CPU	GCC	O.S.	KS	KSI	Cur	Tur	Pro	-O1	-O2	-O3	-Os
[1]	AC15	Sonoma 14.4.1	1142	800	134	156	147	81	79	75	80
[1]	14.2.0	MacOS 15.0.1	1148	735	118	116	120	39	40	40	39
[1]	Cl16	MacOS 15.0.1	1148	734	117	115	121	38	39	39	38
[1]	13.2.0	Sonoma 14.4.1	1790	1189	196	212	199	92	91	80	134
[2]	6.3.0	W11 PRO	1398	946	158	164	164	44	40	38	56
[3]	6.3.0	W11 23H2	1490	885	151	140	128	44	61	65	38
[4]	6.3.0	W11 Pro	1575	997	174	164	106	37	28	29	45
[5]	8.1.0	W10 Pro 22H2	1948	1224	197	191	192	44	46	44	43
[6]	6.3.0	W10 Pro - 22H2	2226	1456	235	223	228	40	36	35	45
[7]	6.3.0	W11 H 23H2	2238	1432	234	221	262	101	89	149	122
[8]	6.3.0	W11 H 23H2	2240	1415	202	192	174	43	39	39	46
[9]	6.3.0	W11 H 24H2	2312	1377	225	216	212	40	38	41	46
[10]	6.3.0	W10 H	2402	1733	309	300	276	38	35	44	31
[11]	6.3.0	W11 H 23H2	2631	4171	292	240	354	41	38	38	56
[12]	14.2.1	FEDORA 41	2753	1874	469	312	307	35	33	40	28
[13]	6.3.0	W11 H 23H2	2759	1727	328	276	222	41	40	65	48
[14]	6.3.0	W11 H 22H2	2817	1712	277	267	269	49	48	73	62
[15]	14.2.0	W10.0.19045.5011	2819	1840	294	286	285	72	71	71	73
[16]	14.2.0	W10 Pro 22H2	2899	2870	293	284	282	47	49	49	58
[17]	9.2.0	W11 Pro 23H2	2903	1661	251	226	235	47	47	62	55

3.5   Turner Combinators

The third intermediate-code optimization the students must perform is to introduce the Turner combinators. As already mentioned, Turner aim was to increase the efficiency of the implementation of the SASL language [3]. Combinators are variable-free; thus, there is no concern of avoiding variable captures, whenever a β-reduction in the λ-Calculus makes a free-variable incorrectly bound. The new set of Turner combinators presented in [12] included four new combinators:

- S1 c f g x $\Rightarrow$ c (f x) (g x)
- B1 c f g x $\Rightarrow$ c f (g x)
- C1 c f g x $\Rightarrow$ c (f x) g
- Y x $\Rightarrow$ x (Y x)

Turner noticed that in "real-world" programs no function (or procedure) takes more than four variables as input. The Y combinator is used in the definition of recursive functions. The students receive the Turner version of the test program and execute it following the same instructions. To avoid using two characters for Turner combinators S1, B1, and C1, they are implemented as D, E, and F, respectively. As one can see in the **Tur** column of Table 1, the performance gain about the **Cur** (Curry combinator) column is minimal or even negative. The reason for that is that there are very few Turner combinators in the benchmark program used, although in real programs they appear very often, bringing a huge code speed-up. In reality, while Schönfinkel's KS-code brings an exponential growth of the combinator code in relation to the size of the equivalent λ-expression, Turner combinator growth rate is theoretically quadratic, but in real programs the growth is linear [8].

Students are also told to test the KS-benchmark on their **Tur** version of the machine, and often they experience a degradation in the performance in relation to the **KS**-machine. They learn that if their code does not take advantage of more powerful commands in their language, the code performance degrades.

3.6   Profiling the Code

One valuable tool for understanding the number of procedure calls and the relative time taken to execute each procedure in a C-program is provided by the Profiler. Surprisingly, no student of the several classes of the Compiler Construction Course taught by the author had ever used a profiler. In this simple intermediate-code optimization, the students are supposed to profile their code and to re-order the case-switch from the most to the least frequently called procedure. Although the students have been recommended to profile their codes to better understand which are the crucial time-bottlenecks in their programs, they were warned that in the present case there would be little performance gain, due to the size of the program, as one can see in column **Pro** of Table 1.

Students also learn that in order to have profiler visibility, the program must be structured in procedures (or functions). They are also told that source-code optimizations will analyze the size of the procedures, compare them with memory-page size to see if it is advantageous to make code inlining.

3.7   Source-Code Optimizations

The GCC compiler provides a very large number of source code optimizations
that are set by compling the code with flags -O1, -O2, -O3, and -Os. None of
the many students of the Compiler Construction Techniques courses taught by
the author of this paper had ever used such flags. After explaining some of the
most important source-code optimizations to the students, they are oriented to
recompile their code with different flags and share their time performance in the
results spread sheet, as may be found in columns **-O1**, **-O2**, **-O3**, and **-Os** in
Table 1.

   Students are advised to discard their code whenever source-code optimization flags degrade the performance of their programs, because that is a clear
indication of poor programming skills.

4   The Turner 2-Strings of Integers Machine

One important aspect that students seldom realize is that the choice of the data
structures used in a program impacts its performance. This becomes straight-
forwardly clear whenever one uses *integers* instead of *characters* in the 2-Strings
of Integers Machine, re-writing the head of the `main` routine as:

```
int main(){
    int *array1, *array2, *array3;
    array1 = input;
    array2 = output;
```

All the ancillary routines also need the corresponding type adjustments.

   All the benchmarks previously tested are re-executed, and students place
their results in the same spreadsheet as the previous machine, allowing them to
see the difference in performance, as shown in Table 2.

5   Assessing Real Programs

At this point, in the theoretical part of the Compiler Construction Techniques
course, students have already learned how to translate a functional program
in a language such as Haskell into a script in the λ-Calculus and also how to
use the Turner Bracket Abstraction algorithm to translate such a script into
Turner Combinatory Logic. The 2-Strings of Integers Machine are enriched with
arithmetic and logic combinators, such as the ones below, in the postfix notation
to execute real programs:

$-$ + a b $\Rightarrow$ a (result of a+b)	- a b $\Rightarrow$ a (result of a-b)
$-$ * a b $\Rightarrow$ a (result of a*b)	/ a b $\Rightarrow$ a (result of a/b)
$-$ T a b $\Rightarrow$ a (True a b = a)	F a b $\Rightarrow$ b (False a b = b)
$-$ = a b $\Rightarrow$ T (True, if a=b)	= a b $\Rightarrow$ F (False, if a$\neq$b)
$-$ > a b $\Rightarrow$ T (True, if a>b)	> a b $\Rightarrow$ F (False, if a$\leq$b)

Table 2. Table presenting the top 20 results ordered by KS execution time in seconds. (**Cur** is the Curry Combinator machine, **Tur** is the Turner Combinator machine with the case switch ordered by the profiler, and **-Ox** is the Turner combinator machine, with the case switch ordered by the profiler compiled with the optimization flag **x** set up. [1] Apple M2-8 GB RAM, [2] AMD R7 5700X@3.40 GHz-16GB RAM, [3] i5-1235U@1.30 GHz-8GB RAM, [4] I7-11880h@3.20Ghz-16GB RAM, [5] i7-9700K@3.60Ghz-16GB RAM, [6] i5-9400F@2.90GHz-16GB RAM, [7] i5-10210U@1.60GHz-8GB RAM, [8] AMD R7 5700u@1.8Ghz-8GB RAM, [9] i7-8565U@1.80GHz-16GB RAM, [10] i5-10210Ux8@4.20Ghz-20GB RAM, [11] i5-1135G7@2.40GHz-8GB RAM, [12] i5-10210Ux8@4.20Ghz-20GB RAM, [13] i5-10210U@2.11 GHz-20GB RAM, [14] i5-7300HQ@2.50GHz-16GB RAM, [15] i5-2400@3.10 GHz-8GB RAM, [16] AMD R5 3600@4.0GHz -16GB RAM, [17] i7-10510U@1.80GHz-16GB RAM.

Machine with 2-Strings of Integers										
CPU	GCC	O.S.	KS	KSI	Cur	Tur	-O1	-O2	-O3	-Os
[1]	AC15	Sonoma 14.4.1	2399	311	236	73	71	67	71	80
[1]	14.2.0	MacOS 15.0.1	1396	143	217	36	46	43	68	39
[1]	Cl16	MacOS 15.0.1	1394	141	137	44	43	43	43	38
[1]	13.2.0	Sonoma 14.4.1	3555	367	357	62	79	79	117	134
[2]	6.3.0	W11 PRO	1411	142	140	46	45	47	46	56
[2]	6.3.0	W11 23H2	2107	192	209	74	84	72	73	38
[3]	6.3.0	W11 Pro	1851	193	233	81	80	79	76	45
[4]	8.1.0	W10 Pro 22H2	2156	218	212	76	84	85	73	43
[5]	6.3.0	W10 Pro - 22H2	2443	243	234	59	58	58	60	45
[6]	6.3.0	W11 H 23H2	2519	663	279	76	71	72	85	122
[7]	6.3.0	W11 H 23H2	2371	232	217	85	81	80	85	46
[8]	6.3.0	W11 H 24H2	2543	250	260	78	65	64	79	46
[9]	6.3.0	W10 H	3785	290	249	81	100	132	98	31
[10]	6.3.0	W11 H 23H2	4331	250	399	64	67	68	67	56
[11]	14.2.1	FEDORA 41	3792	340	582	162	184	158	174	28
[12]	6.3.0	W11 H 23H2	2621	254	244	74	72	72	72	48
[13]	6.3.0	W11 H 22H2	2828	2810	284	87	79	78	93	62
[14]	14.2.0	W10.0.19045.5011	3835	395	392	129	155	152	138	73
[15]	14.2.0	W10 Pro 22H2	3298	333	325	76	78	78	75	58
[16]	9.2.0	W11 Pro 23H2	3672	724	495	93	88	86	79	55
[17]	14.2.0	W11 23H2	2714	284	267	62	73,	73	74	68

- $<$ a b $\Rightarrow$ T (True, if a$<$b) $<$ a b $\Rightarrow$ F (False, if a$\geq$b)
- $\geq$ a b $\Rightarrow$ T (True, if a$\geq$b) $\geq$ a b $\Rightarrow$ F (False, if a$<$b)
- $\leq$ a b $\Rightarrow$ T (True, if a$\leq$b) $\leq$ a b $\Rightarrow$ F (False, if a$>$b)

Table 3. Table presenting 10 results (time in seconds) for the Fat 20 KSI-benchmark for different architectures, operating systems, and Gnu C Compiler version running time executed in the Turner Combinator 2-String of Integer Machine, compiled without and with GCC optimization flags. [1] AMD R3 3200G@3.80 GHz-24GB RAM, [2] i3-1005G1@1.20GHz -12GB RAM, [3] i3-7020U@2.30GHz 16GB RAM, [4] i5-10210Ux8@4.20Ghz-20GB RAM, [5] i5-13420H @2.10 GH -16 GB RAM, [6] I5-6200U@2.3Ghz-8GB RAM, [7] I5-9300H@2.40GHz-8GB RAM, [8] i7-8565U@1.80GHz-16GB RAM, [9] i7-9700K @3.60Ghz-16GB RAM, [10] i7-9750H@2.60GHz -16,0 GB RAM.

Turner Combinator Machine with 2-Strings of Integers							
C.P.U.	GCC	O.S.	Fat 20	Fat 20-O1	Fat 20-O2	Fat 20-O3	Fat 20-Os
[1]	14.2.0	W10 Pro 22H2	6.90	1.15	1.28	1.27	1.26
[2]	6.3.0	W11 H 23H2	8.61	1.75	1.91	1.92	2.44
[3]	14.2.0	W10 H	8.20	1.92	2.38	2.37	2.02
[4]	14.2.1	FEDORA 41	4.92	1.82	2.03	2.34	3.13
[5]	14.2.0	W11 23H2	2.28	0.63	0.83	0.81	0.64
[6]	6.3.0	W10 H	7.98	2.22	2.31	2.31	3.89
[7]	8.1.0	W11 23H2	5.12	5.23	5.16	5.07	5.24
[8]	6.3.0	W11 H 24H2	5.41	1.44	1.93	1.93	2.18
[9]	8.1.0	W10 Pro 22H2	3.72	0.87	1.06	0.92	1.12
[10]	14.2.0	W11 23H2	4.85	0.98	1.36	1.36	1.53

5.1   Factorial

The factorial function may be defined as:

```
fat n = if (n=1) then 1 else (n * fat (n-1))
```

In postfix notation, corresponds to:

```
fat n = if (n1=) then 1 else (n fat (n1-)*)
```

Translating **Fat 20** into Turner-combinatorial logic one gets:

```
Fat 20 = Y((B(S(S(C(C(CI1)=)(K1))))(C(BC(B(SI)(C(BBI)(C(CI1)-))))*))20
```

The result of the execution of the **Fat 20** benchmark in Turner Machine with 2-Strings of Integers may be found in Table 3.

5.2   Fibonacci

The fibonacci function may be defined as:

```
fib n = if (n<2) then x else (fib(n-2)+fib(n-1))
```

In postfix notation, corresponds to:

Table 4. Table presenting 10 results (time in seconds) for the Fib 20 YKSI-benchmark for different architectures, operating systems, and Gnu C Compiler version running time executed in the Turner Combinator 2-String of Integer Machine, compiled without and with GCC optimization flags. [1] AMD R3 3200G@3.80 GHz-24GB RAM, [2] i3-1005G1@1.20GHz -12GB RAM, [3] i3-7020U@2.30GHz 16GB RAM, [4] i5-10210Ux8@4.20Ghz-20GB RAM, [5] i5-13420H @2.10 GH -16 GB RAM, [6] I5-6200U@2.3Ghz-8GB RAM, [7] I5-9300H@2.40GHz-8GB RAM, [8] i7-8565U@1.80GHz-16GB RAM, [9] i7-9700K @3.60Ghz-16GB RAM, [10] i7-9750H@2.60GHz -16,0 GB RAM.

Machine with 2-Strings of Integers							
CPU	GCC	O.S.	Fib 20	Fib 20-O1	Fib 20-O2	Fib 20-O3	Fib 20-Os
[1]	14.2.0	W10 Pro 22H2	12.535,18	2.063,61	2.312,62	2.307,04	2.432,12
[2]	6.3.0	W11 H 23H2	10.141,22	2.211,07	2.220,65	2.224,88	2.137,14
[3]	14.2.0	W10 H	15.149,50	2.993,48	3.913,25	2.793,48	2.886,48
[4]	14.2.1	FEDORA 41	12.030,00	2.121,00	2.111,00	2.341,00	2.222,00
[5]	14.2.0	W11 23H2	4.185,18	1.030,70	1.324,07	1.305,28	1.024,62
[6]	6.3.0	W10 H	11.298,70	2.549,06	2.388,80	2.380,91	2.419,56
[7]	8.1.0	W11 23H2	8.341,34	1.765,37	2.216,61	2.251,78	2.268,09
[8]	6.3.0	W11 H 24H2	8.104,03	1.973,78	1.764,04	1.748,58	1.810,62
[9]	8.1.0	W10 Pro 22H2	6.949,73	1.533,50	1.714,60	1.776,07	1.888,01
[10]	14.2.0	W11 23H2	9.205,80	1.799,88	2.310,50	2.326,06	2.314,02

```
fib n = if (n2<) then n else (fib(n2-) fib(n1-)+)
```

Translating `Fib 20` into Turner-combinatorial logic one gets:

```
Fib 20 = Y(B(S(S(C(CI2)<)I))(FC(S(FDI(C(CI2)-))(FBI(C(CI1)-)))+))20
```

Some of the results of the execution of the `Fib 20` benchmark in Turner Machine with 2-Strings of Integers may be found in Table 4.

After running the YSKI code, students are requested to use Turner Bracket Abstraction algorithm for `Fat 20` and `Fib 20`, and to re-execute their codes to see the enormous performance gains.

6   Conclusions

The Compiler Construction Techniques (CCT) course plays an important role in the formation of professionals in Computer Science as it serves as the point of convergence between programming languages, computer architecture, operating systems, and theory of computation. The practical part of such a course must not only emphasize that Computer Science is an experimental science, but also that theory and practice are strongly bound.

The two Turner 2-Strings abstract machines presented here have been successfully used in the last six years in several one-semester long Compiler Construction Techniques courses taught by the author of this paper at UFRPE. Students have shown no difficulty in performing the tasks described here and have become aware of the need to carefully choose the data structures used in their programs, the suitable implementation language, and the computer architecture. In addition to that, students become aware that the choice of commands can impact the final performance and maintainability of their code. In a straightforward way, students may see that the quality of their code has a stronger impact on the performance of their programs than the quality of their hardware platform, as simple intermediate and source code optimizations may bring a 95% decrease in the time needed to execute the program. Students also become aware that the different versions of the GNU C compiler may provide different time figures and have a performance account of the different operating systems, melting prejudices such as "Ubuntu is fast", "Windows is very slow", etc.

The abstract machine presented shows the importance of using an abstract machine not only to bridge the semantic gap between source and object languages, but also to introduce intermediate code optimizations that may be very simple and significantly increase the efficiency of the final code.

In the courses taught by the author, all students are asked to send their teacher the code for each optimization requested, along with a 1-min video showing that no other processes are running on their machines, the execution result and the elapsed time. It is important to remark that the time figures presented in the tables above correspond to only one-run, and that they are not valid as a strong performance figure for any sort of research or "real-world" application. In such cases, the students should take ten performance measures, discard the outliers, and to take the average and variance. Having made such a remark, it is easy to spot result outliers by looking at the data of the students, by analyzing the spread sheet of results.

The hundreds of students in the Compiler Construction Techniques courses taught by the author had **never** used the code *Profiler* before, but after becoming aware of its existence, they awakened to its importance as a way to better spot the performance bottlenecks in their code. Similarly, the performance gains brought by the source-code optimization flags astonished students, and they were instructed to write code in a way to let the compiler to better "understand" their code yielding expressive performance gains.

The Compiler Construction Techniques (CCT) course is a compulsory part of the syllabuses of the CS courses, both at UFPE and UFRPE. At UFRPE, the author also teaches the Compiler Project (CP) course, which is non-compulsory and has the CCT course as a prerequisite. The first part of the CP course is to implement Lint Turner Graph Reduction machine [6], which is two orders of magnitude faster than the Turner 2-Strings Machines presented here. In addition, the students implement either a mark-scan or a copying garbage collector [14]. The evolution from Turner Graph reduction machine to Thomas Johnsson G-

Machine, is presented following the steps presented in reference [15]. The second part of this course is dedicated to the front-end, in which the students make use of LEX and YACC [5] to implement a subset of SASL [3] plugging it to the Turner Graph Reduction machine back-end.

The C-code for the machines presented and the benchmarks are available under request to the author.

Acknowledgements. This paper is dedicated to Professor David A. Turner (26/Jan./1946 - 19/Oct./2023), a great researcher and a fantastic person.
The author is grateful to Professor Simon J. Thompson for his comments in a previous version of this paper.

Rafael Dueire Lins holds a Senior Researcher Grant from CNPq - Brazil.

References

1. Schönfinkel, M.: Über die Bausteine der mathematischen Logik, From Frege to Gödel: A Source Book in Mathematical Logic, 1879-1931, pp. 355–366. Harvard University Press (1967). ISBN 978-0674324497
2. Wolfram, S.: Where Did Combinators Come From? Hunting the Story of Moses Schönfinkel (2024). ISBN 978-1-57955-044-8
3. Turner, D.A., Joy, M.S.: SASL Language Manual, Document (Functional Language Implementation Project). University of Warwick, Department of Computer Science (1989)
4. Curry, H.: Grundlagen der Kombinatorischen Logik (Foundations of combinatorial logic). American Journal of Mathematics (in German), pp. 509–536. The Johns Hopkins University Press (1930). https://doi.org/10.2307/2370619
5. Aho, A.V., Lam, M.S., Sethi, R., Ullman, J.D.: Compilers: Principles, Techniques, and Tools, 2nd edn. Addison-Wesley Longman Publishing Co., Inc., USA (2006). ISBN 0321486811
6. Turner, D.A.: A new implementation technique for applicative languages. Softw. Pract. Exp. **9**(1), 31–49 (1979). https://doi.org/10.1002/spe.4380090105
7. Turing, A.: Alan Turing's Systems of Logic: The Princeton Thesis, Woodstock, England, editor: Andrew W. Appel, Princeton Univ. (2012)
8. Noshita, K., Hikita, T.: The BC-chain method for representing combinators in linear space. New Gen. Comput. **3**(2), 131–144 (1985). https://doi.org/10.1007/BF03037065
9. McCarthy, J.: History of LISP. Association for Computing Machinery, History of Programming Languages, pp. 173–185 (1978). ISBN 0127450408
10. Backus, J.W., Bauer, F.L., et al.: Revised report on the algorithmic language ALGOL 60. Commun. ACM **6**(1), 1–17 (1963). https://doi.org/10.1145/366193.366201
11. Rojas, R., Göktekin, C., et al.: Konrad Zuses Plankalkül — Seine Genese und eine moderne Implementierung. Geschichten der Informatik: Visionen, Paradigmen, Leitmotive, pp. 215–235. Springer, Heidelberg (2004). ISBN 978-3-642-18631-8. https://doi.org/10.1007/978-3-642-18631-8-9
12. Turner, D.A.: Another algorithm for bracket abstraction. J. Symb. Log. **V44**(2), 267–270 (1979)

13. Diehl, S., Hartel, P., Sestoft, P.: Abstract machines for programming language implementation. Future Gener. Comput. Syst. **16**(7), 739–751 (2000). https://doi.org/10.1016/S0167-739X(99)00088-6
14. Jones, R., Lins, R.D.: Garbage collection: algorithms for automatic dynamic memory management. Wiley, USA (1996). ISBN 0471941484
15. Lins, R.D., Soares, P.G.: Some performance figures for the G-Machine and its optimisations. Microprocessing Microprogramming **37**(1), 163–166 (1993). https://doi.org/10.1016/0165-6074(93)90039-N

A Proof of the De Zolt Postulate
in Three-Dimensional Space

Bruno Cuconato[1,2] and Edward Hermann Haeusler[1(✉)]

[1] Department of Informatics, PUC-Rio, Rio de Janeiro, Brazil
hermann@inf.puc-rio.br
[2] EPGE/FGV, Rio de Janeiro, Brazil

Abstract. De Zolt's postulate is a more mathematically precise restatement of Euclid's geometric principle of "the whole is greater than the part" [8, Book I, Common Notion 5]. While the three-dimensional version of De Zolt's postulate is not consistent with ZFC due to the Banach-Tarski paradox and related theorems, it is consistent with a proof-theoretically weaker theory. In this paper, we provide an implementation of such a weak type theory and a formal proof of De Zolt's postulate in three dimensions in this theory.

Keywords: De Zolt's postulate · Formalization of Mathematics · Banach-Tarski paradox · Lean

We present a proof of De Zolt's postulate in three-dimensional space, formalized with the assistance of the Lean prover [9,10].[1] The three-dimensional version of De Zolt's postulate is not consistent with ZFC due to the Banach-Tarski paradox/theorem [3], which states that a unit ball in $\mathbb{R}^3$ is equidecomposable to the union of two unit balls, and generalizes to a theorem stating that any two finite volumes in $\mathbb{R}^3$ are equidecomposable. De Zolt's postulate is however provable in the weaker type theory Z_p, the system proposed by Giovannini *et al.* [6, §5], since it does not admit such paradoxes as theorems. The Z_p system is a continuation of the work by Giovannini *et al.* in [5], where an abstract algebraic proof of De Zolt's postulate for bi-dimensional space is presented. See Fig. 1 (page 4) for an overview of Z_p.

This paper is structured as follows: we start by introducing De Zolt's postulate and its importance (Sect. 1); we then present the Z_p type system and its rules (Sect. 2); we show how we define the geometric objects we will be working with in Lean (Sect. 3), and then present the implementation of the Z_p system in Lean (Sect. 4). Finally, we prove De Zolt's postulate (Sect. 5) and offer some conclusive remarks.

---

[1] The full Lean code appears in the paper and is also attached to this PDF file for convenience.

M. H. ter Beek and L. Teixeira (Eds.): SBMF 2025, LNCS 16363, pp. 225–241, 2026.
https://doi.org/10.1007/978-3-032-12086-1_13

1   Introduction

We state below De Zolt's original postulate, for the two-dimensional case:

Postulate 1 (De Zolt). *Given a polygon $\mathcal{P}$ and a decomposition $T = \{t_1, \ldots, t_k\}$ of $\mathcal{P}$ into k polygons. Let $t_i \in T$, then $T - \{t_i\}$ is not equivalent to T in the theory of equivalence of plane polygons.*

De Zolt establishes common notions concerning equal magnitude (e.g., area of polygons) and congruence between polygons. There is an important discussion on whether one needs to attach a measure, such as the concept of *area*, to figures in order to make a mereological statement. Hartshorne [7] claims that the words 'lesser' or 'greater' in Euclidean geometry should be avoided because these imply the existence of an order relation among figures which has not yet been established. In fact, the existence of an order relation for content depends on the above postulate. He argues that there is no notion of a *purely geometric* proof of the De Zolt postulate from the definition of content area already given. On the other hand, he observes that De Zolt holds whenever a measure of area function is defined in geometry. Moreover, Hartshorne emphasizes [7, pp. 202–210] that "[Hilbert's] proof [of De Zolt and of area function] is analytic in that it makes use of the field of segment arithmetic and similar triangles".

A geometrical proof (following Baldwin [1]) is one provided in one of these forms:

1. A proof in a formal language for geometry;
2. A proof in a meta-theory (e.g. ZFC) with geometry as a defined notion, or
3. Use (1) to get (2).

Under this perspective, we can observe that Euclid's proofs in his Elements are not geometrical in Baldwin's sense, because they were written in natural language. The same reasoning applies to Hilbert's (1899) proof of De Zolt's postulate.

Again following Baldwin [1,2], a formal proof in geometry should choose:

1. a vocabulary, under some previous conceptual analysis, of the fundamental notions, such as *point, line, incidence*, etc.;
2. a logic, such as first-order logic, second-order logic, $L_{\omega_1\omega}$, dependent or even intuitionistic type theory, for example, and
3. the axioms that reflect the conceptual analysis.

There is much more to discussing Hilbert's proof of De Zolt's postulate from the perspective of a formal geometric proof as provided by Baldwin and Hartshorne. However, we can say that conceptually De Zolt's original postulate is related to what is known as the scissors congruence (decomposition or dissection) or equidecomposability as opposed to Hilbert's and Euclid's notions that are closer to equicomplementability, equal content or area. To compare statements, Hartshorne's version of De Zolt is:

Postulate 2 (Hartshorne version of De Zolt). *If Q is a figure contained in another figure P, and if $P - Q$ has a non-empty interior, then P and Q do not have equal content.*

Equal content, in the version of De Zolt above, can be taken as equal area. For Hilbert and other researchers, the original version of De Zolt can be obtained by connecting the mereological and the analytical equivalences with the following theorem:

Theorem 1. *In every model of Euclidean geometry, two figures are equimeasured iff they are equicomplementable, iff they are equal figures.*

The theorem above holds in Euclidean plane geometry, also known as the Wallace-Bolyai-Gerwien theorem [4, 11][7, §24]. In Giovannini *et al.*. [5], we can find a geometrical formal proof of the plane version of De Zolt. It is proven in the original version of De Zolt and does not need the theorem above, nor does it mention any content measure, such as area. It is a mereological formal proof using algebra as a logic for equality and fundamental notions of point, line and polygons in the basic vocabulary.

A natural continuation of the work by Giovannini *et al.* [5] is to have a proof of De Zolt's for the three-dimensional case, and indeed this is pursued in later work by the same authors [6]. A three-dimensional version of De Zolt's postulate is given [6, §5] as follows:

Postulate 3 (Three-dimensional De Zolt) *Given a polyhedron $\mathcal{P}$, a decomposition Δ_p of $\mathcal{P}$, and a truncation Δ_q of Δ_p, then we have that $\Delta_p \prec \Delta_q$.*

The definitions of decomposition, truncation, and $\prec$ are formalized later in this paper, or see [6].

As previously mentioned, De Zolt's postulate in three dimensions is inconsistent with ZFC. De Zolt conflicts with the ball paradoxes, Hausdorff and Banach-Tarski, which have as a consequence that any two polyhedra, with equal volumes or not, are equidecomposable.

However, the notion of equidecomposability that is used in the ball paradoxes is too broad to be considered seriously in De Zolt's terminology. This point was also made by Giovannini *et al.* [6].

Thus, this paper aims to provide a mereological and geometrical, in Baldwin's sense, proof of De Zolt's postulate in the three-dimensional case. We will be formalizing the work of Giovannini *et al.* in proposing the Z_p type system, and filling in the details of their natural language sketch of the proof of De Zolt's postulate in three dimensions (see [6, §5]). The proof is formal not only in the sense of Baldwin's definition of a formal geometrical proof but also due to its execution in the Lean proof assistant. The Lean proof uses only a basic form of recursive definition and a weak type system, the aforementioned Z_p (Fig. 1), to provide the fundamental geometric vocabulary. Z_p has no way to define what is geometric content, such as area or volume; it does not have even the notion of natural numbers, making our proof mereological in nature. Both the notion of polyhedron decomposition and that of the $\prec$ relation needed by the three-dimensional version of De Zolt's postulate are given by the Z_p system's rules (Sect. 2); the definition of a truncation of a polyhedron decomposition is given in Lean in Sect. 5.

2   The Z_p System

Z_p is a type theory with a closed universe of types. It only contains types for points, segments (actually open polygonal chains), faces, and volumes, represented by $\mathfrak{p}, \mathfrak{s}, \mathfrak{f}, \mathfrak{v}$ respectively.

Z_p describes the construction of geometric objects by the composition of lesser geometric objects, and provides rules to establish mereological relationships (lesser than, and lesser than or equal to) between these objects. We can thus classify the main rules of the Z_p system (see Fig. 1) in two groups: the ones related to the construction of geometrical objects, and the mereological rules. Figure 2 shows an example of a polyhedron and one of its possible decompositions; Fig. 3 shows a derivation—using Z_p rules—of one of its faces.

The former group comprises monomorphic rules only, with the exception of the ε rule which states that the empty object has any type $t \in \mathfrak{T}$. Every other geometrical rule concerns a single type of geometric object, and describes the construction of an object of this type by the composition of other geometric objects. Rule $\mathfrak{s}_1$ describes the creation of a segment by joining two distinct points, while rule $\mathfrak{s}_2$ describes the creation of an open polygonal chain (considered itself of type $\mathfrak{s}$) by joining two segments that intersect at a single point, and whose component segments being joined at those points are not collinear.[2]

The rules for the type of faces $\mathfrak{f}$ are analogous, but for rule $\mathfrak{f}_1$ we build a new face from two segments whose union is a closed polygonal chain (i.e., Jordan).[3] In rule $\mathfrak{f}_2$ we need the intersection of two faces to be a segment so that their union is a well-formed face. Finally, for volumes rule $\mathfrak{v}_1$ requires the union of two faces to be closed for their union to be a valid volume, and rule $\mathfrak{v}_2$ requires the intersection of two volumes to be a face for their union to be a well-formed volume itself.

Because Z_p is a weak theory, it takes the geometrical concepts that guarantee the well-formedness of compositions—such as collinearity and Jordan polygonal chains—as primitive notions, as is done originally by Giovannini *et al.*. Note that these concepts are fundamental to the building of well-formed geometric objects, but are not central to the proof of De Zolt's postulate.

The mereological group of rules ($\varepsilon_0, \varepsilon_1, \varepsilon_2, \preceq_0, \preceq_1, \prec_1, \prec_2$) describe the $\prec, \preceq$ size relations on geometric objects. Rule ε_0 states that the empty object is lesser

---

[2] The non-collinearity requirement is not strictly necessary, it is just a form of normalization: instead of having a line segment $\overline{AC}$ built from two collinear line segments (defined by points A and B, and by points B and C), we make it impossible to define $\overline{AC}$ as such, thus requiring it to be built as a single segment defined by points A and C.

[3] This implies their coplanarity.

Types:

$$\mathfrak{T} : \mathfrak{p}, \mathfrak{s}, \mathfrak{f}, \mathfrak{v}$$

Rules:

$$\frac{n : \mathfrak{p} \quad m : \mathfrak{p} \quad n \neq m}{\langle n, m \rangle : \mathfrak{s}}\,\mathfrak{s}_1 \qquad \frac{p : \mathfrak{s} \quad q : \mathfrak{s} \quad p \cap q : \mathfrak{p} \quad \neg\,\mathrm{Collinear}(p, q)}{\langle p, q \rangle : \mathfrak{s}}\,\mathfrak{s}_2$$

$$\frac{p : \mathfrak{s} \quad q : \mathfrak{s} \quad \mathrm{Jordan}(\langle p, q \rangle)}{\langle p, q \rangle : \mathfrak{f}}\,\mathfrak{f}_1 \qquad \frac{p : \mathfrak{f} \quad q : \mathfrak{f} \quad p \cap q : \mathfrak{s}}{\langle p, q \rangle : \mathfrak{f}}\,\mathfrak{f}_2$$

$$\frac{p : \mathfrak{f} \quad q : \mathfrak{f} \quad \mathrm{Closed}(\langle p, q \rangle)}{\langle p, q \rangle : \mathfrak{v}}\,\mathfrak{v}_1 \qquad \frac{p : \mathfrak{v} \quad q : \mathfrak{v} \quad p \cap q : \mathfrak{f}}{\langle p, q \rangle : \mathfrak{v}}\,\mathfrak{v}_2$$

$$\frac{}{\varepsilon : \mathfrak{T}}\,\varepsilon \qquad \frac{p : \mathfrak{T}}{p \preceq p}\,\preceq_0 \qquad \mathrm{i}{=}1,2\;\frac{p_i : \mathfrak{T} \quad q_i : \mathfrak{T} \quad p_i \preceq q_i \quad p_1\,\mathrm{cmp}\,p_2 \quad q_1\,\mathrm{cmp}\,q_2}{p_1\,;\,p_2 \preceq q_1\,;\,q_2}\,\preceq_1$$

$$\frac{p : \mathfrak{T} \quad p \neq \varepsilon}{\varepsilon \prec p}\,\varepsilon_0 \qquad \frac{p : \mathfrak{T} \quad q : \mathfrak{T} \quad p\,\mathrm{cmp}\,q \quad q \neq \varepsilon}{p \prec p\,;\,q}\,\varepsilon_1 \qquad \frac{p : \mathfrak{T} \quad q : \mathfrak{T} \quad p\,\mathrm{cmp}\,q \quad p \neq \varepsilon}{q \prec p\,;\,q}\,\varepsilon_2$$

$$\mathrm{i}{=}1,2\;\frac{p_i : \mathfrak{T} \quad q_i : \mathfrak{T} \quad p_1 \prec q_1 \quad p_2 \preceq q_2 \quad p_1\,\mathrm{cmp}\,p_2 \quad q_1\,\mathrm{cmp}\,q_2}{p_1\,;\,p_2 \prec q_1\,;\,q_2}\,\prec_1$$

$$\mathrm{i}{=}1,2\;\frac{p_i : \mathfrak{T} \quad q_i : \mathfrak{T} \quad p_1 \preceq q_1 \quad p_2 \prec q_2 \quad p_1\,\mathrm{cmp}\,p_2 \quad q_1\,\mathrm{cmp}\,q_2}{p_1\,;\,p_2 \prec q_1\,;\,q_2}\,\prec_2$$

$$\frac{\langle p, q \rangle : \mathfrak{s}}{p\,\mathrm{cmp}\,q}\,\mathrm{cmp}_\mathfrak{s} \qquad \frac{\langle p, q \rangle : \mathfrak{f}}{p\,\mathrm{cmp}\,q}\,\mathrm{cmp}_\mathfrak{f} \qquad \frac{\langle p, q \rangle : \mathfrak{v}}{p\,\mathrm{cmp}\,q}\,\mathrm{cmp}_\mathfrak{v}$$

Fig. 1. The type system Z_p for polyhedral mereology

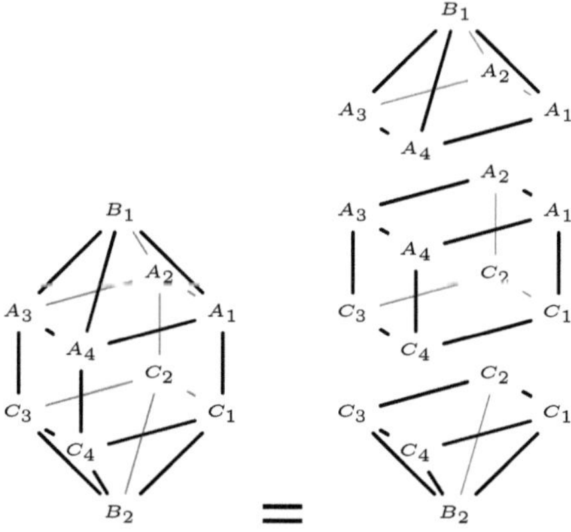

Fig. 2. A polyhedron and one of its decompositions

$$\cfrac{\cfrac{A_4:\mathfrak{p} \quad B_1:\mathfrak{p} \quad A_4\neq B_1}{A_4B_1:\mathfrak{s}}\mathfrak{s}_1 \quad \cfrac{B_1:\mathfrak{p} \quad A_1:\mathfrak{p} \quad B_1\neq A_1}{B_1A_1:\mathfrak{s}}\mathfrak{s}_1 \quad A_4B_1\cap B_1A_1:\mathfrak{p} \quad \neg\,\mathrm{Collinear}(A_4B_1,B_1A_1)}{A_4B_1A_1:\mathfrak{s}}\mathfrak{s}_2$$

Fig. 3. A derivation of face $A_4B_1A_1A_4$. To save space on the page we stack the premises of the leaf rule applications and write A_4B_1 instead of $\langle A_4, B_1\rangle$.

than any non-empty object. Rules ε_1 and ε_2 state that if an object is not empty, an arbitrary object is strictly lesser than the concatenation (denoted by the ; symbol) of this object and the original non-empty object.

For the rules involving concatenation to be correct we must require that the result of the concatenation of the two objects is well-formed; because the conditions on the well-formedness of geometric objects described in the geometric rules are monomorphic and the mereological rules are polymorphic, we introduce the judgement p cmp q (read 'p is composable/compatible with q'). A judgement like p cmp q is derived from the creation of a geometric object that resulted from the application of the geometrical rules, establishing the well-formedness of the concatenation of p and q (see rules $\mathrm{cmp}_{\mathfrak{s},\mathfrak{f},\mathfrak{v}}$).

Finally, we have the general comparison rules. For the lesser than or equal to relation, we have rule $\preceq_0$ which states that any object is the same or lesser than itself, while rule $\preceq_1$ states that if two pairs of objects of the same type are such that the first is pairwise lesser or equal to the second, then the concatenation of the first pair is lesser or equal than the concatenation of the second pair. Rule $\prec_1$ states that if we again have two pairs of objects of the same type, the first element of the first pair is strictly lesser than the first element of the second pair, and the second element of the first pair is lesser or equal than the second element of the second pair, we have that the concatenation of the first pair is strictly lesser than the concatenation of the second pair. Rule $\prec_2$ is analogous, but the strictly lesser relationship is on the second element of each pair.

Compared to the definition of the Z_p system rules in Giovannini *et al.* [6], here we have made the cmp rules explicit. We have also added some missing premises that should have used cmp predicates, and added the ε_0 rule, without which it is not possible to say that the empty object is less than a non-empty object. The latter statement could also be obtained by defining a rule stating that the concatenation of an object p with the empty object is equal to p itself, i.e., $p:\mathfrak{T}\vdash p=\varepsilon\,;p$.

Given this overview of the Z_p system, we can now show how geometric objects and their well-formedness are encoded in the Lean prover.

3   (De)composition of Geometric Objects in Lean

The first step in our formalization is to define the geometrical objects of the Z_p system in which De Zolt's postulate holds.

The first and most elementary object we will implement in Lean is the point. We define it as an opaque type, henceforth written as `Point`. This means that a `Point` is not explicitly described, and so we can't 'look inside' it.

```
opaque Point : Type
```

The treatment given to `Point` is exceptional: all the other geometric objects are represented in Lean by their constructions/compositions (or deconstructions/decompositions, depending on how you look at it). These constructions/compositions are defined by the type

```
inductive Composition (α : Type) where
| e
| c₁ (a₁ a₂ : α)
| c₂ (v₁ v₂ : Composition α)
```

With this type, we can build geometric objects from their base type. For example, the base type for segments is `Point`, so the type for segments would be `Composition Point`: the `e` constructor gives us the empty/null segment, `c₁` would give us a simple segment, and `c₂` would give us a polygonal chain of segments.

The `Composition` type allows us to build invalid objects, however. For example, for two points to make a well-formed segment, we need them to be different. Moreover, for two segments to make a polygonal chain, they must not be collinear, and they must intersect each other at a single point.

We can guarantee the well-formedness of the compositions by creating another type:

```
inductive Composition.Forall
    (P₁ : β → β → Prop)
    (P₂ : Composition β → Composition β → Prop)
    : Composition β → Prop
| e : Forall P₁ P₂ .e
| c₁ : P₁ a₁ a₂ → Forall P₁ P₂ (.c₁ a₁ a₂)
| c₂ : Forall P₁ P₂ v₁
       → Forall P₁ P₂ v₂
       → P₂ v₁ v₂
       → Forall P₁ P₂ (.c₂ v₁ v₂)
```

`Composition.Forall` formalizes the well-formedness of geometric composition by defining a predicate on compositions given a predicate on two elements of the base type and another on two elements of the composition type. It says the empty composition (`e`) always satisfies well-formedness, that the composition of two elements of the base type satisfy well-formedness if the two elements satisfy the supplied predicate on the base type (`P₁`), and that the composition of two compositions satisfies well-formedness if the two compositions are well-formed and so is their composition (the latter is given by the second supplied predicate `P₂`).

With this, we can define the well-formedness predicate for segments:

```
opaque Segment.IsCollinear
  : Composition Point → Composition Point → Prop
```

```
opaque Segment.HasPointIntersection
  : Composition Point → Composition Point → Prop

def Segment.wf : Composition Point → Prop
  := Composition.Forall
      (· ≠ ·)
      (λ p q => ¬ Segment.IsCollinear p q ∧
    Segment.HasPointIntersection p q)
```

All of the geometric objects we will define are `Compositions` that have well-formedness restrictions, so we define a single Lean structure (`GeomObj`) for them. The `obj` field has the composition itself, and the `wf` field has the proof of well-formedness based on the `Composition.Forall` type.

```
structure GeomObj
  (γ : Type) (P₁ : γ → γ → Prop)
  (P₂ : Composition γ → Composition γ → Prop)
where
  obj : Composition γ
  wf  : Composition.Forall P₁ P₂ obj
```

As an example of how we use `GeomObj`, we define the type of `Segment`.

```
def Point.cmp (p q : Point) : Prop := p ≠ q

def Segment.cmp (p q : Composition Point) : Prop
  := ¬ Segment.IsCollinear p q ∧ Segment.HasPointIntersection p q

def Segment := GeomObj Point Point.cmp Segment.cmp
```

The other geometric objects are defined similarly. Here is the definition of `Face`, which are (de)compositions of segments:

```
opaque Segment.UnionIsJordan : Segment → Segment → Prop

opaque Face.HasSegmentIntersection
  : Composition Segment → Composition Segment → Prop

def Face.cmp (p q : Composition Segment) : Prop :=
    Face.HasSegmentIntersection p q

def Face := GeomObj Segment Segment.UnionIsJordan Face.cmp
```

Finally, we define `Volume`, which is the subject of De Zolt's postulate.

```
opaque Face.IsClosed : Face → Face → Prop

opaque Volume.HasFaceIntersection : Composition Face → Composition Face
    → Prop

def Volume.cmp (p q : Composition Face) : Prop :=
    Volume.HasFaceIntersection p q
```

```
def Volume := GeomObj Face Face.IsClosed Volume.cmp
```

4   The Z_p System in Lean

We have just seen the definition of the geometrical objects of the Z_p system in Lean, and how they are constructed. In this section we show how we define the rules of Z_p (Fig. 1) using the definitions from Sect. 3.

Here is the definition of the first set of Z_p rules—the geometrical rules.

```
def s₁ (n m : Point) (P : n ≠ m) : Segment
  := { obj := .c₁ n m, wf := .c₁ P}


def s₂ (p q : Segment)
      (P : ¬ Segment.IsCollinear p.obj q.obj)
      (Q : Segment.HasPointIntersection p.obj q.obj)
      : Segment := {
          obj := .c₂ p.obj q.obj,
          wf := .c₂ p.wf q.wf (And.intro P Q)
      }


def f₁ (p q : Segment) (P : Segment.UnionIsJordan p q) : Face
  := { obj := .c₁ p q, wf := .c₁ P}


def f₂ (p q : Face) (P : Face.HasSegmentIntersection p.obj q.obj)
      : Face := {
          obj := .c₂ p.obj q.obj,
          wf := .c₂ p.wf q.wf P
      }


def v₁ (p q : Face) (P : Face.IsClosed p q) : Volume
  := { obj := .c₁ p q, wf := .c₁ P}


def v₂ (p q : Volume) (P : Volume.HasFaceIntersection p.obj q.obj)
      : Volume := {
          obj := .c₂ p.obj q.obj,
          wf := .c₂ p.wf q.wf P
      }
```

We chose the constructor names of the `Composition` and `Composition.Forall` types so that the construction and well-formedness proofs of the geometric objects mirror each other as in the above code.

The definition of the ε rule is polymorphic:

```
def ε {γ : Type} {P₁ : γ → γ → Prop}
    {P₂ : Composition γ → Composition γ → Prop}
    : GeomObj γ P₁ P₂
    := { obj := .e, wf := .e }
```

We now handle the mereological rules, in the form of two types: `le` (lesser than or equal to) for $\preceq$, and `lt` (lesser than) for $\prec$. Both types are defined inductively over pairs of geometric objects:

```
inductive le
  {γ : Type} {P₁ : γ → γ → Prop}
  {P₂ : Composition γ → Composition γ → Prop}
  : (_ _ : GeomObj γ P₁ P₂) → Prop
| le₀ {p} : le p p
| le₁ {p₁ q₁ p₂ q₂} : le p₁ q₁ → le p₂ q₂
        → (pc : P₂ p₁.obj p₂.obj) → (qc : P₂ q₁.obj q₂.obj)
        → le (concat p₁ p₂ pc) (concat q₁ q₂ qc)


inductive lt
  {γ : Type} {P₁ : γ → γ → Prop}
  {P₂ : Composition γ → Composition γ → Prop}
  : (_ _ : GeomObj γ P₁ P₂) → Prop
| ε₀ {p} : p ≠ ε → lt ε p
| ε₁ {p q} : (pqc : P₂ p.obj q.obj) → lt p (concat p q pqc)
| ε₂ {p q} : (pqc : P₂ p.obj q.obj) → lt q (concat p q pqc)
| lt₁ {p₁ q₁ p₂ q₂} : lt p₁ q₁ → le p₂ q
        → (pc : P₂ p₁.obj p₂.obj) → (qc : P₂ q₁.obj q₂.obj)
        → lt (concat p₁ p₂ pc) (concat q₁ q₂ qc)
| lt₂ {p₁ q₁ p₂ q₂} : le p₁ q₁ → lt p₂ q₂
        → (pc : P₂ p₁.obj p₂.obj) → (qc : P₂ q₁.obj q₂.obj)
        → lt (concat p₁ p₂ pc) (concat q₁ q₂ qc)
```

The constructors of the `le` and `lt` types correspond to the Z_p deductive rules of the same name (substituting `le` and `lt` with $\preceq$ and $\prec$ respectively, see Fig. 1). The cmp relation between geometric objects is given by the predicates on the composition of geometric objects used on the `GeomObj` types, and `concat` is used to represent the ; operator from the Z_p system rules.

```
def concat {γ : Type} {P₁ : γ → γ → Prop}
           {P₂ : Composition γ → Composition γ → Prop}
  (p q : GeomObj γ P₁ P₂) (cmp : P₂ p.obj q.obj) : GeomObj γ P₁ P₂
  := { obj := .c₂ p.obj q.obj, wf := .c₂ p.wf q.wf cmp }
```

Note that `concat` takes an additional argument compared to the ; operator: the proof that two objects are composable. These pertain to the cmp predicates from the Z_p system, and correspond to the predicates on the composition of geometrical objects. We have already shown the $\text{cmp}_{t \in \mathfrak{T}}$ rules; they correspond to `Point.cmp`, `Segment.cmp`, `Face.cmp`, `Volume.cmp`.

5   The Proof of De Zolt's Postulate

Now that have shown how the Lean definitions correspond to the Z_p system rules, we introduce the final piece we need to prove De Zolt's postulate for the three-dimensional case: the truncation of a geometric object. We define truncation inductively:

```
inductive TruncationOf
  {γ : Type} {P₁ : γ → γ → Prop}
  {P₂ : Composition γ → Composition γ → Prop}
  : (_ _ : GeomObj γ P₁ P₂) → Prop
| t₀ {p} : p ≠ ε → TruncationOf ε p
| t₁ {r s v} : (rv : P₂ r.obj v.obj) → (sv : P₂ s.obj v.obj)
  → TruncationOf r s
  → TruncationOf (concat r v rv) (concat s v sv)
```

That is, a `TruncationOf` value is constructed recursively. The base case is that
for any non-empty version of a geometric object, the empty object is a `Trunca-
tionOf` it. So for the case of a `Volume`, for any non-empty `Volume` the empty `Volume`
is a `TruncationOf` it. For the inductive case, given two geometric objects, the first
of which is a `TruncationOf` the second one, we have that the concatenation of the
first object with an arbitrary third object is a `TruncationOf` the concatenation of
the second object with the same third object. This is only true provided we can
perform both of these concatenations, that is, that their results are well-formed
geometric objects; this is guaranteed by the two predicate arguments that satisfy
the third argument of *concat*.

We are finally ready for the statement of De Zolt's postulate:

```
theorem Volume.zolt {q p : Volume}
  (isTrunc : TruncationOf q p)
  : lt q p
```

That is, if p, q are values of type `Volume`, and q is a `TruncationOf` p, we
have that $q \prec p$. Note that the statement of De Zolt's postulate for the three-
dimensional case (Postulat 3) talks about polyhedron decompositions; in Z_p a
polyhedron and its decomposition are the same thing, for the construction of the
polyhedron value is given by its (de)composition.

Proof (De Zolt's Postulate). The proof is by induction on the `TruncationOf` construction: in the base case, we have that q is the empty `Volume` ε, and so we
use the ε_0 rule to show that $\varepsilon \prec p$. In the inductive case we have that p and
q are actually $u \mathbin{;} r$ (`concat u r`) and $w \mathbin{;} r$ (`concat w r`) respectively. Moreover,
we have a proof that `TruncationOf w u` holds, with which we recursively invoke
Zolt's postulate to obtain $w \prec u$. With this proof and the trivial proof of $r \preceq r$
we can invoke the $\prec_1$ rule to show that $w \mathbin{;} r \prec u \mathbin{;} r$ (i.e., $q \prec p$) holds.

Or, in Lean:

```
theorem Volume.zolt {q p : Volume}
  (isTrunc : TruncationOf q p)
  : lt q p :=
  match isTrunc with
  | TruncationOf.t₀ pneq => lt.ε₀ pneq
  | TruncationOf.t₁ (r := w) (s := u) (v := r) wrcmp urcmp wIsTruncOfu =>
    have w_lt_u : lt w u := zolt wIsTruncOfu
    have r_le_r : le r r := le.le₀
    lt.lt₁ w_lt_u r_le_r wrcmp urcmp
```

6   On the Use of `Face.IsClosed` and Similar predicates in the proof of De Zolt's postulate

One might question whether the proof of Theorem `Volume.zolt` in Sect. 5, which establishes the three-dimensional version of De Zolt's postulate, explicitly guarantees that the geometric objects constructed in the inductive step are indeed volumes, as a previous reviewer to this paper did. In particular, the rule v_1, used to construct a `Volume` from two `Face` objects, requires the predicate `Face.IsClosed`. However, the proof of `Volume.zolt` does not mention this predicate directly.

We argue that the use of `Face.IsClosed` is implicitly and correctly ensured in the proof. The reason lies in the definition of the type `Volume` in Lean:

```
def Volume := GeomObj Face Face.IsClosed Volume.cmp
```

Every value of type `Volume` is a `GeomObj` whose construction is governed by a `Composition` over `Face`, with well-formedness ensured by a `Composition.Forall` predicate using `Face.IsClosed` as the base predicate and `Volume.HasFaceIntersection` as the composition predicate.

Furthermore, the recursive case of the `TruncationOf` relation uses the function `concat`, which has the following type:

```
def concat {γ : Type} {P₁ : γ → γ → Prop}
  {P₂ : Composition γ → Composition γ → Prop}
  (p q : GeomObj γ P₁ P₂) (cmp : P₂ p.obj q.obj)
  : GeomObj γ P₁ P₂
```

This function constructs a new geometric object (of the same type) by concatenating two valid geometric objects p and q, provided that a proof of their composability `cmp` is available. In the case of `Volume`, the composability predicate is `Volume.HasFaceIntersection`, and the validity of the new object requires carrying over the well-formedness proofs of both components—which themselves include satisfaction of `Face.IsClosed` due to the type definition of `Volume`.

Hence, although the proof of `Volume.zolt` does not mention `Face.IsClosed` explicitly, the requirement is satisfied by construction. The Lean type system guarantees that every step in the inductive proof operates on valid volumes, and this includes verification of the closure condition needed to apply rule v_1 in the Z_p system.

In conclusion, the omission of an explicit mention of `Face.IsClosed` in the proof is justified: its use is embedded in the definition of the `Volume` type and enforced structurally by the type system and the composition constructors.

Analogous arguments apply to the other well-formedness predicates: `Segment.IsCollinear`, `Segment.HasPointIntersection`, `Segment.UnionIsJordan`, `Face.HasSegmentIntersection`, `Face.HasSegmentIntersection`, and `Volume.HasFaceIntersection`.

7   A Discussion on the Deductive Power of Z_p

One of the essential features of the Z_p system is that it is a *weak type theory*, intentionally designed to avoid the paradoxes that arise in more expressive set-theoretic or topological systems. A central consequence of this weakness is the following: **it is not possible to deduce that a given set of faces forms a closed volume within Z_p unless closure is explicitly assumed.**

Why Closure Cannot Be Derived

1. The notion of *closure* in Z_p is captured by the primitive predicate

$$\mathsf{Face.IsClosed : Face \to Face \to Prop}$$

   which cannot be derived or inferred from the composition of points, segments, or faces. It must be postulated for each pair of faces involved in a composition.
2. The system Z_p intentionally omits any geometric or topological structure such as orientation, angles, curvature, or even natural numbers. Therefore, the idea that three triangular faces (e.g., forming a cap like $\triangle ABC$, $\triangle ABD$, and $\triangle ACD$) close a portion of space is not expressible or provable within the system.
3. This design prevents Z_p from falling into paradoxes like Banach–Tarski, where two solids with the same volume can be decomposed and recomposed into a different volume. Such paradoxes require a global notion of space and measure, which Z_p avoids.

What Z_p Can Deduce

Despite its limitations, Z_p supports important structural reasoning. Specifically, it can handle:

- *Mereological comparisons*, such as proving that one decomposition is strictly smaller than another using the relation $\prec$.
- *Structural well-formedness* of composed objects via the use of compatibility predicates (`cmp`), ensuring that segments, faces, and volumes are constructed from well-formed parts.
- *Truncation-based reasoning*, including the formal statement and proof of the three-dimensional De Zolt postulate: removing a part yields a strictly smaller whole.

Pros and cons of Z_p definition

The inability to derive closure is not a bug but a feature of Z_p. It reflects the system's commitment to a formal and paradox-free mereological framework, grounded in syntactic compositional rules rather than spatial or metric semantics. Closure must always be explicitly assumed via axioms or provided as external input (e.g., in proof assistants), reinforcing the system's robustness against pathological constructions. In Appendix Λ we provide an argument based on Lean's metatheory.

8 Relevance of this Work to Computer Science

The formal proof of De Zolt's postulate developed in this article has a significant impact on the domains of Computer Science concerned with the correctness, verification, and formalization of mathematical reasoning. The use of the Lean proof assistant and the adoption of a weak type theory such as Z_p showcase a concrete and nontrivial case of how Computer Science tools and techniques advance foundational mathematics and its applications.

Proof assistants are increasingly common due to their role in ensuring the correctness of complex systems, programming languages, and algorithms. The formalization carried out in Lean demonstrates how even classical geometric principles can be captured in a computational framework. By encoding geometrical objects, well-formedness rules, and mereological relations, the article exemplifies how proof assistants serve as both verification tools and vehicles for the exploration of theoretical foundations.

8.1 The Need for Correct Proofs in Pure Mathematics and Beyond

Mathematics benefits from the precision and rigor of formal verification, especially when dealing with paradox-sensitive domains. Since the three-dimensional version of De Zolt's postulate is inconsistent with ZFC, its proof requires a carefully restricted logical setting. This paper achieves this through the weak type-theoretic system Z_p, which avoids the well-known paradoxes, such as the Banach-Tarski paradox, thus illustrating how proof assistants can highlight hidden assumptions and formalize reasoning that would be error-prone in informal mathematics.

Applied mathematics and technological domains—such as computer graphics, computational geometry, verification of hardware models, and CAD systems—rely on the correct decomposition and manipulation of spatial objects. The formal mereological treatment of volumes and decompositions in the article provides a rigorous foundation upon which implementations and algorithms can be trusted. In such contexts, even subtle errors in reasoning about parts and wholes may propagate to critical failures in software or engineered systems.

For Computer Science in particular, this work contributes the following ways:

- it offers a concrete case study where a classical mathematical postulate is proved within a machine-verified environment, bridging theoretical logic, type theory, and geometry;
- it illustrates how restricting expressive power, rather than increasing it, can yield consistency and avoid paradoxes, a principle relevant to programming language design, proof-carrying code, and safe specification languages;
- it shows that formal proofs in weak theories can still capture rich mereological and geometric content, enabling future generalizations to higher dimensions and other application domains;
- it reinforces the broader research agenda of formally certifying knowledge once taken for granted or considered too informal for mechanization.

9   Conclusion

As discussed in the introduction, the concept of a formal geometric proof was extensively discussed in meta-mathematics and was finally provided in the works of Hartshorne [7] and Baldwin [1]. Due to its content-based and decomposition-based notions, De Zolt's postulate for the three-dimensional case is not consistent with ZFC.

This challenges us to provide a mereological geometrical formal proof. The logic behind this formal proof had to be very weak; the fundamental geometric vocabulary could not, in any way, give rise to a content-based De Zolt's version statement and proof, or the ball paradoxes would jeopardise the proof.

In this article, we have provided just such a proof, based on the proof sketch by Giovannini *et al.* [6, Thm.5.1]. The use of a proof assistant was of great importance in showing in detail the formal aspect of our mereological formalization of De Zolt's statement and proof.

A shortcoming of the Z_p system is that it is difficult to provide a model for it without it requiring the introduction of concepts that would lead to a form of the aforementioned Ball paradoxes. For the same reason we can not define the well-formedness predicates (such as being a Jordan curve) in Z_p itself.

The well-formedness predicates such as Jordan curve geometrical predicate (`Segment.UnionIsJordan`) or the closure predicate (`Face.isClosed`) predicate are not expressed directly in our type system, and this is by design. To detail any geometrical content of these predicates is not the intention of our type system, as explained in Sect. 6. We want to keep the type system mereological, and hence, it must have abstract models.

We conjecture that our formal proof scheme scales to higher dimensions, so as future work we would like to extend it. The only measure of complexity that seems to grow is related to the size and nesting of the decompositions, due to the new geometrical objects, i.e. n-polytopes, for arbitrary n.

Acknowledgments. We would like to thank Abel Lasalle and Eduardo Giovannini for ideas and discussions on the philosophical underpinnings of this research. We also thank Timo Carlin-Burns for helpful comments on Lean's zulipchat. E. H. Haeusler was partially suported by CNPq grant 309287/2023-5.

Disclosure of Interests. The authors have no competing interests to declare that are relevant to the content of this article.

A   Lean's Foundational Theory and Consistency of Z_p

Lean is based on the *Calculus of Inductive Constructions* (CIC), a dependent type theory that extends the Curry–Howard correspondence: propositions are types and proofs are programs inhabiting those types. This setting supports inductive types, universes, and structural recursion, providing a uniform framework for both mathematical formalization and program verification.

A key requirement for the consistency of Lean is the *strict positivity condition* on inductive definitions. When declaring a new inductive type, Lean checks that all recursive occurrences of the type appear in *positive* positions, i.e. only as outputs or components of data, never as inputs to a function. For instance:

```
inductive Nat
| zero : Nat
| succ : Nat → Nat
```

is valid, since `Nat` appears only positively. By contrast:

```
inductive Bad
| mk : (Bad → Nat) → Bad
```

is rejected by Lean, because `Bad` occurs negatively as an argument to a function. Allowing such definitions would enable paradoxical constructions (e.g. Girard's paradox), collapsing the logic. The strict positivity check thus guarantees that recursive types are well-founded, ensuring termination of functions defined by pattern matching and preserving the overall consistency of Lean's core theory.

The type system Z_p is implemented directly inside the Lean prover, using *strictly positive inductive types* and simple structural recursion. All the geometric objects (`Point`, `Segment`, `Face`, and `Volume`) are constructed as instances of Lean inductive types (`Composition` and `Composition.Forall`) together with opaque well-formedness predicates. The mereological relations ($\preceq$, $\prec$) are also defined inductively.

Because Lean's core type theory enforces positivity and termination, every inductive family in Z_p is automatically well-founded. In particular:

- All recursive definitions are structurally recursive, so Lean ensures termination.
- The empty object ε is definable, but no derivation can inhabit an impossible judgment such as $\varepsilon \prec \varepsilon$.
- No closed term of type `False` (the empty proposition) can be derived within Z_p.

It follows that if Lean's underlying type theory is consistent, then so is the subsystem Z_p formalized within it: Con(Lean core) $\implies$ Con(Zp).

We sketch the inductive proof that no contradiction can be obtained within Z_p:

1. **Base case (reflexivity).** The constructor $\mathtt{le}_0$ yields $p \preceq p$ for any object p. This does not generate a contradiction, since $\prec$ is defined separately.
2. **Composition rules.** For each rule (e.g. $\mathtt{s}_1$, $\mathtt{s}_2$, $\mathtt{f}_1$, $\mathtt{f}_2$, $\mathtt{v}_1$, $\mathtt{v}_2$), the premises require a well-formedness witness (`cmp`). Because such witnesses are opaque predicates in Lean, they cannot be constructed unless postulated. Thus, no derivation of ill-formed compositions arises.
3. **Rules for $\prec$.** The inductive family `lt` has constructors requiring either (i) $\varepsilon \prec p$ for some non-empty p, or (ii) inheritance from strictness in components.

By induction on derivations, the only way to derive $p \prec p$ would be from a subderivation of the same shape. This circularity is blocked by Lean's positivity check and well-founded recursion.

Hence, no closed derivation of $\varepsilon \prec \varepsilon$ exists, and more generally, no contradiction (inhabitation of `False`) can be derived within Z_p.

References

1. Baldwin, J.: What is a geometric proof: reflections on de zolt's axiom. In: Proceedings of the 17th CLMPST (2023)
2. Baldwin, J.T.: Model Theory and the Philosophy of Mathematical Practice: Formalization without Foundationalism. Cambridge University Press (2018)
3. De Rauglaudre, D.: Formal proof of Banach-Tarski paradox. J. Formalized Reason. **10**(1), 37–49 (2017)
4. Gerwien, P.: Zerschneidung jeder beliebigen Anzahl von gleichen geradlinigen Figuren in dieselben Stücke. Journal für die reine und angewandte Mathematik (Crelles Journal) **1833**(10), 228–234 (1833). https://doi.org/10.1515/crll.1833.10.228
5. Giovannini, E.N., Haeusler, E.H., Lassalle-Casanave, A., Veloso, P.A.S.: De Zolt's postulate: an abstract approach. Rev. Symbolic Logic **15**(1), 197–224 (2019). https://doi.org/10.1017/s1755020319000339
6. Giovannini, E.N., Lassalle Casanave, A., Haeusler, E.H.: Sobre el postulado de De Zolt en tres dimensiones. O que nos faz pensar **29**(49) (2021)
7. Hartshorne, R.: Geometry: Euclid and Beyond. Springer-Verlag (2000)
8. Heath, T.L.: The Thirteen Books of Euclid's Elements. Dover Publications (1956)
9. de Moura, L., Kong, S., Avigad, J., van Doorn, F., von Raumer, J.: The lean theorem prover (system description). In: Felty, A.P., Middeldorp, A. (eds.) CADE 2015. LNCS (LNAI), vol. 9195, pp. 378–388. Springer, Cham (2015). https://doi.org/10.1007/978-3-319-21401-6_26
10. Moura, L., Ullrich, S.: The lean 4 theorem prover and programming language. In: Platzer, A., Sutcliffe, G. (eds.) CADE 2021. LNCS (LNAI), vol. 12699, pp. 625–635. Springer, Cham (2021). https://doi.org/10.1007/978-3-030-79876-5_37
11. Wallace, W., Lowry, J.: Question 269, New Series of the Mathematical Repository, vol. 3. W. Glendinning, London (1814)

Author Index